Motherhood and Single-Lone Parenting

Funded by the Government of Canada
Financé par la gouvernement du Canada

Demeter Press
140 Holland Street West
P. O. Box 13022
Bradford, ON L3Z 2Y5
Tel: (905) 775-9089
Email: info@demeterpress.org
Website: www.demeterpress.org

Demeter Press logo based on the sculpture "Demeter" by Maria-Luise Bodirsky <www.keramik-atelier.bodirsky.de>

Printed and Bound in Canada

Front cover artwork: Jewelles Smith

Library and Archives Canada Cataloguing in Publication

Motherhood and single-lone parenting : a twenty-first century perspective / edited by Maki Motapanyane.

Includes bibliographical references.
ISBN 978-1-77258-001-3 (paperback)

1. Single mothers. 2. Single parents. 3. Single-parent families. 4. Motherhood. I. Motapanyane, Maki, 1978-, editor

HQ759.915.M68 2016 306.874'32 C2016-903614-6

MIX
Paper from responsible sources
FSC® C004071

Motherhood and Single-Lone Parenting

A Twenty-First Century Perspective

EDITED BY

Maki Motapanyane

DEMETER PRESS

For my dear mother, Virginia,
giver of life and conqueror of mountains.

Table of Contents

Acknowledgements

A volume that centres the subjective realities of lone parenting, an experience so near and dear to my own life, is truly a labour of love. Furthermore, it is a work supported and enabled by the love of others, by family, and by my children, who graciously and understandingly allowed me hours of work time. For that time, I continue to carry a guilt that is only slightly assuaged by their genuine pride and happiness in holding the physical manifestation of all that typing. I wish to express a heartfelt thank you to the contributors, many of whom are courageously sharing personal aspects of their lives to augment our collective understanding of the contemporary landscape of lone parenting and whose research provides us with a framework and a current language to comprehensibly read the trends before us. My gratitude goes out to Catherine A. Vigue, without whose final formatting and editing skills, I would not have been able to see this manuscript into its end shape. And finally, a tremendous thanks to all who have contributed life-sustaining support to the contributors and to myself along this writing journey.

Introduction

Motherhood, Mothering, and Single-Lone Parenting in Contemporary Perspective

MAKI MOTAPANYANE

THE TWENTY-FIRST CENTURY has one significant commonality with the decades of the preceding century: the majority of individuals parenting on their own and heading one-parent families continue to be mothers. Even so, current trends in globalization (economic, political, cultural) along with technological advancement, shifts in political, economic and social policy, contemporary demographic shifts, changing trends in the labour sector linked to global economics, and developments in legislative and judicial output, all signify the distinctiveness of the current moment with regard to family patterns and social norms. This volume explores and illuminates a more recent landscape of popular public discourse, experience, and policy surrounding single motherhood and one-parent headed families. The perspectives featured here range in approach, method, and analysis. These are scholarly pieces tailored to an academic as well as broader audience. Included are autoethnographic essays, reflective experiential compositions, and contemplative advocacy oriented writing and policy research, with several of the chapters in this collection bearing a combination of two or more of these elements. This collection is aimed at a broad general audience with an interest in the subject of single motherhood and lone parenting as these currently manifest in popular discourse, policy, and experience. The book is designed to be accessible, exploratory, and revealing in its exposition of contemporary deliberations on lone parenting.

The past three decades have revealed notable changes in the way single motherhood and lone parenting is discussed and debated in the North American context. There is an increasingly nuanced landscape of policy recommendations, forms of representation, and family arrangements in the Canadian, U.S., and other geographic contexts that have pushed the basis of discussion beyond the conceptual terrain of the 1990s, which was the last period of visible and heated public engagement in North America over the subject of single motherhood. The discursive terrain has so expanded over the last three decades that we are now (and in many instances more accurately) referring to *lone parenthood* rather than merely *single motherhood*. To this point, the contemporary context, to some extent, reveals the absorption of critiques regarding the erroneous association of motherhood with wifery, critiques which trouble the so often taken-for-granted term "*single mother*."[1] In other ways, and perhaps more commonly, the language of lone parenting reflects the increase in one-parent headed households led by men in both Canada and the U.S., as well as the departure from reductionist gendered language that reproduces a woman-man—mother-father binary. At the same time, the term *lone parent*, which speaks to these issues and shifts in thinking, can itself mask the gendered reality of parenting alone, that it is still predominantly women and mothers ("women's work") who are engaged in the bulk of the labour of childrearing.[2] To the extent that this reality is concealed by the neutral language of lone parenting, there is also a risk of depoliticizing a crucial civic and social issue that hinges on gendered inequality. The perspectives in this collection reflect multiple ways of framing and naming representations and experiences of lone parenting, and, importantly, they collectively highlight the political stakes in play.

A cursory search of academic and popular literature on one-parent headed families indicates a persistent focus, across culture and geography, on single mothers (Duncan and Edwards). A bulk of this literature speaks largely to American experiences, with Canadian, Western European and Nordic contexts following closely behind. There is also a growing yet comparatively small body of scholarship examining the experiences of single fathers (Hamer and Marchioro; Lichter and Graefe). The themes that feature prominently in the literature on single motherhood and lone parenting include discourse and representation (Juffer), policy (Brooks; McLanahan and Sandefur; Russell, Harris, and Gockel; Sidel), economics (Kramer et al.; Myles, Hou, and Picot), social stigma (Jarrett), health (Jayakody and Stauffer; Olson and Banyard), and, more recently, single mothering by choice (Bock; Hertz; Morissette).

The literature more often than not takes heterosexuality as its departing premise and leans strongly towards exposing the hardship of parenting on one's own. For instance, much of the literature focusing on economics and policy highlights financial struggle and overwhelming childrearing responsibility as primary hardships characterizing the experiences of lone mothers (Russell, Harris, and Gockel). This leads to negative judgement of lone moms on the quality of their motherhood, and self-questioning on the basis of social constructions of "good motherhood," which include intensive (emotional and physical) mothering, paying for and engaging in children's extracurricular activities, and participation in and volunteering in the children's school, among other idealized criteria. Additionally, the social stigma and economic hardships associated with lone motherhood in heteropatriarchal contexts,have been shown to have detrimental health effects on women. Chronic stress and fatigue can cause a number of health ailments, the most commonly identified being depression. In fact, depression has a higher likelihood of appearing among single mothers than among other groups of women (Jayakody and Stauffer; Lipman, Offord, and Boyle). In the Canadian context, time-stretched and stressed lone mothers identify a need for help with rearing their children but note that they are frequently blamed for the hardships they face—their challenging realities are deemed a result of their personal failings. They also note that any formal help received (e.g. state aid) comes at the cost of increased surveillance (Russell, Harris, and Gockel), which further demoralizes and constrains them in mobilizing optimal parenting strategies, thereby also reinforcing the illusion of the normative heterosexual nuclear family as the "natural" (read healthy and "intact") family.

Single mothering by choice (SMC) is often presented in the literature as the positive and ideal version of lone mothering. Yet it, too, is shown to struggle with a persistent culture of sexism, in which financially independent women, even in making an empowered choice to parent alone, must continuously justify that choice via class privilege as well as via a racialized and gendered discourse of responsibility and respectability. In single mothering by choice there is not necessarily divestment from differentiating oneself from "bad" single mothers—the teenaged, undereducated, and low-income (Bock). Normalizing or mainstreaming single motherhood by choice appears dependent to some extent on reinforcing the stigma faced by differently positioned and marginalized mothers. As with other lone moms, single mothers by choice must demonstrate economic self-sufficiency and "freedom from any kind of dependency—in order to qualify as 'normal'" (Juffer 5); they must, as Juffer points out, provide a home and upbringing with all the trappings of a middle-upper income and heterosexual nuclear family (minus the dad in the house). Single mothers by choice, more so than other lone mothers, are able to distinguish themselves as particularly capable in this respect, and, therefore, as more socially acceptable than many of their fellow lone-parenting mothers.

Juffer also addresses the realm of discourse and representation and presents an analysis of lone mothers as domestic intellectuals—here, borrowing explicitly from Antonio Gramsci's concept of the organic intellectual, and less explicitly and admittedly a projection of mine onto her work—exhibiting traces of Sara Ruddick's concept of "maternal thinking" (the act of mothering as intellectual work). In giving voice to the joys, victories, and love found in lone-parent households, Juffer's domestic intellectuals are poised to unsettle the dominant heteronormative narrative of the nuclear family as *the* healthy family. Drawing on personal experience and the knowledge produced by the work of mothering, single mothers as domestic intellectuals "act as an antidote to universal claims, connecting rather than transcending places of life and work" (Juffer 10). Nevertheless, heteropatriarchal discourses of "good motherhood" maintain significant clout, which leaves the lone mothering domestic intellectual in a precarious position. If she expresses a future wish for marriage in all the normative ways, she is advanced a certain level of respectability; if she applies her organic intellectualism, in Gramsci's radical sense, and advocates the legitimacy of alternative family formations, she is often accorded less legitimacy (Juffer).

There is a growing body of literature on lone-parenting fathers, demonstrating a few trends with some predictability. For instance, although social stigma remains an unfortunate reality for many single moms, lone-parenting dads are often praised and admired for being single fathers. As Ruth Sidel has insightfully shared, the perception of her single dad "differed dramatically from that of millions of single mothers largely because of his gender: he was a man and therefore given respect, particularly for raising a child and for dealing with all the domestic details connected with maintaining a household" (Sidel 20-21). Single fathers are more likely than single mothers to have relatives and their extended social networks reach out to them with help (Hamer and Marchioro). An American study of attitudes towards never-married single mothers and fathers (DeJean, McGeorge and Carlson) found that the participants viewed single fathers more favourably than single mothers when presented with identical narratives of each. The study points out that because single fatherhood is perceived to ask of men to assume a role that is not "natural" to them, they receive more sympathy, compliments, and support in the process of lone parenting, which serves to augment rather than challenge their self-esteem when compared to their lone-mothering peers. In the case of lone-parenting dads, there are often assumptions made about a woman-related tragedy (wife died) or some kind of deviancy (mother incapable of fulfilling her natural role), which has led to the dad's present situation. Interestingly, this study also found single dads rated more positively than single moms on seven items having to do with parenting, with the exception of single mothers being perceived as better carers for other people's children. As DeJean, McGeorge and Carlson indicate, "single mothers were rated less positively as parents, but were still likely to be hired to care for other people's children" (133). Such a finding points to a persistently sexist biological determinism regarding the grunt work of mothering and motherhood as an institution. Somewhat surprisingly, the majority of study participants who ranked lone dads more positively than lone moms (save in the case of looking after other people's children) were women themselves—indicating the powerful influence of heteropatriarchal ideology surrounding motherhood. Some research suggests that custodial lone-parenting dads are more involved parents than their married counterparts (Cooksey and Fondell; Hawkins, Amato, and King)—a reflection of the gendered biological determinism applied to childrearing and the conflation of wifery and mothering. When men are custodial single fathers, they more closely embody a set of parenting practices typically associated with mothering. With growing numbers of custodial single dads globally (Livingston; Orendain; Maruko; Vaughan), more research is needed to shed light on this terrain.

Three overarching sections form the structure of this collection: discourse, media and representation; the experiential; and policy, resistance and activism. "Discourse, Media and Representation," section one, constructively engages a contemporary landscape of popular discourse on lone parenting, situating current popular cultural frames and trends relative to the patterns of preceding years, and presents a framework for comprehending an increasingly diverse terrain of experiences and interpretations surrounding the lone parent. Section two, "The Experiential," pushes beyond the heteronormative framework characterizing much of the scholarship on single mothering and lone parenting and considers the transformative power of resilience and agency as revealed through experience. The third and final section of this book, "Policy, Resistance, and Activism," examines policy debates and reform from several cultural and geographic perspectives (Australia, Germany, Spain, U.S.) and extols the virtues and contributions of lone mothers' resistance and activism in shifting the parameters of discourse, policy, and experience surrounding lone parenting.

A number of key themes emerge from this collection, which keep with more recent literature on single motherhood and lone parenting (as listed above) and, concurrently, press beyond to contribute fresh perspectives and questions to the field of motherhood studies. In section one, a robust discussion of dominant discursive representations of single motherhood and lone parenting is conveyed by Nancy Bressler and Lara Lengel in chapter one "Mothering in Dystopia," as well as in Katherine Mack's chapter two "Do Two a Family Make?," Dwayne Avery's chapter three "Every Child Needs a Father," and Danielle Russell's chapter four "Courageous Mothering." The authors indicate that the heterosexual nuclear family continues to operate as the assumed standard of normalcy, health, and stability. (In fact, most of the authors in this volume show this to be the case in all of the cultural and geographic contexts explored.) Examining representations of mothering in popular, cultural, twenty-first century, post-apocalyptic, televisual texts (science fiction and horror), Bressler and Lengel in chapter one argue that mediated representations of lone mothers demonstrate "continued cultural anxiety about the changing nature of the American family." They explore how science fiction texts may be used to question dominant social assumptions of family in ways that traditional television genres are not able to do. For instance, the authors suggest that horror films can demonstrate "the contemporary weakening of patriarchal authority and the glaring contradictions that exist between the mythology of family relations and their actual social practice." Mack in chapter two discusses the contemporary culture of motherhood as represented through American film and notes the acceptance of single motherhood according to strictly classed and racialized criteria normative to neoliberal ideology. Using cultural rhetoric as a research method, Mack examines a trio of recent Hollywood feature films focused on single mothers between 2008 and 2011. She finds that positive representations of single mothers are dependent on their collusion with neoliberal capitalism, which reinforces racist and classist constructions of "good" motherhood. In addition, Mack identifies the disheartening "congruence between the motivations and aspirations of actual intentional single mothers and their fictional counterparts in Hollywood films," which reveals the significant influence of conservative "postfeminist" discourses on the ways that single mothers are categorized and judged. In chapter three, Avery also points out that despite "films and television shows like *Brokeback Mountain*, *The Kids Are All Right*, *Transamerica,* and *United States of Tara* bringing attention to the rise in gay and lesbian families, all too often media reproduces dominant images of family life." Avery situates single motherhood within a recent media trend that envisions lone mothers as the head of a legitimate family structure, yet he, simultaneously, reveals the postfeminist ambivalence of popular media regarding single motherhood. As with Mack, Avery notes that single motherhood may no longer be vilified as it was in the past, but it is only a particular group of lone mothers who are often depicted positively—those with socio-economic privilege.

Additionally important in Avery's work is the congruent identification of the contemporary ambivalence of white masculinity. Avery discusses a reinvigorated postfeminist fatherhood consisting of men seeking the reinstatement of an antiquated patriarchal authority (e.g. the men's rights movement in North America, the "crisis in masculinity," and concerns regarding "the problem of fatherlessness"). Avery identifies a contemporary twist in patriarchal discourse of the family, reflected in advocacy of the social good of tough but sensitive men as needed protectors and providers in a society that has grown soft and weak. According to Avery, this is an expression of a postfeminist culture that understands feminism as obsolete at the same time that fantasies about men's return to patriarchal dominance are bolstered. In chapter four "Courageous Mothering," Danielle Russell explores the concept of courageous mothering as displayed through the character of Katniss Everdeen in the popular trilogy *The Hunger Games*. Similar to Bressler and Lengel, Russell indicates the capacity of dystopian novels, and *The Hunger Games* trilogy in particular, to reflect counter-normative realities and to warn readers of real world dangers "by projecting problems into a distant but recognizable future" and by drawing "attention to a variety of issues—ecological concerns, gender and racial stereotypes, political oppression, among others." For Russell, Katniss's various acts of mothering in *The Hunger Games,* which in many ways challenge patriarchal conceptions of motherhood and reflect a diversity of mothering practices, allude to an already existing landscape of multifaceted forms of mothering and represent the positive potential of a future human society.

In section two, Linda M. Burns in chapter six "Single Mother Adoption" and Lara Descartes in chapter nine "Single Lesbian Mothers" exemplify single mothering by choice through experience-centred reflections. In the first instance, Burns uses memoir as the means of contemplating a twenty-four-year journey as a single adoptive mother. She recounts the quick and hassle-free adoption of a four-month-old baby girl of mixed ethnic heritage. Her professional standing as assistant dean at the time, combined with the often invisible manifestations of white privilege, resulted in Burns living with her daughter just six months after beginning a twelve-week parenting class for prospective adoptive parents. Burns's narrative of single mothering by choice is revealing of some of the patterns identified by a few of the authors in this volume (Mack; Avery) in discussing the contemporary terrain of single mothers by choice. The classed and racialized dimensions of "good" motherhood are certainly there, evident in the assessment process through which Burns had to pass in order to adopt as a single mother. Also evident is the resilience of traditional constructions of family, against which Burns and her daughter would collide, despite the security of middle-class status. Lara Descartes presents her own experiences alongside information gleaned from interviews with five other single lesbian mothers and situates these vis-à-vis interviews with five coupled lesbian mothers to highlight the ways in which single lesbian mothers challenge heteronormative family ideas. Situated in southwestern Ontario, Descartes's study investigates her interviewees' experiences before and after motherhood to highlight issues of identity, exclusion, and belonging as important considerations for lesbian single mothers. Single lesbian mothers, Descartes indicates, are often assumed to be heterosexual by both heterosexuals and non-heterosexuals alike (reflecting the heteronormativity and presumed heterosexuality tied to motherhood and single mothering). Experiences of exclusion from lesbian community life are discussed, with some single lesbian mothers describing a sense of alienation from their identity as lesbians. Descartes challenges a literature on single motherhood and single mothering by choice, which, she points out is overwhelmingly heterocentric and in the case of literature on lesbian parenting, couple-centred.

In chapter five "Single Motherhood," Ellen Hauser uses autoethnography to explore leading social constructions and assumptions in the U.S. regarding single mothers as carriers of innate deficiencies. A "mythical madness" argues Hauser, stereotypes single mothers as social misfits, which lies in stark contrast to the lived realities of single mothers struggling to raise their children in a patriarchal and sexist social context that is constructed to discourage their success. Hauser suggests that "many of us single mothers experience our daily lives as 'insanity,' where we must maintain actual sanity to carry on our parenting responsibilities but feel as if the life we live is crazy and unsustainable." She highlights a common psychological conundrum: "to admit the full depth of 'insanity' we feel in our lives is dangerous because some survival techniques involve ignoring just how difficult it is raising children alone; but to not admit the real level of felt 'insanity' is to deny our own challenges, realities, and experiences." Hauser celebrates the resilience of single mothers like herself, whose strength triumphs over a hostile national culture and environment. In chapter eight "The Lone Ranger," Lee Murray further examines the stigma of single motherhood, which Hauser discusses. Murray also utilizes autoethnography to revisit her divorce in the early 1990s and to reflect on the feelings of shame and self-blame that she experienced at a time when, as she points out, there was a palpable culture of suspicion and stigma associated with single motherhood. Murray seeks to challenge assumptions that children of single moms are disadvantaged and that they are subject to deficient parenting. She confronts the societal myth that a "mother-headed" family is an aberration and espouses the possibility that such families are sites of diversified knowledge, strength, and empowerment. In chapter seven "Great Lakes to Great Walls," Natasha Steer—as with Deborah Byrd and Richard Piatt in chapter fifteen "Scripting Stories of Resistance"—focuses on experiences of young single motherhood. Steer explores her experiences living, working, and travelling overseas as a young single mother with her ten-year-old son. Steer reflects on the positive outcomes of her decision to move to China, which included a closer relationship with her son, an expanded worldview for her child, the development of a love of travelling, and a broadened understanding of different ways of parenting.

In chapter fifteen, part of section three, Byrd and Piatt describe a collaborative initiative involving young parents and students from Byrd's upper level women's and gender studies course titled "Single Motherhood in the Contemporary U.S.: Myths and Realities." In this initiative, Byrd and Piatt use the system known as theatre of the oppressed along with forum theatre to engage young parents in the telling of their experiences and stories. The concerns that emerge from the young parents participating in Byrd and Piatt's theatre workshops reflect some of the issues raised by Steer in chapter seven. The stigmatization, negative assumptions, and insulting comments to which young parents are subjected are significant aspects of the narratives that young parents produce with the theatre of the oppressed. The method is used to enhance understanding and build solidarity and to open spaces for sharing and critical analysis. Byrd and Piatt demonstrate the radical potential of this theatre as pedagogy for imagining broader possibilities and a different future, regarding the experiences of young single parents.

Motherwork, as the daily labour of mothering, and its associated forms of agency and resistance are explored by Elizabeth Bruno in chapter fourteen "I Play, Therefore, I am" and by Lydia Potts and Ulrike Lingen-Ali in chapter thirteen "Escaping a Life in Violence?" Bruno critiques a culture of intensive mothering and proposes a particular understanding of "play" as a form of resistance against this dominant ideology. She argues that the ways single mothers are praised as hard workers reinscribe the values of neoliberal capitalism. Bruno articulates "play" as opening possibilities for the construction of "a richer imaginative framework out of which to conceptualize care and attention in rearing children." She explains that "play within the family allows collaborative meaning building and ways to order reality co-operatively that can resist detrimental cultural expectations for perfection and self-sufficiency." Potts and Lingen-Ali examine one-parent migrant families in Germany. Using biographical interviews with migrant single mothers, the authors centre the mothers' voices in the discussion of the experience and labour of mothering. The mothering work of single migrant women in Germany is often done within contexts mired by multiple forms of violence—racism, physical violence, insults, control, and restrictions. Potts and Lingen-Ali indicate that the women whose voices are featured in this chapter seem to prefer single motherhood to their experiences of coupling. Most are aware of the services available through the state and describe their experiences with the limitations of these services. The resilience and agency demonstrated by the interviewees is heartening and present important insights to a still small body of literature on migrant single mothers.

Christin Quirk in chapter ten "Historicizing the Marginalization of Single Mothers," Rosa Ortiz-Monera, Dino Di Nella and Elizabet Almeda-Samaranch in chapter twelve "One-Parent Families in Spain," and Shihoko Nakagawa in chapter sixteen "Single Mothers' Activism against Poverty Governance" present policy-oriented analysis of government legislation and practices surrounding single motherhood, whereas Rachel Lamdin Hunter in chapter eleven "Single-Parent Families, Mother-Led Households, and Well-Being" questions conventions in the collection of well-being data that continue to erroneously present single-mother households as less healthy and happy than dual-parent households. Quirk's look at Australian policy highlights a continuing stigmatization of single mothers, manifested through punitive government reforms that have reduced eligibility and payments for single mothers. Quirk identifies a neoliberal political discourse that promotes "traditional family values" as underlying current discursive and policy-based attacks on single mothers. For Quirk, the impact of this is clear—her oral history interviews with single mothers demonstrate that even the social privileges identified earlier in this volume as pertaining to a more acceptable middle-upper class single motherhood do not take hold in the Australian context, where, as she states, "the conflation of categories of single motherhood is resolute, not only in the popular imagination, but also in the way in which single mothers see themselves." In Spain, as illustrated by the work of Monera, Di Nella and Samaranch in chapter twelve, a similar dominant positioning is accorded to the two-parent heterosexual nuclear family. The authors point out that one-parent families have been crucial in promoting family diversity and expanding existing legislation and policy along more progressive paths. Family and supportive social networks are shown to play an important role in determining quality of life among one-parent families in Spain. These, in turn, are triangulated with material identity markers, such as nationality and ethnicity, gender, and social class.

In chapter twelve, Hunter troubles the continued naturalization of the nuclear family by pointing to its origins in conservative family research. Hunter argues that this genealogy inevitably shapes the direction of researcher questions reproducing skewed data on single-parent families. Moreover, the author indicates that the efforts of lone mothers to provide vital and rewarding lives for themselves and their families are undermined by such views, which "further erod[es] well-being over and above any underlying economic or social disadvantage" that these families may face. Hunter advocates the reframing of "lone mothers" as "mother-led households" to highlight "the strengths, capacity and gifts which mothers readily describe when research methods and values are scrutinized and revisioned." Finally, Nakagawa, in chapter sixteen, presents a persuasive indictment of U.S. state policies and exposes exploitative cultures of discipline in the realm of child welfare. Importantly, Nakagawa calls attention to the activism of single mothers against the dominant paradigm of child welfare policies in the U.S. Relying on interviews conducted with single mothers associated with the activist organization Welfare Warriors (based in Milwaukee, WI), Nakagawa criticizes systemic greed and prejudice in the child welfare system and outlines the powerful organized resistance of single mothers against unrelenting and state-sanctioned incursions on their civil and parental rights.

The themes of contemporary relevance emerging from this volume include the current discursive landscape surrounding single motherhood, fatherhood and lone parenting more broadly (in both popular and policy cultures), manifestations of single mothering by choice, reflections on young single mothering, the experiences of migrant single mothers, the continuing stigmatization and demonization of single mothers (also evident through research and policy practices-including the welfare state's exploitation of single mothers for profit), and the resilience, agency, resistance, and activism of single parents, particularly mothers, who are individually and collectively contributing to more inclusive and just cultures for the benefit of us all. The themes and voices contained here are not exhaustive of the complex and multifaceted realities comprising the realm of lone parenting. They are, however, a rich tapestry and provide a valuable glimpse into the contemporary landscape of issues and discussions surrounding single mothering and lone parenting.

NOTES

[1]As Oyeronke Oyewumi, among others, has indicated, the conflation of motherhood with wifery is a distinctly Western European and

North American ideological practice. The genealogy of motherhood in her Nigerian (Yoruba) cultural context accords recognition and status to women as mothers regardless of marital status.

[2]Custody and the day-to-day labour of childrearing are distinct matters. In both Canada and the U.S., custody is often legally shared or joint between the parents; however, mothers continue to vastly outnumber men as the primary caregivers to children in these situations, with the majority of children having primary residence with their mothers and scheduled visitations with their other parent under a joint or shared custody agreement (Williams).

WORKS CITED

Bock, Jane D. "Doing the Right Thing? Single Mothers by Choice and the Struggle for Legitimacy." *Gender and Society* 14.1 (February 2000): 62-86. Print.

Brooks, Brandynicole. *Black Single Mothers and the Child Welfare System: A Guide for Social Workers on Addressing Oppression.* London: Routledge, 2015. Print.

Cooksey, E.C., and M. M. Fondell. "Spending Time with His Kids: Effects of Family Structure on Fathers' and Children's Lives." *Journal of Marriage and the Family* 58.3 (1996): 693-707. Print.

Dejean, Sarah L., Christi R. McGeorge, and Thomas Stone Carlson. "Attitudes Toward Never-Married Single Mothers and Fathers: Does Gender Matter?" *Journal of Feminist Family Therapy* 24.2 (2012): 121-138. Print.

Duncan, Simon, and Rosalind Edwards, eds. *Single Mothers in an International Context: Mothers or Workers?* London: Routledge, 1997. Print.

Gramsci, Antonio. *Selections from the Prison Notebooks.* Trans. Quintin Hoare and Geoffrey Nowell Smith. New York: International Publishers Co., 1971. Print.

Hamer, Jennifer, and Kathleen Marchioro. "Becoming Custodial Dads: Exploring Parenting among Low-Income and Working-Class African American Fathers." *Journal of Marriage and Family* 64.1 (February 2002): 116-129. Print.

Hawkins, D. N., P. R. Amato, and V. King. "Parent-Adolescent Involvement: The Relative Influence of Parent Gender and Residence." *Journal of Marriage and Family* 68.1 (2006): 125-136. Print.

Hertz, Rosanna. *Single by Chance, Mothers by Choice: How Women Are Choosing Parenthood without Marriage and Creating the New American Family*. New York: Oxford University Press, 2008. Print.

Jarrett, Robin L. "Welfare Stigma among Low-Income, African American Single Mothers." *Family Relations* 45.4 (October 1996): 368-374. Print.

Jayakody, Rukmalie, and Dawn Stauffer. "Mental Health Problems among Single Mothers: Implications for Work and Welfare Reform." *Journal of Social Issues* 56.4 (Winter 2000): 617-634. Print.

Juffer, Jane. *Single Mother: The Emergence of the Domestic Intellectual*. New York: New York University Press, 2006. Print.

Kramer, Karen Z., Laurelle L. Myhra, Virginia S. Zuiker and Jean W. Bauer. "Disparity of Single Mothers and Fathers Across Three Decades: 1990-2010." *Gender Issues* 33.1 (2016): 22-41. Print.

Lichter, Daniel T., and Deborah Roempke Graefe. "Men and Marriage Promotion: Who Marries Unwed Mothers?" *Social Service Review* 81.3 (September 2007): 397-421. Print.

Lipman, Ellen L., David R. Offord, and Michael H. Boyle. "Single Mothers in Ontario: Sociodemographic, Physical and Mental Health Characteristics." *Canadian Medical Association Journal* 156.5 (1997): 639-645. Print.

Livingston, Gretchen. "The Rise of Single Fathers: A Ninefold Increase since 1960." *Pew Social Trends*. Pew Research Center, 2 July 2013. Web. 17 Dec. 2015.

Maruko, Mami. "Single Fathers Emerge from the Shadows." *japantimes.co.jp*. The Japan Times, 20 Aug. 2014. Web. 17 Dec. 2015.

McLanahan, Sara, and Gary Sandefur. *Growing Up with a Single Parent: What Hurts, What Helps*. Cambridge: Harvard University Press, 1994. Print.

Morissette, Mikki. *Choosing Single Motherhood: The Thinking Woman's Guide*. Boston: Houghton Mifflin, 2008. Print.

Myles, John, Feng Hou, and Garnett Picot. "The Demographic Foundations of Rising Employment and Earnings among Single Mothers in Canada and the United States, 1980 to 2000." Ottawa:

Statistics Canada, March 2008 (Catalogue no. 11F0019M–No. 305). Print.

Olson, Sheryl L., and Victoria Banyard. "'Stop the World So I Can Get Off for a While': Sources of Daily Stress in the Lives of Low-Income Single Mothers of Young Children." *Family Relations* 42.1 (January 1993): 50-56. Print.

Orendain, Simone. "Spouses of Philippine Contract Workers Adjust to Single Fatherhood." *Voice of America (VOA)*. N.p., 22 Dec. 2014. Web. 17 Dec. 2015.

Oyewumi, Oyeronke. "Conceptualizing Gender: The Eurocentric Foundations of Feminist Concepts and the Challenge of African Epistemologies." *CODESRIA: Council for the Development of Social Science Research in Africa*. Codesria, 21 Dec. 2015. Web. 10 Nov. 2015.

Ruddick, Sara. *Maternal Thinking: Toward a Politics of Peace*. Boston: Beacon Press, 1995. Print.

Russell, Mary, Barbara Harris, and Annemarie Gockel. "Canadian Lone Mothers Describe Parenting Needs: European Solutions Explored." *Canadian Social Work Review* 25.2 (2008): 169-185. Print.

Sidel, Ruth. *Unsung Heroines: Single Mothers and the American Dream*. Berkeley: University of California Press, 2006. Print.

Vaughan, Andrew. "More Canadian Single Dads Head Rise in Lone-Parent Families." *CBC News*, 19. Sept. 2012. Web. 17 Dec. 2015.

Williams, Charmaine C. "Race (And Gender and Class) and Child Custody: Theorizing Intersections in Two Canadian Court Cases." *NWSA Journal* 16.2 (Summer 2004): 46-69. Print.

I.
DISCOURSE, MEDIA, AND REPRESENTATION

1. Mothering in Dystopia

Lone Parenting in a Post-Apocalyptic World

NANCY BRESSLER AND LARA LENGEL

LONE MOTHERING IS A BLUR and a series of chronic stresses and low-level traumas, which, sometimes, does seem like it happened to someone else—a story narrated amid a bad dream. Within the myriad conflicts of contemporary society, lone mothering is an ongoing survival test and a constant stream of calamities. Those who have experienced lone mothering[1] can attest to the distress and emergent symptoms, similar to that of major depressive, dissociative, and/or anxiety disorders or mild to moderate posttraumatic stress disorder.[2]

Contemporary mothering is often fraught with conflict. In her book *Mothering in the Third Wave*, Amber Kinser analyzes the struggles and complexities of mothering. She attests that contemporary mothers are "mothering through terrorism, war, and the Patriot Act; through eating disorders and meth epidemics; through hurricane Katrina and other disasters—natural and unnatural" (1). These twenty-first century crises, in part, explain the vast popularity of literary and mediated dystopian narratives. In our rational moments, we know that we are negotiating a world that is not necessarily on the brink of collapse. However, we also realize the stresses and complications of everyday life as a mother are more than merely trivial. Financial hardships, exhaustion, and guilt are far more probable to occur than any array of catastrophes likely to emerge after a societal mega-collapse.[3]

Anxieties, whether minor or monumental, can plague even the healthiest lone mother parenting her children in a relatively tranquil environment. Persistent fears of the future, both her children's and her own, are a consequence of the plurality of ways a society could fail. In their study "Everyday Fear: Parenting and Childhood in a Culture of Fear," Leanne Franklin and John Cromby argue that "The family unit is where this culture of fear is perhaps most visible as the relationship between adults and children is seemingly more fraught than ever. Child rearing is no longer a shared social responsibility, but is confined to the immediate family, while strangers are viewed with a mistrust that comes easily" (161).[4] Mothers are abundantly aware of the myriad of afflictions that could harm them and their offspring, including but certainly not limited to abduction, human trafficking, armed conflicts, nuclear Armageddon, global ecophagy (Maras), anthropogenic global warming leading to threatened food insecurity, incidence and prevalence of increasing diseases, and—as detailed in our autoethnographic reflections in "Mothering in a Time of Terror" (Lengel, Birzescu, and Minda)—transnational terrorism, primarily those involving an invisible enemy "other." Mediated discourses of fear exacerbate these concerns (Altheid and Michalowski; Franklin and Cromby; Wuthnow).[5] Any one of the aforementioned crises, let alone a combination, could be the underpinning of a tremendously perilous future for one's children.

HOW DYSTOPIAN FANTASY INFORMS CONTEMPORARY MOTHERING

Perhaps it is the fleeting escape from the challenges of daily life, ranging from those mundane to monstrous, that draws mothers to dystopian fantasy. In the most irrational and emotional moments, we do feel as if we are mothering at the end of the world as we know it. Not only do dystopian filmic and televisual narratives provide temporary diversions, but they also reflect contemporary socio-political contexts of the human condition generally and lone mothering specifically. Representations of lone mothering in popular cultural dystopian televisual texts reflect and affirm the hegemonic construction of family. In these and other mediated narratives a "white, nuclear version of **familialism** continues to be naturalized and privileged" (Chambers 195).

Our analysis contributes to the body of cultural studies and feminist scholarship on the contemporary notion of family and the lone mother's place in it. Scholarship by luminaries including Louis Althusser, Michel Foucault, Pierre Bourdieu, Nancy Chodorow, Patricia Hill Collins, and Raymond Williams[6] all provide important critique of the concept of family in contemporary society. Family has been identified as patriarchy's chief institution, "both a mirror of and a connection with the larger society; a patriarchal unit within a patriarchal whole" (Millet 33) and a central and vital agent for ensuring hegemonic conformity, particularly when other agents, such as political or religious ones, fail to do so.

Despite the "dramatic changes in the structure of the traditional nuclear family, claims regarding the 'death of the family' or a 'decline in family values' fail to grasp the dynamic formulations of family" (Lahad and Shoshana 2) in conceptualization and praxis. Mediated representations of the shifting constitutions of family similarly fail to grasp these changes. The continued ambiguity of the mediated representations of family that diverge from the heteronormative patriarchal structures are even more critical towards lone mothers and their inclusion in mediated narratives. This ambiguity demonstrates "continued cultural anxiety about the changing nature of the American family" (Silbergleid, "'Oh Baby!'" para. 18). Gendered hierarchies, particularly evident in the separation of the public and private sphere (Lengel; Silbergleid, "Women, Utopia, and Narrative"), provide further opportunities for cultural anxiety.

Aside from the few literary critiques of mothering in post-apocalyptic worlds (Haupt; Martucci; Ostman; Schrynemakers)[7] and analysis in blogs and the popular press (Grey; Kearns; Parrinello-Cason; Truitt; Weaver), there is, to date, a lack of work on the complexities of parenting or, specifically, lone mothering in dystopian media texts. Given the absence of work in this area, particularly considering the "dystopian turn" in Anglo American science fiction and fantasy (Baccolini 165; Baccolini and Tom Moylan), this study embarks on an important examination on how mothers in dystopia are framed within their respective narratives as they respond to serious existential threats.

With particular focus on the parent-child relationships in *Falling Skies, Revolution,* and *The Walking Dead*, this study asks with what contemporary contexts and themes do post-apocalyptic narratives resonate. It studies the representation of lone mothers in both science fiction and horror genres and examines the state of family in flux, the difficult decisions mothers face, and the cultural and psychological implications of those choices.

SITUATING LONE MOTHERING IN DYSTOPIAN NARRATIVES

An analysis of lone mothering in televisual dystopian texts provides rich opportunities to critique gendered representations of parenting, family, and community. Previous scholarship on lone mothering in television has critiqued how such texts represent "macrocosmic issues within the microcosm of community life. It is here that cultural and societal values are attached to subjects which may be of topical interest or which have engendered public debate in a wider social context" (Teckman 135). Here, we situate the representation of lone mothering into broader contemporary socio-political contexts, particularly the imagining of mothering in dystopian fantasy narratives to illuminate relevant social issues.

Lone mothers in dystopian landscapes are exposed to the most horrific elements of human- and undead-inflicted violence and the brutalities of both the natural and (entirely or partially destroyed) built environment. As the destruction of modernity occurs, community and family are rebuilt, reformed, and reconstituted. Heba Hosni argues that "the degradation of the atmosphere, the collapse of law and order, and the loss of a material infrastructure lead to, among other destructive effects, the break-up stable, biologically related families" Hosni goes on to suggest that "groups of people, disparate survivors of one kind or another, band together for self-protection."

Following the journeys of the family and communities trying to survive unforgivingly violent post-apocalyptic worlds has captivated tens of millions of viewers. The dystopian landscapes presented in these narratives result from diverse societal, anthropomorphic, or environmental crises, including the following: complete breakdown of telecommunication systems, energy and food insecurity, or the attack of the "other"—a visible or an invisible enemy "other," which can be constituted as a microbial or viral infectious pandemic. Any one of these has the capacity "to reduce our cherished social structures to absolute rubble" (Ozog 140).

Science fiction narratives have a long history of creating "morally informed story lines" (Creeber 31). In response to second wave feminist critiques of sexist media portrayals of women, writers and producers of mainstream science fiction in the late 1960s and 1970s attempted to offer more progressive women characters. Since that time, science fiction has relied on the fantasy and impracticality of storylines and situations to challenge the societal status quo. When science fiction is viewed as fantasy, the genre provides more robust possibilities to present subversive material than other genres, such as dramas, comedies, and, more recently, reality television.

Science fiction narratives, thus, can provide social commentary and resist social norms, however explicitly or subtly, through metaphors and conventionally less realistic settings. By using a combination of relatable characters within a unique and fantastical setting, these texts provide the opportunity to comment on human inconsistencies. Parrinder argues that the strange worlds depicted in science fiction are distorted just enough for audience members to recognize and identify with them (31). Critics and audiences "regard it as the inevitable and necessary expression of the contemporary 'human condition'" (31). Through science fiction texts, social assumptions can be questioned in ways that traditional television genres cannot. Science fiction texts present imaginative futures that still emphasize the flaws within the human condition (Hollinger and Gordon 2). Yet because of the change in setting, science fiction allows for greater social commentary (Milstead xii).

FALLING SKIES: WOMEN ON THE MARGINS OF BROTHERHOOD

Croteau and Hoynes observe that "there is potential social significance in all media products—even those that are clearly make-believe fantasies. Creators of media products are often aware of this fact and use entertainment media to comment on the real social world. In turn, readers and audiences develop at least some sense of the social world through their exposure" (197). Although creators and producers are aware of media's social impact, the texts that they create often fall short of resisting white, hegemonic norms of masculinity and femininity. This deficiency is evident in the science fiction series *Falling Skies*.

A narrative focus on family, familial survival, and brotherhood is central to *Falling Skies*. Through examining various episodes, we analyze how motherhood is situated in a post-apocalyptic world and in a narrative in which brotherhood is an ongoing trope. Given the hype of its executive producer, Steven Spielberg, *Falling Skies* premiered on TNT in June 2011 with 5.9 million viewers (2.6 million of those comprising the key demographic of viewers under the age of fifty). It was the most watched cable premiere of the year, surpassing *The Walking Dead* and *Covert Affairs* (Adalian 1). The drama focuses on the Mason family and their makeshift family of fighters as they battle "Mechs" and "Skitters," sent by the "Espheni" aliens to dominate and exterminate the human race. Within days of the aliens' arrival, the majority of the world's population is killed, leaving only small bands of fighters to maintain the human race. One militia regiment, known as the Second Massachusetts Militia Regiment (2nd Mass), includes the main character, Tom Mason a former Boston College professor of history who is now second in command of the makeshift group of patriot paramilitaries. Tom and his three sons—Hal, Ben, and Matt—must strategize and fight against the alien invasion to ensure the survival of the human race.

The only mother figure in *Falling Skies* is Dr. Anne Glass, a medic for the patriot group. Although Tom's wife, and the mother of the boys, died during the first season, Tom meets and falls in love with Anne; they have a baby girl named Lexi in the third season. Aside from her medical talents, Anne is underappreciated. Her input is frequently devalued or entirely ignored by her new family. Given that Tom and the boys have a stronger, more developed relationship, Anne is left out of any decisions that the men in the family make together. One may argue that Tom and his sons have had more time to bond and develop their relationship, which accounts for the more minimized role accorded to Anne. Yet this is also the beginning of a trend in the show in which fatherhood is valued over motherhood. Developing and sustaining a relationship with a mother becomes an afterthought. Ironically, in a post-apocalyptic world where characters frequently die and each day is a struggle for survival, the implication is that the mother will always be there and that the relationship can be addressed at a later point in time. Fatherhood, in particular the relationships between sons and their father, receives narrative priority.

Eventually, Tom and others from the patriot rebel group rescue mother and daughter and return them to the group. At this point, daughter Lexi continues to exhibit strange behaviours and in a matter of months, she has grown into a teenager. As Lexi struggles to adapt to her hybrid alien human status, she wishes to maintain a relationship with her father, Tom, but not her mother, Anne. Thus, it is the father-child relationship that is, again, emphasized. In the horror genre, Barbara Creed observes that "all individuals experience abjection at the time of their earliest attempts to break away from the mother. She sees the mother-child relation as one marked by conflict; the child struggles to break free but the mother is reluctant to release it" (41). The mother, thus, becomes abject when she declines to release control over her child, which allows the child to take "its proper place in relation to the Symbolic" (Creed 41). Anne struggles to develop a relationship with her daughter and refuses to let her go when the two are separated; when Lexi returns, she is only interested in a relationship with her father. Ultimately, Lexi strives to find her humanity within her father's image. She rejects her mother, who has always emotionally and physically cared for her, in favour of becoming the daughter whom her father desires.

Science fiction theorist Vivian Sobchack observes that when the horror film and family drama converge, a new interpretation of family and patriarchal culture is possible. Horror films can demonstrate "the contemporary weakening of patriarchal authority and the glaring contradictions that exist between the mythology of family relations and their actual social practice" (147). Yet even in the post-apocalyptic world of *Falling Skies,* these gender roles seem firmly fixed. Fatherhood is valued more than motherhood, no matter the gender of the children or the biological ties. In a post-apocalyptic context of "brotherhood," fatherhood is the primary familial relationship.

REVOLUTION: POSSIBILITY, PATRIARCHY, POWERLESSNESS

A post-apocalyptic world mysteriously devoid of electricity is the setting for the science fiction dramatic television series *Revolution.* Set in the year 2027, the series uses flashbacks from fifteen years earlier, 2012, to provide context. The show focuses on the Matheson family—parents, Ben and Rachel, and their children, Charlie and Danny, and Ben's brother, Miles. The harmony within the family is immediately interrupted in the series: Rachel is presumed dead at the beginning of the narrative, and Ben is killed by members of the militia of the Monroe Republic, which rose to power after the U.S. government collapsed. Rachel, however, is alive and has been held prisoner at the Republic's capital under orders of its leader, General Sebastian "Bass" Monroe because he thought Rachel had the technical knowledge to reinstate "the power." Despite her distance from her children, Rachel becomes the central mother figure in *Revolution*'s powerless world.

Similar to *Falling Skies,* the relationships between the central mother and her children are minimized and problematized, whereas the male characters develop richly nuanced relationships with their children or, in the case of Charlie, Danny, and Miles, a niece and a nephew. During flashbacks throughout the first season, Ben is shown as a caring and nurturing father to his children; in contrast, Rachel is portrayed as having willingly deserted her children. Rachel's identity inscription as a deficient mother is not inconsistent with many mediated representations of women. Although some women characters in media representation can break free of traditional gender roles and performances, mothers have often been stereotyped in confined ways.

The pilot episode[8] opens with a flashback of a typical mother-child interaction. While Rachel is speaking with her own mother, she encourages six-year-old Charlie to talk to her grandma via Rachel's iPhone. Transfixed by the television screen, Charlie cannot be bothered to turn her attention away from Bugs Bunny. Moments later, the television screen flickers to static then goes dead, along with all the electrically powered devices in the Matheson home. It is the last time that Rachel would be able to speak with her mother, and it is the final moments of the family's comforts of modernity. In a later flashback in the first episode, hours after the global power outage, Rachel and Ben provide a loving parenting moment for young Charlie, as they realize that this is the final day of the world that they once knew. They do what parents do to comfort young children in the face of catastrophe: they smile as they suppress their tears and allow their child to focus on something happy—in this case, eating as much ice cream as Charlie wants. "Really?" Charlie asks. The mother shares just enough information to provide context for her child: "The freezer, it doesn't work. It's all gonna melt anyway." As Charlie digs into the gallon ice cream container, Ben says, "Whoa! Slow down, kiddo. I want you to really, really remember what it tastes like, okay?" Fifteen years later, Charlie, now a young adult woman, remembers that moment—the taste, texture, and chill on her tongue long forgotten.

Several other flashbacks, which are far less pleasurable, of the days, weeks, and years following the blackout provide context for Charlie's character development and, after her father is murdered, develop the complexities surrounding her relationship with her lone mother. Charlie recalls when a fellow survivor threatened to kill her if her mother refused to give him food and provisions. Later in season one, a coda to this flashback reveals that it was her mother who shot and murdered the survivor, not her father as originally insinuated. In one of Charlie's most devastating memories, a flashback recounts Rachel saying goodbye to her husband and young children to seek food and supplies. Charlie cries and begs her mother not to leave. Rachel is seen walking away from her family without looking back at them, a tough and stoic mother marching away from her family. She never returns and is presumed dead. In another flashback, several episodes later, the audience sees Rachel leaving her family, her expression and tears revealing her devastation.

INTENSIVE MOTHERING IN TRAUMATIC CONDITIONS

Mothers in televisual texts often exhibit "intensive mothering," in which the child is the primary focus, and the mother comes secondary to the child's interests (Ennis; Hays). Such mothers are portrayed as caregivers, who are expected to care for the children and the home foremost, often at the expense of themselves. Idealized images of the mother nurturing and protecting her children reinforce the notion that a woman's sole responsibility is caring for her child. Rachel, by contrast, balances mothering with her pre-blackout career as a contractor for the U.S. Department of Defense (DOD). The series of flashbacks in season one, episode seven, "The Children's Crusade," reveal the immense sacrifice that Rachel makes to arrange for specialist medical care for her infant through the power hierarchy of the DOD.

Another mother who exhibits behaviour focused only on her children is Maggie Foster, the village doctor. Maggie is introduced in the pilot episode with an angelic face and curled blond locks. Maggie is the ideal earth mother, as she has practical intelligence, backed up by her quiet, calming British accent. She tends a makeshift homeopathic herb garden, growing in the carcass of a rusted out Toyota Prius, and identifies the healing benefits of certain herbs to a young girl in their rural community. Shortly thereafter, Maggie creates an herbal remedy for seventeen-year-old Danny, who had an asthma attack while out hunting with his sister Charlie. There are evident tensions between Maggie and Charlie, who resists Maggie's role as de facto stepmother to the Matheson children. Maggie is no pushover, however. Her "bad ass" powers emerge halfway through the pilot when she, Charlie, and another community member, Aaron Pittman, set off to secure assistance to rescue Danny who was taken by militia of the Monroe Republic, one of six regional powers that emerged in North America after the U.S. and Canadian governments collapsed post-blackout. Ambushed by a group of violent male survivors while they slept in an abandoned jet plane during their rescue mission, Maggie saves her group by offering poison that appeared to be whiskey, followed by a serious of fatal self-defence manoeuvres against the men who tried to assault her and Charlie.

The lone mother's backstory is the most compelling of any character in *Revolution*. A glimpse of her life emerges in the final moments of season one, episode three, "No Quarter." A mysterious pendant, given to Aaron by Ben just before he dies, has the capacity to power up electronic devices, including Maggie's iPhone. The iPhone screen reads 6:23 Monday, September 17, over an image of two young children. A moment later, the image breaks up and the screen returns to the blank state that it has been for the past fifteen years. Aaron asks in "No Quarter" why Maggie carries around her iPhone in her pack and she explains that the phone has her only pictures of her children, and she fears she can no longer remember their faces. The following episode, "The Plague Dogs," reveals the extent to which Maggie has tried to reunite with her two preschool sons. Maggie's first flashback in "The Plague Dogs" provides context: she is a working professional single mother and a British national, who happened to have travelled from London to Seattle before the blackout. She is seen preparing for an evening event while talking to her sons via Skype. As the boys' nanny is trying to put them to bed, Maggie's sons ask when she will be home. Maggie responds that she will be home in "two sleeps," after which the boys beg their mummy to read one more chapter of *The Wizard of Oz*. She says, "no," just as the computer screen flickers and dies, along with all the lights on the Seattle skyline. As "The Plague Dogs" progresses, subsequent flashbacks illuminate Maggie's trauma following the blackout and effort to get back home.

After the blackout, Maggie heads eastward on foot from Seattle through Montana to Buffalo, New York. She arrives at the docks in Buffalo, where she says to Rudy, a fisherman, that a man in Montana told her she could get to the Atlantic from there. Rudy responds, "You can't get to England either. There are no more tall ships, no more steamboats. They were all destroyed in the wars or ripped apart for lumber when the militias got 'em. Hell, getting to England? That's like trying to get to the moon." Maggie continues to walk up and down the eastern seaboard, hoping for passage to the UK. Finally, she wanders back westward. Another flashback depicts Maggie sitting at the shores of a lake in Wisconsin, ready to drink some of her poison. Ben Matheson approaches to refill his water bottles, talks to her, and invites her back to his campsite for a meal. She is welcomed into the Matheson family and helps raise Charlie and Danny with Ben. "The Plague Dogs" is the fourth and final episode featuring Maggie. She is killed by another survivor.

Later in the first season, upon reconnecting with her children, Rachel initially tries to develop a relationship with young adult

Charlie, despite still being imprisoned by Monroe. The struggle for survival in the dystopian post-blackout world—further complicated by a subtle narrative of Rachel's negotiation of a past tryst with her brother-in-law, Miles Matheson—overshadows her familial relationship with Charlie. Rachel and Charlie are depicted as having a strained relationship, which neither wishes to discuss. Instead, they each seek romantic relationships: Rachel has a romantic history with Miles, which she rekindles. Charlie's first love interest is Jason Neville, but she also has a brief intimate relationship with Connor, Monroe's son.

By contrast to the strained mother-daughter dyad, the father-son relationship of Tom Neville and Jason Neville, a major and lieutenant in the Monroe Militia respectively, is featured prominently within the series. The two characters frequently have scenes in which they discuss their relationship. Even when Jason begins to challenge the Monroe Militia and defy his father and fellow soldiers, Tom struggles to protect his son and sustain their relationship. In addition, in *Revolution*'s second season, Bass Monroe discovers he has a long-lost son; the majority of his storyline focuses on Monroe's redemption in order to earn a relationship with his son. Overall, the show spends a considerable amount of time building the father-child relationship[9] but avoids the mother-child one. For the women characters of the show, romantic relationships are the primary focus, whereas the male characters develop and sustain their familial relationships.

CRITIQUING PATRIARCHAL DOMINANCE AND NORMATIVE FAMILY STRUCTURE IN *THE WALKING DEAD*

Because it can be a site for critiquing traditional gendered perspectives and normative femininity (Ahmad; Clover; Mubarki), the horror genre serves as the ideal context to analyze shifting conceptualizations of motherhood. The disruption of the perceived natural order of society and the portrayals of gender repression dominate the plots of the horror genre. Although patriarchal dominance, materialism, and normative family structures can all be critiqued within this context, new analysis of the role of the horror genre on television is warranted because these media texts have replaced the idyllic images of the harmonious nuclear family that appeared, and to a certain extent continue to be portrayed, in other television genres. Contrary to other genres, such as drama and sitcom, the horror genre often portrays the family as a site of repression, which confines members of society into symbolic roles, particularly mothers. Consequently, these depictions of the family serve as warnings against conformity to the symbolic order. Thus, when the horror genre and the portrayal of family converge, a new interpretation of motherhood is possible. Tony Williams has argued that horror films provide an ideal opportunity to discuss deeply ingrained social factors that ultimately repress particular members of society. Specifically, the American family and its suppressive authoritarian roles warrant analysis for signs of progression within the horror genre. Parents are often confined, both emotionally and financially, in these roles. Children and women who challenge the totalitarian role of the family are often depicted as monsters. In actuality, it is the family constraints that are monstrous. Stephen Snyder observes that the horror genre's overarching theme is to underline anxieties about measuring up to the standards, both socially and financially, set forth in America. Idealized imaginaries of the traditional family can become more detrimental than supernatural or monstrous entities; yet a post-apocalyptic world has more survival challenges to overcome. Thus, this altered context may provide an even more nuanced interpretation.

Of the various dystopian narratives within either the horror or science fiction genres, perhaps none have received more attention in the current scholarly and popular press as has the zombie one.[10] And rising to the top of the zombie apex is the "walker." *The Walking Dead (TWD)* has received a tremendous amount of news coverage, as AMC's "juggernaut series" has been the number one television program among the eighteen to forty-nine audience group each year from 2014 to the present (Kruse; Kissell). The series has also received a solid amount of scholarly analysis. In his essay "Locating Zombies in the Sociology of Popular Culture," Todd Platts argues that the zombies in dystopian televisual, filmic, and literary narratives can be seen as "significant cultural objects that reflect and reveal the cultural and material circumstances of their creation … emanating from complex culture-producing institutions and (arguably) capturing extant social anxieties" (547). In *The Walking Dead*, both a graphic novel-comic series and a television series on the AMC cable network, anxieties emerge from an invisible enemy that has taken over like "wildfire,"[11] from a disease that may have emerged from any number of sources, microbial, viral, fungal, or parasitic.

Jessica Murray, in her work "A Zombie Apocalypse: Opening Representational Spaces for Alternative Constructions of Gender and Sexuality," explores whether "zombie texts successfully capitalise on the post-apocalyptic social ruptures in terms of their representations of gender and sexuality. Although the texts do suggest alternative constructions, they also reinscribe and reify traditional patriarchal and heteronormative binaries" (1). Although there are numerous ruptures and reinscriptions of gender norms that we could critique in *The Walking Dead*[12] our analysis focuses on the birth and subsequent parenting of Judith Grimes.

Baby Judith is portrayed as the first infant having been born after "the turn."[13] Judith was born to the wife, Lori, of protagonist Rick Grimes. Given that Lori had a brief sexual relationship with Rick's best friend and colleague, Shane Walsh, when Lori assumed Rick had died in a hospital just before the outbreak, Rick's identity as Judith's father is questionable. Lori's mothering has been questioned throughout seasons one and two; she is often unaware of the whereabouts of her son Carl, an inattentiveness that can easily result in the death of a child, as is the case with other children in *The Walking Dead*. Furthermore, in season two, episode six, "Secrets," Lori considers abortion upon discovering that she is pregnant. The season three episode, "The Killer Within," portrays a harrowing birthing process, one that is consistent with the preposterous losses experienced by the characters in both the graphic novel and television series. Lori's baby is born in the "tombs" of the prison inhabited by a survivor group led, in part, by Rick Grimes. Maggie Green delivers the baby by performing an emergency Caesarean section on Lori, slicing her lower abdomen open with a knife. Suffering shock from the pain, because of the lack of anesthesia, and blood loss, Lori dies shortly after the baby is lifted from her. Lori's son, Carl, offers to shoot his own mother so that she would not "turn."

EXPANDING THE DEFINITIONS OF PARENTING AND FAMILY

The narrow definition of "family," is one that often fails to take into account the extended community and family networks that provide support. Specifically, it is important to examine to what extent lone-**mother** families, communal childrearing, co-parenting, and community parenting critique the broader infrastructures of care and the influence of community and family networks on maternal parenting and child and youth adjustment and well-being.[14] The televisual representation of collaborative care in *The Walking Dead* emerges from the moment Judith is introduced to the other survivors and Judith's father, Rick Grimes: Maggie Green walking out of the prison "tombs" holding a bloodied newborn, with the traumatized expression on Maggie's face indicating that Lori did not survive the birthing.

Works by Judith Stacey and Cassie Ozog look at the "broader sentiment in many facets of American culture" (Ozog 134). Ozog suggests that "as the traditional family unit fades from modern life and is replaced by new configurations, and no one particular 'family pattern' exists to which most of society adheres or aspires" (134). Once Lori dies in childbirth, a new family pattern emerges to care for the newborn Judith. The co-parenting of Judith is depicted in numerous episodes. After Maggie and Daryl Dixon make a supply run to a daycare centre for baby bottles and formula, Daryl gives Judith her first bottle in the episode titled "Say the Word." Beth Greene is seen in several episodes holding, playing with, and caring for Judith. The collaborative childrearing of Judith exemplifies a return to more traditional collectivistic cultures. The dystopian aftermath of the breakdown of Western and/or American individualistic modernity leads to new constructions of the family as inclusive communities that extend far beyond blood lines.

Some of the most touching scenes involving Judith depict the co-parenting of the baby by the lone mothers who have lost their own children to the undead. In the first half of season four, for example, after Judith spits up on Beth, she abruptly hands the baby over to Michonne, who, at first, is reluctant to hold the baby and starts to cry while holding her. Later in season four, episode two

"Infected," Michonne reveals her lone mother identity to Carl. She had a son, Andre Anthony, who died in a post-apocalypse encampment while the father and Michonne's boyfriend, Mike and his best friend, Terry were too inebriated to adequately care for the boy. Carol Peletier—mother of Sophia who went missing in the first several episodes of season two and then was discovered undead—has had several painful collaborative parenting moments, most notably when she murdered a preadolescent girl, Lizzie Samuels, who had killed her own sister, Mika, and was preparing to kill Judith as well. Other co-parenting moments for baby Judith include the care provided by Tyreese Williams who saved her from the catastrophic attack on the survivors' home in the prison, from numerous "walker" attacks in the surrounding wilderness, and, most notably, from a direct attack by a cannibal.

One of the touching co-parenting moments occurs in the final moments of the season five premiere of *The Walking Dead*. It is important to note that the various small groups of survivors assume that many, if not most of their makeshift family, have perished. Carol reconnects with the main group including Rick, Carl, Daryl, Michonne, Bob, and Sasha. Carol leads Rick and the group to a cabin in the woods where Judith was nearly murdered. In a visually lovely shot, Carol and Michonne, two important lone-mother characters, walk on either side of Rick as they all approach the dwelling. Tyreese emerges from the cabin holding Judith. Rick and Carl run to Judith to reconnect with the baby whom they thought was dead. The reconnection at the cabin is a rare happy ending, with a father, son, and male co-parent all present. Former lone mothers, Michonne and Carol, look on as their bittersweet smiles hint at the unending grief of losing their own children.

This group of survivors, similar to other zombie apocalypse narratives, constitute a new family in the new world. In her study "Zombies and the Modern American Family: Surviving the Destruction of Traditional Society in *Zombieland* (2009)," Cassie Ozog argues that "the zombies, who have shattered the long-held traditions of our society, have become emblematic of the changing social tides wherein traditional family spheres have fragmented, allowing for new family shapes and processes to emerge" (134).

The Walking Dead family is comprised of lone fathers, newly formed brotherly and sisterly bonds, and lone mothers whose birth children were killed. Furthermore, Ozog suggests that "As survivors reinvent the traditional structure of the family, they also begin to disregard old societal values, including how we value other people and cultures. It is important to understand that both our values and our ways of looking at the world are ingrained in us through the social values we learn, including how we value other cultures" (137).

In her analysis of gender and race in *The Walking Dead*, Kate Steiger argues that "*some* of the *worst gender* dynamics in today's world" (99) are represented in the series. Although the women of *The Walking Dead* exhibit flawed mothering, could it be the narrative limitations that inhibit the mothers from having better options? Lori has been seen by many audience members as an incompetent mother, often not knowing the location of her son, Carl. Carol did not run after her daughter, Sophia, when she sprinted into the woods during a walker attack. Michonne left her son, Andre, with his father, who was too stoned to save the boy from a walker attack. Lilly, mother of Meghan and a lesser-known character, focuses on a distant walker and fails to see the one that emerges from the sand to bite her daughter. By contrast, Tyreese, after dodging a military tank, numerous AK-47s and even more walkers, carries an infant while guiding two young girls, whose parents were killed by walkers, through the prison attack and into the walker-filled wilderness. Out of all the co-parents raising baby Judith, Tyreese is depicted as the most attentive, gentlest, most willing to change the diapers amid a walker onslaught. Tyreese's superlative parenting of baby Judith is not uncommon with the representations of men as parenting heroes in numerous filmic and televisual genres. By contrast, women are represented as deficient parents as their human imperfections are highlighted. In the examples mentioned above, *The Walking Dead* mothers are negligent but are still unable to protect their children, given that the existing storylines have provided these mothers with no opportunities to be parenting heroes. That Tyreese is given the most robust set of narrative possibilities to do so reinforces hegemonic constitutions of parent, both on screen and off.[15]

IS THERE HOPE FOR MORE NUANCED GENDER REPRESENTATION IN DYSTOPIAN NARRATIVES?

In a post-apocalyptic world, hope is fleeting.[16] Baby Judith in *The Walking Dead* represents a rare moment of optimism in its otherwise dystopian landscape. In "The Heaven and Hell of Mothering," Ros Coward notes that "children have come to embody society's sense of itself as good. Children are the place where the best of humanity is expressed. They appear free from the corruptions of the world and they elicit from those around them the nobler emotions of protectiveness and love" (114-115). Because women have bodies that can birth these little hopes, women are "arguably the most important symbols of hope in dystopian landscapes" (Colangelo para. 4).

With particular focus on the familial relationships in dystopian televisual narratives, this study has examined representations of mothering and explored contemporary contexts and themes with which post-apocalyptic narratives resonate. The narratives analyzed in this study provide valuable opportunities to study lone mothering and the state of family in flux, the difficult decisions mothers face, and the cultural and psychological implications of those choices. Kirsten Moana Thompson suggests that "apocalyptic dread's guiding tropes of cataclysmic violence, prophetic revelation, and radical transformation do not exhaust themselves" in familial narratives in dystopia. These tropes "link the familial to the public sphere by pointing to broader historical fragmentation and change" (3).

Given our theorization that lone mothers may actually excel in post-apocalyptic situations and given the trauma that they may have experienced in their pre-apocalyptic lived experience, we had hoped to uncover transformative representations for the women characters in these texts. *Falling Skies, Revolution,* and *The Walking Dead* tell a contrary story, however. Although post-apocalyptic media texts provide for an expansion of the boundaries of family, depictions of motherhood generally and lone mothering specifically remain troublingly transgressive. Even though the post-apocalyptic world remains a fight for survival, mothers in *Revolution* and *Falling Skies* sustain the belief that they can develop or repair their relationships with their children at a later point in time. The fight against aliens and human villains or the development of romantic relationships overshadows any focus on familial relationships. In seasons one and two of *The Walking Dead*, Lori's desire to repair her relationship with her husband—a man whom she thought was dead—eclipses her relationship with her only son. Thus, there appears to be opportunity to focus on the mother-child relationship, despite the urgency of the post-apocalyptic condition.

Moreover, there is a binary distinction that says fathers can enjoy in-depth relationships with their children, but mothers, particularly those who are portrayed as having a prestigious career, are not afforded the same opportunities. Patrice DiQuinzio contends that representations of mothering could depict alternative family structures to "destabilize the distinctions of mothers, fathers, and people who are 'childless' so as to create even more variety of ways that all persons can participate in caring for children" (248-249). This idea is repeated across all three texts, where fatherhood and male bonding with the children are clearly primary plot points; however, it comes at the expense of mothering, particularly lone mothering. In *Falling Skies,* Lexi desires a relationship with her father, who is not biologically related to her, rather than one with her mother. Although both parent-child bonds are problematized, Charlie's relationship with her mother on *Revolution* is not prioritized, whereas Tom and Jason's father-son relationship is highlighted. Despite multiple caregivers for baby Judith on *The Walking Dead,* Tyreese is portrayed as the most competent, devoted, and capable caregiver, whereas Carol and Michonne are shown abandoning their children. Consequently, these three televisual texts represent motherhood as a faltering and unreliable notion in post-apocalyptic societies, in sharp contrast to how fatherhood is portrayed. Rather than providing innovative family connections, as we had hoped would appear in post-apocalyptic narratives because existing social structures have been eliminated, *Falling Skies, Revolution,* and *The Walking Dead* perpetuate the dominant ideology that male characters have the greatest capacity to care for children, even when conquering the various perils of these new worlds.

Televisual dystopian narratives provide the context to examine the human condition and how lone mothering is represented in popular cultural dystopian televisual texts. However, hegemonic constructions of family in post-apocalyptic texts reflect progressive fatherly representations only. Lone mothers not only are situated as faltering in their role as caretakers, but are also portrayed as unable to care for the children without other family or co-parents to assist them. The imagined mothers succumb to a myriad of anxieties of these unfamiliar worlds and rely on others, particularly male characters, to survive and thrive. Even the children are depicted as perceiving their mothers' failures, as they seek to develop relationships with, gain knowledge from, and, overall, be cared for by their fathers.

Representations of motherhood in post-apocalyptic mediated texts should reflect more inclusive perceptions about mothering, the social role mothers play in the family unit, and how family is socially and culturally contextualized rather than perpetuate recurring tropes of symbolic femininity (Greven). As Raffaella Baccolini argues, "dystopia is traditionally a bleak, depressing genre with no space for hope within the story, where utopia(n hope) is maintained outside the story: it is only if we consider dystopia as a warning that we as readers can hope to escape such a pessimistic future" ("Finding Utopia in Dystopia" 165). Perhaps these televisual post-apocalyptic narrative themes about lone mothering instead serve as a cultural warning as well as a call to engage in resistant readings to hegemonic discourse, with "potential to envision different worlds that can work as a purely imaginative (at worst) or a critical (at best) exploration of our society" ("The Persistence of Hope" 519). This study serves as a call for producers of dystopian fiction—be it filmic, televisual, or literary—to create counter-narratives that resist rather than reinforce patriarchal familial norms.

NOTES

[1]The author listed second on this study was a lone mother of an infant and a toddler while negotiating the work-family balance as full-time associate professor appointment. Note: authorship of this study is listed alphabetically to reflect equal contribution from both authors. See "Mothering in a Time of Terror" by Len-

gel, Birzescu, and Minda for details on the trauma of mothering. In this chapter, Lara Lengel analyzes her experience as a mother being 3,800 miles away from her two young children who, with their summer nanny Jennifer Minda, were on a West London bus during the bombings of July 7 2005. Minda recounts their survival experience, whereas Anca Birzescu recalls surviving a different type of nation-wide trauma in Romania sixteen years earlier.

[2]See Maki Motapanyane-D'Costa's introductory chapter in this volume for more on chronic stress and fatigue and depression. For research on mothers, post-traumatic stress symptom, and anxiety disorders, see Butterworth; Chemtob, Gudiño, and Laraque. For a particularly illuminating example of research on trauma and single mothering, see "Single Mother's Adverse and Traumatic Experiences and Post-Traumatic Stress Symptoms" by Joan Samuels-Dennis, Marilyn Ford-Gilboe, and Susan Ray in *Nursing Publications*. Out of a random sample of 247 Canadian single mothers receiving social assistance, the authors note that "31% met the criteria for a probable PTSD diagnosis. Between 78 percent and 80 percent reported one or more lifetime adversity, psychological trauma, and assaultive trauma. Rates of adversities were similar to the general female population. However, rates of psychological and assaultive trauma were six to ten times greater than the general female population." For research on stress level of mothering of children with disabilities, see Michelle Diament who argues that "mothers of adolescents and adults with autism experience chronic stress comparable to combat soldiers and struggle with frequent fatigue and work interruptions" (see also Smith et al.; Smith, Greenberg, and Seltzer). Finally, for research on parenting in a range of situations surrounding severe trauma, from intense poverty to war to surviving hurricane Katrina, see Banyard, Williams, and Segal; Lowe, Chan, and Rhodes; Moscardino, Scrimin, Capello, and Altoè; Sprang et al.; van Ee, Kleber, and Mooren; Zurayk et al.

[3]For research on various challenges of lone mothering, particularly in times of crisis, see, for instance, Boney; Hayes and Hartman; Kotwal and Prabhakar; Moscardino, Scrimin, Capello, and Altoè; Wu and Eamon; and, in particular, "Dispatches from a Displaced Mama: Mothering through Disaster or Re-Membering Home" by Laura Camille Tulley for an account of mothering during the

"personal, social and environmental tragedy" of Hurricane Katrina (38). See, for example, Karen Atkinson, Sarah Oerton, and Diane Burns for research on perceptions of lone mothers in governmental and other discourses.

[4]Along with the body of research on fear and parenting, there is also a wide body of scholarship on the mediated construction of fear more broadly contextualized. See, for instance, Altheide and Michalowski; Del Nero; Franklin and Cromby; Glassner; Pain.

[5]Anxieties emerging from the possibilities of partial or total societal collapse have increased sharply in filmic and televisual mediated narratives, particularly during the past half-decade. Numerous scholars have analyzed how post-9/11 anxieties—fueled by fears of the unexpected, invisible enemy "other" invading the heretofore safe and lovely homeland and exacerbating fears across the U.S.—have been illustrated through dystopian narratives. For a selection of scholarship on post-9/11 dystopian narratives, see Alber; Bishop, "Dead Man Still Walking," "The Sub-Subaltern Monster," *American Zombie Gothic*; Dixon; Dodds; Kellner; Ndalianis; Natoli; Saunders; Whetmore.

[6]Louis Althusser included family as an ideological state apparatus. See Chloë Taylor's study, "Foucault and Familial Power," Jon Simons's "Foucault's Mother," Caroline Knowles's book *Family Boundaries: The Invention of Normality and Dangerousness,* and Katherine Logan's "Foucault, the Modern Mother and Maternal Power."

[7]To date, the only scholarship specifically focusing on mothering in post-apocalyptic worlds in literature is by these authors. See also the work of Bacon and Dickman; Korte; Latimer; Ziarek; Žižek on *Children of Men* (dir. Alfonso Cuarón), arguably one of the most captivating narrative inclusions of lone mothering in film.

[8]*Revolution* first aired on NBC on September 4, 2012. With 11.6 million viewers, the pilot episode was the top television drama premiere between 2009 and 2012 (Collins).

[9]See Haire and McGeorge for scholarship on the negative perceptions of lone mothers vis-a-vis lone fathers.

[10]For a selection of the growing scholarship on zombies, see Balaji; Bishop, "Raising the Dead"; Dixon; Eaton; McIntosh and Leverette; Moreman and Rushton; Natoli; Wallis and Ashton.

[11]Coincidentally, "Wildfire" is the name of *The Walking Dead* season one finale and in the narrative, the nickname of the disease given by the fictional Dr. Edwin Jenner and his fellow researchers at the Centers for Disease Control in Atlanta.

[12]For an analysis of how hegemonic gender norms reinforce patriarchy and, specifically, an analysis of the gender binaries of characters Lori and Andrea in *The Walking Dead,* see Greene and Meyer; Baldwin and McCarthy (84-86). For an analysis of hegemonic masculinity, gender, and sexual identity in *The Walking Dead,* see Kluch and Lengel.

[13]"The turn" is the term used in *The Walking Dead* to denote the start of the zombie apocalypse which, as the narrative indicates, occurred in 2009. Also, "turn" is used as a verb to describe the human post-death reanimation process.

[14]For research on communal childrearing, co-parenting, and community parenting, see, for instance, Altenburger et al.; Blanton; Gonzalez, Jones and Parent; Kessler; Laxman et al.; McHale and Lindahl.

[15]An analysis of the co-parenting of baby Judith by Tyreese Williams (Chad L. Coleman), which is beyond the scope of this chapter, is analysed by Kluch and Lengel (forthcoming). We thank one of the anonymous reviewers for her or his insights on Tyreese's co-parenting in *The Walking Dead* as reinforcing of hegemonic constitutions of men's parenting under patriarchy. In September 2014, AMC announced production had been approved to create a spin-off program to *The Walking Dead.* One of the lead characters in *Fear the Walking Dead* (*FTWD*) was originally described AMC as "a thirty something *single mother* with two kids." Before the August 23, 2015 premier of *FTWD*, AMC revealed a key narrative element of the program would be the blended family of Madison Clark (Kim Dickens) and Travis Manawa (Cliff Curtis). The *FTWD* premier was the most watched season debut in cable television history and featured not only the blended parenting of Madison and Manawa, but also Liza Ortiz (Elizabeth Rodriguez), lone mother to her and ex-spouse's son, Chris Manawa (Lorenzo James Henrie). Season two of *FTWD*, the fifteen episodes of which began airing on April 10, 2016 (Peters), will provide more opportunities for analyzing dystopian lone mothering.

[16]There are some encouraging illustrations of hope in dystopian literature—for example, Nalo Hokinson's novel *Brown Girl in the Ring*. Gretchen Michlitsch and Sharon DeGraw analyze Hokinson's character Ti-Jeanne, whom DeGraw describes as a "young, unwed black mother of low socio-economic standing holds the key to saving her community, not the CEO of a major corporation or a government official" (DeGraw 207). Ti-Jeanne is the "least traditionally powerful member of society; she is young, poor, female, a mother, often accompanied by her baby from an immigrant family, and without weapons. She is disadvantaged, marginalized, and seemingly defenceless, yet she becomes empowered beyond regular humans." DeGraw argues that "Ti-Jeanne's status as 'superhero' revises the Anglo, male, and technological biases of science fiction and Western society more broadly" (207)

WORKS CITED

Adalian, Josef. "Sunday Ratings: Spielberg Scores with *Falling Skies.*" *Vulture Magazine.* New York LLC 20 June 2011. Web. 6 Oct. 2015.

Ahmad, Aalya. "Feminist Spaces in Horrific Places." *Offscreen* 18.6/7 (2014). Web. 26 May 2016.

Alber, Catherine. "Road to No(Where)? Literal and Metaphoric Journeys in the Post-9/11 Zombie Narrative." *The Image of the Road in Literature, Media, and Society.* Eds. Will Wright and Steven Kaplan. Pueblo: Colorado State University—Pueblo, 2012. 118-128. Print.

Altenburger, Lauren E. et al. "Associations Between Prenatal Coparenting Behavior and Observed Coparenting Behavior at 9 Months Postpartum." *Journal of Family Psychology 28.4 (2014):* 495-504. Print.

Altheide, David L., and R. Sam Michalowski. "Fear in the News: A Discourse of Control." *The Sociological Quarterly* 40.3 (1999): 475-503. Print.

Althusser, Louis. "Idéologie et Appareils Idéologiques d'État. (Notes pour une Recherche)" [Ideology and Ideological State Apparatuses: Notes Towards an Investigation]. *La Pensée* 151 (June 1970): 3–38. Print.

American Movie Classics (AMC). "AMC Announces Pilot Order for *The Walking Dead* Companion Series." *Blogs AMC*. AMC, *9 Oct. 2014. Web. 6 Mar. 2016.*

Atkinson, Karen, Sarah Oerton, and Diane Burns. "'Happy Families?': Single Mothers, the Press and the Politicians." *Capital & Class* 21.1 (1998): 1-11. Print.

Baccolini, Raffaella. "Finding Utopia in Dystopia: Feminism, Memory, Nostalgia, and Hope." *Utopia Method Vision: The Use Value of Social Dreaming*. Eds. Tom Moylan and Raffaella Baccolini. Berne: Peter Lang, 2007. 159-190. Print.

Baccolini, Raffaella. "The Persistence of Hope in Dystopian Science Fiction." *PMLA* 119.3 (2004): 518-521. Print.

Baccolini, Raffaella and Tom Moylan. "Conclusion: Utopia as Vision." In *Utopia Method Vision: The Use Value of Social Dreaming*. Eds. Tom Moylan and Raffaella Baccolini. Berne: Peter Lang, 2007. 319-324. Print.

Bacon, Terryl, and Govinda Dickman. "'Who's the Daddy?': The Aesthetics and Politics of Representation in Alfonso Cuarón's Adaptation of P. D. James's *Children of Men*." *Adaptation in Contemporary Culture: Textual Infidelities*. Ed. Rachel Carroll. New York: Continuum, 2009. 147–59. Print.

Balaji, Murali, ed. *Thinking Dead: What the Zombie Apocalypse Means*. Lanham: Lexington, 2013. Print.

Baldwin, Martina, and Mark McCarthy. "Same as It Ever Was: Savior Narratives and the Logics of Survival in *The Walking Dead*." *Thinking Dead: What the Zombie Apocalypse Means*. Ed. Murali Balaji. Lanham: Lexington. 2013: 75-87. Print.

Banyard, Victoria L., Linda M. Williams, and Jane A. Siegel. "The Impact of Complex Trauma and Depression on Parenting: Exploration of Mediating Risk and Protective Factors." *Child Maltreatment* 8.4 (2003): 334–349. Print.

Bishop, Kyle. "Raising the Dead: Unearthing the Non-Literary Origins of Zombie Cinema." *Journal of Popular Film and Television* 33.4 (2006): 196-205. Print.

Bishop, Kyle. "The Sub-Subaltern Monster: Imperialist Hegemony and the Cinematic Voodoo Zombie." *Journal of American Culture* 31.2 (2008): 141-52. Print.

Bishop, Kyle. "Dead Man Still Walking: Explaining the Zombie

Renaissance." *Journal of Popular Film and Television* 37.1 (2009): 16-25. Print.

Bishop, Kyle. *American Zombie Gothic: The Rise and Fall (and Rise) of the Walking Dead in Popular Culture*. London, England: McFarland, 2010. Print.

Blanton, Judith. "Communal Child Rearing." *Alternative Lifestyles*. 3.1 (1980): 87-116. Print.

Boney, Virginia M. "Divorced Mothers' Guilt: Exploration and Intervention Through a Postmodern Lens." *Journal of Divorce & Remarriage* 37.3/4 (2002): 61-83. Print.

Bourdieu, Pierre. "On the Family as a Realized Category." *Theory and Society* 13.3 (1996): 19–26. Print.

Bressler, Nancy. "Good Luck Raising the Modern Family: Portrayals of Sexual Division of Labor on Current Family Sitcoms." Home Sweat Home: Perspectives on Housework and Modern Domestic Relationships. Eds. Elizabeth Patton and Mimi Choi. Lanham: Rowman & Littlefield, 2014. 183-200. Print.

Butterworth, P. "Lone Mothers' Experience of Physical and Sexual Violence, Association with Psychiatric Disorders." *British Journal of Psychiatry* 184 (2004): 21–27. Print.

Chambers, Deborah. "Representations of Familialism in the British Popular Media." *European Journal of Cultural Studies* 3.2 (2000): 195-214. Print.

Chemtob, Claude M., Omar Gudiño, and Danielle Laraque. "Maternal PTSD and Depression in Pediatric Primary Care: Association with Child Maltreatment and Frequency of Child Trauma Exposure." *JAMA Pediatrics* 167.11 (2013): 1011-1018. Print.

Chodorow, Nancy. *The Reproduction of Mothering*. Berkeley: University of California Press, 1978. Print.

Clover, Carol J. *Men, Women, and Chain Saws: Gender in Modern Horror Film*. Princeton: Princeton University Press, 1993. Print.

Colangelo, B. J. "The Burden of Carrying On: The Currency of Women in Dystopian Films." *Btchflicks*. Btchflicks, 29 July 2015. Web. 13 Feb. 2016.

Collins, Patricia Hill. "It's All in the Family: Intersections of Gender, Race, and Nation." *Hypatia* 13.3 (1998): 62-82. Print.

Collins, Scott. "NBC's 'Revolution' is Top Network Drama Premiere in Three Years." *latimes.com*. Los Angeles Times, 18 Sept. 2012.

Web. 17 Mar. 2016.

Coward, Ros. "The Heaven and Hell of Mothering: Mothering and Ambivalence in the Mass Media." *Mothering and Ambivalence*. Eds. Wendy Hollway and Brid Featherstone. London: Routledge, 1997. 111-118. Print.

Creeber, Glen. *The Television Genre Book*. London: British Film Institute, 2008. Print.

Creed, Barbara. *The Dread of Difference*. Austin: University of Texas Press, 1996. Print.

Croteau, David R., and Williams Hoynes. *Media/Society: Industries, Images, and Audiences*. Thousand Oaks: Pine Forge Press, 2003. Print.

DeGraw, Sharon. "Brown Girl in the Ring as Urban Policy." *Blast, Corrupt, Dismantle, Erase: Contemporary North American Dystopian Literature*. Eds. Brett Josef Grubisic, Gisèle M. Baxter, and Tara Lee. Waterloo: Wilfrid Laurier University Press, 2014. 193-215. Print.

Del Nero, Michael V. "Invasion, Surveillance, Biopolitics, and Governmentality: Representations from Tactical Media to Screen." Diss. Bowling Green State University, 2016. Print.

Diament, Michelle. "Autism Moms Have Stress Similar to Combat Soldiers." *Disability Scoop*. Disability Scoop, LLC, 10 Nov. 2009. Web. 22 Mar. 2016.

DiQuinzio, Patrice. *The Impossibility of Motherhood: Feminism, Individualism, and the Problem of Mothering*. New York: Routledge, 1999. Print.

Dixon, Wheeler Winston. *Film and Television after 9/11*. Carbondale: Southern Illinois University Press, 2004. Print.

Dodds, Klaus. "Hollywood and the Popular Geopolitics of the War on Terror." *Third World Quarterly* 29.8 (2008): 1621–1637. Print.

Eaton, Lance. "Spotlight Essay/Film: Zombie Films." *September 11 in Popular Culture*. Eds. Sara E. Quay and Amy M. Damico. Santa Barbara: Greenwood Press, 2010. 209-212. Print.

Ennis, Linda Rose. "Intensive Mothering: Revisiting the Issue Today." In *Intensive Mothering: The Cultural Contradictions of Modern Motherhood*. Ed. Linda Rose Ennis. Toronto: Demeter Press. 2014. Print.

Falling Skies. Turner Network Television, 19 June 2011-30 Aug. 2015. Television.

Foucault, Michel. *Le Désordre des Familles: Lettres de Cachet des Archives de la Bastille*. Paris: Gallimard Julliard, 1982. Print.

Franklin, Leanne, and John Cromby. "Everyday Fear: Parenting and Childhood in a Culture of Fear." *The Many Forms of Fear, Horror, and Terror.* Eds. Leanne Franklin and Ravenel Richardson. London: Inter-Disciplinary Press, 2009. 161-174. Print.

Glassner, Barry. *The Culture of Fear: Why Americans are Afraid of the Wrong Things: Crime, Drugs, Minorities, Teen Moms, Killer Kids, Mutant Microbes, Plane Crashes, Road Rage, & So Much More* (Revised edition). New York: Basic Books, 2010. Print.

Gonzalez, Michelle, Deborah Jones, and Justin Parent. "Coparenting Experiences in African American Families: An Examination of Single Mothers and Their Nonmarital Coparents." *Family Process* 53.1 (2014): 33-54. Print.

Greene, John and Michaela D. E. Meyer. "The Walking (Gendered) Dead: A Feminist Rhetorical Critique of Zombie Apocalypse Television Narrative." *Ohio Communication Journal.* 52 (2014): 64-74. Print.

Grey, Ian. "The Fall and Rise of 'Falling Skies.'" *Roger Ebert.* Ebert Digital, LLC. 13 Sept. 2013. Web. 12 Mar. 2016.

Haire, Amanda R., and Christi R. McGeorge. "Negative Perceptions of Never-Married Custodial Single Mothers and Fathers: Applications of a Gender Analysis for Family Therapists." *Journal of Feminist Family Therapy* 24.1 (2012): 24–51.

Haupt, Melanie. "Mothering Amid *White Noise*: DeLillo's Post-Apocalyptic Mother in the Kitchen." Northeast Modern Language Association 38th Convention, Johns Hopkins University. Baltimore, Maryland. 2 Mar. 2007. Lecture.

Hayes, Jeff, and Heidi Hartman. *Women and Men Living on the Edge: Economic Insecurity after the Great Recession.* Washington, DC: Institute for Women's Policy Research, 2011. Print.

Hollinger, Veronica, and Joan Gordon. *Edging into the Future: Science Fiction and Contemporary Cultural Transformation.* Philadelphia: University of Pennsylvania Press, 2002. Print.

Hosni, Heba. "*Memoirs of a Survivor:* The City and Apocalypse." *iBuzzle*. iBuzzle, n.d. Web. 20 May 2016.

Kearns, Megan. "Nothing Can Save 'The Walking Dead's Sexist Woman Problem." *Btchflicks*. Btchflicks, 1 May 2013. Web. 12 Sept. 2015.

Kellner, Douglas. *Cinema Wars: Hollywood Film and Politics in the Bush-Cheney Era*. West Sussex, UK: Wiley-Blackwell, 2010. Print.

Kessler, Laura T. "Community Parenting." *Journal of Law & Policy* 24 (2007): 47–80. Print.

Kinser, Amber. "Thinking About and Going About Mothering in the Third Wave." *Mothering in the Third Wave*. Ed. Amber Kinser. Toronto: Demeter Press, 2008. 1-16. Print.

Kissler, Rick. "AMC's 'The Walking Dead' Finished as TV's Top Series in Key Demo for Fourth Straight Season." *Variety*. Variety, 6 April 2016. Web. 30 May 2016.

Kluch, Yannick, and Lara Lengel. "**'Heteronormative Masculinity in Dystopian Narratives.**" Gay, Lesbian, Bisexual, Transgender, and Queer Communication Studies Division for the National Communication Association Convention, Philadelphia, November 2017. Forthcoming Manuscript.

Kluch, Yannick, and Lara Lengel. "'If It Were the End of Civilization What Good Would Gays Be?' Ruptures and Reinscriptions of Heteronormative Masculinity in Season 5 of *The Walking Dead*." Gay, Lesbian, Bisexual, Transgender, and Queer Communication Studies Division of the National Communication Association Convention, Las Vegas, November 2015. Lecture.

Knowles, Caroline. *Family Boundaries: The Invention of Normality and Dangerousness*. Toronto: University of Toronto Press Higher Education, 1997. Print.

Korte, Barbara. "Envisioning a Black Tomorrow? Black Mother Figures and the Issue of Representation in *28 Days Later* (2003) and *Children of Men* (2006)." *Multi-Ethnic Britain 2000+: New Perspectives in Literature, Film and the Arts*. Eds. Larks Eckstein et al. New York: Rodopi, 2008. 315-25. Print.

Kotwal, Nidhi, and Bharti Prabhakar. "Problems Faced by Single Mothers." *Journal of Social Science* 21.3 (2009): 197-204. Print.

Kruse, Jarrett. "The One Walking Dead Episode Robert Kirkman Regrets." *Cinema Blend*. Gateway Media and Entertainment, 25 Nov. 2014. Web. 26 Nov. 2015.

Lahad, Kinneret, and Avi Shoshana. "Singlehood in Treatment:

Interrogating the Discursive Alliance Between Postfeminism and Therapeutic Culture." *European Journal of Women's Studies* 22.3 (2015): 334-349. Print.

Latimer, Heather. "Bio-Reproductive Futurism: Bare Life and the Pregnant Refugee in Alfonso Cuarón's *Children of Men.*" *Social Text* 29.3 108 (2011): 51–72. Print.

Laxman, Daniel J. et al. "Stability and Antecedents of Coparenting Quality: The Role of Parent Personality and Child Temperament." *Infant Behavior and Development* 36.2 (2013): 210-222. Print.

Lengel, Lara. "Resisting the Historical Locations of Tunisian Women Musicians." *Gender & History* 12.2 (2000). 336-365. Print.

Lengel, Lara, Anca Birzescu, and Jennifer Minda. "Mothering in a Time of Terror." *Mothering in the Third Wave*. Ed. Amber Kinser. Toronto: Demeter Press, 2008. 48-69. Print.

Logan, Katherine. "Foucault, the Modern Mother and Maternal Power: Notes towards a Genealogy of the Mother." *Foucault, the Family and Politics*. Eds. Robbie Dusckinsky and Leon Antonio Rocha. London: Palgrave Macmillan, 2012. 63-81. Print.

Lowe, Sarah R., Christian S. Chan, and Jean E. Rhodes. "The Impact of Child-Related Stressors on the Psychological Functioning of Lower-Income Mothers after Hurricane Katrina." *Journal of Family Issues* 32.10 (2012): 1303-1324. Print.

Maras, Marie-Helen. *Transnational Security*. Boca Raton, Florida: Taylor & Francis Group, 2014. Print.

Martucci, Elise. "Toxicity in the Mother-Land." Northeast Modern Language Association 38th Convention, Johns Hopkins University. Baltimore, Maryland. March 2, 2007. Lecture.

McHale, James P. and Kristin M. Lindahl. *Coparenting: A Conceptual and Clinical Examination of Family Systems*. Washington, DC: American Psychological Association, 2011. Print.

McIntosh, Shawn, and Marc Leverette. *Zombie Culture: Autopsies of the Living Dead*. Lanham, Maryland: Scarecrow Press, 2008. Print.

Michlitsch, Gretchen J. "Breastfeeding Mother Rescues City: Nalo Hopkinson's Ti-Jeanne as Superhero." *FEMSPEC: An Interdisciplinary Feminist Journal Dedicated to Critical and Creative Work in the Realms of Science Fiction, Fantasy, Magical Realism, Surrealism, Myth, Folklore, and Other Supernatural Genres*. 6.1

(2005): 18-34. Print.
Millett, Kate. *Sexual Politics.* New York: Doubleday, 1970. Print.
Milstead, John W. *Sociology through Science Fiction.* New York: St. Martin's Press, 1974. Print.
Moreman, Christopher M., and Cory James Rushton, eds. *Zombies Are Us: Essays on the Humanity of the Walking Dead.* Jefferson: McFarland, 2011. Print.
Moscardino, Ughetta, Sara Scrimin, Fabia Capello, and Gianmarco Altoè. "Social Support, Sense of Community, Collectivistic Values, and Depressive Symptoms in Adolescent Survivors of the 2004 Beslan Terrorist Attack." *Conflict, Violence, and Health* 70.1 (2010): 27-34. Print.
Mubarki, Meraj Ahmed. "The Monstrous 'Other' Feminine: Gender, Desire and the 'Look' in the Hindi Horror Genre." *Indian Journal of Gender Studies* 21.3 (2014): 379-399. Print.
Murray, Jessica. "A Zombie Apocalypse: Opening Representational Spaces for Alternative Constructions of Gender and Sexuality." *Journal of Literary Studies/TLW* 29.4 (2013): 1-19. Print.
Natoli, Joseph. *This is a Picture and Not the World: Movies and a Post-9/11 America.* New York: SUNY Press, 2007. Print.
Ndalianis, Angela. "Genre, Culture and the Semiosphere: New Horror Cinema and Post-9/11." *International Journal of Cultural Studies* 18.1 (2015): 135-151. Print.
Ostman, Heather. "Staving Off the Apocalypse: Motherhood in Grace Paley's Short Fiction." Northeast Modern Language Association 38th Convention, Johns Hopkins University. Baltimore, Maryland. March 2, 2007. Lecture.
Ozog, Cassie. "Zombies and the Modern American Family: Surviving the Destruction of Traditional Society in Zombieland (2009)." *Thinking Dead: What the Zombie Apocalypse Means.* Ed. Murali Balaji. Lanham, Maryland: Lexington Books, 2013: 127-139. Print.
Pain, Rachel. "Globalized Fear? Towards an Emotional Geopolitics." *Progress in Human Geography* 33.4 (2009): 466–486. Print.
Parrinder, Patrick. *Science Fiction: Its Criticism and Teaching.* London: Routledge, Kegan and Paul, 1981. Print.
Parrinello-Cason, Michelle. "Sex and Laundry: The Role of Women in Apocalyptic Landscapes." *Balancing Jane.* N.p., 9 Mar. 2012.

Web. 13 Oct. 2015.

Peters, Oliver. "Postapocalyptic Post." *Digital Video*. 23.9 (2015): 20-24. Print.

Platts, Todd. "Locating Zombies in the Sociology of Popular Culture." *Sociology Compass* 1.14 (2013): n.p. Print.

Revolution. National Broadcasting Network, NBC. 17 Sept. 2012—21 May 2014. Television.

Samuels-Dennis, Joan, Marilyn Ford-Gilboe and Susan Ray. "Single Mother's Adverse and Traumatic Experiences and Post-Traumatic Stress Symptoms." *Nursing Publications* 211 (2011): n.p. Print.

Saunders, Robert A. "Undead Spaces: Fear, Globalisation, and the Popular [U.S.] Geopolitics of Zombiism." *Geopolitics* 17.1 (2012): 80-104. Print.

Schrynemakers, Ilse. "Nuclear Family Values: Fallout Crimes in Ross Macdonald's Crime Fiction." Northeast Modern Language Association 38th Convention, Johns Hopkins University. Baltimore, Maryland. March 2, 2007. Lecture.

Silbergleid, Robin. "'Oh Baby!': Representations of Single Mothers in American Popular Culture." *Americana: The Journal of American Popular Culture*. 1.2. (2002): n.p. Web. 20 May 2016.

Silbergleid, Robin. "Women, Utopia, and Narrative: Toward a Postmodern Feminist Citizenship." *Hypatia* 12.4 (1997): 156-177. Print.

Simons, Jon. "Foucault's Mother." *Feminist Interpretations of Michel Foucault*. Ed. Susan J. Hekman. Philadelphia: Pennsylvania State University Press, 1996. 179-209. Print.

Smith, Leann E., Jan S. Greenberg, and Marsha Mailick Seltzer. "Daily Experiences among Mothers of Adolescents and Adults with Autism Spectrum Disorder." *Journal of Autism and Developmental Disorders* 40.2 (2010): 167-178. Print.

Smith, Leann E. et al. "Social Support and Well-being at Mid-Life among Mothers of Adolescents and Adults with Autism Spectrum Disorders." *Journal of Autism and Developmental Disorders* 42.9 (2012): 1818-1826. Print.

Snyder, Stephen. "Family Life and Leisure Culture in The Shining." *Film Criticism* 7.1 (1982): 4-13. Print.

Sobchack, Vivian. "Bringing It All Back Home: Family Economy and Generic Exchange." In *The Dread of Difference*. Austin:

University of Texas Press, 1996. 143-61. Print.

Sprang, Ginny et al. "The Impact of Trauma Exposure on Parenting Stress in Rural America." *Journal of Child & Adolescent Trauma* 6.4 (2013): 287-300. Print.

Stacey, Judith. *In the Name of the Family: Rethinking Family Values in the Postmodern Age*. Boston: Beacon, 1996. Print.

Steiger, Kate. "No Clean Slate: Unshakable Race and Gender Politics in *The Walking Dead*." *Triumph of the Walking Dead: Robert Kirkman's Zombie Epic on Page and Screen*. Ed. James Lowder. Dallas: Smart Pop, 2011. 99-114. Print.

Taylor, Chloë. "Foucault and Familial Power." *Hypatia* 27.1 (2012): 201-218. Print.

Teckman, Julie. "Bringing Up Baby: Representations of Lone Motherhood in Modern Popular Culture." Diss. University of Leicester, 2004. Print.

The Walking Dead. American Movie Classics (AMC). 31 Oct. 2010—. Television.

Thompson, Kirsten Moana. *Apocalyptic Dread: American Film at the Turn of the Millennium*. Albany: New York University Press, 2007. Print.

Truitt, Brian. "Girl Power Fuels '*Revolution*." USA *Today*, Sept. 17 2012. Web. 8 Mar. 2016.

Tulley, Laura Camille. "Dispatches from a Displaced Mama: Mothering through Disaster or Re-Membering Home." *Mothering in the Third Wave*. Ed. Amber Kinser. Toronto: Demeter Press, 2008. 38-47. Print.

Van Ee, Elisa, Rolf J. Kleber, and Trudy T. M. Mooren. "War Trauma Lingers On: Associations Between Maternal Posttraumatic Stress Disorder, Parent-Child Interaction, and Child Development." *Infant Mental Health Journal* 33.5 (2012): 459-468. Print.

Weaver, Sean. "When Skies Fall, Bodies Fail: Gender and Performativity on a Dystopian Earth." *Btchflicks*. Btchflicks, 30 June 2015. Web. 27 Feb. 2016.

Williams, Raymond. *Keywords: A Vocabulary of Culture and Society*. Oxford: Oxford University Press, 1983. 131-134. Print.

Williams, Tony. "Trying to Survive on the Darker Side: 1980s Family Horror." *The Dread of Difference*. Ed. Barry Keith Grant. Austin: University of Texas Press, 1996. 164-81. Print.

Wu, Chi-Fang, and Mary Keegan Eamon. "Employment Hardships and Health Insurance Coverage in Single-Mother Families During and after the Great Recession." *Affilia: Journal of Women & Social Work* 28.3 (2013): 273-283. Print.

Wuthnow, Robert. *Be Very Afraid: The Cultural Response to Terror, Pandemics, Environmental Devastation, Nuclear Annihilation, and Other Threats*. Oxford: Oxford University Press, 2010. Print.

Ziarek, Ewa Plonowska. "Bare Life on Strike: Notes on the Biopolitics of Race and Gender." *South Atlantic Quarterly* 107.1 (2008): 89–105. Print.

Žižek, Slavoj. "Comments on *Children of Men*." *Children of Men*. Dir. Alfonso Cuarón. Universal, 2007. DVD.

Zurayk, Hudaet et al. "The Impact of War on the Physical and Mental Health of the Family: The Lebanese Experience." *Center for Migration Studies Special Issues*. 11.4 (1994): 84-85. Print.

2.

Do Two a Family Make?

Hollywood Engages Intentional Single Motherhood

KATHERINE MACK

IT IS HARD TO GET exact numbers, but approximately fifty thousand women each year pursue single motherhood in the United States (Ravitz). Even if you do not know any personally, most of us can name a celebrity whose decision to become a single mother provided tabloid cover copy. The very fact that it is possible and somewhat more acceptable for some women to choose intentional single motherhood is a sign of feminist progress, as that very choice and the families that result from it challenge patriarchal notions of the primacy of the nuclear family. As such, intentional single mothers merit scholarly attention. Much of the scholarship on intentional single motherhood is empirical and draws on statistics, observations, and interviews to understand women's motivations to pursue as well as their varied practices of intentional single motherhood (Bock; Graham; Hertz). Women, however, do not experience intentional lone motherhood in a cultural vacuum; they both respond to and shape the "cultural conversation" about single mothers, intentional and otherwise (Mailloux 54). This chapter uses a cultural rhetoric approach to examine a trio of recent Hollywood feature films from between 2008 and 2011 that contribute to that "conversation" (Mailloux 54). A cultural rhetoric approach aims to reveal the relationship between expressive forms and the social order. This approach tracks the interaction of ideas, arguments, and identity formation across sites, objects, performances, and genres, fiction and non-fiction, as well as public and private spheres.[1] In this chapter, I demonstrate the disheartening congruence between the motivations and aspirations of actual intentional single mothers and their fictional counterparts in Hollywood films. This congruence is disheartening because it reveals how powerfully conservative postfeminist discourses are shaping the *topoi*—places of argument—that North Americans use to categorize and judge single mothers.

In the United States, the 1990s witnessed a rise in the number of unmarried women over the age of thirty-five who became mothers (Ludtke).[2] It is difficult to determine whether these unmarried women were unmarried but still partnered or single. Some must have been those women joining or forming the Single Mothers by Choice chapters that Jane Mattes describes in her 1994 guidebook to intentional single motherhood. Despite this increase in practice, intentional single motherhood was not often represented in popular culture in the late twentieth century, and when it was, it provoked public censure. In 1990, fancy camerawork hid the real-life pregnancy of Susan Saint James, one of the stars of the single-mother (through divorce) sitcom *Kate and Allie* so as to avoid introducing the controversial spectacle of "conception, pregnancy, and birth to an unwed, white, affluent woman" (Rabinovitz 15). Two years later, Dan Quayle infamously expressed consternation about the fictional character Murphy Brown's decision to pursue single motherhood in the eponymous TV series: "It doesn't help matters when primetime TV has Murphy Brown, a character who supposedly epitomizes today's intelligent, highly paid professional woman, mocking the importance of fathers by bearing a child alone and calling it just another lifestyle choice." Quayle was lambasted for his comment for a host of reasons,[3] but in many senses, he won rhetorical ground. Popular culture shied away from the topic, despite the fact that more and more women pursued intentional single motherhood as the decade progressed.

Approximately twenty years later, in the United States, intentional single motherhood seems almost hip. Hollywood, a risk-averse industry, green lit three romantic comedies—*Baby Mama* (2008), *The Switch* (2010), and *Back-Up Plan* (2011)—about intentional single mothers. According to the website *Box Office Mojo*, though not blockbusters, each of these movies made money: *Baby Mama* made 60 million dollars in total domestic gross, *The Switch* twenty-eight million, and the *Back-Up Plan* thirty-seven million. Reviews from mainstream publications—such as the *New York Times (NYT)*, *Entertainment Weekly (EW)*, and *Los Angeles Times*—demonstrate the shift in perception about these mothers. Although the protagonists' pursuit of single motherhood fuels the plot of these films, the reviews focus primarily on other issues. In the case of *Baby Mama*, the reviewers centre almost exclusively on Tina Fey's star power. The first three paragraphs of Manhola Dargis's review in the *NYT* address Fey's career more than the movie itself ("Learning"). Lisa Schwarzbaum of *EW* avers, "More than any other woman working in comedy today, Tina Fey has figured out how to charm men while speaking sisterly truth in a frequency heard only by other women." Although Carina Chocano of the *Los Angeles Times* begins her review by acknowledging that the subject matter of *Baby Mama* may trouble some critics—"Is Tina Fey, former head writer for 'Saturday Night Live' and creator and star of one of the best shows on television, '30 Rock,' going to get hit with a knee-jerk media backlash now?"—she goes on to assert that whatever the response, "it's a pretty safe bet that Fey's exotic status as a funny, smart woman over 35 will be cited." Reviews of *The Switch* from these same publications discuss the maturation of the unintentional sperm donor, Wally, the best friend of the protagonist and ultimately her husband, more than they do the protagonist's pursuit of single motherhood (Gleiberman, "Best Friends Forever"; Holden; Sharkey). Holden's title, "In a Baste and Switch, a New Father Is Born," reflects this focus. Similar to the ways in which reviews of *Baby Mama* focus on Tina Fey, those of the *Back-Up Plan* assess Jennifer Lopez's ability to carry a movie and her beauty (Dargis, "Love"; Gleiberman, "Back-Up Plan"; Phillips). Owen Gleiberman does briefly engage the issue of intentional single motherhood and notes that "Zoe, now in love, would probably say that getting pregnant on her own was not a good idea." Although Gleiberman's comment assumes that a woman's ideal is motherhood in the context of a romantic relationship, he does not critique intentional single motherhood per se. His observation, instead, underscores the fantastical nature of the movie's fairy tale plot. In sum, although the pursuit of single motherhood drives the plots of these three films, it did not drive the reviews.

What do these films do to make their representation of intentional single motherhood seemingly inoffensive and unpolemical? I argue that by mobilizing postfeminist discourses to represent intentional single mothers as responsible, financially secure, and ideologically conservative, these films distinguish "good" intentional single mothers from "bad" single mothers, thereby making the former acceptable heroines. In so doing, these films reinforce racialized and class-based standards of good mothering. These films also foreclose the radical feminist potential of intentional single motherhood. Upon first glance, they seem to reflect and celebrate more inclusive notions of family. In the end, however, they counter the fear that intentional single motherhood obviates men by making the movies about men's continued centrality. This conservative vision implicitly critiques family formations in which men—as biological, legal, and co-residential fathers—do not figure, thus undermining the potential of single-mother headed households to expand the understanding of what constitutes a family.

To understand these films' construction of "good" single mothers, one must understand the overwhelmingly negative perception of single mothers with which they contend.[4] Rhetoricians call these perceptions "constraints" because "they have the power to constrain decision or action" (Bitzer 8). I amplify Bitzer's notion of "decision or action" to include viewers' willingness to identify with and celebrate, rather than condemn, these films' single mother protagonists. The verb "condemn" certainly captures dominant public sentiment about single mothers and non-heteronormative households as well. A 2011 Pew survey found that "seven in ten say the trend toward more single women having children is bad for society, and 61% say that a child needs both a mother and a father to grow up happily." In a follow-up interview, Rich Morin, the author of the Pew study, interprets his findings: "Americans, when they think of single mothers, don't think of a woman who is financially secure, who made a decision to have a child, who has the time and the social support to provide that child with a safe home" (qtd. in Lee). According to public perception then, single mothers are not only irresponsible and resource strapped but also unable to provide the emotional sustenance and security that children require. A February 2014 essay in the *New York Times*,

"How Single Motherhood Hurts Kids," focuses on the economic consequences of single motherhood and claims that "[it] is complicit in our high levels of poverty and inequality" (Hymowitz). These concerns about single motherhood have a long history. In the "Murphy Brown" speech referenced above, Quayle identifies single mothers and their role in "the breakdown of the family structure, personal responsibility, and social order" as the primary causes of the moral crisis befalling the United States. These Hollywood films about intentional single mothers negotiate this rhetorical landscape by constructing *intentional* single mothers as wholly different from the bad ones (i.e., unintentional single mothers) by virtue of their financial security, conscious decision to pursue motherhood, the reservoir of emotional resources on which they can draw, and their intense desire to find a father for their children.

POSTFEMINISM

These three films participate in what popular media describe as a postfeminist moment. Postfeminist texts avoid raising the bugaboo of feminism. They depict a world in which feminism is outdated, "incorporated, assumed, or naturalized" (Tasker and Negra 2), so much so that there is little mention of the "f" word. There is a "pastness" to feminism (Tasker and Negra 1). Postfeminist cultural texts imply that feminism simply has no bearing on the lives of contemporary women because the necessary gains have already been made. Furthermore, they suggest that gender differences exist and should be acknowledged, perhaps even celebrated; their consequences are certainly not detrimental. Moreover, postfeminist culture argues that women do not necessarily want a family *and* a career. What women really want is hetero-nuclear domesticity: a husband, children, and a home. Diana Negra characterizes this homeward trajectory as "retreatism" (3). Postfeminism also trumpets choice, autonomy, and the related ethics of personal responsibility. If a woman makes poor life decisions and is unhappy with the consequences, she bears the burden of responsibility. As feminist critic Angela McRobbie explains, "Individuals must now choose the kind of life they want to live. Girls must have a lifeplan" (261). Postfeminism's odd blend of liberal and neoconservative values creates a "double-entanglement," in that it encourages women to use their freedom and agency to construct identities and life trajectories that have the potential to undermine their much-vaunted independence (McRobbie 256).

In many respects, intentional single mothers are quintessential postfeminist subjects. They emphasize that they chose to pursue motherhood and have the adequate resources to do so, according to middle-class standards of good mothering. Jane Mattes explains the genesis of the name "Single Mothers by Choice" (SMC) for the organization that she founded for intentional single mothers: "We felt strongly that we wanted the name to clearly convey that it was our choice and our decision to become single mothers ... [We are] single women who *chose* to become mothers; single mothers who are mature and responsible and who feel empowered rather than victimized" (xxi, emphasis in original). Mattes implicitly distinguishes SMC from bad single mothers by virtue of their intentionality, maturity, responsibility, and sense of empowerment. Subsequent guidebooks emphasize related characteristics of SMC. Louise Sloan, author of *Knock Yourself Up: A Tell-All Guide to Becoming a Single Mom*, marks their controlled sexuality by bluntly stating: "We got pregnant on purpose" (xv). In *Choosing Single Motherhood: The Thinking Woman's Guide* (2008), Mikki Morrissette defines a "Choice Mom" as "someone who proactively seeks to become a nurturing mother on her own" (Morrissette, *Choosing* xiii). Morrissette's title and definition underline intentional single mothers' thoughtfulness and deliberateness as well as their ability to provide for a child's emotional needs. Her definition suggests that in taking on the responsibilities typically associated with fathers in the nuclear family model, "Choice Moms" do not renege on the roles traditionally associated with mothers.

Also consistent with postfeminism, intentional single mothers tend not to acknowledge feminism's role in making their life path possible, nor do they embrace the potentially feminist implications of their decision to pursue single motherhood. Despite severing the link between sex, marriage, and family formation, they are "reluctant revolutionaries" (Hertz, *Single By Chance* 141) or "reluctant warriors" (Bock 70), as doing so was not their aim. Susanna Graham suggests that intentional single mothers are in fact pursuing a conservative goal, "aim[ing] to salvage at least some of the nuclear ideal they had imagined for themselves" (97). In this same vein, Jane Bock found that intentional single mothers typically legitimize their decision to become single mothers by demonstrating their allegiance to conservative cultural logics (69-70). They describe themselves as "deserving" motherhood by virtue of their age, responsibility, emotional maturity, and fiscal capacity (Bock 70). Although "retreatism" is usually not an option for intentional *single* mothers (Negra 3), their decision to prioritize motherhood suggests their dissatisfaction with professional success alone and could feed into conservative narratives about women's innate and overpowering urge to mother.

Intentional single mothers contribute specific tropes to the rhetorical storehouse of postfeminism as well. Firstly, many seem to adhere to cultural assumptions regarding a child's need and desire to have a father. Although contemporary guidebooks to intentional single motherhood devote fewer pages to the "Do I have a dad?" question than do the guidebooks published in the mid-90s, many intentional single mothers accept the dominant cultural argument that children need a father, preferably a biological and co-habiting one.[5] Susanna Graham concludes that "The absence of a physical father for their child, and the knowledge about him as a person, was a stumbling block for many: they wanted their child to have a father, not some 'genetic fluid in a vial'" (102). Although concerns about the absence of a known father did not stop these women from proceeding to become intentional single mothers, Graham's qualitative study suggests that it lingered for many, even after they had their children. Many intentional single mothers seem to believe that family formations that include a father are more stable and legitimate than their own. Secondly, they refer to their becoming intentional single mothers as Plan B, their "second-choice" or a "back-up plan," thereby underscoring that the ideal consists of marriage and then the baby carriage. Finally, as the guidebooks to intentional single motherhood demonstrate, these mothers legitimize their non-nuclear family structure by pointing to the ways that they adhere to middle-class white norms of good parenting. The misgivings and defensiveness of some intentional single mothers do not undercut the feminist implications of their very existence, but they do suggest how deeply ingrained conservative assumptions about "good" family are in this particular population of women.[6] As I go on to demonstrate, popular cultural representations reinforce rather than challenge or complicate these assumptions.

In the following section, I trace the ways that three Hollywood films develop these tropes, which are specific to intentional single motherhood. To illustrate the influence of postfeminism on the representation of intentional single motherhood, I discuss *The Switch* and *Back-Up Plan*. Then I turn to *Baby Mama*, which simultaneously invokes and challenges the "platitudes of postfeminist culture" (Negra 2). *Baby Mama*, unlike *Switch* and *The Back-Up Plan*, juxtaposes two women whose background and class status make them do motherhood differently. Through its juxtaposition of the two mothers, client and surrogate, the film asks viewers to consider the class prejudices that inform their conceptions of worthy motherhood. It also raises provocative questions about the role of technology and human labour in creating families and the economic realities that undergird both. By taking seriously the differences among single mothers, *Baby Mama* qualifies as a "quality" postfeminist text (Negra 2).

SWITCH AND *THE BACK-UP PLAN*

Despite their initial premise of intentional single motherhood, *Switch* and *The Back-Up Plan* end up being postfeminist romantic comedies, in which the protagonists marry men and form nuclear families. They are postfeminist in the sense that their protagonists engage in the rhetoric of choice and individual autonomy; make feminist statements without acknowledging their debt to feminism and/or mocking feminism; and pursue motherhood as the *sine qua non* of a meaningful life. Additionally, both films imply that the nuclear family is the ideal model by describing intentional single motherhood as, as the title of one suggests, the "back-up plan" and by arguing, if implicitly, that a family without a father is incomplete. These postfeminist tropes help the protagonists to gain viewers' acceptance of their pursuit of intentional single motherhood.

Kassie, the protagonist of *Switch*, is a poster child for postfeminist single motherhood. In the opening scene of *Switch*, she explains her decision to pursue motherhood by asserting her agency and autonomy: "I'm ready to do it now. Life is in session. I'm not going to wait forever." The toast at her insemination party— "We're doing it for ourselves"—encapsulates this ethos. The success of second-wave feminism paved the way for Kassie's professional success as an executive at ABC and her concomitant financial independence. However, she never mentions it; feminism's gains are simply assumed, unworthy of comment. Although certain lines seem feminist, even ironically so in their overtness, the protagonists' delivery undermines their impact. For example, Kassie says: "I don't need a man to have a baby." In a movie that goes on to show how Kassie created and raised that baby without a man as co-parent, this could sound like the clarion call of feminism. *Switch*, however, does not offer viewers that vision. Concerns about the absent father recur throughout *Switch*. Wally, Kassie's friend (and the father of the son she ends up conceiving through the plot device that gives the film its name), worries that Kassie, by pursuing single motherhood, will miss the opportunity to meet a man who could be a father to her future offspring. Sebastian, the son that Kassie ends up conceiving through donor insemination, collects picture frames without removing the stock photos they contain so that he can imagine that they are pictures of the father whom he does not know. In this sense, the movie reinforces the notion that children of intentional single mothers suffer from "absent daddy" issues. The movie ends with Kassie marrying Sebastian's biological father. The final scene is Sebastian's birthday party in their new home, every room of which is filled with framed photographs of the nuclear family that they have formed. Audiences accepts Kassie as an intentional single mother because she is financially secure, desires motherhood, and understands that the single-mother family that she has created is far from the ideal formation. However, they like her even more at the end of the movie when she is married and Sebastian has a father.

Zoe, the protagonist of *The Back-Up Plan*, likewise hits all the points on the postfeminist rubric. Zoe is a successful small business owner, financially secure, and organized. After getting inseminated, she tells herself: "Everything is going to be okay. I have a plan." It is she who reassures Stan, the boyfriend that she met immediately after getting inseminated, that they can handle the financial burden of children: "We're going to be okay; I have money saved." Whereas *Switch* fails to acknowledge Kassie's indebtedness to earlier feminist struggles, *The Back-Up Plan* outright mocks feminism. Zoe attends the meeting of a group called Single Mothers and Proud, which parodies the real organization Single Mothers by Choice. The members of Single Mothers and Proud include the following caricatures: an extremist practitioner of attachment parenting, a defiantly independent feminist, and a lesbian man-hater, among others. The group's mantra, repeated several times by the leader for comic effect, asserts the members' choice and autonomy: "We wanted a child, and we made it happen on our own." As with *The Switch*, however, this seemingly feminist line packs no feminist punch; the delivery primes audiences to laugh at the members of Single Mothers and Proud rather than admire them. Finally, *Back-Up Plan* evades the "absent daddy" question through the character of Stan, Zoe's boyfriend. He serves as a father figure for Zoe's still in-utero babies, even suffering the stereotypical male fears about impending fatherhood—the sleepless nights, the lack of sex, the responsibility, the costs, etc. As with Wally of *The Switch*, Stan eventually overcomes his anxieties. *The Back-Up Plan* ends with his proposing to Zoe and, minutes later, Zoe throwing up because she is once again pregnant, this time with Stan's biological child.

BABY MAMA

In some respects, *Baby Mama* also adheres to the rules of the postfeminist playbook. Like Kassie and Zoe, Kate, the protagonist, is a professionally successful single woman who decides to pursue motherhood. Responsible, empowered, and entitled, she is the quintessential postfeminist heroine. On a first date, Kate explains her situation with a series of "I" statements, which foreground her agency: "I'm thirty-seven, and I want a baby, so I'm pursuing all my options. I met with an adoption attorney who was very encouraging, and I recently began the artificial insemination process. So, with a little bit of luck, I could be pregnant right now." Consistent with the postfeminist ethos, Kate owns her situation and uses the language of "choice" to explain her predicament: "I made a choice ... Some women get pregnant; I got promotions." Her tone here is matter-of-fact but also wistful. Postfeminist texts often represent "single professional women as selfish, emotionally stunted, and ultimately regretful about 'forgetting' their essential roles as wives and mothers" (Negra 4). Although Kate is not portrayed as "selfish" or "emotionally stunted," she does lament later in the movie that "He [her ex-boyfriend] wanted to marry me, and I wanted to focus on work." Kate's comment implies that, contra 1970s feminism, women are unlikely to have it all. Even though intentional single mothers may attain professional success and motherhood, the trifecta that includes romantic love is out of their reach (except in these romantic comedies, which, per the genre, overcome the obstacles to the trifecta that initially lay in the way of their protagonists).

Unlike *The Switch* and *Back-Up Plan*, however, *Baby Mama* lays bare the class privilege that makes intentional single motherhood a possibility and that legitimizes those who pursue it. As sociologist Barbara Rothman explains, "there is pretty much no way to become a mother in America without entering through the door of consumerism" (41). Indeed, Kate prepares for motherhood by purchasing everything from a stack of baby books to an expensive baby-proofing system for her home. Most significantly, she buys the services of a surrogate for a hefty one hundred thousand dollars after her attempts at adoption and insemination have failed. The capitalistic rationality of Chaffee Bicknell, chief executive of the surrogacy service with whom Kate contracts, is both humourous and chilling. Kate asks whether "some poor underpaid woman in the third world" is going to carry her baby. To defend surrogacy, Bicknell responds by defining it as just another form of outsourcing, a daily aspect of many, especially wealthy, Americans' lives. She notes that Kate is planning to hire childcare workers after the baby is born. Why, then, she asks, would she not hire a caretaker for her child before she or he is born? Kate, and by extension viewers, is hard-pressed to dispute the logic of Bicknell's comparison. However, in presenting surrogacy as a capitalist exchange, *Baby Mama* invites viewers to question the morality of anyone, single or otherwise, pursuing motherhood by any means necessary: *should* childbearing and childcare be subjected to the same market forces that govern the way we clean our homes and clothing or buy food, even in pursuit of that most vaunted status—motherhood?

Baby Mama also underscores the fact that women's relationship to motherhood, and specifically single motherhood, is not equal. Class privilege makes intentional single motherhood possible and, more importantly, acceptable to others. Although Angie, the woman who ends up being Kate's surrogate, is not "a poor underpaid woman in the third world," she is a low-income and poorly educated white North American woman, whom Kate calls in a fit of anger "poor white trash." Angie's familial circumstance, as much as her verbal and body language, defines her as such. Although Angie claims that she and Carl are married, they are in fact common-law husband and wife due to their years living together. In this regard, they are part of the growing number of low-income and minority Americans who are opting out of marriage. Indeed, neither Angie nor Carl bathes marriage in a romantic haze. When Kate expresses regret about her choice to pursue work instead of marrying her ex-boyfriend, Angie says: "Of course you did. Because working is awesome and being married sucks." Carl is equally unsentimental. In his and Angie's first meeting with Kate, Carl describes his initial thoughts about Angie becoming a surrogate. Betraying both his incomprehension of the process and his callousness, Carl recalls thinking that someone would have "to pay extra" to have sex with his wife. When Angie says that this would be "out of the question," Carl hurriedly changes his tune, but the point is made: if the price were right, he would be willing to pimp his wife.

Angie eventually finds out that she is, indeed, pregnant but not with Kate's embryo.[7] She considers maintaining the façade that the baby she is carrying is Kate's on the assumption that Kate will be a better mother than she. The camera shows Kate's apartment through Angie's eyes: to her, it seems the lap of luxury. Given the depiction of Angie and Carl, viewers cannot help but take seriously Angie's perspective—that the child might actually be better off being raised by Kate. The viewers' concerns about Angie's maternal readiness are somewhat allayed when, in a later scene, Angie reassures Kate that she is drinking water instead of Dr. Pepper; her choice of beverage implies that she is now making more responsible mothering choices. Though having called into question her readiness for parenthood and class-based prejudices about what makes a good mother, the movie is good natured and generous about Angie's impending motherhood.

Baby Mama concludes as a romantic comedy must: with a marriage scene. The closing credits set a year or so in the future, show the child borne of Kate's one-in-a-million chance pregnancy, staring at Kate's engagement ring. Kate is apparently going to marry Rob, the man whom she started dating during the surrogacy process and the biological father of this miracle child. Viewers, also, overhear Angie telling Kate that Carl is committed to being a father and is even taking parenting classes. When the camera shifts to Carl, who is trying to teach their baby girl how to hold a gun for a video game, she ruefully adds that the classes "haven't yet taken effect yet." It is only in these very final minutes that *Baby Mama* addresses the fatherhood question, which was surprisingly absent for the bulk of the movie. *Baby Mama*'s engagement with the question of paternity is nuanced: the images of Carl invite viewers to consider whether Angie and her child would be better off without him, thereby calling into question the blanket insistence that children are always better off being raised by a mother *and* a father.

Despite adhering to the conventions of the romantic comedy genre, *Baby Mama* smuggles in a good deal of critique. Sociologist Barbara Rothman asks: "How can we understand motherhood outside of the systems, often systems of evil, in which we live? What can we use to weave a family?" (53). Through humour, and in a way that is accessible to general audiences, *Baby Mama* considers how contemporary technologies and vast income inequality complicate viewers' responses to these important questions. On the one hand, we forgive women a lot if motherhood is their goal and are thus primed to like Kate. On the other hand, Angie, a surrogate who initially shows zero interest in mothering, does not win our sympathies. Once she embraces motherhood, however, the audience is more inclined to forgive, or at a minimum overlook, the class-based deficiencies that were fodder for humor and judgment when she was a surrogate. Thoughtful viewers will take from *Baby Mama* a more poignant and keener understanding of how much economics, as expressed through consumerism, shapes evaluations of motherhood, which is ostensibly a most intimate relationship and choice.

CONCLUSION

Feminist critics Tasker and Negra suggest that "the transition to postfeminist culture involves an evident erasure of feminist politics from the popular" (5). In other words, postfeminist popular culture offers images of ostensibly liberated girls and women without engaging the inequities that persist among women and society at large. The U.S. films that I discuss in this chapter, though *Baby Mama* to a lesser degree, make this mistake. Moreover, in these films, the radical feminist potential of intentional single motherhood is lost, as their vision is narrow. As romantic comedies, these films are compelled to end with romantic procreative unions. And, indeed, they do; their single mother protagonists find men with whom to partner and who will father their children. More perniciously, these films suggest that this is the ideal outcome. In so doing, they constrain rather than expand viewers' sense of what is good and desirable for women and, more generally, for families. They affirm rather than challenge the postfeminist platitudes that what women want deep down is romantic love and that the ideal family has a particular structure, number of parental figures, and gender configuration. It does not have to be that way.

It is instructive to consider Marleen Gorris's *Antonia's Line* (1995), a Dutch film that offers an alternative vision of women and family. As the title suggests, Antonia is the matriarch of a family that the film follows for approximately fifty years. Antonia's daughter, Danielle, wants to become a mother, but she does not want to partner. Antonia helps her accomplish her goal. Danielle's daughter, Therese, has a daughter, Sarah, with a man whom she loves but does not want to marry. Janet Maslin's review of *Antonia's Line* mistakenly claims that "Antonia and her descendants come to symbolize the freedom of independent females, with little need for men in their lives." To the contrary, men figure prominently in the lives of the women in *Antonia's Line*, just not with the titles and within the legal bounds of family. The numerous family gatherings depicted include men and women, brought together by friendship, romantic love, shared commitments to childrearing, and community bonds. Just imagine what would happen if Hollywood offered viewers similarly expansive visions of family.

NOTES

[1]For more on the theoretical underpinnings and methodologies of cultural rhetorical studies, see Thomas Rosteck's *At the Intersection: Cultural Studies and Rhetorical Studies*. See also Powell et. al., "Our Story Begins Here: Constellating Cultural Rhetorics" for an alternative notion of cultural rhetorics that focuses as much on performance and objects as it does on text and that calls for the decolonizing of scholarly and disciplinary practices.

[2]Melissa Ludtke, author of *On Our Own: Unmarried Motherhood in America*, finds that "In the past decade, women who are thirty-five and older have experienced a more rapid increase in the rate of out-of-wedlock births than have women in younger age groups" (26).

[3]Michael A. Cohen suggests that "The problem for Quayle was the context of his comment.... It was one thing to criticize the show for glamorizing a so-called poor lifestyle choice, but to link the violence in Los Angeles and the generation-long epidemic of out-of-wedlock births in poor communities to a television program struck many as inappropriate and inaccurate. Moreover, pro-choice advocates, including Murphy Brown's executive producer, pointed to the very real inconsistency of a pro-life supporter such as Quayle criticizing a woman for having a baby. Quayle was attacked anew, not only by Hollywood but increasingly by newspaper columnists around the country" (440).

[4]As Elizabeth Bruno demonstrates, the meaning of single mother is ambiguous: it refers both to mothers who are unmarried and to mothers who parent alone. Intentional single mothers, the focus of this chapter, are by definition unmarried. Some, however, create families in which they do not parent alone. For more on the various family configurations that intentional single mothers create, please see chapter seven, "What Does Single Mean?," in Rosanna Hertz's *Single By Chance, Mothers By Choice: How*

Women Are Choosing Parenthood Without Marriage. Creating the New American Family.

[5]See Blankenshorn; Popenhoe; and Pruett for extended arguments about the necessity of fathers.

[6]Since writing this chapter, I have continued to live and research this topic. My own experience as an intentional single mother, as well as several memoirs, documentaries, and blog posts by intentional single mothers, show that many of us do challenge these assumptions about the necessity of fathers and the necessary components of "good" or "complete" families. These writings also demonstrate that some intentional single mothers do identify as feminists and situate their decision to mother solely in a feminist framework. At the same time, the writings of intentional single mothers reveal that the absence of an explicitly feminist vocabulary and framework does not necessarily indicate the absence of feminist motivations and impulses. To put it simply, many intentional single mothers live as feminists whether they identify as such. My monograph-in-progress, *I Am Murphy Brown: Rhetorics of Intentional Single Motherhood 1994- 2014*, examines this complicated rhetorical scene.

[7]Two weeks after the embryo transfer, Angie does a take-home pregnancy test and discovers that she is not pregnant. She and Carl have sex to commiserate the loss, and Angie decides to delay telling Kate the bad news. In the meantime, Angie has no idea that she has become pregnant with Carl's child. She is on the verge of telling Kate about the failed at-home pregnancy test when, during a routine ultrasound, the doctor discovers a heartbeat. Kate, believing that the heartbeat is that of her embryo, is ecstatic. Angie is ecstatic for another reason: the heartbeat gives her a bit more time before she has to disclose the truth.

WORKS CITED

Baby Mama. Dir. Michael McCullers. Michaels-Goldwyn, 2008. Film.

Bitzer, Lloyd. "The Rhetorical Situation." *Philosophy and Rhetoric* 1 (1968): 1-14. Print.

Blankenshorn, David. *Fatherless America: Confronting Our Most*

Urgent Social Problem. New York: BasicBooks, 1995. Print.

Bock, Jane D. "Doing the Right Thing: Single Mothers by Choice and the Struggle for Legitimacy." *Gender and Society* 14.1 (2000): 62-86. Print.

Chocano, Carina. "Baby Mama." *Los Angeles Times*, 25 Apr. 2008. Web. 14 Aug. 2014.

Cohen, Michael. *Live from the Campaign Trail: The Greatest Presidential Campaign Speeches of the Twentieth Century and How They Shaped Modern America*. New York: Walker & Co, 2008. Print.

Dargis, Manhola. "Learning on the Job About Birthing Babies." *New York Times*, 25 Apr. 2008. Web. 15 Aug. 2014.

Dargis Manhola. "Love Means Having to Say I Feel." *New York Times*, 22 Apr. 2010. Web. 15 Aug. 2014.

Gleiberman, Owen. "Back-Up Plan." *Entertainment Weekly*, 22 Apr. 2010. Web. 13 Aug. 2014.

Gleiberman, Owen. "Best Friends Forever." *Entertainment Weekly*, 20 Aug. 2010. Web. 14 Aug. 2014.

Graham, Susanna. "Choosing Single Motherhood: Single Women Negotiating the Nuclear Family Ideal." *Families beyond the Nuclear Ideal*. Eds. Daniela Cutas and Sarah Chan. London: Bloomsbury, 2012. 97-109. Print.

Hertz, Rosanna. *Single by Chance, Mother by Choice: How Women Are Choosing 'Parenthood Without Marriage and Creating the New American Family*. Oxford: Oxford University Press, 2006. Print.

Hertz, Rosanna. "The Father as an Idea: A Challenge to Kinship Boundaries by Single Mothers." *Symbolic Interaction* 25.1 (2002): 1-31. Print.

Holden, Stephen. "In a Baste and Switch, a New Father is Born." *New York Times*, 19 Aug. 2010. Web. 15 Aug. 2014.

Hymowitz, Kay. "How Single Motherhood Hurts Kids." *New York Times*, 8 Feb 2014. Web. 15 Aug. 2014.

Lee, Amanda. "Single Mothers 'Bad for Society,' Pew Research Center's Latest Poll Finds." *Huffington Post*, 21 Feb. 2011. Web. 8 Aug. 2014.

Ludtke, Melissa. *On Our Own: Unmarried Motherhood in America*. Berkeley: University of California Press, 1997. Print.

Mailloux, Steven. *Reception Histories: Rhetoric, Pragmatism, and American Cultural Politics*. Ithaca: Cornell University Press, 1998. Print.

Maslin, Janet. "A Line of Strong Women With Faith in Destiny." *New York Times*, 2 Feb. 1996. Web. 20 Sept. 2014.

Mattes, Jane. *Single Mothers by Choice: A Guidebook for Single Women Who Are Considering or Have Chosen Motherhood*. New York: Three Rivers Press, 1994. Print.

McRobbie, Angela. "Post-Feminism and Popular Culture." *Feminist Media Studies* 4.3 (2004): 255–264. Print.

Morin, Rich. "Disapprove of Single Mothers." Pew Research Center, 6 Jan. 2011. Web. 8 Aug. 2014.

Morissette, Mikki. *Choosing Single Motherhood: The Thinking Woman's Guide*. Boston: Houghton Mifflin, 2008. Print.

Negra, Diane. "Quality Postfeminism: Sex and the Single Girl on HBO." *Genders OnLine Journal* 39 (2004): n. pag. Web. 29 July 2014.

Phillips, Michael. "The Back-Up Plan." *latimes.com*. Los Angeles Times, 22 Apr. 2010. Web. 15 Aug. 2014.

Popenhoe, David. *Life Without Father: Compelling New Evidence that Fatherhood and Marriage Are Indispensable for the Good of Children and Society*. New York: Martin Kessler Books, 1996. Print.

Powell, Malea et. al. "Our Story Begins Here: Constellating Cultural Rhetorics." *Enculturation: A Journal of Rhetoric, Writing, and Culture* 25 Oct. 2014. Web. 29 Mar. 2016.

Pruett, Kyle D. *Fatherneed: Why Father Care Is as Essential as Mother Care for Your Child*. New York: Broadway Books, 2011. Print.

Quayle, Dan. "Address to the Commonwealth Club of California." Dan Quayle: 44th Vice President of the United States, 1989-1993. N.p., 19 May 1992. Web. 10 Aug. 2014.

Rabinovitz, Lauren. "Sitcoms and Single Moms: Representations of Feminism on American TV." *Cinema Journal* 29.1 (1989): 3-19. Print.

Ravitz, Jessica. "Out of Wedlock Births Hit Record High." *Cable News Network (CNN)*. Cable News Network, 8 Apr. 2009. Web. 9 Aug. 2014.

Rosteck, Thomas Rosteck, ed. *At the Intersection: Cultural Studies and Rhetorical Studies*. New York: Guilford, 1999. Print.

Schwarzbaum, Lisa. "Baby Mama." *Entertainment Weekly*. Entertainment Weekly, Inc., 25 Apr. 2008. Web. 15 Aug. 2014.

Sharkey, Betsy. "The Switch." *Los Angeles Times,* 20 Aug. 2010. Web. 15 Aug. 2014.

Sloan, Louise. *Knock Yourself Up: A Tell-All Guide to Becoming a Single Mom*. New York: Penguin Group, 2007. Print.

Stonesifer, Jené. *When Baby Makes Two: Single Mothers by Chance or by Choice*. Los Angeles: Lowell House, 1994. Print.

Tasker, Yvonne and Diane Negra. "Introduction: Feminist Politics and Postfeminist Culture." *Interrogating Postfeminism: Gender and the Politics of Popular Culture*. Eds. Yvonne Tasker and Diane Negra. Durham: Duke University Press, 2007. 1-26. Print.

The Back-Up Plan. Dir. Alan Poul. CBS Films, 2010. Film.

The Switch. Dirs. Josh Gordon and Will Speck. Mandate Pictures, 2010. Film.

3.
Every Child Needs a Father

The Shield and the Postfeminist Desire for Single Motherhood

DWAYNE AVERY

IN THIS CHAPTER, I explore postfeminist representations of single motherhood, especially the ways in which contemporary television has fostered an ambivalent attitude toward lone parenting. That is, whereas some media forms provide a far more positive image of women parenting alone—as many single mothers are portrayed as competent, educated, and well-respected members of society—there is still the tendency to picture the lone mother as a deviant subject, whose decision to parent outside the heterosexual norm is treated as a threat to society. Furthermore, I contend that although the media's recent celebration of lone parenting is welcomed, many of its representational and narrative strategies are troubling. For example, rather than address the structural issues that make life hard for many single mothers, popular media has tended to paint a positive picture of only affluent mothers, whose financial security and private resources allow them to escape the stigma of deviance and become self-respected citizens within the framework of neoliberalism. Although these depictions serve as a promising example of the real powers *some* women have over their lives, as they can choose to create a non-patriarchal family structure, the media's alignment of female power with the tenants of neoliberalism is disconcerting. By aligning the "good" lone mother with the entrepreneurial spirit of neoliberalism, where survival is made possible only through the productive accumulation of individual resources, the media continues to demonize those single mothers who cannot pull themselves up by their own bootstraps. Finally, I argue that along with ambivalently depicting lone parenting, many contemporary shows, such as *The Shield*, accentuate this uncertainty by giving special attention to a new breed of patriarchal father figures, who attempt to reclaim their status as head of household by combining the traditional masculine traits of violence and aggression with parental sensitivity. Thus, although some facets of these shows offer a promising image of single motherhood, the media's focus on the "trials and tribulations" of the postfeminist father demonstrates the ways in which feminism is still greatly needed to combat the retro-sexist tendencies of popular media.

AMBIVALENT MOTHERS AND DESTRUCTIVE FATHERS: *THE SHIELD'S* PORTRAIT OF DOMESTICITY

In the series finale of FX's *The Shield*, Vic Mackey—television's most notorious crooked cop—is dealt an unexpected form of justice. Unlike his partner in crime, Ronnie, who is escorted to jail, Mackey is shown in the dying moments of the show being trained for a new office job with the Federal Bureau of Investigation (FBI). After seven seasons of highlighting the toxic effects of masculinity gone terribly awry, *The Shield* finally shows Mackey contained. He is brought to his knees, not by the creed of violence that he so openly endorsed, but by a new life as an office stiff. Trading in his street wear for a stuffy, grey, bureaucratic suit, Mackey—the condescending and egomaniacal white patriarch—is rendered obsolete; his days of reigning over the wild, wild West are resolutely over. As Stephen Shapiro writes, "Stripped of his patriarchal powers—no official gun, no family, no team—and leashed by a female manager, Mackey can only plaintively listen to the sounds of the street's freedom, knowing that his struggle for status as a caregiving father and autonomous leader of men has failed" (187).

As with other gritty television shows (*The Sopranos*, *Breaking Bad*, *Sons of Anarchy*, and *Hell on Wheels*), *The Shield* documents the trials and tribulations experienced by "the common white man," especially the emotional, psychological, and spiritual agony associated with hegemonic masculinity. Similar to the anguish experienced by television's other great anti-hero, Tony Soprano, Mackey's moral upheaval speaks to a post-9/11 culture that is unsure about the status of men; his rise and fall a testament to the media's obsession with masculinities in crisis. However, although much has been written about *The Shield's* exploration of troubled masculinities, what interests me about Mackey's failed paternity is how his social disintegration relates to postfeminist representations of single mothers.[1] After all, the most devastating blow to Mackey's ego comes from the loss of his place as the patriarchal head of household, not from his transformation into a bureaucratic stiff. A vigilant, if not pathological believer in the social importance of fathers, Mackey emblematizes the recent pushback by many men who feel that the paternal rights of fathers are under siege—a trend that can be readily seen in the collective efforts that have emerged around "fathers' rights" in North America in the past few decades. Subsequently, when his ex-wife, Corrine, betrays him by working with the FBI and disappears with their kids into a witness protection program, Mackey is pulverized. As the series concludes, Corrine arrives at her new home in Illinois, a single mother about to start a life completely on her own. For Mackey, the self-appointed patriarch, who believes all children need a father, nothing could be worse than this: a man without a family and the reality of single motherhood.

The Shield's image of single motherhood belongs to a recent media trend that envisions lone mothers as the head of a legitimate family structure. Whereas twenty years ago, single mothers were associated with poor family values, in today's media climate, being a single mother is almost hip. From the *Gilmore Girls*' frisky, quick-witted, and kind-hearted depiction of single motherhood to *Friends*' sexy representation of Rachel's fearless decision to parent alone, contemporary television has been increasingly accepting of lone motherhood. However, although a plethora of recent shows (*Ally McBeal, Desperate Housewives*, *Fraser*, *Bones*, *Cougar Town* etc.) have appeared, which feature strong, self-reliant, and responsible single moms, the representational and narrative strategies used to celebrate postfeminist single motherhood has led to a stark representational divide. Whereas many lower-income single mothers continue to be imagined through the stigma of welfare dependency, popular television's new class of postfeminist single mothers are distinguished by their remarkable economic position, as their financial security and private wealth provide them with the freedom to parent alone. In her chapter in this volume on Hollywood images of lone motherhood, for example, Mack describes a special class of single mothers—intentional single mothers—who are championed for their decision to intentionally parent alone. Unlike "regular" single mothers, who do not actively "choose" single motherhood and are often branded as irresponsible and financially insecure, the intentional single mother is shown as an affluent and responsible figure, whose upward mobility allows her to avoid the stigma of deviance. Speaking about the way Hollywood has transformed the intentional single mother into an enviable figure of maternal "goodness," Mack claims that "by mobilizing postfeminist discourses to represent intentional single mothers as responsible, financially secure, and ideologically conservative, these films distinguish 'good' intentional single mothers from 'bad' single mothers, thereby making them acceptable heroines."

Mack's observations about Hollywood's neoconservative depiction of single mothers are important, as they demonstrate the need to critique the problematic alignment of motherhood discourses with a laissez-faire brand of postfeminism, which openly supports the privatization of neoliberalism. In *The Shield*, however, a slightly different approach to single motherhood is evidenced, one that comes with its own set of discursive problems. As I will argue in this chapter, *The Shield's* representation of single parenting captures one of the most important facets of postfeminist media: its ambivalence. As feminist scholar Stephanie Genz argues, postfeminist media does not adhere to any one political stance but straddles many points of view, from the promise of new liberating opportunities for young women to the oppressive commercialization of gender politics. In *The Shield,* this ambiguity translates into a portrait of domestic life, wherein single mothers are both celebrated and denigrated; they are both a real threat to the patriarchal order and a reproachable group that reinforces traditional family structures.

As with many of the neoconservative films described by Mack, *The Shield* draws on the postfeminist idea that feminism is no longer needed, since women can now *choose* their own destinies, even opting to forego a traditional family system for a life of single parenthood. By showing women in positions of power, shows, such as *The Shield*, take great strides towards presenting lone motherhood in a positive light, as the absence of domineering father figures does not automatically conjure up the stigma of the feckless welfare mom. The problem with this approach, however, is that its celebratory depiction of lone mothering is only granted to a select group of mothers. Whereas the "bad" single mother must continue to endure the stigma of irresponsibility, as her inability to climb the ladder of self-sufficiency is seen as destroying the bedrock of domestic stability, the "good" postfeminist single mother is championed as a symbol of the self-rewarding possibilities associated with neoliberalism.

On the other hand, although *The Shield's* depiction of lone motherhood shares in the neoconservative ideology of personal responsibility, it also avoids a blatant celebration of affluence by showcasing the economic burdens of the struggling middle class. That is, even though the show draws attention to the neoliberal tendencies of postfeminist media, it avoids the jubilant Hollywood endings described by Mack. Indeed, even though many of the mothers in the show may be described as heroic women, who challenge the heterosexual norm by choosing to abandon the two-parent family system, they, ultimately, lack the financial resources to sustain any form of domestic contentment. Subsequently, by bringing attention to the financial strains and class restrictions facing single moms, *The Shield* provides a noteworthy critique of many of the affluent representations of postfeminist single moms. This class-based critique is further accentuated by the show's refusal to participate in the heterosexist rhetoric offered by postfeminist media. In many contemporary films and television shows, for example, the single mother's potentially subversive desire to parent alone is all too often dampened by the use of the coupling plot—a narrative device that envisions happiness as the product of the heterosexual union of a healthy man and woman. As Mack claims, although many films feature women who appear to challenge the social norm, in the end, these subversive inclinations are curtailed by the mother's desire to find the "perfect" husband to complement her new family. In *The Shield,* no such resolution is attained—quite the contrary. Instead of using the coupling plot to reinforce the legitimacy of heterosexuality, the show provides this far more destabilizing ending: after seven seasons of trying to endure the violent tendencies of her ex-husband, Corrine is finally released from patriarchal domination, free to live a life as a single mom without the need or desire for a husband. Indeed, by refusing the coupling plot, the show seriously questions the social valence of fathers, as patriarchal authority is shown as a toxic force that has the potential to destroy families rather than restore them to normalcy.

Yet even this questioning of patriarchal authority is not without fault. While the show provides a more realistic depiction of the real struggles and burdens that many single mothers face, ultimately, the focal point of the series is not the lives of single moms but the trials and tribulations of the suffering white male. The failure of patriarchy, especially the devastating emotional effects of hyper-masculinity, is the real story behind the show, and, all too often, the viewer is invited to sympathize with the men issuing the blows, not with its many female victims, who must suffer at the hands of men's violence. This ambiguous perspective on patriarchy can be seen in the way in which Mackey is trumpeted as a necessary evil, a paternal figure required to maintain law and order. In the concluding scenes of the pilot episode, for example, the social necessity of Mackey's extreme violence is pictured in domestic terms: as Mackey is handing out his "tough on crime," renegade justice, the other characters are shown nestled softly in their homes, their safety and security only made possible by the tough and gritty work of "real men." Regrettably, by showcasing this model of toxic paternity, the show does a great disservice to its maternal characters. Although some characters, such as Corrine and Danny, barely escape the paternal clutches of Mackey, other mothers are not so lucky. Death or absence becomes the only viable option for those "bad" mothers who desire or are given the option to parent alone.

DYSFUNCTION IN THE TELEVISUAL HOME: THE FALLOUT OF PATRIARCHY

The tendency to see contemporary television through the canonical gaze of the aftermath of 9/11 is pervasive (Shapiro). This is especially true of *The Shield*, as Mackey's police brutality has been read as an allegory for America's perpetual war on terrorism. Undoubtedly, television's recent portrayal of men who use torture to secure the "homeland" represents a poignant field of critical inquiry; however, a major omission in television studies is the way that shows, such as *The Shield*, demonstrate television's ability to transform all genres into some form of family drama. For postfeminist media cultures, it is within the dysfunctional spaces of the home that today's political and social allegories are played out, as the stresses of domestic life, complex gender identities, and new family structures are used to map another mode of contemporary uncertainty: the demise of the heteronormative family. As Shapiro writes:

> The past order's eclipse by a new way of life is represented through the lens of an increasingly dysfunctional but authentically Americana family or small group whose members are frequently, if not congenitally, incapable of maintaining the roles and responsibilities they have inherited. At the center of this dissolving present stands a morally ambiguous patriarch, whose limited comprehension of the emerging horizon is characterized less by rational contemplation than by his performance of asphyxiating frustration, anger breathing, and the occasional Sturm und Drang of shouting and pointless violence. (196)

From this domestic perspective, Mackey's "asphyxiating frustration" stems not just from his hatred of bureaucratic power; his frequent displays of puffed-up aggression are equally about his twisted attachment to an antiquated image of family life. As Judith Stacey has shown, many of today's families fail to live up to the heteronormative model that continues to occupy the mainstream cultural imaginary in North America. Long gone is the nuclear family structure that celebrates the breadwinning capabilities of fathers and the domesticated prowess of "intensive mothers." Instead, contemporary families abound in diversity: from lesbian and gay families to the rise of single mothers, family structures today do not abide by traditional models of normalcy.

Yet despite this plurality, the word "family" continues to summon a heterosexist tradition, and, in this form, shows itself to be a resilient discursive and disciplinary device. As Stacey writes, "the word family continues to conjure an image of a married, monogamous, heterosexual pair and their progeny. This is still the model of a 'normal family,' not only in the world of soccer moms and Joe six-packs ... but even among some family researchers who should know better" (4).

Missing from Stacey's long list of institutions that continue to endorse heterosexist images of family life is the contemporary media. Although the media has provided, at times, insight into alternative domestic spheres—with films and television shows such as *Brokeback Mountain*, *The Kids Are All Right*, *Transamerica*, and *United States of Tara* bringing attention to the rise in LGBT families—all too often, media reproduces dominant images of family life. This is not to say that all media works to naturalize heterosexist family values, nor does it mean that the media has not shifted over the years in the way that they represent domestic roles and family structures. Representations of single mothers are a good example. In 1992, when Vice President Dan Quayle vehemently attacked the show *Murphy Brown* for what he felt was the show's misguided glorification of single motherhood, the media climate surrounding lone mothers was bleak (Stone). The idea of raising a child without acknowledging the social importance of fathers was deemed irresponsible, even pathological. Unlike the heteronormative mother, who was celebrated for her intensive dedication to her children, the single mom became the scapegoat for a host of social ills, especially the rise in welfare dependency (Jayakody; Stone; Sidel).

The situation has shifted somewhat since then. Although attacks on single mothers continue—a few years ago, for example, *The Washington Post* published an article, "20 years later," declaring that Quayle was right about *Murphy Brown* and unmarried moms—contemporary images of lone mothers have not been as disparaging and one-dimensional. According to gender studies scholar Jane Juffer, within popular culture, there are not only representations of single mothers that run contrary to the stigma of deviance and irresponsibility but also instances in which they are celebrated for their strong work ethic, self-determination, and personal willpower. As Juffer writes,

> Single mothers emerge as a respected identity group in the context of the neoliberal production of the self-regulating citizen-consumer-subject. This conjuncture of forces can be seen in the remarkable explosion of positive media representations of single moms over the last decade; from *Austin Powers* to *The Cat in the Hat*, single mothers are the new darlings of popular culture. (4)

Importantly, for Juffer, these more positive images of single moms cannot be divorced from the normalization of the neoliberal subject, which envisions the productive capacities of the lone individual as the sole arbitrator of personal and social success. As Juffer continues, the prime force of legitimization that has "helped bring single mothers into the national imaginary as respectable 'family' people" (46) is the *lone* mother's unfathomable powers of calculated, self-determination and self-sufficiency. Rather than being stigmatized as deficient, reckless, and negligent, postfeminist single mothers are praised for their autonomy, as they rely on the marketplace's plethora of self-motivating products and services to ensure their families' personal success. As Juffer writes,

> This single mom is palatable because she constantly demonstrates her self-sufficiency, distancing herself from the welfare mom ... The perfect liberal subject, she governs herself. For help, she looks to advice books and Internet support groups, fitting into the self-help movement, which, as Heidi Marie Rimke says, constructs citizens who are "rendered entirely responsible for their failures as well as their successes, their despair as well as their happiness." (47)

What a change of fortune for single moms. Whereas twenty years ago Murphy Brown stood out as a vilified promoter of poor family values, in more recent television shows, such as *Ally McBeal*, *Sex and the City*, *Fraser*, *Desperate Housewives*, and *Six Feet Under*, single mothers are treated as normalized subjects of postfeminist progress. By utilizing their postfeminist powers of choice, these strong, educated, and well-to-do figures are free to create their own destinies. However, although these favourable images may have helped legitimize some single mothers, the postfeminist lone mother does not speak for the majority: the media's preoccupation with affluent moms masks and conceals some of the concrete realities, deprivations, and stigmas that many single mothers in Canada and the U.S. continue to contend with. Indeed, instead of bringing light to the many structural problems that make life hard for single moms (inadequate daycare resources, lack of benefits for part-time workers, the ongoing surveillance of dependant mothers etc.[2]), postfeminist television has produced an exclusionary account of the self-reliant single mom, which, as a by-product, stigmatizes those mothers who cannot meet the neoliberal ideals of personal autonomy. As Juffer writes,

> The neoliberal alternative to dependency is personal responsibility, which has indeed been used to remove the stigma from single mothers who can demonstrate self-sufficiency. It would seem that the self-supporting single mom, through no singular power of her own even though it is represented as such, puts more pressure on the low-income single mother to distance herself from dependency in order to gain respect. (26)

There is also the question of whether the postfeminist lone mother actually subverts the heteronormative family. As Mack shows in her chapter, narratives about women who actively pursue single motherhood tend to reinforce rather than dismantle the normative order, as the protagonist's search for heterosexual love revalorizes the very patriarchal system that the intentional single mother supposedly rejects. Although many narratives engage with the act of choosing to parent alone, the predictable use of the coupling plot, which seeks narrative resolution through heterosexual union, thwarts the possibility of a non-patriarchal system of family attachments. Thus, rather than dealing meaningfully with the material realities of lone motherhood, these narratives use romance as a means to sanitize the threat to a heterosexist world order. As American literature scholar Robin Silbergleid writes,

> The problem, ultimately, is that representations of reproduction inevitably reproduce narrative's reproductive paradigm. Until we can create narratives that operate under a non-heterosexual metaphor, the stories that we tell about the family will continue to reproduce rather than challenge dominant ideas about the family, ensuring that single motherhood remains either the enviable outcome of Hollywood wealth or the deplorable stereotype of the welfare mom.

Juffer's and Silbergleid's criticism of the emergence of the "good" postfeminist single mother righty demonstrates some of the problems and oversights associated with postfeminist discourses that uncomplicatedly equate gender equality with the right to choose. However, I would argue that another pertinent area of investigation, which is rarely discussed, involves the reoccurring use of the trope of "men in crisis" to undermine single moms and re-establish the merits of patriarchy. Indeed, perhaps the most disarming aspect about postfeminist television resides not in its refusal to deal with the structural problems affecting lone mothers but the way in which its insistence that feminism is no longer needed—since women are now free to choose—masks another threat: the arrival of the postfeminist father.

SENSITIVE VIOLENCE AND CONTRADICTORY FATHERHOOD

"Keep your ties; never mind the designer polo shirts and forget the phony-macho perfume. Let me tell you what fathers want. We want our intrinsic authority back" (Safire). William Safire's sentiments on what fathers want encapsulate the political firestorm associated with the supposed waning of men's power and authority. "This essential prerogative of fatherhood," Safire continues, "has been stolen from us by children who want us to be their friends and by those children's mothers who insist on shared parentalism." Several years earlier, Robert Bly published his influential book, *Iron John:*

A Book About Men, a work that explores contemporary issues of manhood, especially the absence of men's paternal authority. Echoing Safire, Bly envisions the plight of men, especially their inability to get in touch with their inner "Wild Man," resulting from the domineering role that women play in the lives of men. "When we walk into a contemporary house," Bly observes, "it is often the mother who comes forward confidently. The father is somewhere else in the back, being inarticulate" (21). For Bly, so many of society's problems, especially the inability to transform young boys into real men, can be attributed to the overbearing and outlandish influence of mothers. As Donna Peberdy writes, "For Bly, fatherhood is a central masculine signifier that has been usurped by the mother figure in the contemporary period. Bly repeatedly returns to this idea of father lack or loss as a significant explanation for the softening of men" (11).

Bly's and Safire's comments came during a time of heightened sensitivity to the idea that North American men were experiencing a widespread crisis in masculinity, especially regarding their role as fathers. The social critic, David Blankenhorn, for example, has openly declared fatherlessness as the most pressing social problem affecting Americans. According to Blankenhorn, the traditional model of the breadwinning father, which envisions men as the family's moral and economic guardian, has been slowly eroded by a system of beliefs that understands fathers as a disposable part of society. Fathers, Blankenhorn bemoans, are no longer given the respect and admiration that they deserve. According to Blankenhorn, society's lack of regard for the institution of fatherhood has single-handedly destroyed the moral fabric of American life. Fatherlessness is seen as the root cause of most American problems, from the rise in poverty to the widespread problems of domestic violence and sexual abuse.

Although Bly and Safire mourn the loss of men's authority, within contemporary television, interestingly, a very different story about the place and power of men is being told. "It's no coincidence," Dave Thier proclaims, "that while the traditional masculine roles may be disappearing in reality, they've only become stronger on television." After *The Sopranos* redefined television as a post-network space of quality entertainment, many shows have portrayed men trying to reclaim their "intrinsic authority." From the grotesque violence espoused by the motorcycle gang fathers in *Sons of Anarchy* to Rick's overbearing paternalism in *The Walking Dead,* contemporary television has worked hard to harden its image of contemporary masculinity, as television's new fathers attempt to salvage their place in a social world that is supposedly unsure about the proper role of men. Indeed, whereas earlier models of fatherhood depended on the straightforward image of the detached, breadwinning father, today's men are expected to straddle multiple gender positions, abiding by what Hannah Hamad calls the rise of "postfeminist paternity," a hegemonic form of masculinity, wherein traditional ideas about masculinity—toughness, rationality, individualism—are coupled with sensitivity, domesticity, and parental care. In the case of Vic Mackey, this model of "sensitive fatherhood" translates into a strange concoction of hyperbolic violence and an accentuation of his capacity to care. In short, Mackey's character entails a re-imagining of the male hero as a domestic gatekeeper, whose ability to protect the hearth does not challenge the dominant structures underlying traditional masculinities (Faludi). As Cynthia Fuchs writes regarding the parental similarities between *The Shield* and the detective show *Kojak*:

> Tellingly, both *Kojak* and *The Shield* have found similar means to make their mad bald anti-heroes even remotely sympathetic ... And that route goes through kids. Whatever they do, they protect kids—from lousy parents, from sexual abuse, from drugs, violence, confusion, and horror ... For Vic, it's one of many motivations for brutality: When he hears that some child has been raped, turned into an addict, prostitute, or mule, Vic implodes, all steamy meanness, his symptomatic sense of entitlement ignited.

Mackey's coupling of paternal sensitivity and brute violence is demonstrated poignantly near the end of the pilot episode. When the detectives Wyms and Wagenbach are unable to get a suspect to disclose the whereabouts of a missing girl, who was sold into sexual slavery, the captain turns to Mackey as a last resort. Entering the interrogation room armed with a bottle of whisky, a zippo lighter, a box cutter, and a telephone book, Mackey proceeds to show why tough and gritty men are needed in a society that has grown soft and weak. "What's that stuff for," inquires the suspect. Mackey's reply: "This is what I'm going to use to get you to tell me where Jenny is." As it happens throughout the series, Mackey leaves the interrogation room miraculously equipped with all the information needed to solve the case. As Nicholas Ray observes, "*The Shield's* symbolic universe is so constructed that when Mackey suspends or is required to suspend law in the name of law, the result is habitually engineered to be safely to the benefit of the juridical order" (185).

I would add that although Mackey's abuse of the law speaks to the use of exceptional acts of violence to restore order and civility, his enforcement of "rugged paternalism" equally highlights the problematic gender politics associated with a postfeminist culture that understands feminist discourses as obsolete at the same time that fantasies about men's return to patriarchal dominance are bolstered. This retro-sexual impulse is particularly evident in the way that Mackey maintains a domineering parental influence over the show's token "bad" single mothers: the prostitute, Connie, whose excessive life of debauchery embodies a monstrous form of maternity, and the manipulative informant, Emolia, who supports her son by snitching on others. As depraved characters, who are unable to gain the respect afforded to affluent single mothers, Connie and Emolia are positioned at the bottom of the family hierarchy. Even worse than the stigma of welfare dependency, these lone mothers are labelled as urban delinquents, selfish, dangerous, and criminal mothers, whose inability to properly care for their children is routinely symbolized through the sickness of their children. Connie's son was born premature due to her excessive drug abuse, whereas Emolia's son possesses some kind of growth problem that requires constant rehabilitation.

Even though depictions of monstrous mothers are commonplace in contemporary media— as the deviant mother's status as an irredeemable figure absolves society of any blame for her debased situation—in *The Shield*, the monstrous mother forms the necessary "other," which allows men to reclaim their authority. According to the self-appointed patriarch, Mackey, all that these women need to pick themselves up again is the spiritual guidance of a strong father figure. Throughout the first season, for example, Mackey is shown taking a special interest in Connie, which goes well beyond his use of her as an informant. The other detectives treat her as a faceless, degenerate prostitute, yet Mackey goes out of his way to care for and protect her, treating her more as a family member than a monstrous deviant. He provides her with money so that she can spend quality time with her son. When she attempts to kick her heroin addiction, he comes to the rescue, caring for her son as if he were one of his own children; he even puts his career on the line by covering up her murder of a violent John. Although the viewer is never told explicitly that Mackey is the father of Connie's son, his relentless care for her family suggests that there is more than meets the eye with their relationship. Whether or not he is the biological father hardly matters, as nothing seems to dampen Mackey's domestic authority, especially his prowess in breadwinning. When he meets Emolia, a single immigrant mother who makes her living by snitching on her low-life associates, Mackey, yet again, comes to the rescue and provides her with the same protective care as he did for Connie. He helps her find an apartment and takes her on as a full-time informant, a job that helps her stay clear of any criminal activity; his greatest involvement, however, comes from his concern with her sick son. Pushing her to leave her life of crime so that she can be an intensive mother for her son, Mackey's paternal reach is far and wide, as he tries to set her on the right path of motherhood.

Despite Mackey's paternal hand, both Connie and Emolia are punished severely for their decision to parent outside the patriarchal order. When Connie rejects Mackey's help and returns to a life of drugs and sex work, she decides to place her son in foster care, a decision that Macket vehemently opposes. Following a long list of contemporary narratives that punish mothers by having them killed off in the story (Karlyn), *The Shield's* treatment of Connie shows just how difficult it can be for some women to escape the patriarchal power inscribed within motherhood. For even though Connie returns in season two as a redeemable character, her decision to abandon her son does not go unpunished. Murdered by a deranged firefighter, who went on a shooting spree at a women's shelter, Corrine is, as with so many other fictional "bad mothers," punished for her refusal to accept men's authority. Although Emolia is able to escape with her life, her punishment is just as severe. When Mackey discovers that she has been working with the FBI to bring him to justice, his fatherly love quickly turns to hatred and aggression, as he threatens to kill her family if she does not recant her statements. As Karlyn argues, depictions of deviant, absent, or missing mothers have become a common strategy within contemporary media that works to reposition the father as an untainted pillar of virtue. This strategy is amply evident in *The Shield*, as its scornful dismissal of Connie and Emolia comes to serve only one purpose: to bolster Mackey's paternal rights. The lone mother's status as a postfeminist media darling is completely undone: fulfilling none of the neoliberal requirements for the self-disciplining and consumerist subject, Connie and Emolia become a haunting reminder of just how easily society's ills can be laid at the feet of lone mothers.

THE SHIELD'S "GOOD" SINGLE MOTHERS: POSTFEMINISM AND THE RETURN OF PATRIARCHY

Whereas *The Shield's* unequivocal "bad mothers" are punished for their inability to break free from the stigma of deviance, the show's other single mothers are depicted far more ambivalently. Their decision to step outside the heteronormative family is treated as a risky affair that entails both hope and despair, both the possibility of avoiding the violence inscribed in hegemonic masculinity and the tragic recuperation of traditional gender structures. Mackey's ex-wife, Corrine, for example, is a single mother who must negotiate between two opposing parental worlds. On the one hand, Corrine's status as a single mother enables her to momentarily escape the domineering world of her husband. When she flees her home at the end of season one, Corrine boldly confronts the toxicity of Mackey's patriarchal environment: she chooses to live as a lone parent rather than become confined to the submissive role of domestic housewife. However, although Corrine's single motherhood provides her with a degree of freedom, her choice to parent alone does not occur in a utopian world free from the tyrannical influence of men. In fact, in some ways, her life as a single mother becomes even more burdensome because she is placed precariously between two equally unjust forms of patriarchy: a privatized form of patriarchy, in which Mackey's fatherly authority pushes her back into the home, and a public form of patriarchy, in which she must deal with the uncertainties and inequalities that come from public institutions, such as the workplace.

In *Theorizing Patriarchy*, Sylvia Walby distinguishes between two forms of patriarchy. Walby writes:

> Private patriarchy is based upon household production as the main site of women's oppression. Public patriarchy is based principally in public sites such as employment and the state. The household does not cease to be a patriarchal structure in the public form, but it is no longer the chief site. In private patriarchy the expropriation of women's labour takes place primarily by individual patriarchs within the household, while in the public form it is a more collective appropriation. (24)

In *The Shield*, Corrine confronts both systems of patriarchy. When she discovers that her son has autism in season one, Corrine is forced to delay her return to work so that she can provide "the best" motherly care for her son, a decision that ends up reinforcing traditional gender roles. Whereas Mackey amplifies his breadwinning role by working overtime to provide money for their son's special needs, Corrine is expected to fulfill her duties as "intensive mother," sacrificing her career in order to care for the family.

Season two focuses on Corrine's rejection of her submissive position within a system of private patriarchy. She divorces Mackey, returns to work part time, and begins dating her son's therapist; in short, Corrine takes charge of her life and uses her status as a single mother to balance her desires with the responsibilities of family. By season three, however, Corrine's attempt to become less dependent on Mackey by returning to work full time only makes her life more difficult because she is unable to balance the demands of her career with the pressures of intensive mothering. Although her decision to parent alone was supposed to free her from private patriarchy, she is, somehow, unable to excise the poisonous influence Mackey holds over her family. When Mackey learns that Corrine is dating their son's therapist, for example, he coerces her into finding a new therapist, a decision that proves costly, since Owen was the only person able to help their son. Later, when their daughter is diagnosed with autism, Corrine is required to deal with caring for two high-needs children alone. Finally, when Mackey rips off the Armenian mob, Corrine becomes embroiled in a life of organized crime, which almost leads to the death of her family. Forced to deal with two equally unjust patriarchal orders, Corrine, in the end, comes completely undone. She begins to rely on various pills and sleep medications to cope with a life filled with constant marital woes and complicated constraints.

According to Juffer, one of the single most pressing concerns affecting single mothers is the need to escape the "bad mother" stereotype, which envisions mothers who invest in their own self-care as selfish and uncaring. As with other mothers, single mothers need to take time for themselves to ensure that they remain happy and fulfilled role models for their children. Unfortunately, single mothers face the extra burden of having to parent alone and, as such, must find additional resources to care for themselves. Subsequently, in order to survive, many lone mothers must depend on various support networks—comprised of family, friends, and communities—that allow them to avoid the renunciation of the self, which is deemed mandatory within the paradigm of the intensive mothering. In *The Shield,* this simple facet of single motherhood—that parenting is always a collective affair and that parents need to rely on one another—is obfuscated. Instead, succumbing to the highly individualized logic of neoliberalism, in which success and failure are always attributed to the merits or shortcomings of the lone individual, the show fails to show the real structural and collective forces that help families succeed. For example, when Corrine gains the courage finally to turn against her ex-husband, her rebellion against patriarchy is depicted as an entirely lonely and solitary affair. Without any hint of outside help, Corrine is destined to suffer as a woman whose role as mother supersedes everything else, including her well-being. Her ability to escape the private patriarchy of Mackey is made possible, not through the assistance of a strong female network, but through another patriarchal institution: state power. Hoping to escape the watchful eye of Mackey by working with the authorities, Corrine, in the end, replaces one form of patriarchy for another, one that entails a far more pervasive system of surveillance.

The character that provides the most ambivalent image of the postfeminist single mother is the police officer Danny. As her name suggests, Danny straddles two gender worlds. On the one hand, she is a competent and capable officer, who can hold her own in a police environment that is ripe with misogyny. On the other hand, Danny retains her postfeminist female powers: she uses her good looks and sexual appeal to attract attention from the male officers. In short, Danny's career and lifestyle choices provide a poignant example of the contradictions associated with postfeminist cultures—the way that feminism is both, as Angela McRobbie writes, taken into account and repudiated. For even though her work environment is a cesspool of racist jokes, homophobia, and crude, sexual innuendos, Danny is, nonetheless, treated as a liberated woman, whose powers of calculated self-determination lead her to a successful career in a male-dominated workplace. These active powers are most notable in season five when Danny becomes pregnant and decides to conceal the identity of the father. An active, "single mother by choice," Danny represents the new freedoms of choice offered to postfeminist women: her decision to forego the traditional, two-parent family structure for a rewarding life of single motherhood attests to the ease by which women can supposedly escape patriarchy. Even the way the police department reacts to her pregnancy attests to the celebratory nature of contemporary gender politics. (The squad uses the father's identity as the base for a festive gambling pool.)

Similar to the conflicting experiences faced by other single mothers in the show, Danny's entrance into the world of motherhood is shown to be quite burdensome. Although season five capitalizes on the festive nature of her choice to parent alone, in seasons six and seven, Danny comes face-to-face with the patriarchal realities of motherhood. When Mackey finds out that he is the father, for instance, his paternal instincts take over and he subjects her to the same patriarchal dominance that he exerts over the other mothers in the show. Danny, however, attempts to fight back. She tries to convince Mackey to sign an agreement removing him of all parental responsibilities, a proposal that Mackey fervently opposes. "Every child needs a father," Mackey pleads, an ironic statement given the way his path to parental domination has destroyed nearly every family that he has contacted. When her use of the law does not work, Danny flees, as her carefree pregnancy quickly transforms into a single mother's nightmare. Again, instead of seizing the opportunity to depict powerful female networks, the show treats Danny's ordeal as an individual affair, wherein success is possible only through the powers of the self-motivating consumer subject. Indeed, although Danny shares the same plight as Corrine, both women are depicted as mortal enemies, who are never given a chance to bond or to forge a network of parental care, which could fight off Mackey's toxic paternal authority.

CONCLUSION

Despite its complexity and array of confusing and ambiguous definitions, postfeminism continues to gain much critical attention. Centred on the youthful energy of the single, career-oriented woman, especially her ability "to have it all," postfeminism, unfortunately, has very little to say about the status of mothers, especially single ones. In this chapter, I have explored how the matter of choice instrumental to equality and choice postfeminism forms a discursive strategy, which the media often uses to represent single mothers. As with the career-oriented woman, whose freedom coalesces around the ability to choose, the single mother, especially the "single mother by choice," has become an icon for neoliberalism's self-determining and self-motivating subject. In *The Shield,* this power of choice is demonstrated succinctly in Corrine's and Danny's decision to exist outside the patriarchal world of motherhood: both choose to parent alone instead of accepting a submissive place within private patriarchy. Yet despite their courageous acts of choosing lone motherhood, neither character is rewarded for their determination, as they try at all costs to escape Mackey's excessive paternalism. Likewise, although contemporary media has not been as denigrating toward single mothers, this does not mean that the stigma of deviance does not continue to be attached to lone mothers. As *The Shield* and other shows demonstrate, for those unable to "choose" the postfeminist ideal of self-regulating autonomy, life can be fraught with the same grave social injustices that besieged the "welfare moms" of a not-so-distant past.

Along with analyzing *The Shield's* ambivalent depiction of lone mothering, this chapter has argued that a continued interest in postfeminist masculinities is required for a more nuanced account of contemporary gender practices. Even though postfeminism has helped shed light on the status of contemporary women, little has been written on the nature of postfeminist men, especially pertaining to their status as fathers. This is unfortunate because the trope of the "sensitive father" has gained prominence in many post-network television shows. As Hamad and Lotz have shown, fatherhood forms an integral part of hegemonic masculinity that has serious consequences for representations of mothers. As with the violent father figures in *Sons of Anarchy*, *Breaking Bad*, and in other shows, *The Shield's* representation of fatherhood relies on an outdated and highly toxic form of masculinity that—in its attempt to navigate through the many uncertain subject positions provided for fathers—has the tendency to override pertinent issues related to contemporary mothering. Subsequently, along with exploring the contradictions associated with postfeminist representations of women, greater attention must be placed on how—at the same time tha feminism is supposedly repudiated—a new enemy surfaces: the ubiquitous, postfeminist father.

NOTES

[1]My use of the term postfeminism refers to what Sarah Projansky calls equality and choice postfeminism, which argues that feminism is no longer needed since young, career-oriented women have gained equal rights, especially in the marketplace. Furthermore, choice postfeminism contends that success and liberation for women results from their ability to choose, a feature that

aligns the term with the consumerist and individualistic logic of neoliberalism.

[2]A wonderful example of the heightened methods of surveillance used to monitor the lives of single moms is found in Jane Pulkingham and Sylvia Fuller's article "The Medicalization of Lone Motherhood through Welfare Reform." Pulkingham and Fuller argue that the trend in neoliberal reforms has placed many single mothers in a precarious position, as their status as productive labourers (capital) takes precedence over their status as mothers (social reproduction). They are now treated as medical subjects, whose worth is determined only by their ability to contribute to the labour market, a policy shift that diverts attention away from the structural problems affecting lone mothers, especially their difficulties in securing stable employment.

WORKS CITED

Blankenhorn, David. *Fatherless America: Confronting Our Most Urgent Social Problem.* New York: Harper, 1996. Print.

Bly, Robert. *Iron John: A Book About Men.* Boston: Da Capo Press, 2004. Print.

Bock, Jane D. "Doing The Right Thing?: Single Mothers by Choice and the Struggle for Legitimacy." *Gender & Society* 14.62 (2000): n.p. Print.

Faludi, Susan. Stiffed: *The Betrayal of the American Man.* New York: HarperCollins, 2000. Print.

Fuchs, Cynthia. "Terrordome." *Flow: A Critical Forum on Television and Media Culture.* N.p., 2005. Web. 9 Aug. 2014.

Genz, Stephanie. *Postfemininities in Popular Culture.* London: Palgrave Macmillan, 2009. Print.

Hamad, Hannah. *Postfeminism and Paternity in Contemporary U.S. Film: Framing Fatherhood.* New York and London: Routledge, 2014. Print.

Jayakody, Rukmalie. "Single Mothers." *Encyclopedia of Social Problems.* Ed. Vincent N. Parrillo. Thousand Oaks: Sage Publications, Inc., 2008. 854-55. Print.

Juffer, Jane. *Single Mother: The Emergence of the Domestic Intellectual.* New York: New York University Press, 2006. Print.

Karlyn, Kathleen Rowe. *Unruly Girls, Unrepentant Mothers: Redefining Feminism on Screen*. Texas: University of Texas Press, 2011. Print.

Lotz, Amanda. *Cable Guys: Television and Masculinities in the 21st Century*. New York: New York University Press, 2014. Print.

McRobbie, Angel. "Post Feminism and Popular Culture: Bridget Jones and the New Gender Regime." *Feminist Media Studies* 4.3 (2004): 255-264. Print.

Peberdy, Donna. *Masculinity and Film Performance: Male Angst in Contemporary American Cinema*. New York: Palgrave Macmillan, 2011. Print.

Projansky, Sarah. *Watching Rape: Film and Television in Postfeminist Culture*. New York: New York University Press, 2001. Print.

Pulkingham, Jane, and Sylvia Fuller. "From Parent to Patient: The Medicalization of Lone Motherhood Through Welfare Reform." *Social Politics* 19.2 (Summer 2012): 243-268. Print.

Ray, Nicholas. "A Different Kind of Cop: Exception and Complicity in The Shield." *Interrogating the Shield*. Ed. Nick Ray. Syracuse: Syracuse University Press, 2012. 166-185. Print.

Safire, William. "Essay; What Fathers Want." *New York Times*, 16 June 1994. Web. 7 Aug. 2014.

Sawhill, Isabel. "20 Years Later, It Turns Out Dan Quayle Was Right about Murphy Brown and Unmarried Moms." *washingtonpost.com*. The Washington Post, 25 May 2012. Web. 3 Aug. 2014.

Shapiro, Stephen. "Crackling Ice: The Shield and the Middle-Class Crisis of Social Reproduction." *Interrogating the Shield*. Ed. Nick Ray. Syracuse: Syracuse University Press, 2012. 186-206. Print.

Sidel, Ruth. *Unsung Heroines: Single Mothers and the American Dream*. Berkeley: University of California Press, 2006. Print.

Silbergleid, Robin. "Oh Baby!: Representations of Single Mothers in American Popular Culture." *Americana: The Journal of American Popular Culture, 1900-present*. 1.2 (Fall 2002) Web. 21 May. 2016.

Stacey, Judith. *Unhitched: Love, Marriage, and Family Values from West Hollywood to Western China*. New York: New York University Press, 2011. Print.

Stone, E. Kim. "Recovering the Lone Mother: Howard's End as Aesthetic Anodyne." *Camera Obscura* 19.1 (2004): 42-76. Print.

The Shield. FX. 12 Mar. 2002-25. Nov. 2008. Television.

Thier, Dave. "FX. Television for Men That Men Actually Want to Watch." *The Atlantic*. The Atlantic Monthly Group, 28 Sept. 2010. Web. 21 May. 2016.

Walby, Sylvia. *Theorizing Patriarchy*. Oxford: Blackwell Publishers, 1990. Print.

4.
Courageous Mothering

Katniss Everdeen as Outlaw Mother in *The Hunger Games* Trilogy

DANIELLE RUSSELL

> *You can't clock out and leave Prim on her own. There's no me now to keep you both alive.... You have to promise me you'll fight through it!* (Collins, *The Hunger Games*, 35)

IN WHAT SHE ASSUMES to be her last interaction with her family, Katniss Everdeen, of the popular *Hunger Games* novels, confronts her mother, highlighting the limitations of the single-parent family in a totalitarian society. Insisting on the necessity to fight for Prim's life, Katniss has serious misgivings about her mother's capabilities. To a large degree, Katniss's fear is justified; her mother has a personal history of incapacitating depression. The other crucial factor in the equation is the undermining of parenthood in Panem. The first novel opens with a deceptively reassuring image of mother and child. On the day of the reaping—the selection of tributes from the rebellious Districts that launched an unsuccessful rebellion decades ago—Katniss awakens to her "little sister, Prim, curled up on her side cocooned in [their] mother's body" (Collins, *Hunger Games* 3). This fleeting sense of security is all the mother can provide. Legal authority pre-empts maternal instincts in Panem.

Mothering is difficult in the best of contexts, but a totalitarian government completely eradicates parental authority. The "Treaty of Treason" imposed oppressive laws and as a "yearly reminder that the Dark Days must never be repeated," The Hunger Games were made mandatory (Collins, *The Hunger Games* 18). "In punishment for the uprising" two children from each District are "imprisoned in a vast outdoor arena" and forced to "fight to the death" while the country watches (Collins, *The Hunger Games* 18). For the citizens of the Capitol, the games are riveting entertainment; for those in the Districts, they are psychological warfare and an incessant form of terrorism. The message of the Hunger Games is clear: "Look how we take your children and sacrifice them and there's nothing you can do" (Collins, *Hunger Games* 19). The government claims ownership of all its citizens, but the practice of selecting tributes from those between the ages of twelve and eighteen is a particularly chilling means of control: not only of parents in the Districts but also of those who survive the years of reapings, who will, ideally, be so psychologically damaged as to render resistance as inconceivable.

Prior to her personal involvement, Katniss's response to this practice is her fierce determination to never be a mother. Already suffering under draconian regulations, she refuses to embrace what she sees as an utterly powerless role. The anguish that she experiences "when they called Prim's name on reaping day" and when she "watched [Prim] walk to the stage to her death" encapsulates Katniss's fears of motherhood (Collins, *Catching Fire* 46).[1] Unlike her actual mother, however, Katniss has a modicum of power; as she observes, "as her sister I could take her place, an option forbidden to our mother" (Collins, *Catching Fire* 46).[2] The rules of the games render parents mute observers. They cannot intercede; indeed, they are required to treat the barbaric spectacle as if it were a festive occasion. It is a distorted and distorting definition of parenthood. Katniss's decision to volunteer in place of her younger sister both compensates for her mother's powerlessness *and* undermines the government's positon of powerfulness. The intervention is to prevent Prim from becoming a victim. By claiming that, albeit limited, power, Katniss resists her officially imposed passivity. She claims a say in her sister's fate and in her own. At this point in the story, it seems to be an act of sacrificial love: Katniss has no real conviction that she will survive because all the power is exercised by others—the government and career tributes who train for the games. Defying the official definition of her as a "tribute," however, Katniss discovers an unlikely source of power: she embraces the role of a single mother in the games. Caring for her sister Prim brings Katniss to the games, whereas caring for Rue—the sister substitute within the games—gives her the added motivation to engineer an unconventional and politically provocative win.

In Panem, the institution of motherhood is crippling: it undercuts any attempt at mothering. The dystopian nature of the trilogy drives home the real-world necessity of separating the two experiences. Dystopian fiction, Chris Ferns observes, "posits a society which—however outlandish—is clearly extrapolated from that which exists" (106). More specifically, "the dystopian writer presents the nightmare future as a possible destination of present society, as if dystopia were no more than a logical conclusion derived from the premises of the existing order, and it implies that it might very well come about unless something is done to stop it" (107). The depiction of motherhood in Collins's novels aligns with a groundbreaking argument that can be traced to Adrienne Rich's *Of Woman Born: Motherhood as Experience and Institution*. Rich distinguishes "between two meanings of motherhood, one superimposed on the other: the *potential relationship* of any woman to her powers of reproduction and to children; and the *institution*, which aims at ensuring that that potential—and all women—shall remain under male control" (13). The patriarchal institution of motherhood is oppressive, even in more benign societies. It imposes and enforces strict definitions of what constitutes "acceptable" mothering. Mothering, however, is a potentially empowering act. Feminist mothering in particular, theorizes Sara Ruddick, "shifts the balance away from ... passivity toward active responsibility and engagement" (222). As a result of this engagement, mainstream values and norms can be actively challenged; as Katniss will discover, the refusal to be contained by the institution of motherhood—implicitly defined in Panem as "provider of victim-tributes"—allows for mothering to be subversive. In the course of the three novels, Katniss will move from a (symbolic) stance of sacrificial mothering to an active practice of courageous mothering. In the process, she will empower a nation. The oppressed citizens of the Districts, inspired by Katniss's example, fight for social change. She helps them envision a more just and compassionate society beyond the limited existence that the Capitol grants them.

Courageous mothering, Rich argues, can counteract the restrictions imposed on women. "The most notable fact that culture imprints on women," she contends, "is the sense of our own limits" (246). Courageous mothering challenges those limitations. For Rich, "the most important thing one woman can do for another is to illuminate and expand her sense of actual possibilities" (246). Katniss's actions spark uprisings, and she becomes the face of the revolution. More than fulfilling a symbolic or inspirational role, however, she also makes the possibility of defying the government an actuality. Rich's depiction of courageous mothering is an apt summary of Katniss—minus the actual daughter. "The quality of the mother's life—however embattled and unprotected—," Rich insists, "is her primary bequest to her daughter, because a woman who can believe in herself, who is a fighter, and who continues to struggle to create livable space around her, is demonstrating to her daughter [and, in this case, the country] that these possibilities exist" (247). A large part of courageous mothering is a willingness to fight against oppressive and destructive forces but equally important are the imaginative possibilities that struggle displays for those who observe it. Katniss rewrites The Hunger Games' script—a clear evasion of the official agenda of controlling the Districts through fear and enforced isolation. Oddly enough, it is only in and through the Hunger Games that Katniss has the opportunity to engage in courageous mothering. In the arena, she redefines the rules of engagement—mothering becomes a means of resistance and a vehicle for rebellion.

Outside the arena, however, Katniss is a suffering observer of her own mother's impotence. Mrs. Everdeen is powerless on both a political and personal level. She is rendered ineffectual by an oppressive government: she can neither feed nor protect her children. Crippled by grief following the death of her husband, Mrs. Everdeen leaves her children even more vulnerable by failing to provide the basic necessities of life. Long after her recovery, Katniss continues to distrust "the woman who sat by, blank and unreachable, while her children turned to skin and bones"—the woman who could not be a courageous mother (Collins, *Hunger Games* 8). The emotional breakdown is inexcusable and unforgettable in Katniss's eyes. It is the fear of her mother's regression that makes Katniss so vehement in the epigraph to this discussion. Terror over Prim's plight supersedes Katniss's concern over her own safety. She spends her final moments with her family instructing *them* on how to survive. In fact, it is Katniss's own survival that is in doubt, but her emotional response must wait until she is alone. At the age of eleven, Katniss stepped into the role of protector for her family; fear of her mother's fragility makes her reluctant to relinquish that role under any circumstance.[3]

In the absence of a functioning parent, Katniss takes on the seemingly masculine role of provider and protector. Survival in District 12 and the Games' arena hinges on her father's lessons: his knowledge of plants, the weapons that he crafted, and the hunting skills that he developed in Katniss allow the family to endure and give the tribute Katniss a fighting chance. The father's protection seemingly continues, despite his physical absence. He is a source of information and inspiration. In contrast, the physically present but emotionally absent mother is a burden. The phrase Katniss uses to describe the family dynamic is telling: "I took over as head of the family" (Collins, *Hunger Games* 27). In light of an earlier exchange between Katniss and her friend Gale, it becomes clear that "head of the family" does not mean mother. The pair dismisses the possibility of running away because they "have so many kids" (Collins, *Hunger Games* 9). Katniss clarifies: "They're not our kids, of course. But they might as well be. Gale's two little brothers and a sister. Prim. And you may as well throw in our mothers, too, because how would they live without us?" (Collins, *Hunger Games* 9). The mothers are grouped with the helpless children: in need of protection rather than sources of it. This disempowerment is one more means of governmental control: the absence of genuine authority in the home further disintegrates the possibility of resistance.[4]

Motherhood equals a state of vulnerability that Katniss refuses to accept; weakness is intolerable in her mind. During the reaping, she refuses to cry because "everyone will make note of my tears, and I'll be marked as an easy target. A weakling. I will give no one that satisfaction" (Collins, *Hunger Games* 23). The division is clear: there are victims and there are victors. Victors rise above emotion, whereas victims succumb to them. The grief that her mother could not battle has driven this point home for Katniss. She is determined to avoid a similar emotional paralysis. The denial of her emotions allows Katniss to project an image of stoicism, self-control, and mental toughness—stereotypically masculine traits. In order to survive, however, Katniss will need to tap into her mother's healing powers and her own compassionate—if not maternal—instincts. The warrior role is incomplete, nor is she the most striking physical presence in the arena—armed with a bow, she is a formidable adversary, but in hand-to-hand combat, she is easily overwhelmed.[5] Katniss must reveal an emotional vulnerability to gain the support of those viewing the games. Physical prowess is commonplace in the Hunger Games. The citizens of the Capitol (the ones with power) crave more of the unexpected from Katniss—the girl who interceded on her sister's behalf and has been Peeta's unsuspecting love interest.[6]

Katniss delivers the unexpected, but the emotional bond that she nurtures is not (initially) with Peeta. It takes a decidedly "maternal" direction. Actual motherhood is not a reality for Katniss until the trilogy's "Epilogue,"[7] but she engages in mothering from the outset. Unlike the institution of motherhood, mothering, argues Elizabeth Silva, is "mostly connected to the caring activity" (2). Emotional connections and sincere efforts to fulfill the needs of the child are at the heart of mothering. It is a process rather than a status. The government of Panem distorts the institution of motherhood by exploiting children as political pawns. The conscious act of mothering resists the official message that the lives of all the citizens of the Districts are expendable and, therefore, void of value. Katniss is intuitively drawn to Rue, the young tribute from District 11, because of her affinity to Prim. Among the other tributes, one stands out "most hauntingly, a twelve-year-old girl ... very like Prim in size and demeanor" (Collins, *Hunger Games* 45).[8] During training, Katniss deliberately distances herself from Rue, but it proves to be more difficult in the actual games. Ultimately, the pair will form an unconventional alliance. Katniss attempts to rationalize the decision— "she's a survivor, and I trust her"—but concedes that "she reminds me of Prim" (Collins, *Hunger Games* 201). She cannot conceive of Rue as her adversary.

The partnership is genuine but built on a shaky foundation. The rules of the games do not accommodate emotional alliances.[9] Each girl glosses over the very real fact that "this kind of deal can only be temporary;" they quickly slip into a mutually beneficial relationship—healing and feeding each other (201). Katniss, however, takes a lead role; she makes "sure Rue's well stocked with food and matches" and insists that she take the sleeping bag (Collins, *Hunger Games* 213). The concern, however, clearly goes beyond practical needs. Separating to enact a plan, the pair share an embrace, and Katniss is left worrying "about Rue being killed, about Rue not being killed and the two of us being left for last, about leaving Rue alone, about leaving Prim alone back home. No, Prim has my mother and Gale and a baker who has promised she won't go hungry. Rue has only me" (Collins, *Hunger Games* 213). The circumstances complicate but do not negate Katniss's protective impulse. The emotional connection to Rue carries with it a weighty sense of responsibility. It also brings a surprizing, if contradictory, sense of security. The night before they set their plot in motion, the girls share a sleeping bag. Katniss discovers that "the warmth of Rue at my side, her head cradled on my shoulder" has "given [her] a sense of security" (Collins, *Hunger Games* 209).[10] The physical presence of Rue is comforting; the contact provides a brief respite from the horror of the arena. Dehumanized by their enforced participation in the games, Katniss and Rue reassert their humanity through the simple act of trusting in each other.

The morning, however, brings fresh horrors for the allies as they turn the tables and target their seemingly invincible opponents. The plan is to level the playing field. Having successfully destroyed the career tributes' food supply, an injured Katniss struggles to escape the scene of her crime. Aware of the ever-present cameras and the policy of mandatory viewing, she forces herself to move and avoid a gruesome death at Cato's hands. Her motivation is quite telling: "the thought of Prim having to watch that keeps me doggedly inching my way toward the hideout" (Collins, *The Hunger Games*, 223). Significantly, Katniss does not say her *family* (or friends); her focus has been, and remains, on the child whom she struggles to feed and shelter. The initial impulse that brought Katniss to the games—to save her sister at any cost—is an extreme example of sacrificial mothering: a selflessness that values the child's life and needs over that of the mother. Katniss recognizes that "in District 12, where the word tribute is pretty much synonymous with the word corpse," volunteering is a kind of martyrdom (Collins, *The Hunger Games* 22). On a practical level, it is a short-term measure: Prim has six more years of reapings ahead of her. Katniss's gesture is noble but, on its own, inadequate. She must move beyond sacrificial mothering to keep hope alive for Prim, herself, and, it will turn out, the oppressed and politically infantilized citizens of the Districts.

The immediate catalyst for Katniss's movement into courageous mothering is the death of Rue. Unable to help Rue in any physical sense, Katniss can only offer emotional succour. It strikes her as woefully inadequate, but the fatally injured young girl draws comfort from Katniss's touch and requests a song. Katniss recognizes the significance of the act to Rue who confided earlier that "what she loves most in the world" is music (Collins, *The Hunger Games* 211). Katniss's thoughts return to Prim, and she once again conflates the pair: "if this is Prim's, I mean, Rue's last request, I have to at least try. The song that comes to me is a simple lullaby, one we sing fretful, hungry babies to sleep with ... the words are easy and soothing, promising tomorrow will be more hopeful than this awful piece of time" (Collins, *The Hunger Games* 234). The choice of a lullaby is particularly evocative and potentially provocative. All of Panem watches as Katniss cradles Rue in her arms: they, however, move beyond the games and share a heartfelt connection. The maternal nature of Katniss's gesture, combined with the lullaby, drive home the horrifying truth that children have been cast as mortal enemies. In their final exchange, the girls refuse to play their parts.

Rue's death is made peaceful by Katniss's actions, but it stirs something aggressive in Katniss. The sight of Rue "smaller than ever ... past harm, but seemingly utterly defenseless" makes the personal political (Collins, *The Hunger Games* 234). The fighter in her recognizes that her true adversary is not the other tributes; although they are clearly threats to her immediate safety, the government is the more pernicious threat. Katniss's hatred for the government coalesces with memories of Gale's "ravings against the Capitol": as Katniss explains, "Rue's death has forced me to confront my own fury against the cruelty, the injustices they inflict upon us. But here, even more strongly than at home, I feel my impotence" (Collins, *The Hunger Games* 236). Katniss's long-suppressed anger needs an outlet. She cannot conceive of one until she recalls Peeta's desire to "think of a way ... to show the Capital they don't own me. That I'm more than just a piece in their Games" (236). Katniss's act of wreathing Rue in flowers is a seemingly simplistic gesture, but the contrast of nature's beauty with the unnatural death is a provocative declaration that they are both "more than a piece in their Games" (Collins, *The Hunger Games* 237).[11] The Capitol has defined them as enemies and forced them into barbaric confrontations. Katniss redefines Rue (and, by implication, herself) by insisting on recognizing her humanity and their emotional connection.

By offering a floral tribute to Rue, Katniss refuses to accept that being a tribute negates her humanity. It also casts an unfavourable light on the forces behind the games—the ones who engineered her death. Her newly conceptualized defiance enables Katniss to create another theatrical moment in the games: the double suicide that she plans to commit with Peeta would rob the Capitol of a victor. By defying the Capitol, she makes a calculated decision, which ends up saving their lives. The powers-that-be have clearly envisioned a melodramatic conclusion to the games: the star-crossed lovers are forced to battle each other. They have, however, miscalculated. Katniss and, to a lesser extent, Peeta are no longer mere pawns; they have discovered the central weakness of the plot being imposed on them. Katniss is the one courageous enough to exploit it. The Capitol needs a victor, but it will only get one by capitulating to her implicit demand that both are allowed to live. The official spin on the act is that it was the desperate action of a pair of star-crossed lovers whom the government magnanimously allowed to live. The storyline is accepted in the Capitol, but has a very different interpretation in the Districts. It is not viewed as an isolated moment but an incendiary lesson in resistance.

The inflammatory nature of Katniss's gambit is not lost on Panem's government. President Snow reveals to Katniss that "people viewed your little trick with the berries as an act of defiance, not an act of love. And if a girl from District Twelve of all places can defy the Capitol and walk away unharmed, what is to stop them from doing the same?" (Collins, *Catching Fire* 23). Katniss's action was a personal resistance to the injustice of the game—a desperate bid for survival tinged with a desire to outwit an oppressor. President Snow recognizes that the second aspect has found an even more sympathetic audience than those emotionally invested in the love story. He concedes that she has "provided a spark that, left unattended, may grow to an inferno" (Collins, *Catching Fire* 23). During the victory tour of the Districts, Snow insists that she follow the official line or a heavy price will be exacted. Katniss's initial reaction is a terrified promise to do all that she can to extinguish the spark. To protect her loved ones, Katniss relinquishes her own (potential) political activism. She slips back into the reactionary and self-negating approach associated with sacrificial mothering. She is once again willing to barter her own life to save others. As was the case with volunteering to replace Prim, even if successful, the act can only provide temporary protection. The political conditions of Panem cannot be altered by the acts of a self-negating individual.

Concerned with the very real and immediate threats to those whom she loves, Katniss can only see the negative effects of her action. As the government of Panem clearly recognizes, fear generates, and is generated by, isolationism. Envisioning a world beyond their personal situation, Gale helps Katniss realize that she had not "hurt people—you've given them an opportunity. They just have to be brave enough to take it" (Collins, *Catching Fire* 99). A collective enterprise is needed: Katniss is the catalyst, but she cannot achieve social change on her own. Through her courageous mothering, Katniss has made the inconceivable conceivable: she has exposed the weakness of the government and demonstrated that alternative possibilities—however improbable—can be fought for and won. Just as the citizens of the Districts must find their courage, Katniss must tap into her own bravery to accept that she has been an agent for positive change. Once again, it is the reality of the children suffering that motivates her:

> Prim ... Rue ... aren't they the very reason I have to try to fight? ... What I am about to do, whatever any of us are

> forced to endure, it is for them. It's too late to help Rue but maybe not too late for those five little faces that looked up at me … in District 11. Not too late for Rory and Vick and Posy. Not too late for Prim. (Collins, *Catching Fire* 123)

The struggle to decide whether the potential gain is worth the probable risks is made easier once Katniss considers the helpless children already endangered and damaged by the current political system. Katniss's protective impulses are triggered, as is her fighting instinct.

In point of fact, the "choice" has been taken out of her hands. Involvement in the rebellion began with Katniss's basic refusal to be a victim and intensified with her act of resistance. The process is one of courageous mothering. Rich's definition of courageous mothering "means that the mother herself is trying to expand the limits of her life. To refuse to be a victim: and then to go on from there" (Rich 246). Katniss is at the "go on from there" stage; she must now map a path from victimhood. She has unwittingly given "birth" to a resistance movement: her strength and compassion spark a grassroots movement that gains in intensity throughout the trilogy. It is only in the final book, while she comforts the wounded, that Katniss realizes "I was their Mockingjay long before I accepted the role" (Collins, *Mockingjay* 90). Katniss's symbolic role can be construed as the continued exploitation of the teenager or as the public recognition of her abilities that she has not been permitted to embrace. In either case, Katniss discovers "a new sensation … Power. I have a kind of power I never knew I possessed" (Collins, *Mockingjay* 91). Katniss's life has been filled with feelings of powerlessness, with the constant threat of being turned into a victim. Involvement in the rebellion—being its inspiration and its face—empowers Katniss in a way that she could never have conceived.

Before she can unleash that power directly on the government—as an armed rebel—Katniss will once again be cast as a victim. The rules for the Hunger Games have changed: tributes will be drawn from the existing pool of victors. Katniss is going back into the arena.[12] Unlike her first games, she enters with a dual agenda: to protect Peeta and to encourage the rebellion. She is, however, once again convinced that she will die in the arena. Katniss prepares herself to be a martyr for the cause. The audience that she will play to are the rebels: "they will be looking for some sign that their battles have not been in vain. If I can make it clear that I'm still defying the Capitol right up to the end, the Capitol will have killed me ... but not my spirit. What better way to give hope to the rebels?" (Collins, *Catching Fire* 243). She is keenly aware of the political ramifications of her behaviour this time. Katniss is constructing a counter-narrative to the official one. Selecting the tributes from the victors is a clear message from the government: even the strongest are vulnerable. It is meant to stifle the rebellion and to instil fear in the already faint-of-heart citizens of the districts.

In defiance of the official agenda, Katniss has found a way to meld the personal with the political—something she did unconsciously in the earlier Games. She reasons that saving Peeta "at the expense of my own life is itself an act of defiance. A refusal to play the Hunger Games by the Capitol's rules ... and it will do more to rally people than anything I could do if I was living" (Collins, *Catching Fire* 244). Her reasoning still smacks of sacrificial mothering but with a crucial distinction. The gift is not her death but her way of living: with courage, compassion, and a concern for the lives of others. Despite the planned sacrifice, Katniss continues her pattern of courageous mothering by encouraging others to envision the possibility that, in the words of the lullaby she sang to Rue, "tomorrow will be more hopeful than this awful piece of time" (Collins, *The Hunger Games* 234). In continuing to engage in courageous mothering, Katniss is assisting those on the side of the rebellion to mature and to resist the infantilized state imposed on them by the government. "The Dystopian rebel," Chris Ferns contends, "inevitably challenges the prevailing ethic of infantile or childlike dependence fostered by the patriarchal state" (121). By insisting on her own agency and pursuing an agenda beyond that of the government, Katniss has rejected "childlike dependence." The example that she sets for the equally oppressed inhabitants of the Districts guides them towards the possibility of their own autonomy, which is all any mother can do.

Motherhood in *The Hunger Games* trilogy has received minimal critical attention. Collections such as *Of Bread, Blood, and The*

Hunger Games: Critical Essays on Suzanne Collins' trilogy; *The Hunger Games and Philosophy: A Critique of Pure Treason*; and *Space and Place in The Hunger Games: New Readings of the Novels* have discussed the novels (and films) in terms of philosophy, politics, spectacle as entertainment, Katniss as heroine, and gender roles. References to motherhood, however, have largely been limited to comments about Katniss's unnamed mother. Jessica Miller disassociates Katniss from a maternal role: "the stereotype of the nurturing mother tends to be associated with warmth and kindness. In contrast, Katniss's protectiveness requires actions more typically associated with masculinity" (147). Miller, rightly, recognizes the fluidity of gender roles in the books but overstates the masculine influence on Katniss's character; her actions need to move beyond physical prowess in order for Katniss to survive the games. Katie Arosteguy does offer a detailed discussion of "othermothering" (non-biological mothering) in the trilogy. She contends that "Katniss's development, survival, and journey to motherhood depend on her reconciliation with her mother—a process fraught with betrayal, negotiation, and resistance" (146). I argue that Katniss's development and survival depend on her reconciliation with her *own* maternal powers. Arosteguy's assertion that "through the character of Katniss, Collins challenges traditional conceptions of motherhood and confronts a multi-faceted maternal identity" does highlight an underexplored aspect of Collins's novels (146).

Dystopian novels in general and *The Hunger Games* trilogy in particular can serve as didactic texts: they warn readers about real-world dangers. By projecting problems into a distant but recognizable future, authors draw attention to a variety of issues—ecological concerns, gender and racial stereotypes, political oppression, among others. "*The Hunger Games* trilogy," assert the editors of *The Hunger Games and Philosophy*, "is a cautionary tale about what human society could easily become" (4). Not surprisingly, they focus on the negative elements that Collins explores: she "depicts a world where children are slaughtered for entertainment, power is in the hands of nearly untouchable tyrants, and workers starve as the affluent look on and laugh" (4). The summary is accurate but the "cautionary tale" can be construed in a positive light. The series is oddly empowering in its engagement with mothering—a topic of interest in both popular and scholarly circles. Katniss's acts of courageous mothering afford a positive lesson "about what human society could easily become." Situating the trilogy within current discussions of motherhood and mothering opens up that discussion by moving it out of the arena of academe and into popular culture.

NOTES

[1]Once a victor, Katniss fears she will be forced to have children, as the offspring of past victors have been reaped at disproportionate levels (Collins, *Catching Fire* 45).

[2]On the day of the reaping, Katniss wears one of her mother's "own lovely dresses" and recognizes that "her clothes from her past are very precious to her" (Collins, *The Hunger Games* 15). The emotional significance is not lost on Katniss, nor can the reader ignore the fact that in volunteering for Prim, Katniss is symbolically taking her mother's place.

[3]In the arena, as she tries to treat Peeta's wounds, Katniss does acknowledge her mother's strengths: "I try to capture the calm demeanor my mother assumes when handling particularly bad cases" (Collins, *The Hunger Games* 256).

[4]It is tempting to read the absence of authority as a feature of motherhood, but Collins (in)conveniently removes the fathers from the equation: Katniss's and Gale's fathers die in an explosion when Katniss is eleven. Her father is dead before his inability to protect her is exposed—reapings begin at age twelve—but Gale, as the older of the two, has already been part of those events when his father dies; the crowd of parents anxiously watching the ceremony drives home the point that it is the adults, not just mothers, who are powerless. The neglect of Katniss's mother's because of depression is countered by the efforts of Gale's mother to care for her younger children.

[5]The image of Katniss, armed with a bow, clearly draws on Diana-Artemis—the goddess of the forest and hunting, the virginal patron of slaves, and the guardian of young children. Katniss, however, is no all-powerful deity; her power will come, not from her bow but from her maternal nature. Significantly, she will marry

and become a (biological) mother in the trilogy's epilogue.
[6]For the citizens of the Capital, the love story is of greater interest, but Katniss adds little to that "plotline" until the rule change—two victors can survive if they are from the same district.
[7]My focus is on the mothering Katniss performs prior to having children with Peeta.
[8]The likeness will strike Katniss in *Catching Fire*: "I squeeze my eyes shut and I don't see Prim—I see Rue" (Collins 40).
[9]Unlike the alliance of convenience formed by the career tributes—they hunt in packs and then have no compunction about turning on each other—Katniss and Rue forge a sincere connection.
[10]The scene echoes the earlier image of Prim, cocooned in her mother's body. In each case, the sense of security, though comforting, can only be temporary.
[11]Indeed, Katniss dares to think of it as murder: a clear violation of the mandate to treat the bloody spectacle as a "game."
[12]Seemingly as a mother: in a bid to protect her, Peeta has announced that they are unofficially married and that Katniss is "pregnant."

WORKS CITED

Arosteguy, Katie. 'I Have a Kind of Power I Never Knew I Possessed': Motherhood and Maternal Influence." *Space and Place in The Hunger Games: New Readings of the Novels*. Eds. Deidre Anne Evans Garriott, Whitney Elaine Jones, and Julie Elizabeth Tyler. Jefferson, North Carolina: McFarland, 2014. 146-158. Print.

Clark, Leisa A., and Mary F. Pharr, eds. *Of Bread, Blood, and The Hunger Games: Critical Essays in Suzanne Collins Trilogy*. Jefferson, North Carolina: McFarland, 2012. Print.

Collins, Suzanne. *Catching Fire*. New York: Scholastic, 2009. Print.

Collins, Suzanne. *The Hunger Games*. New York: Scholastic, 2008. Print.

Collins, Suzanne. *Mockingjay*. New York: Scholastic, 2010. Print.

Dunn, George A., and Nicholas Michaud, eds. *The Hunger Games and Philosophy: A Critique of Pure Treason*. New Jersey: John Wiley and Sons, 2012. Print.

Ferns, Chris. *Narrating Utopia: Ideology, Gender, Form in Utopian Literature*. Liverpool: Liverpool University Press, 1999. Print.

Garriott, Deidre Anne Evans, Whitney Elaine Jones, and Julie Elizabeth Tyler, eds. *Space and Place in The Hunger Games: New Readings of the Novels*. Jefferson, North Carolina: McFarland, 2014. Print.

Miller, Jessica. "'She Has No Idea. The Effect She Can Have': Katniss and the Politics of Gender." *The Hunger Games and Philosophy: A Culture of Pure Treason*. Eds. George A. Dunn and Nicholas Michaud. New Jersey: John Wiley and Sons, 2012. 145-160. Print.

Rich, Adrienne. *Of Woman Born: Motherhood as Experience and Institution*. New York: W. W. Norton, 1976. Print.

Ruddick, Sara. *Maternal Thinking: Toward a Politics of Peace*. Boston: Beacon Press, 1989.

Silva, Elizabeth. "Introduction." *Good Enough Mothering?: Feminist Perspectives on Lone Motherhood*. London: Routledge, 1996. 1-9. Print.

II.
THE EXPERIENTIAL

5.

Single Motherhood

Mythical Madness and Invisible "Insanity"

ELLEN HAUSER

ACCORDING TO THE 2010 U.S. Census Bureau, I am one of approximately ten million single mothers in the U.S. with children under the age of eighteen. With a population that large, one would think that our experiences would be visible. However, the social construction of women who raise children alone stigmatizes us within social institutions as well as through political rhetoric and social stereotypes. Our existence often creates discomfort for others, perhaps because it collides with the dominant heterosexist fairy tale of marriage and motherhood that is taught to most girls at an early age, which continues to be a societal narrative. In order to continue this societal fantasy, single mothers must be found deviant in some way. Social messages about us claim that we must have problems; otherwise, why did we divorce or allow ourselves to have children without husbands? We either cannot find or cannot hold onto men. The stereotypes and stigmas frequently attached to us are based on the assumption that we have personal, social, or ethical deficiencies. In other words, a "mythical madness" becomes our socially constructed identity; we are seen as "mad" social misfits by many in our society. Although this discourse of single mothers as "mad" is mainstream and dominant, it applies to some groups of single mothers more than others, and is one of several competing discourses on single mothers (see other chapters in this work). The more privileges that a single mother enjoys (including race, socio-economic status, and strong family support) the less "mad" she is deemed to be. For example, societal judgment of an upper-class, educated divorced mother with strong family and social ties is likely to be less harsh than that of a minority or lower-class single mother. In contrast, our day-to-day struggles to raise children alone are frequently invisible to those not in our situation, who are usually considered to be "normals," a term coined by Erving Goffman to describe people who are not stigmatized. Many of us single mothers experience our daily lives as "insanity." We must maintain actual sanity to carry on our parenting responsibilities, but we feel as if the life that we live is crazy and unsustainable. The feeling of "insanity" is caused not only by the social repercussions of being stigmatized but also by daily conflicts between our lived realities and societal institutions and processes, which have been constructed based on society's ideal of motherhood and families. To dominant structures and "normals," meanwhile, our lived experience, with all its crazy realities, remains invisible. The surprise is not that we single moms often feel we are going "insane" but that any of us stay sane and strong enough to raise our children, despite the overwhelming challenges. In that survival, single mothers exhibit incredible strength, tenacity, and determination—traits frequently missing in social assumptions about single mothers.

In this analysis, I use the theme of madness and the analytical lenses of gender and deviance to contrast the mythical stereotypes, which society has constructed about single mothers, with our lived experiences. The stigma placed on us contains other negative assumptions besides madness. However, the concept of madness—not in the sense of actual mental illness but rather that of being judged as "not quite right"—is an apt symbolic term for the deviant labelling placed on single mothers. My use of the imagery of "insanity" to describe the lived experiences of single mothers does not imply that single mothers are mentally ill; rather, my use of the term refers to the *feelings* many single moms frequently have that their lives are overwhelming and that they are going "insane" because of the circumstances. I have chosen the term "insanity" because it comes closest to expressing my own experience, which I have found is shared by many other mothers. It also provides a contrast between the stereotypes that society creates about many single mothers as "mad" misfits and the experience of overwhelm that many single mothers actually feel. To help clarify that I am not referring to actual insanity in my usage of the term, I will use quotation marks, viz. "insanity," when referencing single mothers' experiences.

This chapter is written in the style of autoethnography; information for what I present here has been gathered over the past sixteen years from my experiences as a single mother, from my friendships with many other single mothers, and from my observations of how single mothers are treated and represented in American society. The advantages of using this method are that it allows for an expression of personal experience that other methods do not. However, the disadvantages of this method include the potential to use personal experience to overgeneralize to larger societal trends and, therefore, conflate the experiences of all single mothers into that of my own. My conclusions should be taken as an analysis of my own experiences and those of other single mothers whom I know. I recognize that there are competing discourses on single mothers as well as a multiplicity of experiences.

There is a variety of categories of women who raise children alone: unwed teenage mothers; divorced women with significant logistical support from ex-partners or families of origin; lesbian mothers raising children alone after break-ups with their partners; widows with children; single women who chose to adopt or have children on their own; mothers who are single for only a short time until their next marriage or live-in relationship; and women who have been completely on their own for many years with little social support. Any of these mothers may experience, to some extent, the social construction of "mad" social misfits because none of them fit society's definition of acceptable motherhood. However, the women whose reality I believe is the most invisible are those who did not choose single motherhood and who raise their children with little or no family or community support. This is the group most vulnerable to stigma and most likely to experience the "insanity" of single motherhood more intensely.[1]

DEVIANCE AND MADNESS

The culture of the United States has demonized single mothers and has treated them as deviants from colonial times (Sidel 1).

However, with the numbers of single mothers rising in the past forty years, one may think that perceptions have changed. From 1970 to 2003, the number of families with single mothers in the U.S. rose from 3 million to 10 million (Fields 7). In 1970, single mothers represented 12 percent of all U.S. households with children under age of eighteen (8); that percentage grew to 27 percent in 2007 (Jonathan, Lewis, and Kreider 13). Despite the high numbers of single mothers, deviant stereotypes of madness associated with single motherhood have persisted. These stereotypes may be caricatures of reality, but they hold social, economic, and political power. Myths about our madness affect how we are received in social circles, how we are perceived in the job market, whether or not we get help from organizations and the community, and what "solutions" regarding single mothers find their way into political discourse and legislation.

The sociologist Erving Goffman perceptively points out that during stigmatization a person is reduced from being a "whole and usual person to a tainted, discounted one" (3). As mentioned earlier, many single mothers display strength, tenacity, and determination; however, the stigma placed on us only focuses on our lack of marriage partner and the presumed deficiencies that have led to our raising children alone. In contrast to single fathers raising children alone, who tend to be seen as heroic for stepping up to their responsibilities, misogyny takes over in attitudes towards single moms, which hones in on how we are not living up to acceptable societal roles as women. Dominant discourses that frame the institution of motherhood and family in our society and that manifest themselves through media, everyday interactions, political rhetoric, and religious commentary (as just a few examples) reduce the wide variation of roles and situations that single mothers experience. These experiences are cemented into a master narrative of the "single mother," which is defined as lacking appropriate womanly qualities as conventionally defined. In his sociological work on deviance, Howard Becker discusses how deviants frequently feel judged by social rules that they did not have any part in making (15-18). As single moms' realities crash into social rules set up by others society judges the women as deviant.

In many societies, women have been more often stigmatized and declared "mad" than men. In *Labeling Women Deviant*, Edwin Schur analyzes how women in the U.S. have been frequently stigmatized merely for being women: masculine characteristics are taken to be the norm in society, and expectations of women in society are mostly male designated. In the twenty-first century, after various waves of feminism, one would think that these stereotypes (such as "appropriate" characteristics of mothers and what makes women "appropriately feminine") would have fallen by the wayside; however, Schur argues that "(s)ocial stigmatization of the (single) mother ... may be lessening somewhat, but often it remains substantial" (87). The fact that American society still has not rid itself of patriarchy and sexism leads to a lack of recognition of the work women do in raising children and their realities. If women with children—whether married or not—are pushed into unsustainable workloads because society has not come to terms with the amount of energy involved in reproductive labour, how much more difficult is it for those of us who perform the same double workload but do it without a partner or other support? Stir in the stereotypes of what "good" mothers and women are expected to be, and it is not difficult to see how single mothers become poster women for "inappropriate" and "unacceptable" womanhood and motherhood.

Despite advancements in women's rights over the past several decades, which have given women more flexibility in choice of lifestyle, there remains a strong cultural pressure regarding the way things "should be," especially when it comes to marriage and children. Societal stereotypes of women paint them as kind, gentle, and adoring wives, not strong women who survive on their own. Many single moms bought into the married-with-children narrative and did not intentionally set out to have children without a partner. However, when life does not work out as planned, they are subject to scorn because they attempt to survive without men. One possible explanation for this is Schur's discussion of how women are devalued in our society because in many situations, men perceive women to be threats to their dominance (44-47). Perhaps it is the ability of many single mothers to successfully raise children alone that is seen as threatening to certain groups in U.S. society.[2]

The clichés are common gossip: the unreasonable wife who drives her husband to divorce; the woman raising her children alone while on several anti-psychotic prescriptions; or the "mad" ex-wife who refuses to let her ex-husband see their children while she buys furs and Cadillacs with child support. The common theme in these storylines is that there must be something wrong with single mothers. We are not married; we failed at marriage; we failed our children by being divorced; we are "a little off," "too strong," or "unbalanced." If we are in this situation, it is judged to be our fault; according to popular "logic," a sensible, intelligent, capable person would not have let this situation happen. Although a few women may act in ways that feed the myths about single mothers, the majority of us bear little or no resemblance to these stereotypes. As Sidel explains in *Unsung Heroines: Single Mothers and the American Dream*, a few examples of extreme behaviour by a few single mothers become representative of all single mothers, which reinforces stereotypes and leads to misguided social policy (9). Furthermore, stereotypes of single mothers frequently vary depending on a woman's race, social class, and sexual orientation. African American single mothers are held up as examples of the deviance of Black motherhood and what is wrong with Black culture in general. Low-income single mothers become symbols of so-called laziness and irresponsibility. Race, class, and the presence and/or absence of effective support for a mom affect the difficulty of a woman's situation as well as the level of social rejection and blame that she faces.

On a micro level, ex-husbands sometimes describe their children's mothers as "insane" or "wacko" to their friends and family. In these situations, the labels are frequently motivated by legal and financial matters or by personal pain over the separations. Ex-husbands fighting for custody or for some financial revenge during the divorce could suggest that their ex-wives are emotionally unstable. The stress of a bad marriage and subsequent divorce can make even the most emotionally stable person become temporarily unstable. The multiplication of micro-level branding of single moms by ex-partners combined with rampant misogyny in the U.S. is part of the process that creates the macro-level labels of madness and deviance portrayed in the media and in political rhetoric. An extreme illustration of this rhetoric is Ann Coulter's claim that single moms commonly kill their children (52). Cultural and individual viewpoints influence one another, as individuals can make use of cultural stereotypes to bolster their claims of deviance.

No matter what choice a single mother makes, there is a label of mythical madness waiting to be attached to her. When a mother shows strength in raising her children alone and doing what she needs to do to survive, the myths of madness revolve around her being too aggressive. One common stereotype is that single mothers are manipulative "bitches," who are eager to cheat ex-partners or the government out of money. The mother who shows assertiveness in attempting to get her family what it needs is often judged to be a troublemaker. If she sues for child support or applies for government programs to help raise her children, she risks being seen as a greedy social misfit. In the ideology of capitalistic individualism and the myth of meritocracy that is so pervasive in North America, citizens are not supposed to need help; they are expected to pull themselves up and not rely on government programs for help. Furthermore, single mothers who show strength in fighting to help their families survive do not fit societal norms of femininity.

A second common stereotype is that single mothers are weak; they are mentally unbalanced victims who are unable to cope with life. If they do not pursue child support or government programs, they are not being resourceful enough. A single mother struggling with all of the challenges facing her is seen as weak and emotionally unstable. If she would only try harder and make better decisions her life would be better. When single moms, sometimes, suffer from emotional distress their emotional issues are treated as the reasons that they are having difficulty instead of being the result of the overwhelming stress of their situations.

In this case, single mothers are seen as weak, mentally imbalanced parasites, who feed on society. The view is that single mothers need someone to take charge because they are incapable of surviving or raising children on their own. In some ways, it seems as if this is the role society would prefer single mothers to fit because it situates them as non-threatening to the sexist norms of femininity: women being weak and helpless without men. However, patience with single mothers who are seen in this way runs out when women need assistance with logistics to raise their children. The dominant attitude seems to be that if a single mom needs a little assistance, she is completely incompetent. The focus stays on traditional feminine values of weakness and victimhood instead of attempts to be strong and survive even when overwhelmed. Although gendered stereotypes suggest weakness as a desirable feminine attribute, there is little to no societal support when a single mother has trouble coping. Again, the blame is placed on women instead of on the fact that they are living in impossible situations.

Whether or not we have romantic involvement with men while raising our children, we single mothers are often branded with other stereotypes regarding our sexuality. If we are not involved with anyone, we may be seen as defective or undesirable. Or we are seen as so desperate for male attention that we may steal other women's husbands. Because our lives as single mothers are seen as "loose and free," we may entice married women to join our "divorced women's club." We are seen as abnormal; if we were normal, we would be able to find respectable men to marry. Our perceived imbalance not only affects our supposed emotional state but also condemns our sexuality.

Conversely, single moms who have relationships with men can easily be labelled as "whores" and, therefore, bad mothers. The assumption behind this labelling is that we should not be sexually active outside of marriage since we have children. If we are, we must be bad moms. We are judged for a perceived choice of prioritizing sex over our children. In the societal fairy tale regarding romance, we are no longer maidens or respectable princesses: we are the wildly promiscuous shrews.

These judgments set up an impossible situation: single mothers are judged as on the prowl or undesirable if not involved with men; yet seen as irresponsible mothers if they have romantic relationships. None of this labelling takes into account the incredible loneliness and overwhelming responsibility that may lead some single mothers to jump quickly into relationships that do not lead to marriage. Some single mothers choose the freedom of romantic relationships without marriage because they value their personal space and the ability to make their own decisions. The desire to keep this freedom can make these mothers seem pathological by those who think that these mothers are ruining their children by modelling "deviant" behaviour. All of these myths are based on certain assumptions about women—one of which is that all women need men—as well as on sexist definitions as to which conditions must be met before it is acceptable for mothers to be sexually active.

Single moms are also frequently seen as social misfits in social circles of "normals." Despite increased numbers of single mothers, unless they can find groups of other single mothers, they are outliers at many social events, if invited at all. Myths about single moms being "hot to trot," as described earlier, affect how they are seen socially. This social ostracism fits various deviance theorists' descriptions of how once someone is defined as deviant, she tends to be excluded from participating in usual groups in usual ways (Becker 34; Shur 38). An episode from the television program *Mad Men* depicting a single mother, Helen, moving into the neighbourhood and attending a birthday party aptly depicts what still happens in many contemporary social settings. In the scene, the married women gossip about Helen, place the worst interpretation on her behaviour, and never accept her into their group. Numerous conversations that I have had with single mothers regarding similar situations show that even fifty years after the era depicted in *Mad Men*, these kinds of social interactions still occur. The very women who would be most accessible to offer logistical support to single moms through occasional childcare, other neighbourly assistance, or just plain moral support are frequently the most judgmental and often provide little to no support.

Because our circumstances rarely allow us to act in ways that match society's perceptions of good mothers, the mythical label of bad mother is the default judgment placed on us. I am amazed at the comments that I have received over the years regarding my daughter's "normalcy" and how well I am parenting. Although I think that I am a good mom, the frequency with which these comments are made and the contexts in which they are given show that what the people are really expressing is my position as an outsider. If it is so unusual that I am doing a great job raising my child completely on my own, then these comments become the equivalent of praise to a member of a minority group for not acting like those "other" minorities or like telling an immigrant how well she speaks English; none of the people in these instances belong in mainstream society, and we are only seen as positive exceptions to the deviant groups to which we are relegated.

Conservatives in the U.S. periodically discuss legislation to encourage single mothers to marry. Although two-parent households are, indeed, less vulnerable to poverty, the conservative discourse is more interested in punishing women for being single than in providing real support to families. A federal government report titled "State Policies to Promote Marriage" describes ways in which various state policies have encouraged or discouraged marriage, especially among families receiving Temporary Assistance for Needy Families (TANF) , the main U.S. government program to help very low-income families (Gardiner et al). Some conservatives even encourage mothers to stay married, no matter how bad the marriage (Hawkins). My many social encounters and conversations with single moms show that the vast majority of women I have met who are raising children on their own would prefer to have a supportive spouse or partner to assist them in raising their children and to provide adult companionship. Having a partner would likely reduce workloads, but many single mothers have also internalized the societal fantasy of what "normal" families look like. The problem is not that none of the women want to be married; according to the single mothers I have met, the issue is that the many who do desire marriage have not been able to find appropriate partners. The assumption underlying the discussions encouraging us to marry is that somehow we single mothers are too "mad" to understand the benefits of marriage and our appropriate place in society. If only we would do things the "right" way, the numbers of children being raised in single-parent homes would drop and society would function better as a whole. As one example of many negative judgments placed on single mothers, Ann Coulter writes, "Here is the lottery ticket that single mothers are handing their innocent children by choosing to raise them without fathers: controlling for socioeconomic status, race, and place of residence, the strongest predictor of whether a person will end up in prison is that he was raised by a single parent" (37). Coulter's view assumes that all single mothers choose to be single and that we and our children would be better off with any man at all than to be alone.

A publication in *The Atlantic* by sociologist Philip Cohen pointing out inconsistencies in theories claiming single motherhood creates more criminals resulted in a backlash supporting those theories. Although the specific arguments themselves are interesting, what is most disturbing is the focus, once again, on single mothers as deviants and as creators of societal problems. Absent fathers who do not carry through on the responsibilities of parenthood are sometimes mentioned but are not the main focus.

As can be seen from the discussion above, the stereotypical categories that we single mothers are placed in are negative and judgmental; they assume that we have various forms of madness. The myths stigmatize us and do not take into account the realities of our lives. All of these myths of madness share the idea that we are to blame for whatever challenges we face. Our presumed deviant madness and deficiencies are seen as the causes of our problems and difficulties.

Mythical madness can be summed up in the story of a single mother in the U.S. who was arrested and convicted of a felony because her teenage son killed himself (Santora). His suicide note stated that he was tired of other students teasing him about his poor hygiene. Although the boy's mother was working about sixty hours a week in two jobs and just trying to survive, she was accused of not doing enough to help her son. Of course, the absent father was not blamed, arrested, or publicly shamed for not helping his son. The boy's school was not blamed for ignoring the bullying that he was suffering. The mother's workplaces were not blamed for paying her so little that she had to work so many hours. The woman was labelled, arrested, and convicted, despite the fact that she was the person working the hardest to help her son. The Connecticut Supreme Court eventually overruled her conviction of the criminal charges in her son's suicide (Salzman); however, the ruling came after more than four years of suspicion and legal accusation regarding her son's death.

The societal construction of deviance around single motherhood creates mythical madness. This construction of deviance occurs because of sexist norms about appropriate female characteristics and about expectations regarding "normal" motherhood as well as society's narrative about marriage and women's presumed need to have a lifetime male partner.

INVISIBLE "INSANITY"

Although these stereotypes of single moms suggest an unfair labelling of "mad" and deviant, the real feelings of "insanity" most of us experience because we raise children alone remain invisible to most of society. Reality for most single moms is very different from Hollywood movies that romanticize single motherhood. According to many films, we are just a ninety-minute plot away from meeting the man of our dreams, who desperately wants to be an active, loving father to our children. All of the factors that make many single moms feel as if they are going crazy are unacknowledged: the day-to-day stresses in addition to other pressures related to divorce or dealing with ex-partners; the stresses of falling through the cracks and not fitting into society's norms; and the pressures of raising children who have their own challenges because of divorce or abandonment. Many single moms singlehandedly work full-time; handle all household chores, repairs, finances, and responsibilities; and negotiate with teachers, schools, babysitters, and anyone else who interacts with their children. Many of us do this while also experiencing financial instability (Emery 99-103).

What are the everyday realities of single moms? Some of us have more demands placed on us in one day than many adults that we know experience in a week. Many of us juggle the multiplicities of responsibility—human, financial, logistical, and strategic—of some corporate CEOs; however, we do it without any staff. We deal daily with inaccurate labels placed on us that make our lives more difficult. We may, in some cases, internalize these labels and struggle with feelings of inferiority and inadequacy. Unless we are women who have chosen single motherhood, we may have emotional stress because of a divorce or partner's abandonment or death. This does not necessarily make us emotionally imbalanced; however, it does drain our energy.

Once again, there are different categories of single mothers in terms of the level of "insanity" that they may experience. Some single moms get periodic relief if their ex-partners take the children on a regular schedule. These child-free times allow these mothers some time and space—though frequently not enough—to regroup, organize their homes, or work extra hours so that they can feel some control over the chaotic times when their children are with them. Other moms may not have ex-partners who regularly and reliably take the children but have other relatives who help out on a regular basis. Then there are those mothers who have none of the above. They are on duty 24/7 with no evenings or weekends off. Although this group, perhaps, feels the invisible "insanity" the most intensely, I believe the experience of "insanity" of single motherhood is on a continuum. Many of us feel it; however, there are differences in degree and intensity.

A first cause of the "insanity" single mothers feel is the fact that the labour and scheduling requirements of many American workplaces still assume that there is one parent at home to deal with all family and household issues so that workers can focus their energies on their jobs and rearrange their lives around the demands of their work schedules. In other words, society still has not figured out an effective solution to work-family balance. This is difficult enough for married parents, much less single mothers. Logistics of getting it all done are much harder for a woman raising children alone and may, therefore, interfere with the paid workday. However, when predicaments arise that interrupt the workday, many workplaces judge employees across the board as equal, even when single mothers do not live in equal situations. A struggling single mother can be judged as harshly for being late when her childcare falls through as her co-worker who is late due to a hangover.[3] An unmarried worker with no children who volunteers to work on a few Saturdays because—as he openly admits—he has nothing else to do is lauded and given public recognition. On the other hand, his single-mom co-worker is criticized for not volunteering her Saturdays because she has trouble finding weekend childcare or needs the weekend to take care of household and family issues so that she can survive the requirements of her workweek.

Legal scholar Nancy Dowd discusses the unresolved issue of balancing work and family and its relationship to stress in two-parent working families and shows how parenting is supposed to be "invisible in the workplace"; however, as she points out, single moms "stick out like sore thumbs" (xxii). Whereas two-working-parent families do struggle, the situation is more prominent and obvious for single moms with no family support. Because most workplaces in the U.S. do not acknowledge or help parents solve the tension between parenting responsibilities and work duties, single moms, whose work and parenting conflicts are likely to be more frequent and visible, continue to be stigmatized. The larger societal problem of the conflict between paid labour and parenting is ignored, and single moms become the scapegoats: they are the incompetent deviants unable to successfully integrate work and family. Single mothers are required to carry out both instrumental and expressive tasks for their families. Housework, childcare and expressive tasks in general are invisible in society for all parents. Furthermore, parenting tasks are not those that can easily be put off until another day or time. Sick children or family crises need to be dealt with immediately. Like jagged pieces of glass, such crises cut through a parent's schedule and shred any plans for how the day or week or even month was supposed to go. For the single mothers who manage without any logistical support from ex-partners or extended family, the invisibility cloak our society has constructed to mask the problem of work/family balance falls away. A *New York Times* article focusing on the difficulties of a single mother juggling a job at Starbucks with constantly shifting hours emphasizes the problem of her work schedule, although her situation is a clear example of the difficulties of a single mom who does not have a reliable safety net to help her go back to school, keep a job, and fulfill her parental responsibilities (Kantor).

These realities have real implications for job performance and evaluation. A book chapter that I was working on for a year and a half never became published because of a parenting crisis. After spending eighteen months working with the editor on developing the chapter and tailoring it to the specific needs of that book, the editor decided the chapter needed some theoretical changes four weeks before the book was to be sent off to the publisher. Unfortunately, those four weeks coincided with a health crisis for my daughter, an unexpected legal battle with my ex-husband, as well as the end of the semester and the quick turnaround our college expects for preparation of intensive January term classes and spring semester classes. Needless to say, my chapter did not get published in the book. From my employer's perspective, the lack of publication signalled a lack of work productivity. The eighteen months of dedicated work on the chapter and the intense parenting duties I had to perform without the assistance of other adults became invisible and, ultimately, irrelevant. Instead of single mothers' struggles resulting in a solution to work-family imbalances, single mothers are still blamed for their problems and told to find their solutions. Again, the capitalistic societal narratives of self-sufficiency and meritocracy place the blame on individuals who have difficulties. It is up to single mothers to find solutions to their problems, not up to the government or workplaces to provide assistance. Another common response we get when trying to explain our realities is that "everyone is busy," not only single mothers. In other words, our realities and challenges are dismissed as unimportant, non-existent, or no more challenging than what others face. All of this adds to the feeling of "insanity" that some of us feel.

The fact that married working mothers frequently feel some of this pressure makes it even easier for blame to be placed on single mothers. Many times when I have encountered an impossible situation in a clash between work and my child's needs I have been asked why I cannot manage like other working moms. The fact that I do not have a spouse or other family support remains invisible, even when I clearly explain my situation. I have even had other single mothers who have co-operative ex-spouses and extended family helping them held up to me as examples of "successful single moms," before I am asked why I cannot manage as they do. Again, the real differences between my situation and those of the other single mothers remain invisible. The problems and challenges are ours as single mothers to solve as individuals; our work places and society-at-large are not interested in assisting in finding solutions.

A second cause of single mothers' feelings of "insanity" is the assumptions on which various American institutions are set up: they do not recognize the realities that many single mothers live with, and the stigma of deviance negatively influences how these institutions respond to the needs of single mothers, which results in society's unwillingness to adapt to those needs. Judges form decisions during divorce and post-divorce proceedings based on a form of equality that does not consider statistical pay differentials of men and women or the added stresses mothers face while raising children alone (Fineman 36-52). Joint custody gives both parents equal decision-making powers, whereas many single moms do the vast majority (or in some cases all) of daily work raising their children. In some states, when assets are divided during divorces, mothers with primary placement are credited with the financial assets of all of their children's furniture, clothes, electronics, and material property, which reduce the amount of actual financial settlement received. The maze of bureaucracy a mother has to go through in order to track down a child support check that has not arrived is daunting. Meanwhile, our bills need to be paid, and we are further criticized and judged when unable to do so, while many times it is paperwork that an office has lost or an ex-partner's refusal to comply with legal agreements that are at fault. All of these situations are created by legal guidelines that treat individuals as equals, without regard to the actual realities that they are living. Liberal feminism fought for women to be treated equally under the law. However, this equality under the law does not recognize that women still sometimes find themselves in situations that are more disadvantaged than those of men.

There is also more judicial suspicion (whether due to angry ex-partners or judgmental neighbours) regarding our choices and childrearing techniques. The perspective of single mothers is often invisible to government agencies that suggest some other "solution" or "better" way that a mother could have handled a situation, which ignores the reality that there are usually other factors that make such solutions impractical or impossible. The choices that we make do not always seem rational to outsiders because they are based on realities that are not only not acknowledged but also not even imagined. Always considering the perceptions of others when making decisions adds to single mothers' feelings of "insanity."

Social and religious institutions create invisible assumptions that can add to single mothers' stresses. Religious and school events for children are frequently organized around the assumption that the household is two parented, and do not recognize the intense lack of time most single mothers have. The scheduling of events can be difficult for mothers raising children alone; family activities often include different roles for fathers and mothers and heavy volunteering requirements for children to participate in sports or other activities. Again, my point is not that two-parent families have no challenges with these events but rather that the challenges are even more extreme for a mother attempting this on her own.

A third set of causes adding to the feeling of "insanity" is psychological stressors. Many single mothers face additional challenges while dealing with ex-partners and lingering legal issues that demand time and attention. Even after being divorced for years, we single mothers are still frequently required to deal with ex-partners and related legal issues, including the following: custody issues; getting reimbursements from uncooperative ex-partners; legal complaints about how we are raising the children; ex-partners who manipulate children and undermine our authority; ex-partners who put children into dangerous situations; post-divorce court battles; limitations on where we can travel and move that affect our ability to change jobs; and threats of child abduction. In addition, raising a child who has been abandoned by a parent is more difficult; doing it well takes much time and energy, which only adds to our psychological stress. These challenges are invisible to people who have never experienced them, yet for some of us, they fuel our feelings of "insanity."

Quite often it is the loneliness and lack of support that create the greatest feeling of "insanity." I have often received suggestions that I should have my daughter stay with my parents or other relatives for a few days to give me a break. As with many single moms, I do not have such family support. We may joke about the "insanity" of our lives; the reality is that single motherhood poses real mental health risks to women. Stress, social isolation, and financial difficulties are all factors that increase single moms' chances of suffering from anxiety or depression, which are much higher than those of mothers raising children with partners (Bankoff 615-618). However, as mentioned earlier, the most common interpretation of this situation is that whatever emotional issues a single mom may suffer from, they are merely seen as further proof of her deviance, defectiveness, and inability to cope, not as representative of the impossible situation that she is in. In some cases, the felt "insanity" and stress can lead to actual mental health issues. However, felt "insanity" is not the same as clinical insanity. And even when the invisible "insanity" of single motherhood sometimes leads to some mental health concerns, it rarely leads to clinical insanity.

We are often caught up in a psychological conundrum: to admit the full depth of the "insanity" that we feel in our lives is dangerous because some survival techniques involve ignoring just how difficult it is raising children alone, but to not admit the real level of felt "insanity" is to deny our own challenges, realities, and experiences. Hope keeps us going: we think we will meet a great partner and will soon not be attempting the seemingly impossible alone. (The dominant heteronormative romantic narrative remains a strong subconscious force for many of us.) We tell ourselves life will get easier in the near future, or we try to convince ourselves that our situations are not really that bad.

The invisible "insanity" experienced by many single mothers is created by these work-family conflicts and imbalances, which continue because household and family duties remain invisible in our society and because societal institutions are set up with assumptions that clash with the realities that single mothers experience. The label of deviancy adds stress to our lives and creates even more challenges. In sum, the ways in which societal institutions and expectations are set up create the feelings of "insanity." If single mothers' situations are invisible to society, and thereby do not officially exist, our realities and identities are invalidated. This creates a feeling of "insanity" as our real experiences clash with what society expects of us. We know our realities very well, but we are constantly fighting against a system that does not see those realities or chooses to ignore them.

CONCLUSION

What does it say about a society that stigmatizes women who try to do the best for our children, despite huge challenges, which remain largely unacknowledged in mainstream society? As I have discussed in this chapter, one possible cause of this continued stigmatization is the predominance of sexist stereotypes surrounding motherhood and femininity. Women who do not fit into mainstream society's definitions of "appropriate" womanhood or motherhood are frequently labelled as deviants. Single mothers fall into this category by raising children without men and by displaying characteristics that do not fit into idealized and sexist notions of womanhood. The situation also shows that our culture has hidden the problems of work-family balance for all families: single mothers merely live in situations that uncloak the issue. To recognize the stigmatization of single mothers and their everyday challenges necessitates an honest and effective conversation about gender expectations, sexism, and work-family balance issues, yet it is a conversation society is unwilling to have. This silence results in not only increased feelings of "insanity" for single mothers but also the maintenance of a society in which gender concerns and feminism are dismissed as trivial and outdated and those in power need not find solutions to gender discrimination and to the challenges of balancing parenting and paid labour.

NOTES

[1]I recognize that not all women who are single mothers not by choice and are without any outside help in raising their children feel this insanity, and some might even feel empowered. However, in my years of seeking out other single mothers to discuss experiences, I have found very few who do not feel this "insanity."

[2]I am not suggesting that children do not need fathers. Rather, I am saying that the fact that most single mothers survive and manage to raise their children discredits the prejudices and myths regarding women in society.

[3]All of the examples given have happened to women I know.

WORKS CITED

Bankoff, Elizabeth A. "Women in Psychotherapy: Their Life Circumstances and Treatment Needs." *Psychotherapy: Theory, Research, Practice, Training* 31.4 (1994): 610-619. Print.

Becker, Howard S. *Outsiders: Studies in the Sociology of Deviance.*

New York: The Free Press of Glencoe, 1963. Print.

Cohen, Philip. "Single Moms Can't Be Scapegoated for the Murder Rate Anymore." *The Atlantic*. Atlantic Monthly Group, 26 Nov. 2012. Web. 12 Feb. 2015.

Coulter, Ann. *Guilty: Liberal "Victims" and Their Assault on America*. New York: Crown Publishing Group, 2008. Print.

Dowd, Nancy E. *In Defense of Single Parent Families*. New York: New York University Press, 1997. Print.

Emery, Robert E. *Marriage Divorce, and Children's Adjustment, Second Edition*. Thousand Oaks, CA: Sage Publications, 1999. Print.

Fields, Jason. *America's Families and Living Arrangements:* 2003. Current Population Reports, P20-553. U.S. Census Bureau. Washington, DC: Government Printing Office, November, 2004. Print.

Fineman, Martha. *The Illusion of Equality:* The *Rhetoric and Reality of Divorce Reform*. Chicago: University of Chicago Press, 1991. Print.

Gardiner, Karen N., et al. *State Policies to Promote Marriage: Final Report*. U.S. Department of Health and Human Services. Washington, DC: Government Printing Office, Sept. 2002. Print.

Goffman, Erving. *Stigma: Notes on the Management of Spoiled Identity*. New York: Simon and Schuster, 1963. Print.

Hawkins, John. "Ann Coulter on Single Mothers: The Statistics from Guilty." *Right Wing News*. John Hawkins, 1 Apr. 2009. Web. 12 Feb. 2015.

Kantor, Jodi. "Working Anything but 9 to 5." *New York Times*, 13 Aug. 2014. Web. 19 Aug. 2014.

"Marriage of Figaro." *Mad Men*. American Movie Classics, AMC. Los Angeles. 2 Aug. 2007. Television.

Salzman, Avi. "Court Ruling Clears Mother in Son's Suicide." *New York Times*, 29 Aug. 2006. Web. 20 Oct. 2009.

Santora, Marc. "After a Son's Suicide, Mother is Convicted over Unsafe Home." *New York Times,* 7 Oct. 2003. Web. 10 Nov. 2009.

Schur, Edwin M. *Labeling Women Deviant: Gender, Stigma, and Social Control*. Philadelphia: Temple University Press, 1983. Print.

Sidel, Ruth. *Unsung Heroines: Single Mothers and the American Dream*. Berkeley: University of California Press, 2006. Print.

United States Census Bureau. Public Information Office. "Profile America, Facts for Features, Mother's Day: May 13, 2012." U.S. Department of Commerce, 19 Mar. 2012. Web. 16 Aug. 2014.

Vespa, Jonathan, Jamie M. Lewis, and Rose M. Kreider. "America's Families and Living Arrangements: 2012." U.S. Department of Commerce, Aug. 2013. Web. 16 Aug. 2014.

6.
Single Mother Adoption

A Sociologist's Journey

LINDA M. BURNS

THE PRESENT

IT IS ONE YEAR since I retired from a sociology professorship. Although I had contemplated some travel during my retirement, I find myself in a somewhat surprising place on this lovely summer evening. I am sitting in a large outdoor amphitheater in the mountainous area near Dresden, Germany, known as Saxon Switzerland, watching a German production of the 1960s American musical *Fame*. Like other members of the audience, I am focused on the sole American in the cast, a beautiful young woman in a shimmering red dress who has the lead role of Carmen Diaz. As her melodic voice fills the night air, I feel something not felt by the other members of the audience—a swelling of pride. This talented young woman is the daughter I adopted twenty-four years ago. The past twenty-four years have been an adventure filled with the challenges and triumphs familiar to most parents. But my experience of parenting has been tempered by the fact that I adopted as a single parent. I am one of those labelled as a single parent by choice. My approach to raising my daughter has also been influenced by my perspective as a feminist sociologist, and it is from this viewpoint that I share my story.

THE BEGINNING

The motherhood mandate is alive and well in our culture, perhaps particularly for those of us who grew up in the 1950s during the post-war period, when the joys of the traditional family were emphasized and mothers were encouraged to stay at home. As a child, I spent countless hours playing "house" with my huge contingent of dolls, many of which were designed to be like "real" babies who cried and wet diapers. (Yes, *Betsy-Wetsy* was one of my favourites!) As the years went by and I progressed through high school, college, and graduate school, I never stopped believing that one day I would be a mother. Yet at the age of forty, I realized that although I had completed a PhD in sociology, held a professional job at a university, travelled around the world through a shipboard education program, and purchased my own home, motherhood was eluding me. After several relationships that did not end in permanence, I realized that being a parent was really more important to me than being a spouse. For some women in this situation, the experiences of pregnancy and birth are very important, but, as a sociologist, I saw the social relationship between mother and child as more significant than the biological connection. In the back of my mind, I had often considered single-parent adoption as a possibility, so as I entered this new decade, I decided that it was time to pursue this seriously.

Single-parent adoption is a relatively modern practice. As recently as the 1960s in the United States, many states did not permit adoption by single individuals. As single-parent adoption became legal, children placed with single parents were often from groups considered "hard to place," which included older children, children with disabilities, and children of colour. Single-parent adoption is more common and accepted today, and it is often viewed as a good choice for children who may need intense parental involvement, such as children with special needs or children who have had damaging experiences. Some research suggests that single parents are more likely to prefer the adoption of a child who is beyond infancy. [1]

Knowing that the adoption process could be more difficult for a single parent, I began the process of reading and interviewing to learn more about the options available to me. Because I wanted the full experience of parenting, I made the decision to first seek adoption of an infant. At that time, there were some limitations on adoptions to single parents. International adoptions were becoming more popular, but many countries would not consider a single parent. Private adoptions were possible, but preference was generally given to two-parent families, and there could be long waiting periods of several years. In addition, both international and private adoption could be very expensive. Public agencies did consider single parents, and I decided to pursue the possibility of adoption through the local child welfare agency. This agency served children who were removed from their families as well as children who were voluntarily relinquished by their families. I spent hours crafting a letter describing my desire to adopt, what I could bring to the role of mother, and how I was prepared to parent a child from any ethnic or cultural background. I included this last part because I knew that many of the children who were placed for adoption through this agency were children of colour, and I believed that although I was white, my background as a sociologist living in an urban area provided me with knowledge and understanding that would help me to raise a child of a different ethnic-cultural background.[2] Several months after my initial inquiry, I was invited by the agency to join their next parenting class. These twelve-week classes were for prospective adoptive and foster parents and addressed a wide range of issues and culminated in a home visit to determine that the home met all state requirements for the placement of a child.

During the class, I was assigned a social worker, who would get to know me and would represent me in placement decisions. I was also required to provide several letters of recommendation from people who knew me well and believed that I would make a good parent. Several friends and a priest from the ethnically diverse church I attended enthusiastically agreed to write letters. The class included about six married couples, and one other single woman who had already adopted several children. We were encouraged to also think about foster parenting and adopting older children, since these were areas of great need. Although it felt somewhat selfish to me, I made it clear that my interest was in the adoption of an infant. I knew that I would most likely only adopt once, and I looked forward to the full experience of raising a child from infancy to adulthood. I also believed that as a single mother, it would be easier for me to raise a daughter, and I indicated that preference as well.

About one month after the completion of the parenting class, I received a phone call from my social worker telling me that I was being considered for the placement of an infant. A few hours later, I received a call from the social worker who represented my daughter informing me that the deciding group had selected me as their first choice to become the adoptive mother of a four-month-old biracial infant girl. The memory of those calls will stay with me forever. Just as parents who give birth vividly remember the confirmation of pregnancy and the birthing experience, adoptive parents can recall in detail the phone calls and first meetings with their children. These experiences mark one of the most important transitions in life.

A few days later I met my daughter for the first time—a beautiful, smiling baby girl. At that time, she was living in a foster home with a wonderful family who cared for infants waiting for placement. I visited her in the foster home several times, and her foster mother gave me much-needed lessons on infant care. I also worked frantically to finish projects at the university (where I worked as an assistant dean) in preparation for a two-month leave. I had great support from friends and co-workers who gave me three baby showers and provided the essentials, such as a crib, changing table, and high-chair. A friend who is an attorney provided the required legal services as a gift. Two weeks after that phone call, I brought Emily home. As with many adoptive families, in addition to her birthday, we celebrate the anniversary of the day she came home. When Emily was about five years old, she named that day "Becoming Day," since it was "the day we became a family."

The adoption process went more smoothly and quickly than I had ever imagined. Just six months after I started the parenting class, I was living with my infant daughter. This was an even shorter time than a pregnancy! Although I had been optimistic, I was still surprised. My family, friends, and co-workers were shocked. We had all heard stories of couples waiting for years to adopt an infant, so many of them were certain that I was in for a long wait and, probably, a disappointing outcome. Even the experienced social worker who directed the class told me later that she was very surprised that the placement had happened so quickly and that an infant had been placed with me. I also learned later that I was the first person in the class to have a placement. Why did this process go so smoothly? The spiritual side of me believes there was some divine intervention—from the beginning, it has always seemed to me that Emily and I were somehow meant to be together. The sociological side of me recognizes the possibility that the deciding group may have been influenced by my educational background. Perhaps it was a combination of factors. My social worker told me that he read my initial letter to the group, and they were apparently swayed by my words. Based on my interactions with members of the parenting class, it did not seem that other members had advanced degrees or academic careers and, for that reason, I may have stood out. In any case, it is sometimes daunting to think of how the fates of my daughter and me were determined by social workers gathered around a table on a Friday afternoon.

EARLY YEARS

I remember those first years of motherhood as an almost magical time. I was able to take a leave from my job for several months, which gave us relaxed time together with many visits from friends and relatives who wanted to meet Emily. My brother and his family visited from Michigan during those first weeks and bought us a beautiful baby stroller. We also took a number of excursions, attending a family reunion and making a trip to visit my mother who lived about five hours away. I received nothing but support during those early months. Although my white working-class family network included no single parents, no adoptions, and no one of colour, everyone was very excited and supportive. I have since heard horror stories of children of colour adopted into white families whose extended family members were not welcoming and never truly accepted the adopted child as equal to the other children. My mother immediately fell in love with Emily and to this day, they have a very special relationship. Motherhood is very important in my extended family, and I had finally reached that rank.

At the end of my two-month leave, I enrolled my daughter in the university daycare centre. I was fortunate to be working at a large university that had high-quality, onsite daycare. Nevertheless, like many parents, the first few times that I left Emily at daycare were very difficult, and I shed quite a few tears on my way to the office. It was not long, however, until I realized what an asset an excellent daycare can be to working parents and, perhaps, especially to single parents. Since the daycare was on campus, I could visit Emily at lunch time, and I also came to enjoy the company of other parents and daycare staff as we sat and fed our babies. The daycare families quickly became another social and support group, as both parents and children became friends. Many of the children remained in the centre from infancy until they left for kindergarten, so there were many birthday parties and outings together. Like the university, the daycare population was quite diverse with other single parents and families of different ethnicities. The staff was also ethnically diverse, with very little turnover. During these early years, I had a great deal of support outside the daycare as well. My mother, who was living alone, moved near us when Emily was eighteen months old and became our primary babysitter and back-up caregiver. It was also really beneficial for Emily to develop a close relationship with her grandmother, who loved to play games and do puzzles with her. My friends were also great supporters, although I had to learn to ask if I needed some help or just some company.

Were there times during the first years when I would have appreciated a second parent on the scene? Absolutely. Before Emily was a year old, it became clear that she had fairly serious asthma, and she had to be hospitalized several times during her early life. I remember the first hospitalization very well. I had taken her to the pediatrician, and we were seeing a doctor who did not know us. As it became clear that her wheezing was not going to be successfully treated in the office, the doctor told me that she would need to be admitted to Children's Hospital. As I was trying to cope with this news, he guided me to a private room, and in a gesture of support, he told me to just relax, have a cup of coffee, and call my husband! I believe that I burst into tears, as I blubbered that I had no husband. It did get easier, and I learned that I could handle crises. Once when I was carrying my bundled, wheezing child to the car in the middle of a cold, winter night to make the trip to the emergency room, I just kept saying to myself, "I'm handling this … I'm handling this." I learned to manage the difficult times, and it truly helped to know I had good friends that I could call on anytime day or night.

Those difficult times were a small part of my parenting experience, yet there were other times when I thought about a second parent. Because I so much enjoyed Emily, who grew into a spirited, laughing little girl who kept me laughing, I thought, at times, it was unfortunate and somewhat selfish that I had all of this joy to myself. But friends and family shared our good times and, overall, those early years were very satisfying, fun, and joyful.

As I thought about writing this short memoir, I was certainly aware that my decision to become a single parent affected Emily's experience of growing up. My journey was also her journey. Although we often talked about my decision, and I was always open with her about the adoption, I never asked her some hard questions, such as whether she often wished that she had a second parent. Since she is currently working in Germany, I emailed her a number of questions, and she sent back her responses, some of which were surprising to me. In the next sections, I include her voice as I continue with our story.

SCHOOL DAYS

As the time approached for Emily to leave daycare and begin kindergarten, I was faced with a number of options for her next school, and it became clear to me that it would be hard to duplicate the diversity that we had experienced in the daycare. After much consideration, I chose the Catholic school near our home. This was a small school with a good reputation for academics, and I also wanted Emily to have the religious education. It was also at this time that I made a career move from a full-time administrative job at a large university to a faculty position at a small Catholic women's college. We joked that we both entered Catholic school at the same time. This change was not financially beneficial, as I had to take a sizable reduction in salary, but I made this decision to have a more flexible schedule and also because I wanted to be more immersed in my field of sociology. This turned out to be a very good decision—I loved my job, and I had a great group of colleagues. It was very helpful to have summer breaks, during which Emily and I were able to have relaxed time together.

Emily's new school was not as diverse as the daycare centre—the student body was primarily white and middle class. This was not ideal in my mind, but the school was close to home, had a strong curriculum, and a sense of community, which I appreciated. I was not prepared, however, for the lack of diversity in family structure. Aware of statistics on divorce and single parents, I was surprised to find that Emily was the only child in her class with a single parent and no siblings. Although our situation was very different, I felt quite comfortable with the other parents at Emily's school, who were very positive about our situation, and we quickly became good friends with several families. Parents were very involved with their children and school activities, and being part of this close community compensated for the lack of diversity. Many of the mothers were stay-at-home moms who would offer to cover for me when there were school days off. Emily also seemed to thrive at her new school. She did well academically and was well liked by students and teachers. During kindergarten, she became friends with an adopted girl from Nepal. I suspect it was the status of adoption and the fact that both girls looked somewhat "exotic" among the mainly white faces that first drew them together. But as they came to know each other, they became great friends, and we also developed a wonderful relationship with the entire family. Our families have spent much time together over the years, including vacations and jointly celebrated holidays. They are still among our closest friends.

Although Emily was very well accepted at her school, she does recall feeling very different having a single mother. In one question, I asked her if she felt that she was at a disadvantage or whether she was uncomfortable having a single mother. Her response suggests that she was comfortable with her situation, but she was uncomfortable with her classmates' reactions. In her words,

> I do not recall ever feeling at a disadvantage because of having a single mother. I do, however, recall feeling *different* in school-age years. From kindergarten through eighth grade, I was surrounded by classmates with stereo-

> typical families—a mother, a father, and many siblings. I can remember many occasions when I was asked what my parents did and when I responded that it was just my mother and me, I sometimes heard, "Oh, that must be really hard not having a father" or "Wow, I'm sorry. Is this hard for you to talk about?" When I was faced with these questions and responses, I did feel uncomfortable. I was never uncomfortable because I had a single mother, but I was uncomfortable because of my classmates' reactions. Their normal was not my normal, and they often made me feel different and assumed I was missing something.

I recall wanting to protect Emily from feeling different. Her school had two days when parents were invited for breakfast: Muffins with Mom and Donuts with Dad. Even though all dads did not attend, I would try to plan with whom she could sit. And I always dreaded Father's Day. Since my own father was deceased, Emily had no father or grandfather, and her only uncle lived 750 miles away. Some years, we would buy cards for her Godfather and for a friend's father who had spent time with her. I usually tried to plan a special activity for that day, and I was always relieved when it was over. Looking back, I suspect those days were actually harder for me than for Emily.

Emily and I were both viewed as different in many contexts. We certainly may have been the first single-parent adoptive family in the school's history. People like the idea of adoption, so I suspect that I was viewed more positively than if I had been a single mother through divorce or childbirth. As Emily grew up, I think we both grew to enjoy the status of being different. We even joked about all the ways that she was different: adopted, of mixed ethnic heritage, and from a single-parent home. Being different has been mainly positive for me—I admit to enjoying people's surprise when they learn that I am Emily's mother and that I am a single adoptive parent. Emily usually seemed positive with respect to her differences, and I asked her if that was still true. Here are her words:

> I did enjoy being different growing up. Kids always found me interesting and wanted to get to know me. I always

> felt lucky to be able to see the world from a different perspective. I moved to Germany five months ago and being different has been very positive for me and my career.... I grew up feeling accepted and loved and that would make anyone feel comfortable with themselves.

As a sociologist who taught women's studies and sociology of the family courses, I was determined to raise a daughter who would not be limited by traditional gender roles. I assumed that growing up with only one parent, who took all roles in the family, would facilitate a more gender-neutral outlook. I was taken aback then when something in our house was not working, and my young daughter announced, "We better call a man!" I realized then how easily we learn these traditional roles. I was not particularly handy with household repairs, and when we had someone come into the house to help, it was usually a man, so Emily's observations easily led her to the conclusion that men fix things. After that, I often enlisted the help of a more competent female friend when I needed to fix or assemble something. Of course, children also learn gender from media, and when I asked Emily about her experiences growing up with a single mother, she revealed another traditional role that she had absorbed—one that I had never even considered.

> As I became older and more aware of the role gender plays in society, I became wary that my mom wouldn't be able to fill the role of "protector" that is most often taken by the father. In movies, the father is always the one protecting the family in a crisis. I kept thinking of what would happen if an intruder came into my house of females—even our dog was female.

I was quite surprised by this response, but it helps to explain why Emily was often the one to check that the front door was locked before we went to bed.

An intriguing aspect of parenting is the process of watching children's interests and talents emerge. This may be especially true for adoptive parents, who have made no genetic contributions, but even biological parents are often surprised. During her elementary school years, Emily was interested in some sports, and I truly did enjoy the soccer-mom role, rooting from the sidelines and taking my turn to paint lines and provide snacks. I also encouraged her to take skating lessons at a nearby rink, and she seemed to excel at figure skating in ways that my weak ankles would never allow. But the greatest surprise for me came when Emily was in middle school—she discovered that she had a beautiful singing voice! Although Emily had always enjoyed singing, it was around the age of twelve that other people began to notice her voice. This was remarkable to me because of all the ways that I had imagined Emily's future life, I had never anticipated that she would excel in music. There is very little musical talent in my extended family, and like many of my family members, I cannot even carry a tune. So we were all quite astonished when this beautiful voice emerged right on key!

It soon became clear that singing was not just a passing interest for Emily. She spent extra time with the school music teacher learning to harmonize and was invited to sing solos at school events. At this time, we heard about a regional girls' choir, and I encouraged her to audition. She was accepted, and the choir became a very important part of her life for the next five years. Through this choir, she acquired a love of classical vocal music, developed sight-reading skills, and learned the importance of practice. When Emily was in eighth grade, she decided to audition for our city's performing arts high school. She was accepted into the vocal performance program, and there her singing skills and understanding of music really blossomed.

HIGH SCHOOL

As Emily was learning more about music, I was learning as well. I knew very little about the performing arts world, and as I came to know her music teachers and choir directors, I learned more about music professions and the dedication required to have a successful career in this field. It was clear that Emily had the talent, but she also had the determination and the strong work ethic that was required. She acquired professional attitudes and skills at this early stage. Teachers always commented on how hard she worked and how she was always prepared. The Performing Arts High School was also a wonderfully diverse school. Emily was no longer the different one—the student body was ethnically and socio-economically diverse, and there were students from all sorts of family structures. Unlike many high schools, students did not seem to be judged by the clothes that they wore or their hairstyles—it was all about the arts.

During ninth grade, Emily successfully auditioned for the Pennsylvania Governor's School for the Arts. This was a prestigious program for talented students that provided intensive instruction and performance opportunities at no cost. Although she had been away to week-long summer camps, Governor's School was a five-week residential program on a college campus.[3] I was quite concerned about this first major separation and invited a friend to accompany me when I drove Emily to the program so that I would have support on the way home. It was difficult leaving her there, but she quickly made friends, and as I saw that she was enjoying the program, I was able to relax and enjoy my free time. The campus was just two hours from our home, so I was able to visit several times and attend the final performances. Emily flourished at the Governor's School, and we learned that there were other summer programs for high school students that provide similar intensive experiences. The next summer, Emily attended a precollege program at Carnegie Mellon University, which was just minutes from our home, and the following summer, she attended the well-known Interlochen Performing Arts Camp in Michigan. Interlochen was about ten hours away, and I made the trip there by myself. Saying goodbye and driving home alone were difficult for me. Again, it was not too long before I could tell that Emily was thoroughly engaged in the program and I could stop worrying. These separations during high school summers were especially difficult for me due to being a single mother. I can see how a second parent could have eased my separation anxiety. But these separations were probably very healthy for both of us, as it increased Emily's independence and helped to keep our close bond from becoming a constraint.

These were exciting years as it became clear that Emily had found her passion. I have known parents who discouraged talented children from pursuing careers in the arts because the competition is so fierce and the work is unpredictable. But I could not have done anything except to encourage her and cheer her on. During high school, Emily joined our church choir and another outside choir and also had the opportunity to perform in the chorus with a local opera company. The schedule was sometimes hectic, as there were many rehearsals and performances. I never missed a performance, and our friends became loyal fans as well. It was wonderful to watch Emily grow within this strong supportive structure of teachers, families, and friends.

During the high school years, I often thought that being a single mother with one child allowed me to focus on giving Emily extra support by encouraging her, driving her to rehearsals, and just learning more about the field of vocal performance. Some might say that I became a stage mother. I tried to let Emily make her own decisions, but, at the same time, I was quite invested in her progress. I did not know whether Emily ever saw any advantages to having a single mother, and I asked her this in one of the questions.

> Absolutely. My mom was always there. She was my everything. I don't think I would have the same bond with my mom had I grown up in a two-parent household. I was always my mom's first priority no matter how much work needed to be done at home or at work.

We did develop a strong bond during those years, and I believe that bond was made stronger by the support that I could give Emily as she pursued her interest in music. I had heard so many negative stories about the teen years that I was surprised at how much fun they were. I showed Mary Pipher's film *Reviving Ophelia* in several classes and often thought about her conclusion: girls who pursue and develop strong interests—such as sports, horseback riding, or art—often have an easier time during adolescence and are more likely to avoid the, sometimes, toxic and sexually provocative teen culture. I do believe that was the case for Emily. We were more likely to hear Italian arias at our house than MTV music videos.

Although I generally found these years as a single mother to be satisfying and positive, there was a number of ways in which I could see the benefits of two parents. Certainly, it was easy to see the financial advantages of dual incomes. My financial situation was decidedly better than those of many young single mothers who live below the poverty line and struggle to provide for their children, and I was grateful for that. These are the mothers who are often criticized for being mothers at all and who are usually the focus of the media's coverage of single-parent families. But these mothers were not my reference group. I generally compared my lifestyle to those of my closest friends, who were academics or other professionals raising their children with the benefits of two professional salaries. During the early years of my faculty job, I often took on overload and summer courses, which added to the complexities of our schedule. I was aware of the amenities that we sometimes lacked, and I was not able to save as much as my friends saved for college expenses or for retirement. Although being a single parent almost always carries a financial disadvantage, I was, nevertheless, acutely aware of my good fortune in having an interesting, stable job that I truly liked, and I was certainly able to provide for our needs and more. I was also very fortunate that a good friend who had no children frequently helped with some of the expenses of Emily's summer programs and college tuition.

Everyone who has children eventually develops a parenting style that is most likely based on their parents' childrearing approach, their temperament, and advice from friends and professionals. I have seen families where parents have conflicting parenting styles—one more permissive, one more authoritarian. Generally, I enjoyed being able to develop my own style without any compromise. During Emily's teen years, however, I sometimes had doubts about my judgments and could see the benefits of a second opinion. Although Emily's adolescence went quite smoothly, the issues and decisions that needed to be made, eventually, became larger and more serious. Many issues emerge with the activity most parents dread: driving. Because we lived in the city and had access to reasonable public transportation, Emily delayed learning to drive until she finished high school. Still, some of her friends were driving at age sixteen, and there were decisions to be made about when and where she could go in cars, how late she could stay, etc. These were difficult decisions to make, and I often consulted with friends who had already experienced those issues, but, in the end,

I had to make the decisions myself. I will also never forget the experience of teaching Emily to drive. We started by having her practise in a nearby cemetery. If it had been up to me, she would still be driving in the cemetery, but, eventually, we moved to regular streets. Those were not our best moments. As hard as I tried, I could not stop clinging to the armrest on the passenger's side, which made Emily feel that I had no faith in her ability to learn to drive. Friends offered to help, but Emily did not want to learn to drive with a friend. Finally, I signed her up for lessons at a driving school so that she could, gradually, move onto the interstate. She is a fine driver and was always cautious, but that was one area that I would have gladly shared with a second parent.

COLLEGE, GRADUATE SCHOOL, AND BEYOND

By the end of high school, Emily knew for certain that she wanted to pursue a performance career in vocal music, and her years at a performing arts high school with the summer programs had prepared her to audition at some excellent schools. She was accepted at her first choice—Carnegie Mellon University, in our hometown. I was delighted that she wanted to attend Carnegie Mellon—it had an excellent reputation, and I would be able to continue to see all of her performances. Emily lived on campus during her first two years. I encouraged this, since I thought it would help her to continue to gain independence and would give her the full college experience. During three summers of college, Emily worked as a counsellor at a local music and art day camp. She really enjoyed the experience, and as a parent, it was gratifying to have her working full time and being able to cover some of her school expenses. During several summers, she also performed in musicals at a local theater. Throughout Emily's college years, our friends and I attended all of her performances and recitals—she always had an enthusiastic audience. For her senior recital, she had a full house, including friends and relatives from out of town. It was the tradition for parents to provide a reception after the recital. My amazing book club, which twenty-two years earlier had given me a baby shower, stepped forward and offered to provide the reception. I was very grateful for this help, and it allowed me to thoroughly enjoy the day without the concern of hosting a reception. This is another example of the amazing support that I had as a single mother.

During Emily's junior year at Carnegie Mellon, a professor recommended that she audition for a summer music program in Germany. She was accepted, so we prepared for her to spend eight weeks in Germany. This would be the longest and farthest separation yet. I felt that it was important to take her to the airport myself, but as I stood watching her go through the security check, I could not hold back the tears. I am sure that she was anxious about flying alone on her first trip abroad and that I just added to her anxiety. As with our previous separations, we both adjusted, and she absolutely loved Germany and the music program. I was able to go to Germany for her last performances in a German production of *Little Shop of Horrors*. While in Germany, Emily studied with a private voice teacher, who was a professor at Arizona State University. After completing her undergraduate degree, she decided to pursue graduate study at Arizona State so that she could continue to study with her teacher. Arizona was two thousand miles away, but it was much closer and more accessible than Germany. I was able to make two trips a year to Arizona, and I was able to see Emily's primary performances. During her graduate school summer, she returned to Germany for additional study. Through the professional connections that she made in Germany, she was offered the role of Carmen Diaz in a 2013 summer production of *Fame*. So right after she received her master's degree, she left for Dresden, Germany. That role led to offers of several other roles in musicals and operas, and she has stayed in Germany for the time being. I do miss Emily and wish she lived closer, but the bond that we have established in the past twenty-four years can endure any distance. I was fortunate to be able to visit her and see her in *Fame* this past summer, and she was able to come home over the Christmas holidays. We stay in touch through texts and phone calls. She will be home for an extended visit this summer and will be performing with a local opera company. I am thankful that our closeness was not an impediment to her career—I am proud that she has the confidence to pursue opportunities and create a life four thousand miles away. The balance of emotional closeness and independence seems to be steady right now. As a single parent of one child, my "empty nest" is indeed empty, but I, too, have learned to create a separate life with family and friends while cheering for Emily from the other side of the ocean.

REFLECTION

It is important to me to share my story because so much information regarding single mothers emphasizes the negative.[4] In writing this short memoir, I do want to suggest that single adults who strongly desire to be parents should not be discouraged by such reports. There are, of course, no perfect lifestyles, but single parenthood does not need to be viewed as a deficient parenting style. Single parenting can be very satisfying and successful for both parents and children. My personal journey was challenging yet joyful and immensely rewarding. It was helpful to have strong support from family and friends, and I believe that it was important that during those years parenting was my highest priority.

NOTES

[1]For a comprehensive history and review of issues related to single-parent adoption, see the following: Behnaz Pakizegi, "Single-Parent Adoptions and Clinical Implications" and Vic Groze, *Adoption and Single Parents: A Review*.

[2]The adoption of children by parents of a different ethnic or racial background has been often referred to as "transracial adoption" and has been a controversial issue in the United States for decades. Some viewed the practice as humanitarian and others viewed it as a means of weakening the Black community by removing so many children. In the early 1970s, the National Association of Black Social Workers (NABSW) took a strong stand against transracial adoption. Unfortunately, the number of children of colour waiting for placement increased, and in 1994, the U.S. Congress passed the Multiethnic Placement Act, which prohibited agencies from delaying or denying the placement of children based solely on race or ethnicity. A number of studies emerged from this change in policy that focused on the effect of transracial adoption on the children, particularly related to self-esteem and racial identity. In

general, children whose parents encouraged them to learn more about their ethnic roots and who came in contact with people who looked like them tended to have a stronger and more positive sense of identity. For a review of this issue and research, see the following: Rhonda M. Roorda, "Moving Beyond the Controversy of the Transracial Adoption of Black and Biracial Children" and Marsha Wood, "Mixed Ethnicity, Identity and Adoption: Research, Policy and Practice."

[3]After thirty-six years of operation, the Pennsylvania Governor's School for the Arts was discontinued in 2009 due to budgetary issues. This was very unfortunate because the program provided many students from all socio-economic situations the opportunity to receive high-quality intensive study in the arts.

[4]As a faculty member in sociology I taught sociology of the family courses and always wanted to skip the sections on single parents. The texts often highlight the negative consequences of growing up in a single-parent home. For example, Sara McLanahan, a leading researcher in this area, recognizes that low income is the single most important factor that results in low achievement of children, but she also suggests that other factors play an important part. As she states,

> They are twice as likely to drop out of high school, 2.5 times as likely to become teen mothers, and 1.4 times as likely to be idle—out of school and out of work—as children who grow up with both parents. Children in one-parent families also have lower grade point averages, lower college aspirations, and poorer attendance records. As adults, they have higher rates of divorce. These patterns persist even after adjusting for differences in race, parents' education, number of siblings, and residential location.... Thus the parents' socioeconomic status cannot explain why children from one-parent families are doing worse.

More recently, Kimberly Howard and Richard Reeves of the Brookings Institute presented an analysis of reasons that "children raised by married parents typically do better in life on almost every available economic and social measure." They suggest that "both the higher incomes and the more engaged parenting of married parents count for a good deal." They suggest that married parents have more time to engage in "high investment parenting," which includes activities like reading to children. See Kimberly Brookings and Howard V. Reeves, *The Marriage Effect: Money or Parenting.*

WORKS CITED

Brookings, Kimberly, and Howard V. Reeves. "The Marriage Effect: Money or Parenting." *Brookings*. The Brookings Institution, n.d. Web. 9 Sept. 2014.

Groze, Vic. "Adoption and Single Parents: A Review." *Child Welfare: Journal of Policy, Practice, and Program* 70.3 (1991): 321-332. Print.

McLanahan, Sara. "The Consequences of Single Motherhood." *The American Prospect*. The American Prospect, Summer 1994. Web. 22 May 2016.

Pakizegi, Behnaz. "Single-Parent Adoptions and Clinical Implications." In *Handbook of Adoption: Implications for Researchers, Practitioners, and Families*. Ed. Rafael Art Javier. Thousand Oaks: Sage Publications, 2007. 190-216.Print.

Pipher, Mary. *Reviving Ophelia: Saving the Selves of Adolescent Girls*. Media Education Foundation, 1998. Video Presentation.

Roorda, Rhonda M. "Moving Beyond the Controversy of the Transracial Adoption of Black and Biracial Children." *Handbook of Adoption: Implications for Researchers, Practitioners, and Families*. Ed. Rafael Art Javier. Thousand Oaks: Sage Publications, 2007.133-148. Print.

Wood, Marsha. "Mixed Ethnicity, Identity and Adoption: Research, Policy and Practice." *Child and Family Social Work* 14.4 (2009): 431-439. Print.

7. Great Lakes to Great Walls

Reflections of a Single Mom on Young Motherhood and Living Overseas

NATASHA STEER

EVERYTHING ACCORDING TO PLAN

WHEN I GRADUATED from York University with two degrees,[1] I had plans. I had lived with my mother my entire life, and once I had my career settled, my son and I would be able to move out into a place of our own—I could finally gain full independence. Looking all around me, it seemed that things were supposed to go in a certain order, and since I had deviated from that norm, I was striving to return to the original route. I fully expected to find a house, a husband, and potentially have more children (with as small an age gap between the children as possible) in the near future. But China changed all that.

Having become a single parent at the age of nineteen in 2003, my coming-of-age timeline had been atypical. Although single motherhood no longer seemed to involve the major stigmatization that once existed, I knew that many would continue to judge me, and they did (whether they knew me or not). That I had successfully graduated from high school did not matter: I was single, I was a teen, and I was pregnant. In *Fighting Stigma: An Adolescent Mother Takes Action,* Lewis et al. explore the stereotyping of young mothers and claim that "[t]een mothers are especially vulnerable to being stigmatized due to their age, class, and racial/ethnic backgrounds. With few exceptions, media stories, professional discourse, and advocacy organizations portray teen mothers as irresponsible and inept parents whose lives are forever derailed by parenting" (Lewis 303). Having grown up in a female-led household myself,

I knew that it would seem inevitable to some that I would follow the same predestined path as my mother; that in fact, my mother's social-economic background and the lack of a father in the home would point to a path already prescribed for me.

As Silva aptly points out in *Good Enough Mothering? Feminist Perspectives on Lone Mothering*, moral stigmatization is a common aspect of lone motherhood (regardless of age). Yet despite the "apparent sociological evidence in support of the belief that the children of lone parents do less well in life and cause more trouble than those brought up by their two biological parents" (McIntosh 148) and the claims that teenage parenthood is, somehow, a failure in and of itself, my single parenthood had a lot less to do with how my own single mother raised me or what type of person I was and a lot more to do with the biological father of my child, who chose to leave when I was pregnant. Although many women today choose to parent independently and have dropped the notion that a partner is needed to have a child, my ideals at the time were to co-parent with my child's biological father, and it was difficult to be thrown into a new situation through no choosing of my own.

I raised my son with the love and helpful support of my mother, not of a male partner. Yet a deficit discourse follows young parents who continue to live with their own parents. I, too, was occasionally criticized for choosing to live with my mother rather than moving out before I was financially prepared to do - as many are forced to do. Nevertheless, in spite of critics and naysayers, I found the experience of living with my mom to be wholesome and nurturing for us all. Western society's implication that it was not the ideal situation meant that a happy, healthy household of three generations was considered less of an ideal family than a traditional nuclear family—regardless of the health of that family. I could not understand why a family's acceptance should be based on how many genders were in the house, as opposed to how many loving people were in it. My son grew up surrounded by love both inside and outside the home, and as far as I have always been concerned, this is the most important thing that children can receive, regardless of what gender those people may identify with or what generation they may belong to.

It was my mother who taught me about standards. My mother could have remained with someone who did not treat her as she deserved, but instead she left my father when she was pregnant to give us a better life. My mom raised me with the immense help and support of my grandfather, and for the first years of my life, I lived with them both (my grandmother passed away two years before I was born) and happily bestowed all Father's Day gifts on my grandad. As my mother has often noted, it was because of the support of her father that she was then able to model such support for me when I became a single parent. I know of many other experiences in which that level of parental support did not and does not exist, and I credit much of my life to being fortunate enough to have had such support from so many family members and friends. In particular, it was always my mother, who, from a very early age, encouraged me to decide what I wanted out of life and to work towards my goals—as well as to form new goals when my original plan did not go as expected. So many young single mothers have not been given the same level of support that I was so fortunate enough to receive.

After giving birth to my son, I was grateful to remain home and devote almost two years doting on him. Then, amid knowing looks and comments of "Sure, you'll go back to school, one day " and "You say you'll go back now, but..." I entered determinedly into university life in 2005 with toddler in tow. There was a daycare on campus, and the two-hour trek via train and buses provided ample time to read and play (and handle tantrums) with my little one. I was the only student carting a stroller on and off the buses, and I had my share of dirty looks during a memorable two-hour tantrum, but, overall, I enjoyed defying the stereotypical teenage mom template and did not relate to it at all. I was strong, and I would be successful; having a son at the age of nineteen would not affect that in the slightest. He provided me with only more reason to succeed.

Fast forward five years later, and it was graduation time—my son was six years old, and I was twenty-six and ready to finally spread my wings. But finding a job in my field and close to home proved near impossible—our society is full of teachers trying to find a classroom. I joined a fundraising organization for charities, which I grew to adore, and two years later, I had risen in the ranks of the organization to become campaign manager. Still, it was intense work and contract only—I was still ready to teach in a classroom setting.

Then came the email. It was a beautiful Saturday, and I had planned a fun day for my son and me, but this email changed all that. It was about an international job fair—starting only one hour from that moment. What followed was an extremely stressful and discouraging day that would change my life. Having finally found a babysitter, a working printer for my resumes and cover letters, a working scanner (the printer ran out of ink—of course!), and a parking space in downtown Toronto, I arrived at the job fair far too many hours later—two hours before the official end time and with only a few vendors left at the fair. Despite my dismay, I met a woman who interviewed me on the spot and told me that had I arrived earlier, she would not have had the time to talk to me. That horrible detour earlier had resulted in success—I had a job offer to teach in a real school, in China.

So there it was: my first full-time "real" job offer. It would also be my first time moving out of my mother's house. Some of my family and friends were big supporters of this exciting opportunity, whereas others were dismayed by the idea of China. As Edward Said explores in *Orientalism*, people often make arbitrary geographical distinctions in their minds, which often results in an "us vs. them" mentality (54). Such distinctions were clear in the minds of some, who not only had never been to China to form their own opinions of the country but relied solely on mainstream media and stereotypical portrayals to form certain viewpoints. As Said relates, "[t]ruth, in short, becomes a function of learned judgement, not of the material itself" (67). At times, there were veiled comments (some within earshot of my son) that reflected certain problematic, prejudiced beliefs and assumptions. These were often not reflected in the specific words used as much as the tone and underlying attitudes of disdain and superiority. For as Said notes, Asia "has helped to define ... the West ... as its contrasting image, idea, personality, experience" (1-2). The view was clear: Canada and the West are appealing, refined, civilised locations in which to spend time, whereas Asia is not. Even after we made the move, I heard others making condescending comments during summers at home proclaiming that they would never be enticed to go to such a country—they preferred much more "scenic" experiences. Despite my frustration, I could not also help feeling somewhat amused.

It felt natural for me to include my son in the decision to move, and I asked Zac what he thought. It was of great importance to me that my son embraced such a big change in our lives. At eight, Zac was brave, curious, and excited to move to another country on the other side of the world and to start grade four somewhere new. This was such a relief, but I still had my doubts and agonized over the decision until the very last moment. I worried the most about safety issues. What if an earthquake struck? Was it safe enough? The knowledge that my son's physical safety rested on my shoulders alone in a foreign country was unsettling. At home, I had the support of family and friends whenever I needed it. And I often did. Once my son started kindergarten in our hometown, my mother or another family member often picked him up from daycare if a university class went beyond six in the evening. My mom was the one who watched Zac any time I had to take a night class. (Although occasionally I had to bring Zac to classes with books and toys, and my professors were always supportive of this.) I had been incredibly fortunate and had the freedom to learn, to socialize, or to go out for an evening or for dinner because I had an abundance of support around me. Could I really give that up?

My fear was not only for Zac's safety but also for how I thought I would cope as a mother. I feared for myself as a parent in transition—could I do enough, be enough? Could I manage this change in a spirit that allowed Zac to transition in his own way, at his own pace, and in a way that was healthy and safe for him? I knew that I would not have the same kind of support network in China. Despite having been a mother for almost nine years, my sense of independence was not yet secure. As Silva points out, "[l]one motherhood has ... been discussed in association with women's independence and gender equality" (1). She questions whether "women have the right to pursue careers, to live independently from men and to raise children on their own ... The politics of gender is at the centre of these debates" (Silva 1-2). Among all these questions came one more—did I really have the right to pursue my chosen career if it meant uprooting my son from his family?

Something that I had to consider carefully before moving, as both an educator and a mother, was my son's future education. I learned that Zac would be attending a small private Canadian school on campus with other international children and that it was tiny. There were fewer than twenty children in the school, and the teacher-student ratio was high. I was reassured that it would be a positive alternative to Zac's previous school experiences, but it also meant removing him from French immersion. I had always enjoyed hearing him chatter to his friends in French, and I was torn about removing him from that atmosphere, but I also knew that through moving, Zac's learning would be extended far beyond the confines of the classroom. Although it was hard, I knew that I could not simply regulate the education conversation to learning that occurs inside schools. The experience of moving overseas would be so much more holistic than that.

I had to actively fight against letting fear and uncertainty stand in my way. I had always tried to live my life in such a way as to not pass down unnecessary or excessive fears to my son (yelling "isn't this fun?!" as we raced down a rollercoaster with my heart in my throat), and this was my big test. I remember distinctly telling myself, "If I do this, I will know, for the rest of my life, that I can do anything." I now realize that I was telling myself that fear of such a big change is normal, but that it should not prevent me from moving forward. I would always question how different my life may have been had I not gone through with it. But if we did go, and then decided that this was something that did not sit well with us or feel right, we could always come home. I decided that we had to go and try, not only for me but for Zac. Zac knew about the job offer; it had been discussed. Was I going to teach him to reach out to new experiences and to grab hold of life with both hands? Or was I going to teach him to make his decisions based on fear of the unknown? I wanted to show Zac that he could do anything and go anywhere, if he so wanted.

A DIFFERENT LIFE

And then just like that (okay, twenty-four hours and three plane rides later) we were in Wuhan, China. The night of our arrival—heavy with humidity so strong that it smacked us in the face as we walked off the plane—the principal of my school said something to us that really shaped how we would view our experiences. He said that we would notice a lot of differences here and that the important thing to remember was that China was not better or worse than Canada—simply different. As Said notes, for those of us from the Western hemisphere, the East exhibits "those mysteriously attractive opposites to what seem to be normal values" (57). Although I knew intellectually that mine was not the "normal" culture, I was challenged on this many times. I had had a lifetime of being told what was normal and what was not, but now it was essential to me that we explore the culture with an open mind and without judgement, although I confess that this was sometimes difficult. For example, the first time we used a public washroom, I was repeatedly bumped into by people as I waited for Zac, despite the wide open space right beside me. I wondered in frustration why nobody seemed to respect the invisible bubble of space surrounding me, but I soon realized that people in my new home do not take the extra time to walk around someone; they more often push past if someone is in their direct path. With some time, I grew largely unconcerned with this. (Though on a bad day, it can be the last straw!) I was a guest in a new culture, and it was hard to accept that I was the one who needed to adapt—not those around me.

The reality that many people in China are not that concerned with waiting in line was another experience that frustrated Zac and me, and was also something that my students complained of constantly. In Beijing, one month into our time overseas, Zac waited patiently for some children to finish an activity at a museum, and when they were gone, he walked up to the activity only to be flooded by other children who never gave a thought to waiting. In that moment, as he melted down in frustration, I wondered how I would continue to parent Zac. Most of us parent with some instruction as to how we think it is socially acceptable for our children to behave—this is one of the reasons that we teach them manners in the first place. How could I continue to ask Zac to follow a set of cultural expectations when we lived in a country that did not have the same ones? Did that mean that I needed to throw them out the window? But then what would happen when we returned home? Was it a case of "When in Rome..." or was it as our principal warned at a staff meeting, "If you find yourself behaving in ways that you wouldn't normally in Canada, you need to check yourself"? Or maybe, as I later considered, it was not going to be an either-or type of decision, and I needed to learn to be more fluid with my parenting.

On the other hand, the protectiveness of children that I observed in China was something I was thrilled to discover. Having worried previously about safety issues, it became clear early on that no matter where Zac was, everyone would be looking out for him. Once, when I was out for coffee with a fellow parent, our boys were outside play fighting, which is not as common in this culture. So when an elderly woman carrying a baby saw them fighting, she called out to them and told them off, as she was worried someone would get hurt. As my friend and I laughed from afar at the picture our children painted, the boys plastered big grins on their faces as they continued to pretend punching each other, miming enjoyment to reassure the woman that everybody was fine. My son continues to be told by perfect strangers that he is not wearing enough layers of clothing and that he is going to catch a cold. People point to his untied shoe laces constantly. He is well looked after.

The cell phone culture in China was something I did not love, however. We rarely encountered people walking, riding their bike, or driving their car or even scooter, without their heads down, eyes glued to the little plastic screen that they held in their hand or had positioned on their vehicle. I saw mothers with infants lovingly gaze at their iPhones. I saw couples stare at their phones while on dates. I had students tell me that six hours of daily cell phone use was acceptable but that perhaps eight hours suggested addiction. And I had students tell me that their parents do not listen to them anymore—that dinner time has become simply another time of interruptions and distractions, as parents eat with chopsticks in one hand, their phone in the other. As I looked around us, I realized that I had to be vigilant about ensuring that Zac be in control of the technology he used – rather than the other way around. One family member voiced my thoughts perfectly when she said that she is not as concerned with what her children are using technology for, as much as what they are missing out on while using it.

The roads were another experience to behold, and within days of being in Wuhan, we experienced entering the highway via the exit ramp, driving on the opposite side of the road, and driving on the sidewalks to avoid traffic, horns blaring. The real adjustment came when we returned home each summer and had to sit in traffic like everyone else, although when I am out walking, I never fail to appreciate that in Canada, pedestrians always have the right of way. I very carefully tried my best to have open-minded conversations with Zac as we explored our new world. In our first few months in Wuhan, we sometimes played a game when I felt that Zac (or was it me?) was having a hard time adjusting. In this game, we simply sat and observed everything around us while pointing out not only differences but the similarities. (Some of the cars look different, but they have four wheels, too!). Despite the fact that we were often overwhelmed by differences, we always found more similarities between the two countries.

Our first few months were hard. An early test came the first time that we went to get groceries, when we encountered just how difficult it could be to get things done when you do not speak the language of the country you are living in. After a fun game of charades (during which I seemed to be the only one playing), we got lost in the store, unable to find the exit. We finally left an hour later in frustration, without half of the things that we needed. For the first time, I thought of the practicalities of daily living in China and was appalled at myself for not having really considered them earlier. Now, I can easily get by on what we call "Taxi Mandarin" and use the most basic of commands, whereas Zac's ability to speak the language increases year after year.

My own personal struggle stemmed from the fact that the teachers at my job were all straight out of university, with fewer responsibilities and different ideas of what it means to have a good time. I was not interested in drinking every weekend, and could not even if I had wanted to; I felt isolated from this group of people, who were not much younger than I was—but we were separated by so much more than years. I soon found out that spending time with these co-workers exposed Zac to adult content inappropriate for his age, so, for some time, we were truly on our own. I remember cooking dinner one night and crying silently in the kitchen while maintaining what I hoped sounded like an upbeat conversation with Zac, who was playing Wii in the living room. I remember thinking to myself, as tears spilled down my cheeks: "I'm so lonely. I'm just so lonely." I had not planned for this. I had not even anticipated it.

Despite the initial pain and growth one might expect from such a big change, after several months of adjustment, I realized that moving to Wuhan, China with my son had helped me to discover what I am truly capable of. At twenty-eight years of age, I finally felt settled in my own skin, sure of who I was and what I wanted out of life. In many ways, I thought I had known these things beforehand, but it felt different and more authentic. I finally believed it when I told myself who I was. And then, I didn't need to tell myself anymore.

The decision to move led us to have our share of adventure and discovery. In our first year in China, we went off the beaten path and climbed the Great Wall well outside of Beijing, hiking it peacefully for eight hours straight among beautiful, green surroundings. When we hiked across the Wall the night before, it was pitch black, and I had to reign in the fear that Zac would slip or fall, as it was a long way down. This was to be one of my first challenges as we settled in China: being able to give Zac the freedom to roam and explore while being aware of safety concerns. But I soon realized that I could not control everything, and if we were to hike the Great Wall on Moon Festival and share a piece of mooncake with old and new friends by the light of the moon, some risk would be involved in that adventure. Because of experiences such as these, Zac is now a fairly independent kid.

We did not just contain our experiences to China, however. Travelling as a duo with my son was sometimes overwhelming, particularly as I had never travelled like this before. The first time we backpacked outside of the country, I promptly lost my wallet with every single bank card and credit card I had, along with some cash. This meant the trip had me really thinking on my feet, and although it turned out to be amazing, at one point, I found myself brightly asking Zac in Koh Tao, "Wouldn't it be fun to sleep on the beach tonight?" while I inwardly panicked that the island's internet was down, which would mean accessing funds to our one emergency credit card was impossible. Yet had this not happened, we never would have made a new friend (whom we later visited in Sydney, Australia the following year), who overheard us and stopped to generously offer help.

Through our travels, I managed to lose my camera (and precious pictures of us in Borneo, Malaysia, trekking through the oldest rainforest in the world), had none of my credit cards or bank cards work all throughout Morocco, and missed several flights. Once, I realized mid-taxi ride that I did not have enough in the correct currency to get us to the airport; another time I forgot to bring the hotel address with us while we were out exploring Dubai, resulting in hours of driving in circles as the metre on the taxi kept rising. Although we often travelled with family and friends, many of these situations occurred with just the two of us, and they were overwhelmingly stressful. Frustrated and discouraged, I would usually berate myself that I should have known better, planned better, and been better organized. I wondered if I was cut out for this after all. Such experiences were notably less stressful when other adults were travelling with us, yet when we were on our own, I tried my very best to move past my dismay and to treat these experiences as an opportunity to learn. Zac has certainly learned to go with the flow; he laughs whenever I am forced to spend time yelling at an ATM that will not give me my money. Many times I have wished for an extra adult in our tiny overseas family. (Even if just so I can stop being one for a moment!) Yet although these experiences were difficult, they were also the times when people offered their homes, their cars, their money, their advice, and their time to us, complete strangers. Despite some difficult experiences, travelling alone is now part of our lifestyle, and there's no doubt it's worth every second.

One of the things that I love most about travelling with Zac is that he is exposed to such rich experiences, yet even the decisions of where to travel initially came with a sense of fear and uncertainty that I had to overcome. My family thought I was crazy for wanting to backpack with Zac through developing countries in

Southeast Asia, and I began to question it seriously myself. As Said notes, "[t]here is the motif of Asia as insinuating danger," (57) which is something some of my family members clearly believed. I decided that knowledge was power, and rather than let fear guide my decisions, I researched thoroughly and made informed decisions after speaking to people who had actually travelled to the countries that we would be visiting. Once I did this, I felt much more comfortable about our options, and we had a much better time because of it.

Said encourages us to observe how Asia became known historically in the West and argues that out of this history, including what is learned from "discoverers" such as Marco Polo, "comes a restricted number of typical encapsulations: the journey, the history, the fable, the stereotype, the polemical confrontation. These are the lenses through which the Orient is experienced, and they shape the language, perception, and form of the encounter between East and West" (58). As Said demonstrates, our understanding of history plays a large part in our (mis)understanding of different cultures and countries. I often see such misunderstanding being manifested through and perpetuated by media content and depictions, and I wanted to avoid passing on such seemingly inevitable, engrained prejudices to my son.

What parts of history are told is a selective and often biased process, sometimes very different depending on the national viewpoint from which it is told. Despite one family member telling me, "I would never bring my kids to an underdeveloped country" with the underlying assumption being that it was perhaps irresponsible of me, Zac and I have had very positive experiences in countries that are too often viewed as dangerous and too different. Some of our most significant experiences came when we visited the Killing Fields in Cambodia, and the Ho Chi Minh Tunnels in Vietnam, where Zac got to understand ideas of war and genocide beyond just reading about them in a textbook at school. After seeing children in Cambodia who had very few material items playing with a tire, Zac now has a very different idea of what it means to truly live in poverty. Our travels have also given him the opportunity to reflect on how more materialistic cultures affect happiness levels.

Our trip to Australia and New Zealand was, in contrast, seen as more acceptable. And although I would like to think that going to watch the Sydney Symphony at the Sydney Oprah House was a thrilling exposure to the world of art and music, Zac was asleep by the end of the show. On the other hand, when it has come to connecting with nature, Zac has been fortunate enough over the years to learn about the dangers that animals face (usually at the hands of humans) in a variety of national museums and has had up-close encounters with kangaroos, koalas, pandas, tigers, and endangered orangutans in the wild. We have had the opportunity to play tug-of-war with a Tasmanian devil at the Bonorong Wildlife Sanctuary in Tasmania and to ride elephants in Thailand and camels in the Sahara Desert. However, ensuring that we support the right organizations while participating in these activities can be difficult to determine, and it is an ongoing struggle as we strive to do our homework.

I also use our trips as opportunities to value experiences over things. I cannot deny that a big benefit of living in China for us was the opportunity to escape our consumerist culture back home. Despite the many temptations, on our trips we focus on the simplicity of making memories and try to keep our packs free of extra stuff. Still, the idea of keeping our backpacks light is thrown out the window when it comes to combining our love of books with our love of travelling, as both Zac and I buy one book from each country that we visit. Not only does this grow our book collection, but it gives me peace of mind—I have discovered that when waiting during an airplane delay or buying tickets at a train station in a country whose language I do not speak, I am much more comfortable knowing that Zac is immersed in a book (preferably set in the culture that we are experiencing at the moment or written by a national author) rather than in an iPad.

Even further, as an educator and a mother, I have been able to see first-hand what international travel experience can mean to the world of education. Our trip to the Peace Memorial Park in Hiroshima, Japan, was a deeply moving experience that simply could not have been replicated in a classroom. It has long been questioned whether or not conventional schooling is the best, most meaningful way for most children to learn, to be engaged in their learning, and to retain what it is that they are exploring. Our travels have opened up spaces for learning and have had me questioning traditional schooling and alternative options, both as a teacher and as a parent.

For one of our most worthwhile trips, we spent over a week at an orphanage in Guiyang, China, for children with special needs—most of whom were little girls. Ebenstein notes that China's "missing" girls are one of the unintended consequences of the one-child policy. Another unintended consequence from the policy is that too many children who have special needs are left behind. Although in the city ideas of boys and girls are changing (the national holiday "Boy's Day" has been altered to be more inclusive, now called "Children's Day"), according to my students, rural areas still have strong ideas of preferring a strong, able-bodied son to continue to help with life's work. Although there have been recent reforms to China's one-child policy, a Chinese co-worker came into the office one day and told me that she would not be at school for a while because she was pregnant. When she saw my face light up as I reached in to give her a hug, she backed away and told me, "I don't need the happy congratulations. I can't keep this baby if I want to keep my job." My co-worker already had a son, and I was dismayed to hear that even when employed by a Canadian International school, such a policy was in place. It was not fair. Just as unfair is that despite doing similar work and often working longer hours, my Chinese co-workers are paid far less than Canadian teachers. The privileges that we have as foreigners working in this developing country are undeniable. We are paid according to our nationality, not our workload.

I had always wanted to involve Zac in significant volunteer work. Yet in Canada, I consistently came up against closed doors: Zac was always proclaimed too young, as there were many safety rules in place for minors. But in China, the possibilities seemed to be endless. Another year, we attended a Stepping Stones retreat in Anhui, China, for "left behind" children—children who live in rural areas while their parents live and work elsewhere, usually in a big city, such as Shanghai. The children live at their school and share tiny beds in tiny rooms. We arrived prepared only to teach the children English but it became so much more than that.

According to Michael Reist, the author of *Raising Boys in a New Kind of World*, due to the way our society constructs gender norms, boys are "not given many chances [to be nurturing and empathetic]" (150) because these traits are often seen as feminine characteristics rather than human ones. Reist claims that one of the best ways to give boys this chance is to "create opportunities for them to be around younger children, even babies and infants" (150). In both Anhui and Guiyang, Zac was able to have this experience, and I do feel it made a significant difference in fostering empathy in Zac at a young age. In particular, it was incredible to watch Zac interact with the children at the orphanage and alter his communication skills. No longer could a typical question and response conversation be carried; he would need to engage with these (mostly non-verbal) children while not expecting a response in return. Yet Zac also understood that it was important that these children were shown love. Feeling awkward and shy at first, he learned how to communicate in a way that felt right to him, sometimes with words and other times with actions. (The children had a trampoline, and Zac and another boy would jump together, with big smiles spread across their faces as they looked across at one other).

AN ALTERED MINDSET

Doing this on my own can be tough. The decision to move and stay overseas is a difficult one, as is the decision about when to return home. Back in Wuhan, two years into our time overseas, I struggled as I tried to figure out where we would go next. I knew that we needed to move on, but which way to turn? To a new culture in a new country? Back home? Another city in China? I could not decide, and the indecision became overwhelming. As I now realize, there was no "right" decision—I have realized that no matter which way I might have turned, everything would have been okay, because we would have made it okay. Nonetheless, at that time, I felt pressured to make the best decision that I possibly could. As I cried in a cold staff washroom all by myself, I criticized myself not only for still not having a permanent job or a permanent home, but also for not having a permanent man in my life yet, either. A man, I reasoned, would have eased this transition, helped me to feel better, and given me moral, emotional, and financial support. I thought of others with this level of support and yearned to have the same experience. Not only was I a mother who made tough choices around the well-being and education of my son, but I was also a woman who wanted someone to look out for her, too. Sometimes, I still get the occasional pang as I think of how nice it could be to have a partner in my life, but this has become increasingly rare. And at thirty-two years of age, I still think that I have a long time to find that—if I want it.

I cherish the independence that comes from single parenthood. Bzostek notes that

> Results ... indicate that mothers with more financial independence (those with only one child, those who went back to school, those who are employed, and those living in cities with generous welfare benefits) are less likely to be in new co-resident partnerships. This finding is consistent with marriage market theory, which suggests that greater financial independence allows mothers to prolong their search rather than "settling" for a new partner who may not meet their standards. (qtd. in Bzostek, McLanahan and Carlson)

I take my responsibility as a mother very seriously, and being someone's life partner is another form of responsibility. I know that I am not fitting into the culturally expected timetable in which people typically enter into marriage, and I am not sure why that feels so normal for me when it is not viewed by everyone else as normal. This begs the question, what exactly is "normal," anyways?

According to Mary McIntosh, social anxieties about lone mothering and ideologies about the family are two sides of the same coin and there is a pervasive belief that "[t]he single mother is free and irresponsible, sexually promiscuous and available to men" (154). It seems that my single parenthood is threatening to the so-called ideal nuclear family. Nevertheless, I revel in the freedom that I have, and despite some views that I may be disadvantaged, I consider myself to be extremely privileged. Although we may be living off of one income, I know many expatriate families living here in China that are four-person families, with two parents living from one (typically the mother's) income. Zac and I travel much more than these families do, although the responsibility of all decisions weighs on my shoulders alone. Something I love about being a single parent is the fact that I do not need to consider someone else's opinion about my own educational or career opportunities, or about what is best for Zac. Although I seek out and read mountains of information and often consult with trusted friends and family members, the choice of where to move and when is, ultimately, up to me, and Zac of course.

Having a job that supports and respects our family is essential. I know that may seem like a luxury, but as a friend of mine said to me a couple of years ago, if I believe there is something better out there and insist on continuing to look for it, I will eventually find it. What led us to Shanghai, in part, was that I wanted more teaching experience, but after my two years in Wuhan, I also recognized that I needed an employer who could respect my role as a mother more completely. And although there were things that I loved about Zac's school (he was in a class of eight students!), I did not feel Zac's education in Wuhan was ideal. Although we contemplated job offers in London, England, and La Estrella, Colombia, I felt that it would benefit Zac to have more exposure to Mandarin, and we both agreed that staying in China had its benefits. One thing that I have realized on this path is that I have gained the courage to keep searching for a life that embodies my ideals. But it can be hard—I have so many. When there are bumps in the road, I wonder in frustration if it is fair to Zac to keep searching for better, although I am searching it out for him as well.

Moving to Shanghai allowed us to still visit friends in Wuhan occasionally. This eased our transition as Zac made new friends—always a stressful part in moving—but the friends we have had the chance to make are incredible. (And we now have them scattered all around the world). However, when after a year in Shanghai, I was contemplating returning home, Zac was adamant that we stay another year. Although I had my doubts, I listened to him, and this led to an amazing opportunity—one year later, we are now on the same campus. Although I looked forward to teasing him mercilessly in the halls, he has flipped the tables on me several times. But the best has been working in the staff office and knowing when he comes down the hall because of his signature whistle or hearing him laugh from his locker, right next to my office. We have lunches together often, though for Zac, the allure is in avoiding cafeteria food and enjoying ordered-in food, rather than my company. He even comes to visit me in the office occasionally, whenever he wants money for a drink or a snack. It's touching.

Consistently moving outside of my comfort zone forces me to understand my capabilities and become a more present and connected parent. It can be a lot of pressure knowing that I am the one who has to ensure that I meet almost all of my son's needs, without the ease of family and friends to supplement it all, but the rewards in our relationship have been immense, and I treasure the closeness that Zac and I have established. But I work at our relationship all the time. As Pollack notes, "a boy's natural language is usually action language ... empathy and love can emerge simply from a shared game of baseball, a joint building project, or a walk around the block" (100). Although I have often enjoyed playing soccer, tag, or hide and seek with my child, it is the walking together—whether walking our rescue dog, Lucky, or walking to and from school—that gives us the time we need to slow down and share information and thoughts about our day. When we see or hear something upsetting, we use that time to talk about it. This includes the many homeless people that we see on the streets, most frequently with a disability of some kind. In response, we started an Act of Kindness Project, which has simply morphed into our new lifestyle and includes making sandwiches for the homeless or buying milk tea for the ladies we see every time we cross the bridge to the subway. Most important to me are the smiles that I see Zac exchange with those we meet. In Dan Harris's book *10% Happier*, he looks at evidence that explains how "[b]rain scans showed that acts of kindness registered more like eating chocolate than ... fulfilling an obligation. The same pleasure centers lit up when we received a gift as when we donated to charity. Neuroscientists referred to it as 'the warm glow' effect. Research also showed that everyone ... saw their health improve if they did volunteer work" (Harris 184). I see a noticeable difference in Zac because of these changes. For example, in a surprise trip to Barcelona to bring Zac to watch his favourite soccer team in action (they lost), Zac was about to start drinking a soda he had just gotten with excitement. (It was not available in China but had been a favourite back home). As we approached a homeless woman, he did not give a second thought to simply twisting the cap back onto the drink and handing it to her with a grin. It was automatic, without hesitation, and completely beautiful.

I know that I don't do everything right, but I try to do some things right through a reflection of the privilege that we have been granted. I have raised my son to advocate for those less fortunate than us and to ensure that he understands social justice in many of its components. Some days, he is a better feminist than I am. One thing I have always believed is that if I think my son should know something about the world, I cannot rely on anyone but myself to teach it to him. As Jennifer Ajandi points out, "single mother households may be more constructive and healthy than some traditional heterosexual and two parent households" (qtd. in Lee 411). My son is a thriving, socially aware young man, and I am often touched to have compliments on the person he is becoming, or to receive positive comments on our relationship.

A couple of years ago, we were sitting down to breakfast in Phnom Penh, Cambodia, right across from the Kings Palace during the Kings Fathers Cremation. As Zac and I munched on our breakfast, we talked about our options for the day. One thing we had discussed was visiting the Killing Fields, a site where many Cambodian people were killed. I had been concerned that this may be too much for Zac but had spoken to colleagues before going who had reassured me that the experience was not frightening so much as historical, tragic, and moving. As I asked Zac what he thought, I became aware of a man, perhaps in his fifties, watching us. We began chatting with him about our vacations, and, as it always happens, he asked me if I was travelling with my brother. When I explained that Zac was my son, the man was shocked. He laughed, and said, "Well I was listening to the way you two were talking, and I certainly never talked to my children like that! I didn't ask them, I told them." The surprise that we are met with when others overhear our conversations is something that always makes me grin. I take so much delight from the way Zac and I communicate that I simply cannot imagine it being any different.

I have learned, and am continuing to learn, that as a person and as a mother, I can do anything—that in fact, it is not our children who hold us back, but our own preconceptions. I remember overhearing an American couple discussing their travel plans on a bus from Phnom Penh to Siem Reap, Cambodia, and they were very clear that they had chosen not to have children yet because they did not want to be held back from their travels. I could not help but grin as I sat next to Zac continuing to read my book; he was immersed in his own beside me, excited to explore ruins in only a few hours.

Travelling with my kid has made each trip that much more meaningful. In moving to China and travelling often, I began to challenge some of the ideas that I previously had as a parent, and I think I have become a better parent because of it. In Tasmania, Australia the old adage "Don't get in the car with strangers" became very different when I gratefully accepted a ride from another mother with whom we had been chatting at the park. I had already asked her for directions, but when she drove by us after we left, and we were still clearly lost, I trusted my intuition, and we got in the car with her and her two daughters. I realized that rather than hard and fast rules for being safe, Zac also needed to learn to trust his intuition. Similarly, when we were in Christchurch, New Zealand, on the last night of our trip, we spoke to a sweet couple in their 60s, who had just sent their grandchildren back home. They invited my mother, Zac, and me over for a BBQ and to sleep in real beds. (And after the three of us had slept in the campervan for eight nights straight, we were pretty excited about this!) We smiled with delight and had an incredible evening, and we keep in touch to this day.

Still, nothing about this life has been easy. I have started to get tired of asking myself, "What about next year?" I know people who live their entire lives this way and shift their families from continent to continent. It seems glamourous and exciting, and in many ways it is, but I am not sure that I want to be one of them. Yet if my time in China has taught me anything, it is that our lives do not have to be an either-or experience. I think that our future will become a meld of these two options (living overseas versus settling down in Canada), which would allow me, I hope, to provide Zac with a settled base while we continue to embrace our curiosity of the world. I am grateful for the life that we have created together, and I look forward to so many more experiences—World Wide Opportunities on Organic Farms (WWOOFING) in Germany, biking across the Netherlands, building a school in Zimbabwe, homeschooling, or sailing the Atlantic onboard a "school that floats" for one year are just a few of the possibilities that we have talked about. But I also look forward to going back home and being with those who love us best. Yet although we often miss our life back home, Zac also knows how fortunate he is to have explored so many countries and cultures. In fact, when on our road trip through New Zealand, we came across a chalkboard sign by the beach that asked, "What do you want to do before you die?" Zac promptly wrote down, "Explore the world."

I can say with complete certainty that my life, and my son's, would not be as wonderful as it is now had I not raised Zac as a single parent, given my choices at the time. Perhaps this sounds like a bold claim, but as MacCollum and Golumbok point out, "children in fatherless families experience ... more interaction with their mother, and perceive her as more available and dependable ... the children's social and emotional development [is] not negatively affected by the absence of a father, although boys in father-absent families showed more feminine but no less masculine characteristics of gender role behaviour" (x). When feminine characteristics are often associated with traits such as kindness, sensitivity, and empathy, I can only agree with Ajandi that there are "many rewards and possibilities that make this [single mother] family status desirable and rich with possibilities" (410). What is most important to me is that my son is well loved, with an abundance of positive role models, both men and women, to help guide him as he grows into the young man that he is becoming. Although this unconventional way of single mothering can have its challenges, it is also exhilarating, rewarding, and extremely satisfying. Our life is its own reward.

NOTES

[1]Bachelor of English, Specialized Honours and Bachelor of Education (primary and junior).

WORKS CITED

Ajandi, Jennifer "Single Mothers by Choice: Disrupting Dominant Discourses of the Family through Social Justice Alternatives." *International Journal of Child, Youth and Family Studies* 43.4 (2011): 410-431. Web. 2 Mar. 2015.

Bzostek, Sarah H., Sara S. McLanahan, and Marcia J. Carlson. "Mothers' Repartnering after a Nonmarital Birth." *Social Forces* 90.3 (2012): n.pag. Web. 23 Mar. 2015.

Ebenstein, Avraham. "The 'Missing Girls' of China and the Unintended Consequences of the One Child Policy." *The Journal of Human Resources* 45.1 (2010): 87-115. Web. 27 Feb. 2015.

Harris, Dan. *10% Happier*. New York: HarperCollins, 2014. Print.

Lewis, C. M. et al. "Fighting Stigma: An Adolescent Mother Takes Action." *Journal of Women and Social Work* 22.3 (2007): 302-306. Web. 25 Mar. 2015.

Macculum, Fiona, and Susan Golombok. "Children Raised in Fatherless Families from Infancy: A Follow-Up of Children of Lesbian and Single Heterosexual Mothers at Early Adolescence." *Journal of Child Psychology and Psychiatry* 45.8 (2004): 1407–1419. Web. 22 Mar. 2015.

McIntosh, Mary. "Social Anxieties about Lone Motherhood and Ideologies of the Family: Two Sides of the Same Coin." In *Good Enough Mothering? Feminist Perspectives on Lone Mothering*. Ed. Elizabeth Bortolaia Silva. New York: Routledge, 2003. Print.

Pollack, William. *Real Boys*. New York: Henry Holt, 1998. Print.

Reist, Michael. *Raising Boys in a New Kind of World*. Toronto: Dundurn Press, 2011. Print.

Said, Edward. *Orientalism*. Toronto: Random House of Canada Ltd., 1978. Print.

Silva, Elizabeth Bortolaia, ed. *Good Enough Mothering? Feminist Perspectives on Lone Mothering*. New York: Routledge, 2003. Print.

8. The Lone Ranger

Single Mothering, Then and Now

B. LEE MURRAY

THE SOCIO-CULTURAL NORMS and values regarding single parent families are in flux, as the number of single-parent households has almost tripled in the last two decades. Mothers constitute the majority of individuals heading one-parent families and parenting on their own. Single mothers, to some degree, still carry a stigma of shame and blame. By the dawn of the twenty-first century, single mothering began to be seen as more of a lifestyle choice. However, the notion of it being optional is still mostly attributed to mothers who are able to support themselves and their children. My experience of becoming a single mom/divorced woman occurred in the early 1990s, when there was still a degree of stigma and suspicion surrounding the experience. As a result, I felt related feelings of shame and self-blame. Single mothering was not a lifestyle choice for me at that time; however, over the last twenty years, I have come to embrace my "single mom" identity. This paper explores my personal growth and change along with the socio-cultural and socio-political changes that have occurred over the last two decades.

SINGLE MOTHERING THEN

Divorce was definitely not in my life plan. I honestly thought it would never happen to me. I must have believed that people just limp along forever together and that unless something catastrophic happens, they just keep limping. And so I kept limping, and the catastrophe came. It did not really come out of the blue. The clouds slowly built up, the wind got stronger, and the environment became chilly, dark, and ominous. I saw the storm gathering, but when it hit, I was still surprised and unprepared. Even after the storm hit, I told no one. I wanted to pretend that everything was alright. I did not want people to know that I had failed. I did not want people to know I was undesirable. I kept it a secret as long as I could. Breaking the news to my family and friends was extremely difficult, but it did not hold a candle to telling my children. I wanted more than anything not to deliver that message. I wished for a miracle to make everything okay or, at least, to allow us to continue limping and still cross the finish line.

It is moving day. The kids have gone to stay with their grandparents. I watch as the movers load up all our belongings and empty out the mansion in the wilderness. The movers keep commenting on how difficult it must be to leave this beautiful home and yard. I just nod, but I think, "This is not a home; this is only a house, a house built in an attempt to make us happy as a family." I cry and smoke most of the day. I was never a good smoker. I only smoked at work to fit in, and I needed to keep my smokes in the fridge, or they would dry out before I smoked them all. They don't have a chance to dry out now. I am "chain smoking," and I can't eat. I am awake for eighteen to twenty hours a day and rarely sit down. I have lost twenty pounds, and I am on my way to losing ten more. I blame myself for my predicament, and I am too ashamed to tell anyone my husband has left me. Mixed in with that is anger. But because it is mixed up in a pot of emotion, my anger is fragmented. Pieces of anger are mixed in with pieces of shame and blame. The anger never comes together; it is never whole and, thus, has no power. I think that I am also afraid of my anger. If the angry pieces start coming together and gaining force and power, I will probably explode, and the anger will leech out from behind the mask.

MY SECRET

It took me a long time to tell my colleagues about my marital separation, and even then, I told only a few. The news spread like a prairie fire. Most people were very surprised; they had no idea that my husband and I had been having problems. Most people thought we had a great relationship. How would they have known any differently? I wore the mask well; I never complained. I convinced them that everything was okay in my attempt to convince myself of the same, as I projected the image of a happy couple, a happy family, a good wife and, a good mother.

My mask was cracking. My relationship with my husband was fractured; our family was breaking apart. The image of "good wife" was shattered, and the image of "good mother" was tenuous. In *The Mask of Motherhood*, Susan Maushart explains that all masks are props for pretending. Whether comic or tragic, a mask projects uniformity, predictability, and stasis: "Masks portray emotion inert and unmixed in a tradeoff of range for impact" (1). I needed my mask to stay in control. This self-control helped me deny, repress, and misrepresent how I was really feeling and how distorted and chaotic my experience was. Maushart makes sense of this as she recognizes the construction of a situationally appropriate mask as both an advantage and a curse: "The critical distance ... lies between self-control and self-delusion" (2).

I had tipped the scale and fallen into self-deception and self-delusion. But as my mask began to crack, I had this fear that everybody would know. They would know that I did not have it together. I was not happy, I was discontent, and I hated where I had ended up. My life was not perfect; my marriage was a farce; and my children were hurting. I was out of control, and everybody knew it. I still wanted to hide the fact that I was separated, about to be divorced and alone. I was ashamed of where I had ended up, and I blamed myself for my predicament. But there was no turning back—to be or not to be separated and divorced was out of my control. Yet I still tried to hide and avoid the issue.

I am in line to pay at a busy bookstore. The book I am holding is titled Rebuilding: When Your Relationship Ends, *by Bruce Fisher and Robert Alberti. I have really been struggling since the separation, and someone has recommended that I read this book. I hold the front cover close to me so that no one can read the title. I don't want anyone to see the title, and then realize that I am probably a dejected and lonely woman. I usually get into conversations with other people when I am in line, but not today. Someone might ask me what book I am purchasing. I finally get to the cashier, and the young girl behind the counter announces, "My mom is divorced, and she found this book very helpful." I smile at her lamely, and I am mortified that everyone in the bookstore now knows the truth about me. If I could only speak, I might lie and say it is for a friend. How sad is that?*

I read Fisher and Alberti's book, and some things made sense to me. They outline a nineteen-step process of adjustment to the loss of a love relationship. The first few building blocks seemed the hardest. These included denial, fear, loneliness, guilt and rejection. I tried to work through the steps and move up the pyramid. One step on the second level is called openness and is described as coming out from behind a mask or removing the mask. This resonated with me. The authors explain how a mask that we choose is probably appropriate, but a mask that chooses us is probably not. A mask chooses us because we are not free to expose the feelings that are underneath. And in that sense, the mask controls us.

I recognized that I was wearing a mask to protect myself and also to hide how I was feeling from others. My mask portrayed someone who was strong and in control, someone who was not wounded, someone who could manage the situation. But on the inside, behind the mask, I felt dejected, unlovable, and ashamed. I felt as if I were a failure—a failure as a wife but mostly as a mother. I felt helpless and confused. My mask provided a safe emotional distance, but it was also getting in the way of connecting with others and, perhaps, getting the support that I so desperately needed. Reading *Rebuilding* by Fisher and Alberti helped me recognize that my mask was preventing closeness, intimacy, and safety with another person—the very things I longed for. What is more, my mask was also keeping me from knowing myself. By blaming myself and portraying a strong exterior, I was denying my hurt and loneliness. But I had worn a mask for a long time. I was socialized within my family and through normative sexist discourse to portray more positive emotions than I was actually feeling. Also taking off the mask could have put me at risk to be hurt or rejected again. I was losing my inner self and lacked an identity. The shame and self-blame surrounding the divorce was overwhelming at times. However, I was learning that my mask had become somewhat inappropriate and unproductive. Upon reflection, I also realized that I was in the role of single mom even when married, as my husband was away from home for extended periods of time, and I was left to my own devices to manage the home, the children, my work, and all the related responsibilities.

It is now almost two years since our separation. We have been in court for three days. I didn't know divorce was so difficult. We take a break from the proceedings, and I go outside for air. I am surprised to see my soon-to-be ex-husband walking towards me. I look at him and feel sorry for him. Why? I go to say something to him, but he just looks at me with disdain and crosses to the other side of the street. I feel it again. I haven't felt like this for a long time. The shame and blame return.

SHAME AND BLAME

On a cognitive level, I knew it did not make sense. Where did this shame come from? Was it separate from my self-blame or connected? Why was it that his presence or any encounter with him made me question myself, doubt myself, and dislike myself? Perhaps, it was because he held my secrets. He was the only one who knew how unhappy, bitchy, and discontented I was. He was the only one who knew how badly I struggled and how frustrated and angry I was. He frequently accused me of hiding my ugly side from others. Maybe I needed to understand why I felt that a part of what he accused me of might be true. Was my shame about not being true to myself and not being the person I wanted to be or was it about not wanting others to disapprove of me? Was my shame connected to the normative discourse related to being a "good mother" and a "good wife?"

When the divorce settlement comes out many months later, it is fair and equitable. I don't feel sorry for him anymore. I feel understood, legitimate, and deserving. Suddenly, the word "divorce" doesn't sound so bad. I am a divorced woman, a free woman, an independent woman and, most importantly, a single mom. Custody was never an issue. I am truly a single mom. I can parent my way. I can merely say "thank you" when people tell me how great my kids are.

This sense of legitimacy and entitlement removed the shame and blame to some degree and, for the moment at least, I did not feel the need to keep the divorce a secret any longer. I began to tell people with some degree of pride that I was, in fact, divorced. I realized that the shame and blame were partly of my own making. But if I felt shame, and I blamed myself for my circumstances, it was a call to examine those circumstances and begin to understand the societal climate of the time, including the normative discourse related to being a "good wife" and a "good mother."

I was very aware of the normative discourse of the time that characterized single mothers as personally pathological and undesirable and, in a broader context, as neglectful of their children and destructive of their children's "normal upbringing." There was a false and simplistic view of single moms being dependent on the system, a view that permeated throughout social services, education, health care, and the broader community (Bashevkin; Jones-DeWeaver; Sidel). Within this discourse, single mothers were blamed and made responsible for all that society deemed morally wrong and undesirable; their children become scapegoats for a perceived increase in crime rates and a breakdown of social cohesion (Ajandi). Single women were blamed for their circumstances and their success was often hidden. Blaming the victim was a political strategy to hide the inequitable distribution of resources and power (Carniol). This attitude was discriminatory based on family status. At that time, I was very aware that people perceived my children as coming from a "broken home." What was not recognized was my resilience and resistance to the discourse that labelled our family as dysfunctional, as I moved forward to raise my children in a non-traditional, one-parent household.

SINGLE (GRAND) MOTHERING NOW

In general, I no longer feel the shame, blame, and guilt related to being a single mom and a divorced woman. Perhaps, that is because there are more women joining the ranks of single motherhood, whether by choice or by chance. There are many more women who are willing to tell their single mothering stories; and perhaps with each story that is told, the shame, blame, guilt, and stigma decrease. I reflect on my experience in an attempt to sort out the reasons behind this change, not only from a personal perspective but also from a socio-political and socio-cultural one. I also wonder if things have really changed that much. Although single mothers seem to be more accepted, are they still regarded as inferior to parents who have maintained their heterosexual relationships with their partners and, thus, their dual-parent households? *Have things changed?*

Approximately two-thirds of Canadian mothers work; however, the structures of the family and the workplace have not changed substantially (Almey). Mothers with male partners still perform approximately twice as much childcare and housework as their partners (Bianchi, Wright, and Raley). According to sociologist Barbara Rothman, men's responsibility in parenting, when partnered with a woman, has increased only slightly, and more and more women are raising children as sole parents. Mothers, in particular single mothers, realize that they are working a twenty-four-hour shift when it comes to raising their children. Furthermore, the patriarchal norms of Canadian and other societies still stress that mothers should devote their time to their children at their own expense. Despite the increasing pervasiveness of feminist thought over time, it is still overwhelmingly women who are raising children. However, many single mothers feel fortunate—even privileged—to have the opportunity and freedom to parent children on their own, without the need to negotiate parenting approaches with a partner. They can be the decision makers and raise children according to their own values and beliefs; this independence often contributes to an increase in self-esteem and self-worth (Ajandi).

According to Rothman, single motherhood is a place, a position that one occupies. She also states that single mothering *has* changed and is no longer viewed as a tragedy but as "a way of life, a perfectly ordinary way to raise children" (324). I do not know if it is viewed as a perfectly ordinary way to raise children, but the perception of dysfunction surrounding the single mother household is changing. In fact, Jennifer Ajandi puts forward the notion that "single mother households may be more constructive and healthy than some traditional heterosexual and two parent households" (411). Ajandi also finds that single mothers no longer apologize or feel ashamed or inferior to two-parent families; on the contrary, they thrive and are grateful and proud that they and their children are contributing members of society and play a role in advocacy and social justice.

EXTENSIVE VERSUS INTENSIVE MOTHERING

Sociologist Karen Christopher attributes part of this change to a shift away from the idealist notion of intensive mothering to a more realistic idea of extensive mothering. Intensive mothering, according to another sociologist Sharon Hayes, is defined by three themes: "First, the mother is the central caregiver; second, such mothering requires lavishing copious amounts of time, energy, and material resources on the child; and finally, the mother regards mothering as more important than her paid work" (8). Hayes also indicates that the ideology of intensive mothering is constructed "as child-centred, expert guided, emotionally absorbing, labour intensive and financially expensive" (8). By comparison, Christopher defines "extensive mothering" as a result of navigating between the "intensive-mother" and the "ideal-worker" ideologies; it is how employed mothers construct their own accounts of good mothering. In her study, married mothers explained extensive mothering as the delegation of childcare to others and reframed good mothering as being responsible and in control of their children's well-being. However, single mothers were less accountable to the intensive mothering model and emphasized the importance of employment for both themselves and their children while rejecting the long hours of the ideal-worker model.

As single mothers, we know that we have to work; therefore, perhaps we feel less guilt for doing so. The obvious justification is economic need, but according to Christopher, most single mothers would work for pay even if they did not have to because their jobs were personally fulfilling or they needed a break from caregiving.

I struggle with this because in academe, it is very hard to reject the "ideal-worker" model. It appears that in order to cope with the demands of both academic life and family life, women make the choice to either reduce their work hours or limit their careers (Becker and Moen; Castaneda and Isgro). The academic work model usually includes a sixty-hour work week, travel, and concentrated work time, and family life is generally discouraged (Mason and Goulden). University settings have been known to be "hostile," "toxic" (Fothergill and Feltey 9), and "chilly" (Williams) towards women, especially mothers. The pre-tenure years are notably filled with anxiety and stress.

I tried to mother during those first five years in academe as I strived to achieve tenure and I felt pressured, exhausted, and as if I were failing at both endeavours. Trying to do it all was a recipe for failure or, at the very least, some form of disaster in the making. Mothering encompasses a million things and so does academe. As mothers in academe, we do not often silence academe, but we often "hide the baby" (Walden), which is associated with feelings of failure and guilt. We are reluctant to talk about our struggles to do it all, to cope, and to still look good with at least half of our hair in place and our teeth brushed. Alice Fothergill and Kathryn Feltey identify this in the context of the following dilemma for mothers in academe: "We want to excel in both realms, but there is no structural support for those goals" (228). As a consequence, there are more women pursuing PhD degrees but fewer women pursuing tenure-track positions (Fothergill and Feltey), and women are still a minority in the full-professor world (Castaneda and Isgro).

Rejecting the ideal-worker model is an option but will it limit our careers as single mothers? Or can we delegate caregiving tasks to others (without guilt, of course) and still remain ultimately responsible for our children? And can we also justify and enjoy our employment based on our own needs for fulfillment and balance in our lives? Promotion to full professor is the next step for me, but I often contemplate not bothering. My colleagues encourage me to set my sights on the full professor gold ring to improve my salary and pension. I understand their point, but the climb, the hoops, the CV building, the grant writing, the publishing, the research, the community development, and project expansion all seem quite onerous and overwhelming at the moment.

If it is difficult for a married woman (especially a married woman with children) to succeed in academe, imagine what it is like for a single mother with children. I agree with Jane Juffer in that the pressure in academe to show self-sufficiency as a single mom is intense. Although Juffer points out that single mothers are "domestic intellectuals" and the "new darlings of popular culture" and the media, members of the legal system and medical field still assert that heterosexual couples make the best parents. For single mothers, proving and governing themselves depends on their ability to be totally independent (Juffer).

The grand narrative of employed women does not address gender and motherhood. It does not reflect the messiness, complexity, and multiplicity of mothers' lives, nor does it address the challenges and struggles most employed mothers face. As single mothers navigate between the ideal-worker model and extensive mothering, they begin to write their own narratives to justify their employment as they reconcile the tension between their identities as mothers and workers. Single mothers often see employment as making them better mothers; employment not only provides financial benefits but enables single mothers to serve as role models for their children (Johnson and Swanson). I believe that I have been a role model for my children, and they have developed a strong work ethic as a result. Often as a single mother, I have reconciled my busy work life with the fact that my children have survived and are thriving in many ways. I do not see them as trophies, but as independent individuals who have done well and are succeeding in society. They appear to be happy, responsible, well adjusted, involved in healthy relationships with family, friends and significant others—and most days, they like me. They are happily married, and I would not want anything to happen to their relationships or any one of them to become a single parent by chance, as was my experience. This makes me wonder if I still maintain that bias, that need for a happy relationship with a significant partner. Or have relationships changed, especially for those of us who have learned to embrace single mothering over time and wish to maintain that approach as parents and grandparents? Are relationships changing?

I look around and admire the ivy growing along the trellis and enjoy the sun on my face. I am outside at a local restaurant waiting for Susan, a friend since high school, to arrive. We don't see each other as often as we would like, and we immediately become deeply engrossed in our conversation upon her arrival in an attempt to catch up on all the news and the happenings in our lives, including our children and grandchildren. We talk about a close friend of ours who has just recently lost her husband, and we are both struck by the profound sadness she is experiencing. Her husband died suddenly of a heart attack just as they were planning their retirement. Susan and I are silent for a moment and then Susan says, "I really hope nothing happens to Bob [her husband-partner], God forbid, but if it did I would never live with another man... a woman perhaps."

I am a bit surprised but also relieved that my wish not to live with another man may not be as weird as I thought. But live with another woman, I don't think that would work for me either. And then I startle myself. That is exactly what I am doing!

I live with my youngest son Jordan, who has Down syndrome, and his caregiver-nanny, Sarah, and I really enjoy our lifestyle. Although my son is basically independent now, and Sarah no longer needs to be his caregiver, she continues to live with us, and we have become friends. Sarah is now employed full time in a special care home, so we share household tasks.

I like the sense of freedom to "do my own thing" and to make all the decisions related to parenting and managing a household. Jordan is easy to get along with and just OCD enough (like me) to keep the house tidy most of the time. My three older children are married with children of their own, and I care for my grandchildren whenever I can. Having them for sleepovers is the highlight of my life. I feel the freedom to do that because I live without a partner. But I also realize that if my partner also happened to be the grandparent of these little darlings, then it would be different. However, I did not stay married to him, and despite the anguish of the divorce, I believe that was definitely the best decision... for all of us. As Rothman so eloquently states "People should marry and stay married because—and only because—they love each other.

Marriage is a central crucial relationship, too important to waste on the wrong person" (327). I do not believe people should or must strive to get married, but if they do, it is a huge decision and commitment, especially when it is not their first marriage.

I am in a long-term relationship with someone who also has a son at home with Down syndrome; primarily for that reason, we have decided not to cohabitate. This creates different kinds of problems in our relationship, but for the most part, it works for me. I have been "on my own" and a "single mom" for a long time, and it would be difficult to teach this old dog new tricks. Our relationship situation raises eyebrows sometimes, as most people who do not know us assume we are married or, at the very least, are living together.

So, perhaps, it is not so much that single mothering has changed but that relationships have changed. "Examining single motherhood is less about the motherhood end of it—hard work and rewarding—and more about marriage, arguably also hard work and considerably less rewarding" (Rothman 327). There has been a definite decline in marriage and an increase in divorce over the last several decades. Perhaps, the meaning of marriage has changed, as it has become less significant practically and more important symbolically (Rothman). Marriage is now much less about sex, cohabitation, and raising children than it used to be, and there are now very few differences between the rich and the poor regarding their attitudes and values towards marriage (Edin and Kefalas).

And perhaps that is the difference for me. I no longer feel the need to necessarily be in a relationship, and I no longer feel the stigma of being a single mom (or a single grandmother, for that matter). Sure it would be nice to have a little assistance from a partner when my grandchildren visit, but I also have the opportunity to grandparent my way and drop everything in order to care for them and play with them when they are around. I have come to enjoy the freedom and independence of being a single mom, and I no longer feel shame or blame for my experience; it has ceased to be my situation or my circumstance. Single mothering is an experience that is challenging at times but is also very rewarding, as it offers many opportunities and possibilities.

CONCLUSION

In the previous century, single mothers were referred to as unwed mothers, widows, and deserted or divorced wives (Brady). They were defined in terms of their relationship or lack thereof with another person or partner but not as an individual, woman, or mother. The dominant discourse of mothering and norms surrounding the nuclear family continues to reinforce, define, and categorize single mothers as "other" (Ajandi). Because single mothers do not fall into the traditional heteronormative conceptualization of the family, they become the undesirable "other" mother. Single mothers are often seen as marginalized and vulnerable victims who rely on social services to support their children (Brady) and their strength and self-reliance often go unnoticed. If these qualities are noticed, suddenly the single mother becomes a hero or saint (Sidel), who was able to overcome insurmountable obstacles. Typically, very real socio-political and socio-cultural issues are ignored or go unrecognized.

Single mothering is complex and messy, and it is also wonderful, rewarding, and even desirable. Single mothering may be difficult, but it is also rich with possibility. There is an alternate discourse emerging, and it is ours to construct. Susan Maushart challenged us to construct or to de-construct motherhood in 1999, and I believe that challenge remains relevant today, particularly as it applies to single mothers:

> Motherhood lies—today, as it has always done—at the very core of the experience of being female. The bearing and raising of children is no longer our inevitable biosocial destiny. Yet it remains the single most potent tie that binds the diversity of our experience as women. Whatever else it may or may not be, motherhood is non-negotiably ours to construct—or to deconstruct. (Maushart 241)

We need to create a new narrative of single mothers that reflects the strengths and possibilities of single mothering; challenges the dominant discourse and recognizes the positive impacts of the experience; recognizes that children can thrive in single mother households; supports the positive characteristics of single mothering, as opposed to the negative consequences of single mothering put forth by the dominant discourse; and recognizes single mothers and their children as legitimate family units. I am a lone ranger, but I am not alone; I do not feel lonely in my single mother status. I feel independent and autonomous, and my children seem to be doing okay. So I say, "Hi-Ho, Silver!" and gallop forward along with my fellow single mothers as we co-create this new narrative.

Parts of this chapter were adapted from my PhD dissertation. Please see: Murray, B. Lee, Secrets of Mothering, *Diss. University of Saskatchewan, 2010. Print.*

WORKS CITED

Ajandi, Jennifer "Single Mothers by Choice: Disrupting Dominant Discourses of the Family through Social Justice Alternatives." *International Journal of Child, Youth and Family Studies* 43.4 (2011): 410-431. Print.

Almey, Marcia. "Women in Canada: Work Chapter Updates." *Statistics Canada*. Statistics Canada, 20 Apr. 2007. Web. 12 May 2014.

Bashevkin, Sylvia. *Welfare Hot Buttons: Women, Work, and Social Policy Reform*. Toronto: U of Toronto P, 2002. Print.

Becker, Penny Edgell, and Phyllis Moen. "Scaling Back: Dual-Earner Couples' Work-Family Strategies." *Journal of Marriage and the Family* 61.4 (1999): 995-1007. Print.

Bianchi, Suzanne, Vanessa Wright, and Sara Raley. "Maternal Employment and Family Caregiving: Rethinking Time with Children in the ATUS." Presentation at ATUS Early Results Conference, Bethesda, MD. 9 Dec. 2005. Print.

Brady, Michelle. "Institutionalized Individualism and the Care of the Self: Single Mothers and the State." *Contested Individualism: Debates about Contemporary Personhood*. Ed. C. Howard. New York: Palgrave Macmillan (2007): 187-208. Print.

Castaneda, Maria, and Kirsten Isgro, eds. *Mothers in Academia*. New York: Columbia University Press, 2013. Print.

Christopher, Karen. "Extensive Mothering: Employed Mothers'

Construction of the Good Mother." *Gender & Society* 26.73 (2012): 73-96. Print.

Edin, Kathryn, and Maria Kefalas. *Promises I Can Keep: Why Poor Mothers Put Motherhood before Marriage.* Los Angeles: University of California Press. 2005. Print.

Estes, Clarissa Pinkola. *Women Who Run with the Wolves: Myths and Stories of the Wild Woman Archetype.* Toronto: Random, 1992. Print.

Fisher, Bruce, and Robert Alberti. *Rebuilding: When Your Relationship Ends.* 3rd ed. Atascada: Impact, 2000. Print.

Fothergill, Alice, and Kathryn Feltey. "'I've Worked Very Hard and Slept Very Little:' Mothers on Tenure Track in Academia." *Journal of the Motherhood Initiative for Research and Community Involvement* 5.2 (2003): 7-19. Print.

Hayes, Sharon. *The Cultural Contradictions of Motherhood.* New Haven: Yale University Press, 1996. Print

Johnson, Deirdre, and Debra Swanson. "Cognitive Acrobatics in the Construction of Worker-Mother Identity." *Sex Roles* 57 (2007): 447-459. Print.

Jones-DeWeaver, Avis A. "When the Spirit Blooms: Acquiring Higher Education in the Context of Welfare Reform." *Journal of Women, Politics & Policy* 3 (2005): 113-133. Print.

Juffer, Jane. "Domestic Intellectuals: Freedom and the Single Mom." In *Maternal Theory: Essential Readings,* Ed. Andrea O'Reilly. Toronto: Demeter Press, 2007. 726-755. Print.

Maushart, Susan. *The Mask of Motherhood.* New York: New Press, 1999. Print.

Mason, Mary Ann, and Marc Goulden. "Do Babies Matter? The Effect of Family Formation on the Lifelong Careers of Academic Men and Women." *Academe.* 88.6 (2002): 21-27. Print.

Rothman, Barbara Katz. "Mothering Alone: Rethinking Single Motherhood in America." *Women's Studies Quarterly.* 37.3/4 (2009): 323-328. Print.

Sidel, Ruth. *Unsung Heroines: Single Mothers and the American Dream.* Berkeley: University of California Press, 2006. Print.

Walden, Gale. "Hiding the Baby." *Parenting and Professing: Balancing Family Work with an Academic Career.* Ed. Rachel Bassett. Vanderbilt University Press, 2005. 78-81. Print.

Williams, Joan C. "How Academe Treats Mothers." *Chronicle Careers*. Chronicle of Higher Education, 17 June 2002. Web. 4 Oct. 2014.

9.
Single Lesbian[1] Mothers[2]

LARA DESCARTES

I BECAME A single lesbian mother when my child was born in 2008. This was in an era in North America in which reproductive technologies were available to all who could pay for them; prominent LGBT (lesbian, gay, bisexual, and transgender) people publically discussed their children's conception or adoption, and popular media regularly depicted such scenarios. In this environment, my identity as a lesbian seeking motherhood did not seem to be deemed unusual by most. At least to my face. Being *single* and pursuing motherhood, however, was. I repeatedly heard phrases, from heterosexual and LGBT people alike, such as "You're amazing! I can't imagine doing it alone" or, more chidingly, "That's a big responsibility, you know." The repeated nature of these utterances underscores cultural norms; having children still seems to be perceived as something couples should do, not single people. This couple-centric conception of parenthood points to a heteronormative ideology—standard heterosexual conception requires two people. The idea that two people are required to have children seems to go largely unquestioned, even by those who do not practice that form of conception. It cannot be simply an issue of spreading the time, financial, and energy commitments of parenting across more than one adult, as few ever seem to suggest that childrearing be shared by three, four, or more people.

These intertwined issues of parenting, couple-centrism, and heteronormativity were foregrounded for me a few years ago. A male friend and I were walking along a street in an LGBT-friendly section of Toronto, accompanied by my child. Suddenly, we were passed by a car full of energetic young men, all of whom were hanging out of their windows, jeering "Breeders! Breeders! This is *our* neighbourhood!" This was startling yet funny due in part to the irony of yelling this at a gay man, a lesbian woman, and her donor-conceived child, all on their way to the LGBT community centre. As I reflected on this interaction, however, it occurred to me how culturally *outside* it can feel to be a single lesbian mother—outside not only the norms and expectations of heterosexuals but also of sexual minorities.

As noted, parenthood has become a more accessible part of sexual minorities' experiences in the past several decades. The relaxation of laws prohibiting LGBT people in North America from adopting and fostering children and increasingly common reproductive technologies have created a "gayby boom" (Dunne 12). Psychology scholars Fiona Tasker and Charlotte Patterson note, however, that the cultural context of lesbian and gay parenting remains relatively unstudied (Tasker and Patterson 11). It is known that the two-parent, heterosexual family ideal remains potent, shaping North American discourse about families, even as reality continues to diverge from it (Juffer 4, 15; M. Nelson 781-783, 793-794; Smith 51-53). Single lesbian mothers (SLMs) occupy a position that is marginalized with respect to this conventional understanding of family because their families are headed by parents who are neither coupled nor heterosexual. Their experiences can be illuminated by the work of queer family theorists, who seek to decentralize conventional understandings of gender, sexuality, and family and to understand how those norms intersect and interact (Oswald, Blume, and Marks; Oswald et al.). Family studies scholars Ramona Oswald, Libby Blume, and Stephen Marks argue that binaries shape our understandings of these categories, with gender perceived as the oppositional dyad of male-female, sexuality as natural (heterosexual)/unnatural (non-heterosexual, or queer), and families as genuine (married heterosexual couples and their children)/false (any deviation from that) (144-146).

Single lesbian mother families occupy the marginalized halves of the three binaries. Single mothers, in general, up-end conventional gender norms. They combine traditionally male and female roles by performing breadwinning and protective functions as well as nurturing and caretaking. Lesbians challenge sexuality norms simply by not identifying as heterosexuals. And SLM families, of course, depart from the idealized male-female two-parent nuclear family. Despite calls for attention to the diversity of gay and lesbian families (Allen and Demo 111-112, 122-124), single lesbian mothers have for the most part been absent from family research literature. Most research on single-mother families has focused on presumptively heterosexual women (for example, Joshi, Quane, and Cherlin) and most research on lesbian mother families has been with couples (for example, Goldberg and Smith). The omission of SLMs holds true as well in popular literature that is aimed at those who wish to become or already are parents (Lapidus 229).

An examination of the academic and popular literature aimed at single and lesbian mothers makes it clear that even among those sensitive to minority sexual or family status identities, dominant categories can remain unchallenged. One type of popular literature is aimed at single women who are considering motherhood as "single mothers by choice." These are women, often in their thirties, who purposefully pursue motherhood on their own, usually through adoption or donor insemination (Mattes 3-6). Although this definition can encompass lesbian women, the language used in the "choice motherhood" books often seems to assume that the readers are heterosexual. Most such books make an initial statement indicating that women seeking motherhood might be lesbian or bisexual, but once that is acknowledged, they tend to subsequently display heteronormative assumptions. One passage, for example, from Jane Mattes's classic *Single Mothers by Choice* reads, "During the toddler years your child will probably be very interested in the *man* you are dating" (emphasis added, 197). Similar phrasings can be found in Mikki Morrissette's *Choosing Single Motherhood*. Throughout the book, heterosexuality is the referent state, as in the chapter "Grieving the Childhood Dream," which addresses the feelings of loss women may have over not finding a man with whom to have a child before age makes fertility difficult. Women's potential grief over not finding the right woman in time to have a child together is left unacknowledged as a possibility.

Books about single motherhood in general, whether that status comes about by choice or not, tend to use the same type of language. Popular books, such as *Soaring Solo* (Keller), often do not even mention the possibility of a single mother being bisexual or lesbian. The Canadian textbook *Single Parent Families* does not focus on non-heterosexual parents in any of its twenty-two chapters (Hudson and Galaway). It ends with a call for further attention to the diversity of single-parent families, and although groups such as incarcerated and older women are mentioned, mothers of minority sexual identities are not. Academically oriented texts and edited volumes (Yarber and Sharp) also, thus, tend to reinforce the assumption that single mothers are heterosexual, although the current volume (Motapanyane) provides an exception to that trend.

Texts addressing lesbian parents, again both academic and popular, reveal, in turn, a couple-centric bias. They might initially acknowledge that a lesbian mother can be single, but subsequent language often excludes that possibility. A chapter in the edited volume *An Introduction to GLBT Family Studies* states, for example: "For women, the biological clock continues to set an upper limit for the realization of motherhood, an issue relevant both for heterosexual women and women in a *lesbian union*" (emphasis added, Cohler 33). Psychologists Suzanne Johnson and Elizabeth O'Connor use similar phrasing: "For gay and lesbian *couples* who have conceived using any form of reproductive technology…" (emphasis added, 24). Yet Johnson and O'Connor are reporting data from the National Study of Gay and Lesbian Parents, in which 47 of 256 surveyed families are single parent. Even research that includes SLMs as part of their sample thus can omit them in the language used to report and discuss results. Sociologist Fiona Nelson's 1996 *Lesbian Motherhood* draws on a sample, one tenth of which was single, yet much of the discussion conflates "lesbian families" with "two-parent lesbian families." Sociologist Amy Hequembourg's text about lesbian mothers uses a sample that is one eighth single. Yet she notes: "some lesbian *couples* with children demonstrate the need to secure their child's rights to access his or her biological father's identity" (emphasis added, 73). The sentence construction limiting the results to two-parent families is unnecessary; it is unlikely that this is something with which couples, but not singles, are concerned. The research with lesbian mothers that these authors present is significant, highly valuable, and moves our understandings of family diversity forward, yet the presence and voices of the single women in their samples are obscured.

When single-mother families are mentioned in works for and about lesbian parents, they often seem to be mentioned in a deficit context. The *Lesbian Parenting Book*, for example, aimed at a lay audience, discusses single parents twice (as referenced by the index), but both mentions imply comparative insufficiency: they state that single mothers need to work harder than coupled mothers to get social support from friends and family, as they have no partner (Clunis and Green 173, 214). This type of language reinforces assumptions that single-parent families are lacking in comparison to coupled-parent families, rather than simply different. In this way, this literature is in keeping with dominant representations of single mothers in general. In a review of popular and scholarly media, sociologist Margaret Usdanksy finds persistently negative portrayals of single-parent families (222-223). The results of a recent study show that public perceptions of single-mother families continue to be quite disparaging (Haire and McGeorge 42-43).

Exceptions to the trends noted here definitely exist. In publications originating out of the National Lesbian Longitudinal Family Study by psychiatrist Nanette Gartrell and her colleagues, SLM families receive some specific mention and the families' strengths as well as challenges are discussed ("The National Lesbian Family Study: 1"; "The National Lesbian Family Study: 2"). Data from this study and others do indicate that there may be challenges specific to being an SLM, but they are more complex than simply not being part of a couple. Fiona Nelson, for example, reports that SLMs in her study felt isolated both from the lesbian community and from heterosexual mothers ("In the Other Room" 57). A number of scholars point out that women who are mothers are coded by others as heterosexual, unless there is evidence to the contrary (Gartrell et al., "The National Lesbian Family Study: 2)" 367; Goldberg 84; Nelson, *Lesbian Motherhood* 101; Weston 168). Lesbian couples provide that evidence through the fact of their couplehood. SLMs, however, must actively proclaim their sexual identities if they do not wish people to assume that they are something they are not. These sources of potential challenge, then, revolve around exclusion and identity, the attitudes and beliefs of others, and the impact of those attitudes and beliefs on SLMs.

To explore these issues further, I initiated my own study and recruited lesbian mothers living in southwestern Ontario for interviews. The age range of the children was restricted to minors in order to limit the discussion to current and recent parenting experiences. Advertisements for the study were placed electronically and via postings in coffee shops, bookstores, and other public establishments. As a thank you for the women's time, forty-dollar gift cards to a bookstore were provided to participants. Data from five SLMs are presented in this chapter. All had utilized donors to become pregnant. The women used a mix of known donors, whether friends or acquaintances, and unknown donors, obtained via a clinic. Interviews were conducted with five coupled lesbian mothers (CLMs) for purposes of comparison. All of the CLMs similarly had used donors, both known and unknown, to have their children. Three of the CLMs were their children's birth mothers. The SLM and CLM mothers were almost all white, financially secure women in their thirties and forties. Exceptions included one SLM in her twenties, one Latina SLM, and two SLMs who had more limited incomes. The SLMs' and CLMs' children were all age ten and under. The interview guide was comprised of several broad questions, which asked about the women's experiences before and after having children and focused on their interactions with family, friends, neighbours, clinicians, and daycare providers, among others.

Thematic analysis revealed differences and commonalities between the two groups of women that highlight the relevance of identity and exclusion. One emergent theme was the discomfort experienced by some of the SLMs as they navigated various obstacles in what they described as the often couple-centric and heterocentric world of parenthood. Some of these challenges began before the women even became mothers. Audra,[3] for example, a mother of two, had noticed the heteronormative assumptions made by popular birthing books. She described one such book as "totally heterosexist ... there's all this 'smooching your man' kind of crap; it's all through the whole thing, it's kind of annoying." Audra mentioned, however, that when such books otherwise had "good messages, [then] I can get through the heterosexist stuff." Jillian, perhaps the most financially constrained mother in the sample, described feeling completely outside the audience for whom the books for prospective parents seem to be intended. She connected this to her socio-economic status as well as to being lesbian and single: "The 'single mothers by choice' stuff was class-wise really not me, but also really, really straight and then the queer stuff was like logistically informative and whatever ... but I felt like it was really designed for couples." As with Audra, Jillian noted, "I'm able to sort through it and get useful information," but she added that "it never feels like it's for me."

Single lesbian mothers also talked about the ambivalent feelings arising from being assumed to be heterosexual simply by virtue of their motherhood. Friends and family who knew of their lesbian identity, and were sources of reinforcement, usually were part of the women's lives. New acquaintances, such as children's teachers, daycare providers, babysitters, and clinicians, however, often assumed that the women were heterosexual unless specifically told otherwise. I experienced this myself when I told a kindergarten teacher that my daughter had been conceived via a donor, and I said that I hoped family diversity was supported in her classroom. The teacher replied, "Oh yes, we have all sorts of situations here. We had another child from a donor last year. And a few years ago, we had a family with two moms." The teacher looked down, pursed her lips, and said "Now *that* was unusual!" She clearly assumed that I was not lesbian, despite having no data to support that conclusion. One SLM, Audra, told of similar experiences: "I get identified absolutely as heterosexual," and she noted that it feels "weird. I almost feel like I don't come out anymore and I feel weird coming out. I used to be super-out, but now I know that I'm violating all of these expectations. [Pre-motherhood] it didn't used to be a violation of expectations in the same way." Audra stated that she thought the misidentification happened "partly [because of my] femme presentation, and partly having kids, being a mom, people want to put you in that mom, single mom, category." These assumptions were made by heterosexuals and non-heterosexuals alike: Audra recalled one time she and her child attended a party where the guests were all lesbian. Audra felt that the other women assumed that, as a single mother, she must be heterosexual and that they acted in a guarded way around her until she made the truth known. Audra did not discuss her lesbian identity often with new acquaintances, and stated that she is not out at her children's schools. Another SLM, Sydney, told a similar story: "When I go out everyone just assumes I have a husband ... I wish I was more brave, sometimes I'm very brave, and other times I'm not. Other times I feel awkward. And it's terrible; it's like internalized homophobia or something, I don't know, where I feel embarrassed and most of the time, I am not embarrassed about my orientation or anything. So it bothers me when I am." Sydney described an encounter with a man who, upon meeting her and her baby, asked after her husband. Sydney replied "Oh, I'm not married," but noted that "He still thinks [there is] a man, and I just left him thinking like that. But, of course, I wish I had said 'No, actually I'm a lesbian.' ... But ... some days you're just not up to that, you know?" When I asked Sydney how those types of encounters made her feel, she replied "It makes me feel like I am different in a bad way. I don't believe that's true. But yeah, that's the negative thing that it does."

One of the interviewed SLMs, Peg, was content to let such assumptions be made, as she felt they made life easier for her son. Some of the other women, however, related how such interactions left them with a sense of feeling "less lesbian" and how that felt odd and self-alienating. This simply did not seem to be an issue for the CLMs, two of whom discussed how parenthood had made their lesbian identities *more* apparent to others. The women stated that pre-baby when they were in public, they felt others perceived them simply as two female friends. But once they had a child, they thought that strangers likely recognized them as a family unit based on their interactions together with the child. In formal settings, such as school, where alternate contacts and pick-up arrangements were on file, the CLMs felt that those records had made their lesbian identities known, whether they explicitly stated that they were a couple or not.

Single lesbian mothers' narratives indicate that they sometimes felt quite outside of lesbian community life. Audra said, for example, "I feel like I don't get much interaction with the lesbian community." Sydney spoke of feeling left out upon no longer being invited to parties and events with her lesbian friends once her child was born. It is true, of course, that any mother can become somewhat isolated during the first few years of motherhood, just by virtue of the time- and energy-intensive nature of parenting small children. Coupled and single lesbian mothers spoke of how motherhood decreased their participation in the fairly structured activities that make up much of lesbian community life, such as concerts, dances, and volunteer activities. Both SLMs and CLMs also spoke of seeing less of their lesbian friends, particularly those who were not parents themselves, after their children were born. These friendships were often replaced over time by friendships with other parents, who usually were heterosexual. The SLMs, thus, could find themselves without many lesbians around them. This seemed to contribute to some of the women feeling separated from their sense of themselves as lesbians. Peg stated, for example, of how "the lesbian part of [me] has taken a backburner." She and another mother spoke of how it can be hard to feel lesbian when there are no other lesbians around to be lesbian with. CLMs, though, had at least one other lesbian, their partner, regularly in their lives, and the question of feeling lesbian simply did not come up in their discussions.

This chapter has considered various aspects of the cultural context shaping single lesbian mothers' lives. Evidence from academic and popular literature, as well my own and other SLMs' experiences, supports the idea that North American family discourse remains constrained by the dyadic categorizations of gender, sexuality, and family, critiqued by Oswald, Blume, and Marks. Heteronormativity and its linked two-parent paradigm continue to define expectations and assumptions about mothers. There was evidence for this among heterosexuals and non-heterosexuals alike. As Oswald, et al. note, "being lesbian or gay is not in itself enough to transcend heteronormativity" (45). The SLMs experienced feelings of exclusion and alienation in different domains because of others' assumptions. In the literature that some read, they found assumptions that lesbian-headed families are two-parent families. In literature and in their interactions with others, the women encountered assumptions that mothers are heterosexual, and that they, therefore, must be heterosexual. These assumptions, combined with a decreased ability to participate in lesbian friendships and community activities, had some negative ramifications for the SLMs. Some felt anxious or ambivalent about whether they should come out as lesbian in the fairly frequent situations in which they found themselves mislabelled. Some felt isolated from lesbian community life, and, for a few, this affected their sense of themselves as lesbians. The experiences of the SLMs described here indicate some of the challenges that they face—challenges caused not by their status as single mothers per se but rather by the persistence of heterocentric and couple-centric ideals of family.

NOTES

[1]The term "lesbian" is used in this chapter as the majority of the women who participated in the interviews on which it is partly based self-identified as lesbian. The rest identified as queer.

[2]Funding for this project was provided by Brescia University College.

[3]All of the women's names are aliases.

WORKS CITED

Allen, Katherine R., and David H. Demo. "The Families of Lesbians and Gay Men: A New Frontier in Family Research." *Journal of Marriage and Family* 57 (1995): 111-127. Print.

Bigner, Jerry J., ed. *An Introduction to GLBT Family Studies.* Binghamton, NY: Haworth Press, 2006. Print.

Clunis, D. Merilee, and G. Dorsey Green. *The Lesbian Parenting Book: A Guide to Creating Families and Raising Children.* 2nd ed. New York: Seal Press, 2003. Print.

Cohler, Bertram J. "Life-Course Social Science Perspectives on the GLBT Family." *An Introduction to GLBT Family Studies.* Ed. Jerry Bigner. Binghamton, NY: Haworth Press, 2006. 23-49. Print.

Dunne, Gillian A. "Opting into Motherhood: Lesbians Blurring the Boundaries and Transforming the Meaning of Parenthood and Kinship." *Gender and Society* 14.1 (2000): 11-35. Print.

Gartrell, Nanette et al. "The National Lesbian Family Study: 1. Interviews with Prospective Mothers." *American Journal of*

Orthopsychiatry 66.2 (1996): 272-281. Print.
Gartrell, Nanette et al. "The National Lesbian Family Study: 2. Interviews with Mothers of Toddlers." *American Journal of Orthopsychiatry* 69.3 (1999): 362-369. Print.
Goldberg, Abbie E. *Lesbian and Gay Parents and Their Children: Research on the Family Life Cycle*. Washington, D.C.: American Psychological Association, 2010. Print.
Goldberg, Abbie E., and JuliAnna Z. Smith. "The Social Context of Lesbian Mothers' Anxiety During Early Parenthood." *Parenting: Science and Practice* 8 (2008): 213-239. Print.
Haire, Amanda R., and Christi R. McGeorge. "Negative Perceptions of Never-Married Custodial Single Mothers and Fathers: Applications of a Gender Analysis for Family Therapists." *Journal of Feminist Family Therapy* 24.1 (2012): 24-51. Print.
Hequembourg, Amy. *Lesbian Motherhood: Stories of Becoming*. Binghamton, NY: Haworth Press. 2007. Print.
Hudson, Joe, and Burt Galaway, eds. *Single Parent Families: Perspectives on Research and Policy*. Toronto: Thompson Educational Publishing, 1993. Print.
Johnson, Suzanne M., and Elizabeth O'Connor. *The Gay Baby Boom: The Psychology of Gay Parenthood*. New York: New York University Press, 2002. Print.
Joshi, Pamela, James M. Quane, and Andrew J. Cherlin. "Contemporary Work and Family Issues Affecting Marriage and Cohabitation Among Low-Income Single Mothers." *Family Relations* 58.5 (2009): 647-661. Print.
Juffer, Jane. *Single Mother: The Emergence of the Domestic Intellectual*. New York: New York University Press, 2006. Print.
Keller, Wendy. *Soaring Solo: On the Joys (Yes, Joys!) of Being a Single Mother*. Berkeley, CA: Wildcat Canyon Press, 2001. Print.
Lapidus, June. "All the Lesbian Mothers Are Coupled, All the Single Mothers Are Straight, and All of Us Are Tired: Reflections on Being a Single Lesbian Mom." *Feminist Economics* 10.2 (2004): 227-236. Print.
Mattes, Jane. *Single Mothers by Choice: A Guidebook for Single Women Who Are Considering or Have Chosen Motherhood*. New York: Three Rivers Press, 1994. Print.
Morrissette, Mikki. *Choosing Single Motherhood: The Thinking*

Woman's Guide. Boston: Mariner Books, 2008. Print.

Motapanyane, Maki, ed. *Motherhood and Lone-Single Parenting: A Twenty-First Century Perspective*. Bradford, ON: Demeter Press, 2016. Print.

Nelson, Fiona. *In the Other Room: Entering the Culture of Motherhood*. Black Point: Fernwood Publishing, 2009. Print.

Nelson, Fiona. *Lesbian Motherhood: An Exploration of Canadian Lesbian Families*. Toronto: University of Toronto Press, 1996. Print.

Nelson, Margaret. "Single Mothers "Do" Family." *Journal of Marriage and Family* 68.4 (2006): 781-795. Print.

Oswald, Ramona F., Libby B. Blume, and Stephen R. Marks. "Decentering Heteronormativity: A Model for Family Studies." *Sourcebook of Family Theory and Research*. Eds. Vern L. Bengtson, Alan C. Acock, Katherine R. Allen, Peggye Dilworth-Anderson, and David M. Klein. Thousand Oaks: Sage, 2005. 143-154. Print.

Oswald, Ramona F., et al. "Queering 'The Family.'" *Handbook of Feminist Family Studies*. Eds. Sally A. Lloyd, April L. Few, and Katherine R. Allen,. Thousand Oaks: Sage, 2009. 43-55. Print.

Smith, Dorothy E. "The Standard North-American Family—SNAF as an Ideological Code." *Journal of Family Issues* 14.1 (1993): 50-65. Print.

Tasker, Fiona, and Charlotte J. Patterson. "Research on Lesbian and Gay Parenting: Retrospect and Prospect." *Journal of GLBT Family Studies*. 3.2/3 (2008): 9-34. Print.

Usdansky, Margaret L. "A Weak Embrace: Popular and Scholarly Depictions of Single–Parent Families, 1990–1998." *Journal of Marriage and Family* 71.2 (2009): 209-225. Print.

Weston, Kath. *Families We Choose: Lesbians, Gays, Kinship*. New York: Columbia University Press, 1991. Print.

Yarber, Annice D., and Paul M. Sharp. *Focus on Single-Parent Families: Past, Present, and Future*. Santa Barbara, CA: Greenwood Publishers, 2010. Print.

III.
POLICY, RESISTANCE, AND ACTIVISM

10.
Historicizing the Marginalization of Single Mothers

An Australian Perspective

CHRISTIN QUIRK

IN AUSTRALIA, there are an estimated 743,000 single mothers raising dependent children in a population of twenty-thee million. Data from the Australian Bureau of Statistics (ABS) indicates that one-parent families account for 22 percent of all families with children under the age of fifteen; mothers head 87 percent of these. Although these families may share some similarities in their experience of raising children without the added financial and emotional support of a live-in partner or parent, these families are just as likely to represent a diversity of experience that is often overlooked. This is significant because of the tendency among health professionals, government policymakers, and the media to represent and treat single mothers as a homogenous group. This is also problematic not only in the way it has been used to define the identity of single mothers in overwhelmingly negative terms but also in the way it has been used to justify a raft of punitive welfare reforms in response to the perceived threat these women pose to "traditional family values" and the nuclear family model.

With 63 percent of lone-mother families relying on government pensions and allowances as their principal source of income, the discourse on welfare reform can be used to explore attitudes towards the single mother. Indeed, the significant percentage of single mothers in receipt of welfare benefits serves to reinforce a homogeneous negative stereotype as well as to obscure and negate alternative experiences. In tracing the historical subjectivity of the single mother in Australia, this chapter will argue that the parenting abilities of the single mother have been brought into question as a strategy to justify her management and control. Although this was achieved through adoption policies until the early 1970s (by separating mother and child), welfare reform, more recently, has been invoked as the way to police her behaviour. Furthermore, the media participates in this negative representation through its persistent attacks on the welfare-dependent single mother. Although Aboriginal mothers have also been targeted by the systematic removal and control of their children through so-called Protection Acts, this racialized discourse operates notwithstanding marital status (Australian Human Rights Commission). The complexity of the intersecting challenges faced by Aboriginal women falls outside the scope of this work. Instead, this chapter aims to historicize the changing meaning and stigmatization of the single mother in Australia since World War II by exploring welfare discourses and the lived experiences of single mothers across this timeframe.

By definition, the single mother is described by her marital status, specifically in the way that she is positioned in opposition to the ideal married family. Contemporary understandings of single motherhood now include women who have been deserted, divorced, widowed or, more recently, those women who have made a conscious choice to conceive a child on their own— historically, however, that label was reserved only for those "immoral" girls who had children out of wedlock. In 1969, the term "single mother" was embraced by a group of unmarried mothers who formed the Council for the Single Mother and her Child (CSMC) in Melbourne to provide a more positive description of their marital status (West 172); the term "single mother" replaced earlier pejorative labels such as "unwed mother" or "single girl." The distinction between never married mothers and their married counterparts—who were ostensibly single by virtue of desertion, divorce, or death—was deliberate and resolute. Those women who had been married had made the effort to abide by social customs; marriage conferred an imagined maturity on a woman, regardless of her age. On the other hand, the implied immaturity of the "single girl" was a lifelong affliction. Other terms that have been used to denigrate the single mother include "out-of-wedlock birth" and "illegitimate birth" (referring to the mother through the child's status of "nullius filius"). Although "illegitimacy" was officially removed from the legal vernacular through various state-based Status of Children Acts (enacted from the mid-1970s), births outside of marriage continue to be recorded in official state publications as "ex-nuptial births." While acknowledging the potentially disparaging nature of the term "unmarried mother," for the purposes of clarity and consistency, this chapter will adhere to the historical terminology where required. The initial focus will be on the experiences of the unmarried mother prior to 1969, followed by an exploration of the experiences of single mothers from that point onwards, which will reflect the evolution of the term as it was reclaimed and, finally, as it is currently used to encompass the wider range of experiences that predicate lone parenting.

HISTORICAL CONTEXT

The emergence of the modern welfare state in the wake of World War II heralded a conscious effort by Western governments to embrace the concepts of social justice and fair distribution of wealth and income, particularly towards workers and women. Andrew Herscovitch and David Stanton argue that upon the inception of Australia's system of pensions, the Commonwealth viewed the entitlement to social security as a "right based on need" (52). Furthermore, this model of social security is financed from general taxation revenues, not employer or employee contributions as in most other countries. Sheila Shaver points to World War II as a pivotal moment in the expanding program: "Australia entered World War II with only a fragmentary welfare provision: by the end of the war it had constructed a welfare 'state'" (411). However, it must also be noted that income support was far from inclusive at this time; although widows, divorcees, and deserted wives were eligible for pensions, the exclusion of unmarried mothers continued until 1973. Aboriginal women were uniformly excluded from all government benefits (Commonwealth of Australia 9; Haebich). Still, the rights-based approach on which Australia's welfare state was built remained a key feature of policy into the 1990s.

Another key concern of the post-war government was population and demography, which was driven by the ambition to dramatically increase the population of the nation, particularly for reasons of defence. The popular belief that Australia must "populate or perish" was reinforced to encourage not only immigration but also the growth of Australian families. The nuclear family structure was at the forefront of such efforts, and the unmarried mother did not fit this plan. Marilyn Lake argues that the family remained a patriarchal institution in which "a mother's right to custody of her own children was conditional on her being not an exemplary citizen, but a good woman: white, married, chaste and economically dependent on a husband" (86). A system of strict social values and underlying moral and religious assumptions upheld the sanctity of marriage; the family was a male breadwinner and his dependent wife. Women who did work continued to earn significantly less than their male counterparts, which compromised any chance of them remaining financially self-supporting. At the 1988 International Conference on Adoption and Permanent Care, Deborah Lee, a mother who was forcibly separated from her child by adoption, reflected on the experience of the unmarried mother during the 1960s:

> If a woman was without a breadwinner she was almost by definition poor economically, socially and sexually. Mothers who were not married were stigmatized and considered disgraced by a prejudiced community. They were the most undeserving of the undeserving poor. Child-care facilities, career and educational opportunities, equal pay and public housing were not considered necessary. (19)

These structural inequalities undermined a woman's chances of keeping and raising her child. Combined with a discourse of traditional family values and the dominance of two-parent families, no space existed in which to question an unmarried mother's desire or willingness to keep her child. Within this context, the unmarried mother was a social pariah. It was believed that she should want to be rid of her own child, as her capacity to parent was rendered impossible. However, the unmarried mother would be offered salvation through the sacrifice of adoption, which was viewed not only as "a necessary pain" but—and more importantly within this construct of censure and blame—as "the only way in which she could regain her respectability" (Swain and Howe 140). It required the unmarried mother to be complicit in her own punishment, as her absolute silence—about her pregnancy and relinquishment—was essential for her redemption and, indeed, for her to "get on with her life." Adoption was also designed to free the child from the stigma of illegitimacy, which, supposedly, had functioned to deter women (but not men) from engaging in extramarital intercourse. The rising rate of illegitimacy seen throughout the 1960s was attributed to "declines in religious or economic sanctions against unwed mothers" (Cutright 28). This is consistent with the contention that this decade marked "the beginning of the collapse of Christian morality in an increasingly secular Australian society" (Thompson 140). However, the shame of illegitimacy was preserved in the practice of religious-based maternity homes through segregating these "single girls" as well as through the lack of widely available government benefits.

In line with views of the unmarried mother as an immature girl, it was believed that she was incapable of making decisions about her future. Her family, social workers, and the medical profession made decisions on her behalf—supposedly in her and her child's best interest. These expert opinions were based on perceptions of her (in)ability to adequately care for her child. Indicative of prevailing attitudes within the medical profession, Doctor Lawson of the Royal Women's Hospital (RWH) in Melbourne recommended the following course of action to his fellow obstetricians in 1960: "The prospect of the unmarried girl or of her family adequately caring for a child and giving it a normal environment and upbringing is so small that I believe for practical purposes it can be ignored. I believe that in all such cases the obstetrician should urge that the child be adopted." Social workers also held onto an unwavering belief that the obstacles facing the unmarried mother were insurmountable. The advice of the professional always trumped the wants of the unmarried mother. For example, twenty-year-old Lynda Stevens had decided to keep her baby. Her mother supported this choice and would have provided practical support; however, the RWH social worker had other ideas about Lynda's ability to raise a child as an unmarried mother. Lynda recounted that: "The only thing I can remember is that horrible final meeting with her, when she told me that the child would grow up in the gutter and I'd be forced to become a prostitute to support her. Oh, it was quite horrible. And, she really did get red-faced. I remember it vividly" (qtd. in Quirk, "Separated at Birth" 57).

Such attitudes underpinned a booming "market in babies" (Quartly, Swain, and Cuthbert). During the period from 1945 to 1975, the demand for adoptable babies for infertile couples in Australia was at its peak, with over forty-five thousand adoptions legalized in Victoria alone. This period, often referred to as the "heyday" of adoption, saw up to 68 percent of never-married mothers get separated from their babies.[1] It must be noted that adoption was a consumer-driven market, with the "healthy fair baby girl" preferred above all others; babies who were less than "perfect" were transferred to institutional care (Swain and Howe 135; Quirk, "The Business"). Adoption was characterized as a mutually advantageous solution that guaranteed the moral and social redemption of mother and child; adoptive parents were cast as benevolent and sympathetic. Within this context, the relinquishing mother was marginalized, stigmatized, and unable to acknowledge her grief and loss. At a time when the social norm was an idealized nuclear family, fears abounded that the increasing incidence of illegitimacy would dissolve the moral foundations of society. In 1966, sociologist Shirley M. Hartley reasoned:

> If the family is the prime instrumental agency through which institutional needs are met, and if a high individual or family commitment to a given norm such as legitimacy is dependent on social integration—the commitment of the community to the cultural norm and the strength of its social controls—it hardly seems possible to eliminate the stigma attached to illegitimacy without at the same time weakening the family as a social institution. (545)

Aimed directly at the unmarried mother, these views exemplify longstanding (and continued) fears about the impact of "alternative" family structures and the decline of the "traditional" family. The unmarried mother was problematic to the right order of things. As such, her clinical and medical "management" became entrenched in Australian hospitals throughout the 1950s and 1960s. The rise of social work as a profession saw the unmarried mother move from the position of victim-in-need-of-redemption to one of problem-in-need-of-treatment: "in removing unmarried mothers from the evangelical narrative and placing them within the scientific scripts of feeblemindedness and sex delinquent, social workers had gone a considerable distance towards achieving recognition as experts in the field of illegitimacy" (Kunzel 63). Following the establishment of professional training bodies by the end of the 1920s, Australian social workers were largely influenced by British and American texts and movements, with the work of American casework professor Leontine Young featuring prominently (Lawrence ix-x, 3). Young asserted that unplanned pregnancies were willfully premeditated, an indication of the unmarried mother's dysfunctional family relationship and unfulfilled desires. Indeed, Dianne Gray's understanding of her unplanned pregnancy in 1970 mirrors Young's pseudo-psychiatric analyses: "I had a real need to have a baby because I had no love. There was no love at home. Children who have been very deprived—and where there has been abuse—often the women or female children of that type have a strong desire to have a child because they have something to love and someone to love them" (qtd. in Quirk, "Separated at Birth" 41).

However, by the early 1970s attitudes appeared to be shifting. This time was characterized by a mood of hope and anticipation, a concern about Australia's place in the world, and great social change. A complex combination of changing social values, community attitudes, and legislation peaked in the mid-1970s. The increasing affluence and expanded educational opportunities that had arisen out of the post-war boom provided fertile ground for the blossoming of a new radical and idealistic generation. The election of the Whitlam government in 1972 represented the culmination of social agitation by the counterculture and the women's liberation movement (WLM) in the preceding years, as the conservative government that had been in power for twenty-three years was unseated (Robinson). The sweeping social changes introduced included abolishing conscription, withdrawing the remaining troops from Vietnam, providing free university education, and establishing a universal health scheme (Medibank). For unmarried mothers, the passage of the Supporting Mothers Benefit was the most celebrated success and, finally, introduced government payments similar to the pre-existing Widow's Pension.

Community attitudes to extramarital intercourse began to relax. As a result, unmarried mothers became more visible, which suggests that they and their families had become less concerned with the disgrace previously associated with illegitimacy. CSMC founding member Rosemary Kiely argues that the more permissive attitudes found in the community at this time corresponded with "the liberalization of sex mores and the growing independence of women in modern industrialized societies" (155).[2] The establishment of CSMC would have been impossible had the stigma attached to illegitimacy and unmarried motherhood remained strong. But once in existence, the organization created a strong voice to pressure for change, in particular for statutory changes, such as the abolition of the status of illegitimacy and the introduction of government benefits (Swain and Howe 80). CSMC was both evidence for and a cause of the changes that simultaneously occurred with the trend towards more unmarried mothers keeping their babies.

DEFINING FAMILY

The response to the increased visibility of diverse family forms has been an explosion of family studies literature over the last forty years. In preparing a literature review for the Australian Psychological Association, Elizabeth Short, Damien Riggs, Amaryll Perlesz, Rhonda Brown, and Graeme Kane argue that the basis of this expanding research has been twofold: "to explore and document increasing numbers of newly emerged family forms, and to investigate concerns that have been expressed by some about families other than those headed by cohabitating married heterosexual couples who are the biological parents of their children" (4-5). Despite the continued prominence of the nuclear family, there is an increasing number of families who no longer conform to this structural norm. Sociologists Sherry Saggers and Margaret Sims argue that this is the result of a number of post-war developments, including "the cultural diversity of Australia's Indigenous and migrant populations and social trends extending over more than thirty years which have resulted in more single-parent, step and blended, multiple household and same-sex families" (82). More importantly, family studies literature from the past fifteen years has consistently shown that diversity in family structure is not adversely affecting children; it finds that "it is family *processes* (such as the quality of parenting and relationships within the family) that contribute to determining children's well-being and 'outcomes', rather than family *structures*" (Short et al. 4). The simplistic distinction between "traditional" and "alternative" families is socially constructed. Sociologists agree that ideas about what families are, or ought to be, have been constructed from the belief systems of a society's influential elites, including political, religious, economic, and academic leaders. Through constant repetition, these beliefs come to define cultural norms. The present "traditional" or "natural" family in Australia still requires heterosexuality of its adult members. Families that fall outside of this norm have been described as "deviant" or "unnatural," thereby raising the spectre of the "bad mother." Linda Nicholson argues that language used to categorize family structure in such a simplistic and dualistic manner serves only to further stigmatize a range of "non-normative" families:

> Not only gays and lesbians, but also heterosexuals living alone; unmarried heterosexuals living together; married couples with husbands at home caring for children or wives working outside of the home; and children living in single-parent, stepfamily, or alternating households are either "in the closet" or somewhat embarrassed about how they live. (27)

Defined as such, the single mother must constantly defend her ability to be a "good mother." Indeed, the research literature on single mothers indicates that as a group, they have always been subject to an unchanging stereotype: poor, young, and vulnerable. Shurlee Swain and Renate Howe argue that these assumptions fit within a nineteenth-century discourse of innocence and seduction, which was replaced by one of romantic love in the twentieth: "the victim of seduction became in turn the product of poor heredity, poor social conditions or neurotic tendencies" (15). The stereotype is resolute. Kiely claims that despite ever-evolving social theories explaining single mothers' behaviour, the belief that "single mothers are generally disturbed adolescents in the grip of fantasies which make them unfit mothers has never quite lost its appeal" (156). Furthermore, Swain and Howe argue that single mothers remained largely hidden prior to the 1970s, which served to strengthen social stigma and establish the conflation of categories of single motherhood in the popular imagination: "the invisibility of the single mothers who were supporting their own children served to intensify the social disapproval of the more visible and hence the disapproval which they would face should their situation ever become known" (153).

Presently, single mothers continue to have these stereotypes reflected back at them through a never-ending kaleidoscope of tabloid media representations. For example, in January 2013 around one hundred thousand single parents—mostly women—with children aged between eight and fifteen were removed from the social security income support Parenting Payment (Single) and placed on the lower Newstart Allowance (a payment originally intended for short-term unemployed individuals without children). Contemplating the effects of this change, historian and social commentator John Hirst defended the policy decision on the grounds that: "[M]any single-parent households are not good places for children. The mothers are given to junk food, daytime TV and no-good boyfriends, who might develop designs on an adolescent daughter. The worst mothers are addicted to drugs and alcohol and under their influence neglect and abuse their children." And more recently, Sue Dunlevy revealed that being raised by a single parent was the greatest risk factor for childhood obesity. Neither of these opinion pieces, veiled as "reports," problematized the issue of increased poverty among single-mother families. The common thread in these representations is the underlying assumption that the single mother is incapable of being a good parent: at best, she has fat kids; at worst, her addictions compel her to abuse her children or her promiscuity leaves them open to abuse by her lovers.

The pressures inherent in constantly being confronted with representations of single-mothers-as-failures take a toll on women. Although, individually, single mothers may be able to distance themselves from such inflammatory reporting—buoyed by the fact that *they* are not that caricature—they can still find it difficult to maintain composure. During a personal interview, Sue Drummond confessed that she sometimes questions her decision to raise her children alone, particularly when going through a tough time. She said, "I think sometimes you can internalize those stereotypes. If there is something going wrong, people are quick to judge. They say that it's because you are a single mother. On the other hand, if things are going well, no one notices." Drummond is a single mother who, by all accounts, represents the exception to the stereotype: she enjoys her chosen career, she owns her own home, and her teenage children are successful and well adjusted. She considers herself to be among a small group of "lucky" single mothers; she does not rely on income support and, therefore, is not subject to the coercive management and scrutiny of welfare providers.

WELFARE REFORM AND THE "GOOD MOTHER"

ABS statistics reveal that 63 percent of lone-mother families currently rely on government pensions and allowances as their principal source of income. This is not to say that these mothers are not also participating in paid work, but that the proportion of money received from government payments is greater and more secure than that received from other sources—particularly part-time and casual work. Despite evidence of workforce participation, the seemingly high percentage of lone-mother families receiving welfare serves to reinforce earlier stereotypes of the poor and vulnerable single mother. Research consistently indicates that single-mother families are at higher risk of poverty as well as of increased disadvantage in areas of housing, employment, and social participation (de Vaus). Income support for unmarried mothers was first introduced in 1973. The division between the Widow's Pension and the Supporting Parents Benefit continued until 1989 when they were combined under the Sole Parent Pension. That the two existed as distinct payments for so long marks the continuation of earlier moral approaches toward the so-called deserving and undeserving poor. Megan Blaxland indicates that pensions have a higher earnings disregard "a more generous rate of payments, greater annual increases in payment rate, and more additional benefits than allowances" ("Everyday" 27). The policy shift to recognize all single mothers as equal (regardless of whether or not she had ever been married) is consistent with changing public understandings of "the single mother." In the early 1980s, CSMC had a slight name change (but retained the initialism) by way of acknowledging the shifting demographic of its clients. Initially established to support unmarried mothers who were excluded from government support, the introduction of benefits in 1973, along with the introduction of no-fault divorce in 1975, saw the services of CSMC increasingly being accessed by divorced mothers (Carson and Hendry 106). As a lobby group, CSMC henceforward advocated on behalf of all single mothers.

Until the late 1990s, welfare for single mothers acknowledged full-time care for children as a fulfillment of a mother's social citizenship contract. Indeed, Blaxland argues that income support recognized that "mothers have a moral responsibility to their children to be carers" ("Everyday" 26). As such, the payment model was based on a belief that parents (namely mothers) could be either a carer or a worker, but not both. Caring work trumped workforce participation. However, the 1996 introduction of the federal government program Work for the Dole and the concept of "mutual obligation" for jobseekers cemented a new belief in the reciprocal nature of income support. Though not immediately targeting single mothers, welfare was no longer being viewed as a right based on need but was being reimagined as a coercive measure with the power to target personal behaviour.

In 2002, John Howard and the Liberal-National Coalition government introduced a new initiative in social security support payments in the policy program Australians Working Together. This legislation was the first step in drastic welfare reform directed at single mothers, which would continue to the present day. Further changes were enacted in July 2006 with the Welfare-to-Work legislation, which targeted principal carer parents in particular; and in January 2013, further consolidation of this legislation saw single parents in receipt of Parenting Payment (Single) placed instead on the lower Newstart Allowance. Moreover, the 2014-15 budget proposes to cut funding and expenditure on a range of additional payments, allowances, and supports that are essential for single mothers, although these have yet to be passed. In analyzing the underlying motivation for these changes, Blaxland observes that

> The key rhetorical elements of these policy transformations were welfare claimant's obligation to employment for their own sake and for that of the community; parental obligation to employment as an element of good and "normal" mothering; and the need to ensure compliance through mandated activities tied to penalties for non-compliance. ("Mothers" 143)

Since the 1990s, debates have shifted from conditions of entitlement to the question of whether the behaviour of welfare recipients contributes to their disadvantage. Though clearly focused on economic reform, this faux concern for alleviating disadvantage opens the door to further debates about the single mother and her capacity to be a "good mother."

Placing a child's best interests at the centre of debates on the supposed validity and viability of certain types of family is not new, as it also played a role in past adoption policies and practices. Barbara Baird identifies this as a discourse of "child politics" and refers to the logic of such politics as "the fundamentalism of the child" (Baird 292). Baird argues that such discursive positioning is alarming in the way in which it constitutes "the child" as a fixed and absolute category and how this abstracted concept can be mobilized to fit a range of scenarios.

The child is not always specified in any detail, although it is often laden with racialized, gendered, classed and sexualised cultural assumptions. The child is a highly mobile signifier that, despite and because of the mobility, brings meaning over and above reference to real historical children into the various spheres where it is deployed (291).

Political debate in the 2000s set the interests of the child in opposition to those of the mother, particularly those "bad" single and lesbian mothers who fail to fulfill the criteria associated with good citizenship. Jennifer Lynne Smith argues that good citizenship is conveyed by those who are "professional, pay taxes, and are employed" and that much of the demonization stems from a flawed logic linking all single and lesbian mothers to the negative stereotype of the welfare-dependent single mother (141). Baird argues that the neo-conservative Howard years (1996-2007) were characterized as a period centred on policy about families and that this focus on the family was "driven by the figure of the 'father', implicitly if not explicitly" (300). It is, therefore, the absence of the father that becomes central to parliamentary debates about the family and its most appropriate form in Australia. The significance of parliamentary discourse as an analytical tool, particularly in examining the discursive construction of motherhood identity, has been emphasized by Smith, who argues that "it is not merely important because of its ability to produce legislation, but because the personal opinions of members are uttered from a position of influence" (81). Indeed, Senator Cory Bernardi cashed in on the "absent father" and his position of influence with the release of his 2014 book that denounced all single mothers as breeders of promiscuous daughters and criminal sons. Concerns about the absent father serve to reinforce the conception of the Australian family as a patriarchal institution in which women remain economically dependent on men.

CONCLUSION

Oral history interviews with single mothers express the way in which media, welfare, and parliamentary discourses continue to perpetuate the stigmatization of single mothers in Australia, which was earlier maintained by medical and scientific discourses. The impact is clear: although individuals attempt to exclude themselves from the negative stereotype, the conflation of categories of single motherhood is resolute, not only in the popular imagination but in how single mothers see themselves. Sociologists agree that social ideas about what families are, or ought to be, are constructed from the belief systems of a society's influential elites. As long as single mothers continue to be negatively stereotyped as a homogenous group by political, religious, economic, and academic leaders, the stigmatization of single mothers will continue. This is reflected in the narrative identity presented by participants. Pressure for families to conform to particular models of normativity affect not only the experiences mothers choose to share but also the way in which these experiences are constructed. Single mothers are constantly being told that they are doing it wrong: not working enough (or working too much), not feeding their children the right food, and not investing time with their children. In a personal interview with "Pamela,"[3] she commented on the perceived failures of the single mother:

> I do think that single women in general are somehow seen as having failed. They haven't got the family; they haven't got the man or the partner that would make them more viable. I think the sense is that single parent families do struggle with things. The dialogue in society is that women and couples can't have it all, so what about single mothers? They are either in poverty or they have worked too hard and the kids don't see them.

In the meantime, and despite the ongoing stigmatization, single mothers continue to parent effectively from the margins.

NOTES

[1]Percentage for peak year 1948 (Quirk, "Separated at Birth" fig. 4, 97).

[2]Swain and Howe argue that by the late 1960s and 1970s, "radical changes in attitudes to sexuality, the family and the status of women enabled single mothers to move from a position of negotiation within the system to one of greater social and economic independence" (196).

[3]Pseudonym.

WORKS CITED

Australian Human Rights Commission. *Bringing Them Home:*

Report of the National Inquiry into the Separation of Aboriginal and Torres Strait Islander Children from Their Families. Sydney: Australian Human Rights and Equal Opportunity Commission, 1997. Print.

Baird, Barbara. "Child Politics, Feminist Analyses." *Australian Feminist Studies* 23.57 (2008): 291-305. Print.

Bernardi, Cory. *The Conservative Revolution.* Ballarat: Connor Court Publishing, 2013. Print.

Blaxland, Megan. "Everyday Negotiations for Care and Autonomy in the World of Welfare-to-Work: The Policy Experience of Australian Mothers, 2003-2006." Diss. University of Sydney, 2008. Print.

Blaxland, Megan. "Mothers and Mutual Obligation: Policy Reforming the Good Mother." *The Good Mother: Contemporary Motherhoods in Australia*. Eds. Susan Goodwin and Kate Huppatz. Sydney: Sydney University Press, 2010. 131-151. Print.

Carson, Deanne, and Fiona Hendry. *Single but Not Alone: The First 40 Years of the Council of Single Mothers & Their Children*. Melbourne: Council of Single Mothers and Their Children, Inc., 2012. Print.

Commonwealth of Australia. Australian Bureau of Statistics. "2011 Census Quick Stats." *Australian Bureau of Statistics*. Government of Australia, 28 Mar. 2013. Web. 10 June 2014.

Commonwealth of Australia. *Royal Commission on National Insurance, Third Progress Report: Destitution Allowances*. Melbourne: Government Printer, 1927. Print.

Cutright, Phillips. "Illegitimacy: Myths, Causes and Cures: A Family Planning Perspectives Special Feature." *Family Planning Perspectives* 3.1 (1971): 25-48. Print.

De Vaus, David. *Diversity and Change in Australian Families: Statistical Profiles*. Series edited by the Australian Institute of Family Studies. Melbourne: Commonwealth of Australia, 2004. Print.

Drummond, Sue. Personal interview. 13 Feb. 2014.

Dunlevy, Sue. "Single Parents Are More Likely to Have Obese Kids, Australian Institute of Health and Welfare Finds." *News.com.au*. News Limited, 12 June 2014. Web. 12 June 2014.

Haebich, Anna. *Broken Circles: Fragmenting Indigenous Families, 1800-2000*. Fremantle: Fremantle Arts Centre Press, 2000. Print.

Hartley, S. M. "The Amazing Rise of Illegitimacy in Great Britain." *Social Forces* 44.4 (1966): 533-545. Print.

Herscovitch, Andrew, and David Stanton. "History of Social Security in Australia." *Family Matters* 80 (2008): 51-60. Print.

Hirst, John. "Welfare Underpins the Regular Abuse of Children." *smh.com.au*. Sydney Morning Herald, 16 Jan. 2013. Web. 27 May 2016.

Johns, Nan. "The Health of Babies Kept by Their Single Mothers: A Study of the First Years of Life of a Melbourne Sample." 1974. Print.

Lake, Marilyn. *Getting Equal: The History of Australian Feminism*. St Leonards: Allen & Unwin, 1999. Print.

Lawrence, R. J. *Professional Social Work in Australia*. Canberra: Australian National University, 1965. Print.

Lawson, D.F. "The R.H. Fetherston Memorial Lecture: The Anxieties of Pregnancy." *The Medical Journal of Australia* 30 July (1960): 164-166. Print.

Lee, Deborah. "The Growth and Role of Self Help Groups." *To Search for Self: The Experience of Access to Adoption Information*. Eds. Phillip A. Swain and Shurlee Swain. Sydney: Federation Press, 1992. 67-78. Print.

Nicholson, Linda. "The Myth of the Traditional Family." *Feminism and Families*. Ed. Hilde Lindemann Nelson. New York: Routledge, 1997. 27-42. Print.

Kiely, Rosemary. "Single Mothers and Supermyths." *Australian Journal of Social Issues* 17.2 (May 1982): 155-60. Print.

Kunzel, Regina G. *Fallen Women, Problem Girls: Unmarried Mothers and the Professionalization of Social Work, 1890-1945*. New Haven: Yale University Press, 1993. Print.

"Pamela." Personal interview. 6 Feb. 2014.

Quartly, Marian, Shurlee Swain, and Denise Cuthbert. *The Market in Babies: Stories of Australian Adoption*. Melbourne: Monash University Publishing, 2013. Print.

Quirk, Christin. "Separated at Birth: Adoption and Delivery Practices in Relation to Single Women Confined at the Royal Women's Hospital 1945-1975." MPhil. Australian Catholic University, 2012. Print.

Quirk, Christin. "The Business of Adoption: Past Practices at the

Royal Women's Hospital Melbourne." *Lilith: A Feminist History Journal* 19 (2013): 46-59. Print.

Robinson, Shirleene. "1960s Counter-Culture in Australia: The Search for Personal Freedom." *The 1960s in Australia: People, Power and Politics*. Eds. Shirleene Robinson and Julie Ustinoff. Newcastle upon Tyne: Cambridge Scholars Publishing, 2012. 123-142. Print.

Saggers, Sherry, and Margaret Sims. "Diversity: Beyond the Nuclear Family." *Family: Changing Families, Changing Times*. Ed. Marilyn Poole. Crows Nest: Allen & Unwin, 2004. 66-87. Print.

Shaver, Sheila. "Design for a Welfare State: The Joint Parliamentary Committee on Social Security." *Historical Studies*. 22.88 (1987): 411-431. Print.

Short, Elizabeth et al. *Lesbian, Gay, Bisexual and Transgender (LGBT) Parented Families: A Literature Review Prepared for the Australian Psychological Society*. Melbourne: Australian Psychological Society, 2007. Print.

Smith, Jennifer Lynne. "Idealised and Demonised: The Construction of Motherhood in the IVF Policy Debate in Australia." Diss. University of Queensland, 2004. Print.

Swain, Shurlee, and Renate Howe. *Single Mothers and Their Children: Disposal, Punishment and Survival in Australia*. Cambridge: Cambridge University Press, 1995. Print.

Thompson, Roger C., *Religion in Australia: A History*. Melbourne: Oxford University Press, 1994. Print.

West, Rosemary. "How Single Mothers Overcame Discrimination." *Actions Speak: Strategies and Lessons from Australian Social and Community Action*. Eds. Eileen Baldry and Tony

Vinson. Melbourne: Longman Cheshire, 1991. 168-186. Print.

Young, Leontine R. *Out of Wedlock*. 1954. Westport: Greenwood Press, 1978. Print.

11. Single-Parent Families, Mother-Led Households, and Well-Being

RACHEL LAMDIN HUNTER

WIDESPREAD INTEREST in human well-being is evident in social policy and science research journals, health and family research, government statistics, and, more recently, organizational and economic research. Human psychology, increasingly prominent since the early twentieth century, has prioritized individual well-being in Western, democratically orientated societies. Research into well-being should improve individual human health and happiness (Pollard and Lee 59; Angner 5), whereas other research into wellness evaluates the satisfaction of material, physical, affective, and psychological needs and how they are affected by societal, familial, and community wellness (Prilleltensky, Nelson, and Peirson 143). Aspirations for and assessments of wellness are often positioned in government policy and health-focused research as the shared responsibility of government agencies, local community bodies, families, and individual citizens (Cook 143; New Zealand, Ministry of Social Development). Understanding and improving well-being remains a challenge. In this chapter, my interest lies with the assessment and enhancement of the well-being of mothers and their children in mother-led families. Health and social researchers overwhelmingly report poorer well-being for women and children in lone-mother or single-parent families, as compared with two-parent households (Haskins 129). Tensions between the value of producing objective data and reporting subjective experience are well documented. I question how well these research findings represent the experiences of the people whom they purport to represent and, importantly, to what effect? My focus is on the use of purportedly objective data (such as income and housing statistics) as well as the subjective statements taken from scales pre-prepared by researchers (Rablen 300) in research purporting to depict the status of this population for interventionist intent. I begin with a review of the literature concerning the well-being of children and families, dealing with lone-parent families in particular, and examine the relationships between lone-parent resilience, creativity, and self-efficacy, which are commonly glossed over or absent from the literature. I urge a deepened self-reflection on the part of researchers, whose work often exposes sole mothers to the gaze of policymakers, with the intent of enhancing the well-being of mother-led families, their communities, and, by extension, their wider society.

RESEARCHING WELL-BEING

Health and social well-being practitioners have been seen as "experts" on humanity and health for more than a century. Many hold that a society's success is predicated on its children thriving; thus, children have become a major focus of social and humanitarian research. Growing capacity in the surveillance of children and their circumstances enables increased exposure of their lives to adults, including those who wish to help them and those who have the power to define and direct them and their equally exposed caregivers. Researchers are at the forefront of such definition, direction, and exposure. Research into child well-being is justified by the belief that a prompt investment of society's resources in children returns dividends once they reach adulthood, as it results in their productive contribution to society and independence from ever-diminishing social and economic support (McAuley, Morgan, and Rose). These investments may come in the form of health or early childhood education provisions, which are believed to mitigate against lost worktime and to reduce costly social services. According to UNICEF (*Child Wellbeing in Rich Countries* 4), child well-being is a moral imperative for governments as well as a basis for social policy and economic distribution of resources, which is encapsulated in their statement: "The true measure of a nations' standing is how well it attends to its children" (UNICEF, *An Overview of Child Wellbeing* 1).

WELL-BEING IN CHILDREN AND FAMILIES

Child-focused research indicates that for children to thrive, their caregivers must flourish also. Indicators of child well-being are directly linked to the lives, actions, habits, behaviours, skills, potential, and economic status of the children's parents and caregivers (Frech and Kimbro 605; Garbarski and Witt 484). Mothers remain more likely to be the primary caregiver, despite changes in the public, employment, and educational status of women (Crompton and Lyonette 602; Crabb; Esping-Anderson 169). A mounting critique concerns the justice, and effects, of holding one individual entirely responsible for all aspects of the well-being of children (Fisher 596; Kinser 319). Some researchers have contended that much of the literature blames the mother for a child's suffering (Carpenter and Austin 660; Kinser). Shari Thurer calls attention to this culture of "mother blaming" (162), which was identified earlier by Adrienne Rich, in popular media, and also the disempowerment, anger, and despair felt by mothers, who are solely responsible for their children but lack the concomitant resources to better their circumstances.

For children, caring relationships are also evident in connections with fathers, siblings, extended family, paid caregivers, teachers, and other close adults, all of whom, ideally, contribute to the child's attachment and well-being (Gonzalez, Jones, and Parent 36; Yoshida 453; McAuley, Morgan, and Rose 43). However, the complex interconnectedness of humans, in particular between children and their mothers or other caregivers, is poorly represented in research on well-being in families. Historically, researchers have conceptualized people, including dependent children, as discrete, self-contained actors (La Placa, McNaught, and Knight 117; Sointu 255). Views of people as intimately interconnected beings are given occasionally but are rarely acknowledged as a reality from which to begin well-being research (White 9). Discourses of humans as responsible and self-contained individuals (Giddens) dominate Western thought, and resonate with the ideals of twentieth-century individual psychology, wherein well-being research first became a focus. The post-Enlightenment construction of people as autonomous individuals is exemplified in advice given by child experts such as John B. Watson in the 1920s, whose work is detailed by Kathryn Bigelow and Edward Morris (26). Watson and others disapproved of showing affection towards children and, instead, favoured the development of independence and staunch self-sufficiency. Such perspectives are now widely understood to be detrimental to the well-being of children; they arose at the time when "well-being" was under initial conceptualization.

Well-being determinants, such as the disparate lists produced by the UNICEF reports, appear separately as distinct and separate silos. Approaches to well-being which see it as an isolated experience in which individuals are autonomous, ignore entire groups, including families and societies in which collective identities predominate (White 9). For researchers contemplating complex relationships in families, both as a research phenomenon and as a determinant of well-being, individualized measures of well-being are inadequate to understand relationships and interdependent lives.

WELL-BEING AND LONE-MOTHER FAMILIES

Family structure as a determinant of well-being appears in research that names lone-mother families as suffering a greater risk of harm. Research into life in mother-led or lone-mother households is dominated by negative accounts of deficit or survival. This negative bias is depicted in article with titles such as "Has the Association between Parental Divorce and Young Adults' Psychological Problems Changed over Time?" (Gahler and Garriga) and "Attitudes of Children from Complete and Single-Parent Families towards Consumption of Narcotic Substances" (Narbute 62). Amato and Sobolewski's claim that children's well-being is endangered into adulthood after parental divorce, uses data from the 1980s and 1990s as evidence of poorer socio-economic "achievement," poorer relationship skills and quality of parent-adult child relations, poorer self-control, and higher use of adult mental health services, compared with adults whose parents never divorced. However, other research has also shown that sustained intra-familial conflict—not only divorce—creates negative life effects and harms long-term well-being, even in two-parent households (Woessmann 43; McKay 125; Amato and Sobolewski). The effects of familial conflict, divorce, and single-parent family life are easily conflated but poorly distinguished (Riggio 100; Davis 36), indicating that families require access to robust conflict resolution and post-divorce support rather than avoidance of lone-mother status as some may recommend (Haskins). Another purported comparison of well-being between families of one parent and families of two parents features in UNICEF's *Child Wellbeing in Rich Countries*, which identifies "relationships," including family structures, as an external negative indicator of well-being. The writers paradoxically admit that this approach appears "unfair and insensitive," as similar difficulties are experienced in two-parent families and many children thrive in single-parent families. However, they insist that at a "statistical level," growing up in single-parent families and stepfamilies is hazardous and quote "a greater risk of dropping out of school, of leaving home early, of poorer health, of low skills and low pay" (23). The gendered external economic factors that shape this are mentioned elsewhere in this chapter and in many other studies; however, the hazards of large quantitative surveys attempting to form a broad snapshot of well-being are rarely acknowledged - yet are noted by Richard Eckersley (2) in a critique of studies that, he claims, may feature contradictory questions leading to skewed or inaccurate responses.

The negative stereotyping of lone-parent families remains visible in popular media, in which lone motherhood is conflated with unplanned teen parenthood. Although most single-parent households are headed by middle-class mothers, they are persistently depicted as never-married and state-dependent teens (Hutt 77). A Pew Research Center paper reports that public discomfort with households whose main or sole earner is a mother belies the fact that "breadwinner moms" frequently represent two-parent families (Wang, Parker, and Taylor 2). The qualities forged by women in lone-mother families, including safety or resilience, remain largely invisible or minimized in public discourse. The effect on such families of such pitying or damning rhetoric is significant, including the debilitating effects of discrimination and the struggle to overcome these negative stereotypes (Zartler 607). Among people who experience chronic stress, economic disadvantage, and discrimination, single mothers are overrepresented. Even mothers who successfully create support networks for themselves, using every available resource, are taught to see themselves as failed human beings if they are unable to meet all of their own and their children's needs (Goldscheider; Belle and Doucet 101).

The economic disadvantage experienced by those in single-parent families has, in New Zealand, become a topic of conversation illuminating the risks of economic social inequality in relation to well-being. Max Rashbrooke, in his book "*Inequality: A New Zealand Crisis*," discusses how well-being can be enhanced by addressing the inequalities that are experienced by citizens positioned as inferior or lower class, even though such relationships are complex. Economic disadvantage experienced by those in lone-mother households relates to reduced earning power by lone adults who care for children and a failure of governments to adequately address such inequalities, which are persistently gendered in nature. Further gendered analysis of societal structures in order to address gender pay gaps, availability of childcare, and taxation to redress economic imbalances is needed, particularly as burgeoning inequality in many OECD countries has been shown to disadvantage whole populations, not merely those at the bottom (Rashbrooke). My focus in this chapter, however, surrounds the research generated by those who are alarmed at such inequalities and the unintended effects of their positioning of families.

A basic internet search including such broad terms as "problems," "two-parent family," and "single-parent family" attributes various problems to the supposed inadequacies of single-parent families, which are mostly headed by mothers (Narbute 62; Demirblilek et al. 2; Schroeder, Osgood, and Oghia). The pervasive "othering" of any family not a two-parent nuclear one reinforces a dysfunctional view of single-mother families. A series of research articles arising from The Fragile Families study—which was initiated in the United States in 1998 and whose findings continue to be disseminated in a number of studies (McLanahan et al; Osborne and Knab; Harknett and Hartnett)—draw conclusions from a pool of research that casts a negative slant on families who exist outside a nuclear-family frame. The study's periodic interviews with parents, who are unmarried at the time of their child's birth, are based on a premise that such parents are at far higher risk of poor social outcomes, not only economic peril but poor education and decision-making capacity, and a higher propensity to "instability" and "risk" than the "non-fragile" (two-parent) families, with whom they are compared. The terminology of families as "fragile" denotes a deficit-burdened family, who is less than resilient. The ethic of positioning families as fragile, a term synonymous with "flimsy" or "insubstantial" is questionable. Results from the study present single or unmarried parents in deficit-laden terms across indicators not limited to income or social support, but encompassing self-concept, relationship success, and other indicators. No outcomes of the Fragile Families study laud the capabilities or advantages of such parents, many of whom respond nimbly to factors outside of their control. The recruitment of participants, whom the *authors* decide deserve the "fragile" label, glorifies a time-specific and culture-specific social ritual (marriage), which, according to Robyn Penman, is diminishing in social value and occurrence. The moral intonations arising from such studies infer that improved family well-being relies on women remaining or getting married, (Haskins 147). The lack of concern and critique regarding the ethical presuppositions underpinning the Fragile Families study is concerning, as it suggests that the dominance of the nuclear-family discourse is naturalized enough as to be largely invisible to researchers, ethics committees, and prospective participants.

RESEARCHER INTERESTS

In countries where much of the twentieth-century family and social research originated, including the United States and the United Kingdom, well-being and family research favoured the nuclear family form of two heterosexual parents and their biological children. This structure was presented as typical, easily researchable, and preferred. Single-parent families (struggling post-World War one and then after the Great Depression) along with grandparent-headed and extended families, were understood to be a result of misfortune more than choice and were likely to reside at the social and economic margins. The espoused benefits of nuclear families were promoted as a way to improve society and human well-being. Uniformity and conformity rather than diversity were valued in health and political policy. The increased valuing of "expert" scientific knowledge in psychology and health reinforced the external authority held by professionals, among them academic researchers (Ehrenreich and English). During World War II, many mothers demonstrated the ability to care for families while working, and without husbands by their side. Yet after World War II, conclusions regarding attachment relationships, drawn from studies by John Bowlby and Mary Ainsworth, were used by policymakers to encourage mothers to remain at home with children in order to ensure those children's well-being and to provide support to an earning husband or father, reinforcing their economic dependence on him and rendering single-mother homes ever more precarious. Poor employment opportunities for women were ensured by the reality that full-time employment would be reserved for men returning from war service. Since then, family sizes and forms have shifted in response to various forces, such as technology, contraception, women's employment, and urbanization. Yet the nuclear family retains a dominant position in research and in policy considerations, despite the limitations and vulnerabilities engendered by such forms.

The classification, for statistical purposes, of women (and by association their households) as married, single, divorced, or separated deserves closer scrutiny. Many studies of women and families prioritize interest in women's marital status but fail to explicate the rationale behind the categorization (Demo and Acock; Schwarz and Walper). Within each category, there is a vast range of life experience (Hutt) and across categories, many similarities exist, such as those investigated in Arlie Hochschild's studies of families managing work and home life. Researchers could focus attention on other variations and commonalities that affect well-being—such as the numbers, ages, age gaps and genders of children, individual histories or preferences of each person, and salient events, including hospitalization or trauma, dietary requirements, quality of housing, and cultural or religious practices. These aspects of family life and their relevance for well-being may prove as relevant as universal classifications of maternal marital status or monetary income, yet they are still neglected in studies of maternal and child well-being.

Other scholars draw attention to the relationships between marital status and health in their reporting of the negative effects of living in inequitable or conflict-ridden marriages, including lower levels of personal happiness and self-esteem and higher incidences of depression (Demo and Acock; Kamp-Dush; and Taylor). They posit the importance of maternal satisfaction with, and preference of, current circumstances as a predictor of well-being among women not wishing to remarry or return to an inhospitable relationship, despite the supposed statistical benefits. Non-egalitarian marriages are at higher risk of dissatisfaction and conflict (Kamp-Dush; and Taylor 15). Other researchers claim that women are more likely than men to initiate separation and cite lack of support, financial problems, and abuse among reasons for leaving (Amato and Previti; Rosenfeld). Separation and divorce are shown to occur across income and social gradients, whereby financially poorer and unsupported families separate more readily than more affluent and supported couples (Bradbury and Norris). It is likely that some single mothers' financial difficulty or isolation as lone parents reflects ongoing stress, and financial difficulty predates the separation itself. Researchers citing concern for well-being in lone-mother households (Chapple; Dush and Amato; Perry-Jenkins and Gillman) may find that some struggling single-mother families have escaped similarly pressured marriages, yet this is absent in research focused on simple comparisons between one-parent and two-parent families. In such comparisons, poorer two-parent families remain obscured by higher-income two-parent families until such time as those households split and become visible in lower-income, single-parent household data.

Women's preferences for lone parenting are under-researched, though visible in online forms of inquiry, including blogs and online social media forums. Here, women share their sense of freedom, hopefulness, empowerment, resilience and renewed focus upon their children. For instance, on the online blog *MsSingleMama*, the author declares "Every single mother I've ever met has been so strong, like a rock, fortified in her own solitude completely aware of the challenges and the rewards" (Sheer). Online social media sites for single parents feature comments about empowerment, emerging problem-solving skills, and coming to value oneself to care for others. Evidence which includes users of Facebook and Twitter is emerging (Wilson, Gosling, and Graham). However, academic (ethical and methodological) requirements continue to privilege forms of research inquiry which have commonly silenced informal or unsolicited voices like these (Oakley, *Experiments in Knowing*). Ethically grounded insight available on such sites deserves further investigation and will eventually supplement as well as challenge traditional data-collection tools.

The invisibility of lone mothers' stories in formal research is exemplified by Fawzia Ahmad's quest to overcome the fear and responsibility of raising children alone. She is eased, she says, by telling the story of her mothering experience to take control of how she gives her life meaning. Researchers have found that such empowerment can boost well-being (Prilleltensky, Nelson, and Peirson; Fielding).

RESEARCHER POSITIONING

The positivist origins of formal social science research were based on principles developed for natural science research and valued detachment between researcher and participant to avoid researcher bias or influence and to maintain quality and rigour in research (Crotty; Oakley, *Experiments in Knowing*). By following this standard, researchers hoped that their findings would remain pure and unsullied by the vagaries of human emotion, to map and document a neutral external world waiting to be empirically discovered. Other social researchers argue the impossibility and undesirability of maintaining such a position in research (Gergen and Gergen; Adams, Holmes Jones, and Ellis; Oakley, *People's Ways of Knowing*). They urge researchers to recognize and explore the personal and ethical and social dimensions of their work; indeed, the influence of the researcher on the study cannot and should not be avoided. Researchers must be mindful that their values and intentions unavoidably influence research questions and topics, findings, and discussions (Ellis, Adams, and Bochner). These and other theorists recommend researcher reflexivity, in which these influences are acknowledged, as a nobler and more pragmatic goal for those who wish to carry out worthwhile research. Researchers who ignore the effects of their gendered, cultural, and social assumptions and values on others risk dismissing or harming participants, whose realities and values ought to be the focus. In well-being research, participants from backgrounds dissimilar to researchers (including women, children, and people of ethnic minorities) may question the representation of their cultural realities in the research (Oakley, *Experiments in Knowing*).

Research academies have been found to reflect a particular conservative, individualistic, and patriarchal valuing of well-being, women and children, as well as a preference for certain gender functions and the promotion of normative (nuclear) family forms. As such, these structures provided foundations for research that now addresses shifting features of families, such as single and working mothers, late childbearing, shared household responsibilities, and evolving roles of fathers at home—research that remains influenced and distorted by longstanding normative perspectives. Some researchers demonstrate a visible preference for the supposed benefits of living in two-parent families (Maginnis); beside such an agenda, lone-mother families continue to be viewed as deviant. Unless sole-parent families headed by mothers are recognized as intentional and resilient embodiments rather than an aberration from a time- and culture-specific norm, belief in the superiority of the two-parent nuclear household will continue.

Feminist thinkers pose a challenge to traditional academic and research structures in institutions that uphold patriarchal values shown to undermine women and the needs of those in their care (Belenky; Gilligan; Oakley, *People's Ways of Knowing*; Reinharz). Such writers advocate for a critical and nuanced understanding of apparently innocuous concepts, such as "well-being" and "family," terms that have been discursively constructed according to patriarchal values. Moving forward, researchers must acknowledge the effect that their work has on the lives and well-being of women and wider society (Hood, Mayall, and Oliver; Oakley, *Experiments in Knowing*). Research that reinforces and reproduces a deficient evaluation of single-parent families requires re-examination.

CONCLUSION: ENVISIONING THE MOTHER-LED HOUSEHOLD

Well-being is a term with various definitions, as chosen by researchers in health, economics and psychology. Findings drawn from purportedly objective measures of well-being prevail in policy responses. Methods encompassing participants' own accounts of well-being continue to draw on previously established research findings, which reflects a continued tradition in research design and orientation that centres two-parent family. Constructing people as atomised individuals, these methods have failed to grasp the complexities of interconnected mother-child relationships. When issues of income, social support, the interrelatedness of child and maternal well-being, and the limitations of traditionally dominant methods of research (including ignorance regarding the gravity of researcher positioning) are recognized, findings are much less clear, and the strengths and advantages of single-parent families come to light. Going beyond blunt positivist comparison of married and single-parent households to generate richer and more meaningful interpretive knowledge provides a nuanced account of life in mother-led households and is a necessary development in well-being-focused research. A committed effort is needed to extend forms of fieldwork to include informal, narrative, and online sources as well as to commit to researcher reflexivity across all methodologies which acknowledge rather than ignore the embedded values of the researcher. Findings drawn from research projects that reflect limited views of multidimensional realities must be challenged; the persistent denigration of sole-parent families in research undermines well-being in lone-parent families. The reframing of "lone mothers" as "mother-led households" is intended to highlight the strengths, capacity, and gifts that mothers readily describe when research methods and values are scrutinized and revised. More qualitative research informed by nuanced findings regarding both two-parent and one-parent households is required. This chapter encourages such a methodological reframing in future research and urges researchers to listen more carefully to the voices of women and respect their accounts of their own lives.

WORKS CITED

Adams, Tony E., Stacy Holman Jones, and Carolyn Ellis. *Autoethnography*. New York: Oxford University Press, 2015. Print.

Ahmad, Fawzia. "Despite All Odds: Single Mothering's Empowerment." *Journal of Feminist Studies in Religion* 27.2 (2011): 140-143. Print.

Amato, Paul, and Denise Previti. "People's Reasons for Divorcing: Gender, Social Class, the Life Course and Adjustment." *Journal of Family Issues* 24.5 (2003): 602-626. Print.

Amato, Paul, and Juliana M. Sobolewski. "The Effects of Divorce and Marital Discord on Adult Children's Psychological Well-Being." *American Sociological Review* 66.6 (2001): 900-921. Print.

Angner, Eric. "The Evolution of Eupathics: The Historical Roots of Subjective Measures of Wellbeing." *International Journal of Wellbeing*. 1.1 (2011): 4-41. Print.

Belenky, Mary. *Women's Ways of Knowing: The Development of Self, Voice, and Mind*. New York: Basic Books Inc., 1986. Print.

Belle, Deborah, and Joanne Doucet. "Poverty, Inequality and Discrimination as Sources of Depression among U.S. Women." *Psychology of Women Quarterly* 27.2 (2003): 101-113. Print.

Bigelow, Kathryn M., and Edward K. Morris. "John B. Watson's Advice on Child Rearing." *Behavioral Development Bulletin*. 1 (2001): 26-30. Print.

Bradbury, Bruce, and Kate Norris. "Income and Separation." *Journal of Sociology* 41.4 (2005): 425-446. Print.

Carpenter, Lorelei, and Helena Austin. "Silenced, Silence, Silent: Motherhood in the Margins." *Qualitative Inquiry* 13.5 (2007): 660-674. Print.

Chapple, Simon. *Child Well-Being and Sole-Parent Family Structure in the OECD: An Analysis*. Paris: OECD Publishing, 2009. Print.

Cook, Kay. E. "Single Parents' Subjective Wellbeing Over the Welfare to Work Transition." *Social Policy and Society*. 11.2 (2012): 143-155. Print.

Crabb, Annabel. *The Wife Drought*. North Sydney: Random House Australia, 2014. Print.

Crompton, Rosemary, and Clare Lyonette. "The New Gender Essentialism—Domestic and Family 'Choices' and Their Relation to Attitudes." *The British Journal of Sociology* 56.4 (2005): 601-620. Print.

Crotty, Michael. *The Foundations of Social Research: Meaning and Perspective in the Research Process.* Crow's Nest: Allen & Unwin Australia, 1998. Print.

Davis, Chris. "The Long-Term Effects of Divorce and Parental Discord on the Adult-Child's Socioeconomic Attainment." *The Park Place Economist* 16.1 (2008): 36-44. Print.

Demo, David H. and Alan C. Acock. "Singlehood, Marriage and Remarriage." *Journal of Family Issues* 17 (1996): 388-407. Print.

Dush, Claire M.K, and Paul Amato. "Consequences of Relationship Status and Quality for Subjective Well-being." *Journal of Social and Personal Relationships* 22.5 (2005): 607-627. Print.

Eckersley, Richard. "Population Measures of Subjective Wellbeing: How Useful Are They?" *Social Indicators Research* 94.1 (2009): 1-12. Print.

Ehrenreich, Barbara, and Deidre English. *For Her Own Good: 150 Years of the Experts' Advice to Women.* London, England: Pluto Press, 1979. Print.

Eckersley, Richard. "Beyond Inequality: Acknowledging the Complexity of Social Determinants of Health." *Social Science and Medicine* 147 (2015): 121-125. Print.

Ellis, Carolyn, Tony E. Adams, and Arthur P. Bochner. "Autoethnography: An Overview." *Forum: Qualitative Social Research* 12.1 (2011): n.pag. Print.

Esping-Andersen, Gosta. *The Incomplete Revolution: Adapting Welfare States to Women's New Roles.* Cambridge: Polity Press, 2009. Print.

Fielding, David. "How Much Does Women's Empowerment Influence Their Wellbeing? Evidence from Africa." Economics Discussion Papers No. 1307. Dunedin: University of Otago, 2013. n.pag. Print.

Fisher, Pamela. "Wellbeing and Empowerment: The Importance of Recognition." *Sociology of Health and Illness* 30.4 (2008): 583-598. Print.

Frech, Adrianne, and Rachel T. Kimbro. "Maternal Mental Health, Neighbourhood Characteristics, and Time Investments in Children." *Journal of Marriage and Family* 73.3 (2011): 605-621.

Print.

Gahler, Michael, and Anna Garriga. "Has the Association Between Parental Divorce and Young Adults' Psychological Problems Changed Over Time? Evidence from Sweden, 1968-2000." *Journal of Family Issues* 34.6 (2012): 784-808. Print.

Garbarski, Dana, and Whitney Witt. "Child Health, Maternal Marital and Socioeconomic Factors, and Maternal Health." *Journal of Family Issues* 34.4 (2012): 484-509. Print.

Gergen, Kenneth J., and Mary Gergen. *Social Construction: Entering the Dialogue*. Ohio: Taos Institute Publications, 2004. Print.

Giddens, Anthony. *Sociology*. 5th ed. Cambridge: Polity Press, 2006. Print.

Gilligan, Carol. *In a Different Voice: Psychological Theory and Women's Development*. Cambridge: Harvard University Press, 1993. Print.

Goldscheider, Frances. "Rescuing the Family from the Homophobes and Antifeminists: Analyzing the Recently Developed and Already Eroding 'Traditional' Notions of Family and Gender." *Case Western Reserve Law Review* 64.3 (2014): 1029-1044. Print.

Gonzalez, Michelle, Deborah Jones and Justin Parent. "Coparenting Experiences in African American families: An Examination of Single Mothers and their Nonmarital Coparents." *Family Process* 53 (2014): 33-34. Print.

Harknett, Kristen, and Caroline S. Hartnett. "Who Lacks Support and Why? An Examination of Mothers' Personal Safety Nets." *Journal of Marriage and Family* 73.4 (2011): 861-875. Print.

Hochschild, Arlie R. *The Second Shift: Working Parents and the Revolution at Home*. New York: Viking Penguin Inc., 1989. Print.

Hochschild, Arlie R. *The Time Bind: When Work Becomes Home and Home Becomes Work*. New York: Metropolitan Books, 2001. Print.

Hood, Suzanne, Berry Mayall, and Sandy Oliver. *Critical Issues in Social Research*. Buckingham: Open University Press, 1999. 1-9. Print.

Hutt, Rachael. "New Zealand's Sole Parents and Their Marital Status: Updating the Last Decade." *New Zealand Population Review* 38 (2012): 77-93. Print.

Kamp-Dush, Claire M, and Miles G. Taylor. "Trajectories of Marital Conflict across the Life Course: Predictors and Interactions with Marital Happiness Trajectories." *Journal of Family Issues* 33.3 (2012): 341-368. Print.

Kinser, Amber E. "At the Core of the Work/Life Balance Myth: Motherhood and Family Dinners." *What Do Mothers Need? Motherhood Activists and Scholars Speak out on Maternal Empowerment for the 21st Century*. Ed. Andrea O'Reilly. Bradford, ON: Demeter Press, 2012. 316-330. Print.

La Placa, Vincent, Allan McNaught and Anneyce Knight. "Discourse on Wellbeing in Research and Practice." *International Journal of Wellbeing* 3.1 (2013): 116-125. Print.

Maginnis, R.L. "Single-Parent Families Cause Juvenile Crime." *Juvenile Crime: Opposing Viewpoints*. Ed. A.E. Sadler. Farmington Hills: Greenhaven Press, 1997.62-66. Print.

McAuley, Colette, Roger Morgan, and Wendy Rose. "Children's Views on Child Well-Being." *Child Well-Being: Understanding Children's Lives*. Eds. Colette McAuley and Wendy Rose. London: Jessica Kingsley Publishers, 2010. 39-66. Print.

McLanahan, Sara, Irwin Garfinkel, Nancy Reichman and Julien Teitler. *Unwed Parents or Fragile Families? Implications for Welfare and Child Support Policy*. Princeton University: Center for Research on Child Wellbeing Working Paper #00-04. 2004. Print.

New Zealand. Ministry of Social Development. *Children and Young People: Indicators of Wellbeing in New Zealand*. Wellington: Ministry of Social Development, 2008. Print.

Narbute, Jurate. "Attitudes of Children from Complete and Single-Parent Families towards Consumption of Narcotic Substances." *Applied Research in Health and Social Sciences: Interface and Interaction* 1.9 (2012): 62-67. Print.

Oakley, Ann. *Experiments in Knowing: Gender and Method in the Social Sciences*. Cambridge: Polity Press, 2000. Print.

Oakley, Ann. "People's Ways of Knowing: Gender and Methodology." *Critical Issues in Social Research*. Eds. Suzanne Hood, Berry Mayall and Sandy Oliver. Buckingham: Open University Press, 1999. 154-170. Print.

Osborne, Cynthia, and Jean Knab. "Work, Welfare and Young Children's Health and Behaviour in the Fragile Families and Child Wellbeing Study." *Children and Youth Services Review*

29.6 (2007): 762-781. Print.

Penman, Robyn. "Current Approaches to Marriage and Relationship Research in the United States and Australia." *Family Matters* 70 (Autumn) (2005): 26-35. Print.

Perry-Jenkins, Maureen, and Sally Gillman. "Parental Job Experiences and Children's Well-being: The Case of Two-Parent and Single-Mother Working-Class Families." *Journal of Family and Economic Issues* 21.2 (2000): 123-147. Print.

Pollard, Elizabeth L, and Patrice D. Lee. "Child Well-being: A Systematic Review of the Literature." *Social Indicators Research.* 61.1 (2003): 59-78. Print.

Prilleltensky, Isaac, Geoffrey Nelson and Leslea Peirson. "The Role of Power and Control in Children's Lives: An Ecological Analysis of Pathways toward Wellness, Resilience and Problems." *Journal of Community and Applied Social Psychology* 11.2 (2001): 143-158. Print.

Rablen, Matthew. "The Promotion of Local Well-Being: A Primer for Policymakers." *Local Economy* 27.3 (2012): 297-314. Print.

Rashbrooke, Max. *Inequality: A New Zealand Crisis.* Wellington: Bridget Williams Books, 2013. Print.

Reinharz, Shulamit. *Feminist Methods in Social Research.* New York: Oxford University Press, 1992. Print.

Rich, Adrienne. *Of Woman Born: Motherhood as Experience and Institution.* New York: W.W. Norton & Company, 1995. Print.

Riggio, Heidi R. "Parental Marital Conflict and Divorce, Parent-Child Relationships, Social Support, and Relationship Anxiety in Young Adulthood." *Personal Relationships* 11.1 (2004): 99-114. Print.

Rosenfeld, Michael J. *Who Wants the Breakup? Gender and Breakup in Heterosexual Couples.* Draft Paper, 2015. Print.

Schroeder, Ryan, Aurea K. Osgood, and Michael J. Oghia. "Family Transitions and Juvenile Delinquency." *Sociological Inquiry* 80.4 (2010): 579-604. Print.

Schwarz, Beate, and Sabine Walper. "Adolescents' Individuation, Romantic Involvement, and Mothers' Wellbeing: A Comparison of Three Family Structures." *European Journal of Developmental Psychology* 6.4 (2009): 499-520. Print.

Sheer, Alaina. "Being a Single Mom with a Glass Half Full". *Ms*

Single Mama: Musings on Life, Love and Motherhood. WordPress, 2007. Web 10 Dec. 2013.

Sointu, Eva. "The Rise of an Ideal: Tracing Discourses of Wellbeing." *The Sociological Review* 53.2 (2005): 255-274. Print.

Thurer, Shari L. *The Myths of Motherhood: How Culture Reinvents the Good Mother.* Middlesex: Penguin Publishers, 1994. Print.

UNICEF. *An Overview of Child Wellbeing in Rich Countries.* Report Card 7. Florence: Innocenti Research Center, 2007. Print.

UNICEF. *Child Wellbeing in Rich Countries: A Comparative Overview.* Report Card 11. Florence: Innocenti Office of Research, 2013. Print.

Wang, Wendy, Kim Parker, and Paul Taylor. *Breadwinner Moms.* Washington, D.C.: Pew Research Center, 2013. Print.

White, Sarah C. *Analyzing Wellbeing: A Framework for Development Practice.* WeD Working Paper 09/44. 2009. University of Bath: Bath, UK. Print.

Wilson, Robert E, Samuel D. Gosling, and Lindsay T. Graham. "A Review of Facebook Research in the Social Sciences." *Perspectives on Psychological Science* 7.3 (2012): 203-220. Print.

Woessmann, Ludger. "An International Look at the Single-Parent Family: Family Structure Matters More." *Education Next* 15.2 (2015): 42-49. Print.

Yoshida, Akiko. "Dads who do Diapers: Factors Affecting Care of Young Children by Fathers." *Journal of Family Issues* 33.4 (2011): 451-477. Print.

Zartler, Ulrike. "How to Deal with Moral Tales: Constructions and Strategies of Single-Parent Families." *Journal of Marriage and Family* 76.3 (2014): 604-619. Print.

12. One-Parent Families in Spain

Exclusions and Social Networks

ROSA ORTIZ-MONERA, DINO DI NELLA, AND
ELISABET ALMEDA-SAMARANCH

THE GOAL OF THIS project is to analyze one-parent families in Spain, particularly those led by women, and to study their strategies for survival and well-being and their access to support in socio-community networks in the context of crisis and social exclusion. Throughout this chapter, we interrogate the normative model of the two-parent, patriarchal, and heterosexual nuclear family, particularly how it is socially imagined and represented in the realm of public policy. In addition, we measure its impact on the burdens of discrimination, exclusion and inequality that fall on those persons who lead families but do not comply with dominant precepts. This chapter provides a reflection derived from a process that led to the progressive configuration of a specific approach model to analyze one-parent families from a gender perspective in the context of family diversity.

It is important to make clear that the chapter does not aim to generalize about the socio-economic realities of one-parent families, which are already very diverse and represent a wide range of social and economic situations. What it analyzes are the survival and well-being strategies of those one-parent family groups who are vulnerable and socially excluded. Therefore, our goal is not to simply demonstrate that one-parent families represent diverse economic realities, as this issue has already been addressed in other research; rather, we intend to verify the interdependence between situations of exclusion of some one-parent family groups and the patriarchal model of the capitalist welfare system.

This chapter articulates some of the principal conclusions of the studies. Firstly, we consider the theoretical context regarding the exclusion of one-parent families and the vulnerabilities that they face in Spain. Secondly, we present a range of results and reflections obtained in our research, with a brief discussion of the methodology used to produce the principal source of the information presented. Finally, we provide a series of final reflections, which discusses the processes that make one-parent families vulnerable.

A BRIEF THEORETICAL CONTEXT: EXCLUSIONS AND VULNERABILITIES OF ONE-PARENT FAMILIES

One-parent families are a growing phenomenon with a significant importance within the framework of family transformations occurring in Western societies in recent decades. According to census figures, one-parent households represented almost 18.3 percent of the total households with children in Spain in 2001; and ten years later, it had increased to almost 30 percent (Almeda-Samaranch and Di Nella, "Monoparentalidad"). This has caused, on one hand, an increase in the interest in the topic among communication media. On the other hand, this has led to the development of a strong national and local association network consisting of diverse organizations that provide support to these families and channel their demands, and to an ever-growing importance and resonance for the topic within the Spanish political and academic agenda.

One-parent families in Spain find themselves, on the whole, in worse social and economic conditions than two-parent families, both in reference to their job opportunities as well as in relation to public policies that respond to their needs, as dual parenthood is still the norm through which the family welfare and social policies are configured (Almeda-Samaranch and Di Nella, "Hacia un Enfoque"). In this case, in-depth study of one-parent households, both quantitatively and qualitatively, is necessary, as this is fundamental not only to being able to channel situations of exclusion and poverty and shed light on the discrimination that these families face but also to understanding the familial and social changes occurring in recent decades in Spain, in which one-parent households play a major role.

The gender dimension is fundamental to understanding the discrimination, living conditions, and survival strategies for this type of family, led principally by women. Capitalism and welfare regimes are supported by the sexual division of labour. These regimes use and emphasize gender inequalities, and it is in the heterosexual nuclear family where this division works best. This type of family is presented as the only possible option and the ideal configuration for proper childhood development, as it is composed of men and women who fulfil the different reproductive and child-raising functions. Feminist economists and sociologists of gender have shed light on the use that capitalism and welfare states make of childcare, and they have illustrated the value this work has because of its indispensable ability to sustain human life (Benería; Carrasco, Borderías, and Torns; Pérez; Picchio). One-parent families break from this conception of the "ideal family" and challenge this traditional, sexist, and patriarchal family, which is being questioned in its foundations and structure. But they also challenge capitalism and the current welfare regimes, which are supported on the two-parental notion of family life, and shed light on the unsustainability of a model that devalues childcare, which is fundamental for life.

In fact, the reality of one-parent families encourages the acceptance of family diversity and helps to shed light on the excessive demands on female work and the challenges of work-life balance (Fernández and Tobío). Also, these families promote the redefinition of relations between family, state, and market as well as the reconsideration of the role that social and community networks carry for the well-being of these family groups (Almeda-Samaranch, Di Nella, and Obiol Francés). For all these reasons, and from a non-androcentric perspective, families led principally by women constitute one of the most difficult challenges for modern welfare regimes: the recognition of the importance of childcare and the need to assume a social responsibility for care, which comes from the market, the state, the community and also the family, including the men who are mostly absent in childcare.

One-parent families are fundamental in promoting family diversity. However, the women leading these families experience the effects of non-compliance with the two-parental, heterosexual family social mandate with its asymmetric role distribution, in which sexual division of labour works in its ideal and sustains welfare states and corporate profitability. In a non-taxonomic and non-hierarchic statement, one can observe, among other effects, the higher rate of poverty among one-parent families; the extra difficulties of balancing the different times of life for one-parent families; health consequences due to the double or triple work shifts (such as psychosomatic disorders, stress and continual exhaustion); a precarious labour state and lesser female participation in the labour market; biases in the legal sphere with discrimination towards family situations that do not adhere to dual-parenthood; the weakness of the Spanish family-based welfare system; and the lack of family support policies (Almeda-Samaranch). All this causes one-parent families to be at serious risk of poverty and social exclusion (Flaquer, Almeda-Samaranch, and Navarro).

In this context, it is important to recognize the similar difficulties that paternity and maternity face in conditions of single parenthood. However, it is also possible to observe the intrinsic heterogeneity that the different situations of single parenthood (and dual parenthood) contain regarding their potential responses to these challenges. It is, therefore, important not to forget when conducting sociological research into one-parent families the centrality of the historic and traditional sociological variables of analysis, such as social class, ethnicity, lineage, sex, or children's age. All these continue to have great explanatory power regarding the social reality to which individuals and social groups are subjected (Di Nella, "Familias Monoparentales").

MAIN RESEARCH RESULTS: EXCLUSION AND SOCIAL NETWORKS

Methodological Reference: Feminist Perspective and Participatory Action Research

The referenced works of research have been contemplated and developed from a feminist perspective. Thus, the resources and the welfare generated from the social networks and local communities have been taken into account, and the set of goods and services produced in the domestic sphere have been re-evaluated. It is necessary not to fall into the traditional androcentric bias in measuring the living conditions and survival strategies, a bias that frequently makes these resources invisible by exclusively considering only what is generated in the public sphere through productive activities and support provided by the state. The interview designs and the One-Parenthood and Family Diversity Survey (EMODIF) consider the set of goods and services originating in the state, the market, the family, and socio-community networks.

Furthermore, the feminist perspective requires emphasizing that all research is imbued with political and social beliefs and goals (Di Nella, Almeda-Samaranch, and Ortiz-Monera; Thompson). In our case, in order to discover these goals and to take advantage of the transformational potential of social research, we have used a participatory active research (PAR) focus, which involves the individuals in the research as active subjects in the study process itself. In this sense, in several of the projects to which this chapter makes reference, one-parent associations and groups have actively participated, especially the *Federació de Famílíes Monoparentals de Catalunya* (One-Parent Family Federation of Catalonia, FEFA-MOCA). This organization has been a prime actor in the research projects that we have carried out, as it formed part of the working group, participated in defining the variables, helped to design the interviews and the survey, co-ordinated its application, and analyzed and disseminated the results.

Finally, as part of methodological proposal, it is important to mention that our intention is to advance towards studies that consider the paradigmatic context of family diversity. That is, we intend to perform research from a non-stigmatizing perspective for one-parent families. This point of view is fundamental to understanding the material and social difficulties present for one-parent families, not as a result of the physiology of this family configuration but rather as the consequence of non-compliance with underlying social mandates. This is an attempt to connect the personal experience of families with a broad social context and to document the discrimination and inequality deriving from the current social structure.

Presentation of EMODIF: *Some Relevant Data*

With the principal lines of our methodological focus indicated, we briefly, in this section, present the principal results obtained regarding the importance of social and community networks as building blocks of well-being strategies for one-parent families in the two research projects mentioned about the social exclusion and precarious situations that one-parent families face. [1]

The EMODIF is a self-administered survey through an online tool (e-survey) organized in six thematic blocks: it features profiles of one-parent families; living conditions; strategies for survival and well-being; violence against women; children of one-parent families; and socio-demographic information.

The sample is not representative, not random, and is based on two types of sampling: strategic and snowball sampling. In the first case, the families representing the set of one-parent families of Catalonia were strategically defined as those who were associated with FEFA-MOCA, which has a registry with the necessary information to access the sample. The snowball sample was used to achieve a broader sample of one-parent families. The poll was sent to 443 individuals, of whom 300 finished the survey. It is important to note that the application of the survey, though self-administered, was monitored by the project's methodological team.

To define the sample profile, the team decided to use the following variables: access pathway to single parenthood; social class[2]; age of youngest child; sex-gender and origin of the person surveyed. Table 1 presents how the sample is distributed according to these variables:

As can be observed, one-parent families who have begun their situation of single parenthood without a stable relationship with a partner are the majority (48 percent). Furthermore, regarding the age of the child, one can appreciate that one-parent families with very young children are the most prevalent, which may indicate that there are more and more women and men who decide to start a family without a stable partner. In terms of social class, these families tend to be better situated in comparison to those families whose one-parent status is due to a break in the relationship or due to the lack of living with a partner (a group in which over 20 percent are situated within lower class).

Precarious Labour and Social Exclusion: Market, Public Policies and Material Difficulties

In the interviews for the qualitative research, the majority of

Table 1: Access Pathway to Single Parenthood by Social Class, Age of Youngest Child, Sex-Gender, and Origin

	Access pathway to one-parenthood									
	Due to pregnancy or start of adoption without stable relationship with live-in partner		Due to breakdown of relation-ship with stable live-in partner		Due to absence of living with partner for six months or longer		Due to partner's death		*Totals*	
Social Class										
Lower Low	11	8%	30	23%	2	25%	3	19%	46	15%
Upper Low	4	3%	5	4%	1	13%	1	6%	11	4%
Lower Middle	6	4%	13	10%	1	13%	2	13%	22	7%
Middle Middle	42	29%	43	33%	3	38%	2	13%	90	30%
Upper Middle	13	9%	5	4%	0	0%	3	19%	21	7%
Lower Upper	57	39%	32	24%	0	0%	4	25%	93	31%
High Upper	12	8%	3	2%	1	13%	1	6%	17	6%
Totals	145	100%	131	100%	8	100%	16	100%	300	100%
Age of Youngest Child										
Child between zero and two years	28	19%	8	6%	3	38%	0	0%	39	13%
Child between three and five years	61	42%	34	26%	1	13%	5	31%	101	34%
Child between six and twelve years	45	31%	52	40%	2	25%	3	19%	102	34%
Child between thirteen and eighteen years	8	6%	24	18%	2	25%	6	38%	40	13%
Child over nineteen years	3	2%	13	10%	0	0%	2	13%	18	6%
Totals	145	100%	131	100%	8	100%	16	100%	300	100%

Sex-Gender										
Female	144	99%	125	95%	7	88%	11	69%	287	96%
Male	1	1%	6	5%	1	13%	5	31%	13	4%
Totals	145	100%	131	100%	8	100%	16	100%	300	100%
Origin										
Spain	129	89%	108	82%	5	63%	14	88%	256	85%
Rest of Europe	5	3%	6	5%	1	13%	0	0%	12	4%
Latin America	10	7%	14	11%	2	25%	2	13%	28	9%
Rest of the World	1	1%	3	2%	0	0%	0	0%	4	1%
Totals	145	100%	131	100%	8	100%	16	100%	300	100%
		48%		44%		3%		5%	100%	100%

Source: Analysis by the research team based on EMODIF data (2014).

women discussed the difficulty of labour insertion as a key element burdening them and preventing them from escaping precarious economic situations and, thus, achieving stability. Insertion into the labour world is made particularly difficult for three reasons. The first reason is due to the precarious situation and labour flexibility that they experience in the labour market, which is further accentuated for groups who do not have specific educational qualifications. Some of the women interviewed between 2008 and 2009 highlighted that the economic crisis had generated even greater difficulties. Secondly, insertion into the labour market is also made difficult, and for this group specifically, due to the lack of existing possibilities that the labour market offers to conciliate personal, family and professional life. These difficulties are present in two senses: the lack of flexibility in the workday and work schedules, and the very low salaries. For a majority of these women, earning such low salaries creates a situation that if they do work, they have to dedicate their entire salary to services that provide work-life balance; nursery services, for just one example, have a very high cost. Thirdly, in the labour market, there are negative biases against women and single mothers, an element that exacerbates the lack of possibilities for employing them. Being a single mother in a company is already accompanied by a perception that there will be difficulties in the work schedules and greater absenteeism, a perception that does not work in the mothers' favour. These difficulties of insertion and achieving stability are also observed in the quantitative study. As Table 2 shows, unemployed individuals are situated at 14 percent but reach 21 percent in the case of individuals who are in charge of one-parent families as a result of breakdown in relationships. The number reach 25 percent in the case of one-parent families due to the absence of a live-in partner, and 7 percent in situations when single parenthood already without a stable live-in partner. Regarding origins, for individuals coming from Latin America unemployment reaches 32 percent.

It is important to note that although the unemployment rate in Catalonia during the same period was 22 percent,[3] in the case of individuals who lead one-parent families, not having gainful employment has serious effects on the family unit, as economic maintenance falls principally on these individuals. Furthermore, other variables must be considered that can hint at a certain underemployment in the types of labour contracts, in part-time employment, and in work in the underground economy. Table 3 shows how 14 percent of the individuals with employment have a temporary contract, 5 percent work without a contract, and 21 percent work part time. Individuals from lower social classes and non-Spanish nationalities are those with the highest percentage of temporary, partial or non-contractual work. Specifically, 45 percent of individuals from lower class have temporary contracts, 18 percent work without contracts, and 55 percent work part time.

Labour market discrimination is perceived above all to be derived from pregnancy or motherhood (23 percent of the individuals polled have felt discriminated against at least one time due to this reason, which affects above all the individuals from lower-income groups at 32 percent), and from gender (a factor observed by 26 percent of the persons polled). It is also important to note that 46 percent of the individuals from Latin America have felt discriminated against due to their origin.

As such, social class and origin are important for studying the precarious labour state for individuals who lead one-parent families.

Table 2: Labour Situation by Access Pathway to Single Parenthood and Origin

	Labour Situation					
	Employed (with or without contract)	Unemployed	Retired, early retired	Student or in training without work	Permanently incapacitated for work	Totals
Access Pathway to Single Parenthood						
Due to pregnancy or start of adoption without stable live-in partner	132	10	1	1	1	145
	91%	7%	1%	1%	1%	100%
Due to relationship breakdown with stable live-in partner	99	27	0	0	5	131
	76%	21%	0%	0%	4%	100%
Due to absence of living together with partner for 6 months or more	6	2	0	0	0	8
	75%	25%	0%	0%	0%	100%
Due to partner's death	13	3	0	0	0	16
	81%	19%	0%	0%	0%	100%
Totals	250	42	1	1	6	300
	83%	14%	0%	0%	2%	100%
Origin						
Spain	217	31	1	1	6	256
	85%	12%	0%	0%	2%	100%
Rest of Europe	12	0	0	0	0	12
	100%	0%	0%	0%	0%	100%
Latin America	19	9	0	0	0	28
	68%	32%	0%	0%	0%	100%
Rest of the World	2	2	0	0	0	4
	50%	50%	0%	0%	0%	100%
Totals	250	42	1	1	6	300
	83%	14%	0%	0%	2%	100%

Source: Analysis by the research team based on EMODIF data (2014).

Table 3: Type of Contract and Workday for the Individuals Who Have Gainful Employment by Social Class and Origin

	Type of Contract				Type of Workday		
	Temporary	Indefinite	Without Contract	Totals	Full Time	Part Time	Totals
Social Class							
Lower Low	0	0	0	0	0	0	0
	0%	0%	0%	0%	0%	0%	0%
Upper Low	5	4	2	11	5	6	11
	45%	36%	18%	100%	45%	55%	100%
Lower Middle	6	15	1	22	15	7	22
	27%	68%	5%	100%	68%	32%	100%
Middle Middle	11	72	5	88	75	13	88
	13%	82%	6%	100%	85%	15%	100%
Upper Middle	2	19	0	21	16	5	21
	10%	90%	0%	100%	76%	24%	100%
Lower Upper	9	79	4	92	71	21	92
	10%	86%	4%	100%	77%	23%	100%
High Upper	1	15	0	16	16	0	16
	6%	94%	0%	100%	100%	0%	100%
Totals	34	204	12	250	198	52	250
	14%	82%	5%	100%	79%	21%	100%
Origin							
Spain	24	184	9	217	176	41	217
	11%	85%	4%	100%	81%	19%	100%
Rest of Europe	5	6	1	12	7	5	12
	42%	50%	8%	100%	58%	42%	100%
Latin America	4	13	2	19	13	6	19
	21%	68%	11%	100%	68%	32%	100%
Rest of the World	1	1	0	2	2	0	2
	50%	50%	0%	100%	100%	0%	100%
Totals	34	204	12	250	198	52	250
	14%	82%	5%	100%	79%	21%	100%

Source: Analysis by the research team based on EMODIF data (2014).

These factors intersect and make gender inequalities and inequalities deriving from discrimination against motherhood worse, in particular for lower-class and immigrant women. The lower educational level of women from lower-social classes and the discrimination that they face reduce their labour opportunities. Regarding origin, the greater legal and social vulnerability of immigrant individuals provokes discrimination and a lower capacity for choice, which leads them to accept worse working conditions. In fact, more than 10 percent work without a contract, which leaves them without any social protection, as they are unable to enjoy the state services and resources linked with formal employment.

The lack of public services, which could allow time to be better balanced, has clear repercussions for one-parent families. The difficulty in balancing life can lead to certain lack of attention to infants, especially at the emotional level. As such, in the interviews, some of the women explained that they are not working and that they are supported thanks to family or social support. Added to the precarious state of the labour market and the insufficient services to help balance life is the lack of aid and economic contributions that would promote support for mothers or one-parent families.

The quantitative study shows that only 12 percent of the individuals polled receive economic aid from the state. One-parent families have difficulties in accessing certain contributions, such as the minimum insertion income, which is the only resource that they can choose once the unemployment subsidy has ended. This subsidy has a family character, as it is only provided if there are no other employed individuals in the home. This condition makes it difficult for mothers who live with other adult persons to access this aid. Only one of the individuals interviewed receives this aid.

Some of the demands made in the interviews and in the open-ended survey questions include policies to provide work-life balance, public financial support for one-parent families, and the provision of equal advantages as the ones available for large families.

The discrimination and lack of labour opportunities, together with the insufficient resources and public services, mean that some one-parent families (above all, immigrant and those in the lower socio-economic strata) have great difficulties in making ends meet.

It must once again be emphasized that in this type of home,

only one person is responsible for the economic maintenance of the family, as such the consequences of insufficient economic income by the individual leading the family is more serious for the family unit. The quantitative study shows that 47 percent of the individuals polled state that their ability to make ends meet is situated between zero and four on a scale from zero to ten. Once again, the individuals from lower social classes and immigrants find themselves in a worse situation. These difficulties in making ends meet translate into a serious risk of poverty, which means that a considerable percentage of the individuals polled, around 9 percent, have found themselves facing difficult situations, such as the threat of eviction.

Family Support and Social Networks

Regarding family support, the qualitative study clearly reflects that for many women, family has a vital role in economic life, in balancing work and family life, and in providing emotional support. In most cases, the families of these women accept the one-parent family model. The quantitative study shows that 60 percent of the individuals polled receive support for child and family care and 28 percent from their friends. Also, 27 percent receive economic support from their families and 12 from their friends. Finally, 30 percent receive emotional support from their families and 62 percent from their friends. However, through the interviews and survey, we find a group of women for whom family help is less important or almost non-existent: immigrant women. Table 5 shows how for individuals coming from Latin America, only 36 percent receive help for childcare and 21 percent receive economic support from family. However, they rely more on their friendships, from which forty-three percent receive help in childcare and 25 percent receive economic support. The interviews show that despite the difficulties of creating new networks connected to the migratory processes, single parents can depend, in some cases, on certain individuals who are willing to provide them with help. The individuals interviewed said that having women in similar situations nearby is of invaluable help, particularly at the emotional level. Many of them have met one another through various one-parent family associations. Both the qualitative and

Table 4 Ability to Make Ends Meet and Threat of Eviction by Social Class and Origin

	Ability to Make Ends Meet													**Threat of Eviction**		
Social Class	0	1	2	3	4	5	6	7	8	9	10	Totals		Yes	No	Totals
Lower Low	14	6	6	5	8	4	1	0	1	0	1	46		8	38	46
	30%	13%	13%	11%	17%	9%	2%	0%	2%	0%	2%	100%		17%	83%	100%
Upper Low	2	0	1	1	4	1	1	0	0	0	1	11		3	8	11
	18%	0%	9%	9%	36%	9%	9%	0%	0%	0%	9%	100%		27%	73%	100%
Lower-Middle	2	3	4	4	3	2	0	3	1	0	0	22		2	20	22
	9%	14%	18%	18%	14%	9%	0%	14%	5%	0%	0%	100%		9%	91%	100%
Middle-Middle	11	5	7	14	7	16	11	8	6	1	4	90		7	83	90
	12%	6%	8%	16%	8%	18%	12%	9%	7%	1%	4%	100%		8%	92%	100%
Upper-Middle	2	1	2	3	2	4	1	3	2	1	0	21		1	20	21
	10%	5%	10%	14%	10%	19%	5%	14%	10%	5%	0%	100%		5%	95%	100%
Lower Upper	3	1	4	6	8	16	15	17	4	7	12	93		6	87	93
	3%	1%	4%	6%	9%	17%	16%	18%	4%	8%	13%	100%		6%	94%	100%

High Upper	0	1	0	0	0	1	1	2	6	1	5	17		0	17	17
	0%	6%	0%	0%	0%	6%	6%	12%	35%	6%	29%	100%		0%	100%	100%
Totals	34	17	24	33	32	44	30	33	20	10	23	300		27	273	300
	11%	6%	8%	11%	11%	15%	10%	11%	7%	3%	8%	100%		9%	91%	100%
Origin																
Spain	26	15	19	30	26	38	25	31	19	8	19	256		19	237	256
	10%	6%	7%	12%	10%	15%	10%	12%	7%	3%	7%	100%		7%	93%	100%
Rest of Europe	0	0	3	1	2	2	1	1	1	0	1	12		1	11	12
	0%	0%	25%	8%	17%	17%	8%	8%	8%	0%	8%	100%		8%	92%	100%
Latin America	7	2	2	2	4	4	2	1	0	1	3	28		7	21	28
	25%	7%	7%	7%	14%	14%	7%	4%	0%	4%	11%	100%		25%	75%	100%
Rest of the World	1	0	0	0	0	0	2	0	0	1	0	4		0	4	4
	25%	0%	0%	0%	0%	0%	50%	0%	0%	25%	0%	100%		0%	100%	100%
Totals	34	17	24	33	32	44	30	33	20	10	23	300		27	273	300
	11%	6%	8%	11%	11%	15%	10%	11%	7%	3%	8%	100%		9%	91%	100%

Source: Analysis by the research team based on EMODIF data (2014).

Table 5: Support Received in the Previous Twelve Months for Childcare, as Economic Support or Emotional Support, and Participation in Associations Based on Origin

			Spain		Rest of Europe		Latin America		Rest of the World		Totals	
Receive support for the care of their children	From family members	Yes	164	64%	6	50%	10	36%	1	25%	181	60%
		No	92	36%	6	50%	18	64%	3	75%	119	40%
		Totals	256	100%	12	100%	28	100%	4	100%	300	100%
	From friends	Yes	72	28%	1	8%	12	43%	0	0%	85	28%
		No	184	72%	11	92%	16	57%	4	100%	215	72%
		Totals	256	100%	12	100%	28	100%	4	100%	300	100%
Receive economic support	From family members	Yes	71	28%	4	33%	6	21%	1	25%	82	27%
		No	185	72%	8	67%	22	79%	3	75%	218	73%
		Totals	256	100%	12	100%	28	100%	4	100%	300	100%
	From friends	Yes	27	11%	1	8%	7	25%	1	25%	36	12%
		No	229	89%	11	92%	21	75%	3	75%	264	88%
		Totals	256	100%	12	100%	28	100%	4	100%	300	100%

Receive emotional support	From family members	Yes	80	31%	2	17%	8	29%	0	0%	90	30%
		No	176	69%	10	83%	20	71%	4	100%	210	70%
		To-tals	256	100%	12	100%	28	100%	4	100%	300	100%
	From friends	Yes	160	63%	8	67%	17	61%	2	50%	187	62%
		No	96	38%	4	33%	11	39%	2	50%	113	38%
		To-tals	256	100%	12	100%	28	100%	4	100%	300	100%
Participate in associations		Yes	147	57%	7	58%	10	36%	2	50%	166	55%
No		109	43%	5	42%	18	64%	2	50%	134	45%	
Totals		256	100%	12	100%	28	100%	4	100%	300	100%	

Source: Analysis by the research team based on EMODIF data (2014).

the quantitative studies emphasize participation in associations as a fundamental source of support for these families.[4] These associations offer both material and emotional help and make space available for socialization. They also provide services that are essential for these individuals' lives, which help to provide life balance, material support, psychological help, or even programs for women who have fled from gender violence.

Our study confirms that fifty-five percent of the individuals polled participate in associations and other groups. In the case of individuals from Latin America, the percentage is 36 percent. The types of groups in which most people participate include sporting, artistic and youth associations (seventy-one cases); associations for education as well student parent associations (sixty-nine cases); and informal groups of mothers and/or fathers (forty cases).

FINAL REFLECTIONS

One-parent families allow us to visualize the unbreakable communion existing between the patriarchal system, the welfare state, and the capitalist system. They singularly express the intricate links that sustain the sexual, international, generational, and classist divisions of productive and reproductive work. Consciously or not, one-parent families are breaking these traditional patterns of the patriarchal family and encouraging family plurality and diversity. This, however, is not a neutral reality for those who suffer different types of exclusion and discrimination. Among these, it is important to highlight how these families face very disadvantageous conditions, including a lack of public protection, social exclusion, and are more vulnerable to a precarious employment.

Facing this, family and community networks play a fundamental role in the development of survival and well-being strategies. Once again, however, social class and ethnic and/or national origin are particularly relevant factors to consider, given that in these circumstances, a lower presence of family networks and lower participation in associational networks are observed. This is an important point for persons immigrating from outside the continent because they find themselves with a decreased possibility to develop survival strategies that go beyond their family and community networks and become more vulnerable to the processes of exclusion.

In this context, it is essential for single parenthood studies to tackle, from a systematic and structural perspective, the connections with social exclusion that one-parent families are exposed to on the micro-social level. Without this, it is easy to point to conditions of the one-parent families themselves as the cause for their social exclusion.

Little can be done in this respect if researchers do not use a participatory active research method in their research and scientific productions, which gives a leading role to the individuals researched. Such methodology is essential to assume a non-androcentric perspective that performs structural analyzes and takes into account the micro-social and immediate implications of the sexual division of labour and social exclusion of women. Researchers have to focus especially on those women who exercise their rights to maternity in situations in which their citizen rights are practically deprived.

As such, the necessary non-androcentric and participatory perspective requires reconsideration of the total time and work for the care of a human being, particularly in the domestic and socio-community sphere, which has major influence on the living conditions in which one-parent families develop.

NOTES

[1]We refer to the following two research projects: a) "Strategies for Survival and Well-Being of One-Parent Families from a Gender Perspective" (IMU 130/07), with twenty interviews with women who lead one-parent families in precarious situations, marginality and social exclusion in different cities in Spain, from 2008 to 2010. The goal of the project was to understand the well-being strategies developed by one-parent families in situation of "social exclusion" in Spain. These families are led principally by women (80 percent according to the 2011 census in Spain); b) "One-Parent Families in the New Century. Challenges and Dilemmas in Times of Change" (CSO 2011-29889), in which the preliminary results of the One-parenthood and Family Diversity Survey (EMODIF) applied to three hundred individuals who lead one-parent families in Catalonia are shown between 2012 and 2015.

[2]The reference to social class is elaborated by the research team through the systematization of diverse sources, and it is defined through the following variables: labour situation, socio-professional category, and income level. To do so, a cluster analysis has been performed. The lower-low class corresponds with unemployed individuals with up to 600 euros per month; the upper-low class corresponds to unqualified workers with incomes up to 600 euros per month; the lower-middle class corresponds to service sector workers with secondary education or middle level educational cycles and with monthly incomes from 601 to 1001 euros; the middle-middle class corresponds to accountants and administrative workers, with secondary educations and incomes from 1001 to 1600 euros per month; and the lower-upper class corresponds with scientific and intellectual experts and professionals with university studies and monthly incomes from 1601 to 3000 euros.

[3]Data is taken from the Active Population Survey by the National Statistics Institute (INE). The unemployment rate for Catalonia and for those individuals above twenty-four years of age has been considered for this survey, as this is the age range of the individuals to whom the EMODIF has been applied. The application period of this survey covers the fourth quarter of 2012 and the first and second quarters of 2013.

[4]In the same way that the community and associations are important for the welfare of single mothers, other authors show how they are also a fundamental support for other non-normative families, such as lesbian mothers (Federer).

WORKS CITED

Almeda-Samaranch, Elisabet. "Género, Diversidad y Familias Monoparentales." *España 2015. Situación Social*. Ed. Cristobal Torres Albero. Madrid: CIS, 2015. 360-367. Print.

Almeda-Samaranch, Elisabet and Dino Di Nella. "Hacia un Enfoque Integral de la Monoparentalidad." *Introducción a Las Familias Monoparentales. Colección Familias Monoparentales y Diversidad Familiar*, 10 (Las Familias Monoparentales a Debate, Volumen I). Eds. Elisabet Almeda-Samaranch and Dino Di Nella. Barcelona: Copalqui Editorial, 2011. 27-39. Print.

Almeda-Samaranch, Elisabet and Dino Di Nella. "Monoparentalidad, Genero y Benestar." *Bienestar, Protección Social y Monoparentalidad. Colección Familias Monoparentales y Diversidad Familiar*, 11 (Las Familias Monoparentales a Debate, Volumen II). Eds. Elisabet Almeda-Samaranch and Dino Di Nella. Barcelona: Copalqui Editorial, 2011. 93-123. Print.

Almeda-Samaranch, Elisabet, Dino Di Nella and Sandra Obiol Francés. "L'Experiència de la Monoparentalitat: Percepcions, Dificultats i Demandes." *Arxius de Sociologia* 19 (2008): 19-29. Print.

Benería, Lourdes. "Introducción. La Mujer y El Género en la Economía: Un Panorama General." *Economía y Género. Macroeconomía, Política Fiscal y Liberalización. Análisis de su Impacto Sobre sas Mujeres*. Ed. Paloma De Villota. Barcelona: Icaria Editorial, 2003. 23-74. Print.

Carrasco, Cristina, Cristina Borderías, and Teresa Torns. "Introducción. El Trabajo de Cuidados: Antecedentes Históricos y Debates Actuales." *El Trabajo de Cuidados. Historia, Teoría y Políticas*. Eds. Cristina Carrasco, Cristina Borderías, and Teresa Torns. Madrid: Los Libros de Catarata, 2011. 13-96. Print.

Di Nella, Dino. "Familias Monoparentales. Hacia una Conceptualización Crítica Desde la Perspectiva de los Derechos de la Infància". *Entre la Ley y la Experiencia. Nociones y Redes de Familias Monoparentales. Colección Familias Monoparentales y Diversidad Familiar*, 12 (Las Familias Monoparentales a Debate, Volumen I). Eds. Elisabet Almeda-Samaranch and Dino Di Nella. Barcelona: Copalqui Editorial, 2011. 33-55. Print.

Di Nella, Dino, Elisabet Almeda-Samaranch, and Rosa Ortiz-Monera. "Perspectiva No Androcéntrica en los Estudios Sobre Familias Monoparentales. Reflexiones e Implicaciones Metodológicas." *Athenea Digital. Revista de Pensamiento e Investigación Socia* 14.2 (2014): 181-207. Print.

Federer, Lisa. "We Are Family: Creating Lesbian Motherhood through Online Community." *Motherhood Memories*. Eds. Justine Dymond and Nicole Willey. Bradford, ON: Demeter Press, 2013. 205-217. Print.

Fernández Cordón, Juan Antonio, and Constanza Tobío Soler. *Las Familias Monoparentales en España*. Madrid: Ministerio de Trabajo y Asuntos Sociales, 1999. Print.

Flaquer, Lluís, Elisabet Almed, and Lara Navarro. *Monoparentalidad e Infancia. Colección Estudios Sociales*, 20. Barcelona: Fundación "La Caixa," 2006. Print.

Pérez Orozco, Amaia. *Perspectivas Feministas en Torno a la Economía: El Caso de los Cuidados*. Madrid: Consejo Económico y Social, Colección Estudios, 2006. Print.

Picchio, Antonella. "Visibilidad Analítica y Política del Trabajo de Reproducción Social." *Mujeres y Economía. Nuevas Perspectivas para Viejos y Nuevos Problemes*. Ed. Cristina Carrasco. Barcelona: Icaria Editorial, 1999. 201-242. Print.

Thompson, Linda. "Feminist Methodology for Familiy Estudies." *Journal of Marriage and Family* 54.1 (1992): 3-18. Print.

13.
Escaping a Life of Violence? Migrant Mother-Families in Germany

Coping with Gender-Based Violence, Undermining Stereotypes, and Claiming Agency

LYDIA POTTS AND ULRIKE LINGEN-ALI

SINGLE PARENTING IN Germany is a well-covered field of research, yet adequate policy answers, welfare state provisions, and labour market structures are still desiderata. This is not least reflected by the attention single parenting receives in publications and projects initiated and promoted by various ministries (e.g., the Federal Ministry for Family Affairs, Senior Citizens, Women and Youth; the Federal Ministry of Labor and Social Affairs or the Federal Ministry of Education and Research). One-parent families constitute a considerable share of families in Germany: almost 20 percent of the approximately 8.1 million families with underage children are mother- or father-led families. Studies show a differentiated image of single-parent families and challenge common prejudices. They focus on the evaluation of living situations, coping strategies, labour market integration, and organization of childcare.

To date, German studies on single parenting do not systematically address or even include migrants, although migrant[1] one-parent families constitute more than 20 of one-parent families—and also almost 20 percent of all migrant families in Germany. In absolute numbers, there are more than 350,000 one-parent families with a migration background and among them, there are about 200,000 parents with a foreign nationality. How do migrant single parents describe and evaluate their living conditions? What are their self-perceptions, coping strategies, and needs?

The research project ALMIN[2] studies migrant mother- and father-led families through exploring their dynamics, complexities, and diversities. The study comprises sixty qualitative biographical interviews with lone-single parents of various nationalities and backgrounds. The theory-based sample was selected based on an analysis of statistical data: accordingly, half of the interviewees selected are parents with a foreign passport; the other half are naturalized Germans or second-generation migrants. Four interviews were conducted with fathers. Most of the interviewees originate from Turkey, various Arab states, Eastern Europe and the former Soviet Union, but migrants from Africa and the Caribbean were also included. Overall, the sample reflects the diversity of the migrant population in Germany.

As a primarily qualitative study, the data generated in ALMIN show the range of topics and issues with which the interviewees are concerned. In addition to those shared with other single-parent families, there are also migration-specific dimensions: residence permits and legal status, recognition of foreign certificates and qualifications acquired abroad, language barriers, experiences of racism or global fragmentation of extended families, to name only a few.

The interviews began with the expectation that poverty and lack of income would be key topics, as the risk of poverty is dramatically high for migrant single-parent families. Although in the overall population in Germany the poverty risk is 16.1 percent (in 2013), it is double for single parents, affecting more than one in three. For single-parent migrant families, the situation is even worse: the overall poverty rate is 50 percent and for certain nationalities (e.g., Turks), it is even higher.[3] But in the interviews—rather surprisingly for the authors—poverty and related issues were not a dominant topic, instead, experiences of violence came up in almost half of the interviews and featured prominently in many.

These experiences include physical and sexual attacks and harassment, which often led to the end of the marital relationship, and various other forms of violence, such as sexual violence in political conflicts and towards refugees, abuse of children, racist violence, and oppression. The perpetrators were husbands, fathers and other family members, in-laws, partners, members of the cultural community, state institutions, and strangers. Most of these dimensions are present in the interviews with Beatha, Fatma, and Maryam,[4] whose cases were chosen to shed light on some significant questions. How do they articulate their experiences? What enables them to do so? What coping strategies do they develop? What does it mean for them to be head of a single-parent family? Which resources are important for them?

THE JANUS-FACE OF THE EUROPEAN REFUGEE REGIME

At the time of the interview, Beatha is thirty years old, and she has a teenage daughter. Beatha was born in Congo (DRC), her father being Congolese and her mother Rwandan. During the Rwandan genocide, the family was living in Rwanda, and both her parents were killed; Beatha and her siblings fled to Congo, where a relative took care of them. In the course of the First Congo War (1996-1997), the family fled again, from the east of the country to the west, where they found shelter in a refugee camp. During the Second Congo War (1998-2003), they at first sought refuge in a city in the centre of the country and then—with support by the UN—moved on to an eastern city, where Beatha's brothers were immediately handed over to the militia. Her older sister "disappeared" within the context of a disordered European rescue operation, and Beatha and her younger sister remained for at least two years unaccompanied in the camp. In the camp, Beatha, who was not older than thirteen years of age, was continuously raped by different men. After Beatha and her sister managed to escape to Tanzania, Beatha discovered that she was pregnant. The sisters found refuge in a church community, and Beatha gave birth to her daughter. Although she was now hoping for a "normalization" of her troubled life, doctors discovered her daughter's chronic illness, and shortly after that, Beatha herself was diagnosed as HIV positive—it remains unclear if this was caused by rape or by unprofessional medical treatment during and after the delivery. To ensure treatment with the proper medication for both herself and her daughter, Beatha decided to apply for asylum in Germany, as a relief organization had found out that her older sister was alive and in Germany and helped to re-establish contact between the sisters after years of separation.

Beatha's biography demonstrates that being a mother and being a *single* mother can be intrinsically linked with political crises and violent conflict—going far beyond what is usually considered family affairs or questions of lifestyle. Her situation is the result of brutal sexual attacks and exploitation of women and girls in the context of war and of the gendered shortcomings of refugee protection and policies.

Beatha got financial support by her older sister and applied for a visa. She arrived, however, not in Germany, as she expected, but in a neighbouring country where she received neither proper treatment for her disease nor information on the next steps of the procedure. She eventually left the country, met her sister in Germany, and applied for asylum. She was immediately provided with the necessary medical treatment.

After the long narrative sequence explaining the complex and tragic stages that she went through, Beatha stopped talking and reflected on her situation, before concluding, "This is ... a very bad and sad story of me.... So this [is a] sad story I'm talking about." She then explained the normality of her current daily life—which is again under threat:

> Then I take every day my medication. I have a normal life like everyone. I wake up in the morning. I go to work. I go shopping. I eat. I have fun like everybody. But, now the very big problem is ... two weeks ago, I received this thing from *Bundesamt* [Federal Office for Migration and Refugees] ... They rejected my application. So, they told me: "We found out that you came from the neighbouring country and we are taking you back there."

Since arriving in Germany, Beatha and her daughter have experienced, to some extent, safety, support, and relief. Medical treatment for herself and her daughter, which was her top priority, has been met. Still, other needs and wishes have not been fulfilled. Beatha spoke about her reluctance to enter into relationships, not only with a male partner but also with friends, because of the HIV stigma and her traumatic experiences of insecurity and instability: "I would love so much to have a partner, to have a husband, to have a family. To wake up in the morning and I know my husband is there, my daughter is there and he is going to work, I'm going to work. When I'm not there he picks up my daughter at school ... to have someone. I don't have friends." Beatha often spoke about her isolation and emotions with professionals—doctors and counselors—to address the antagonism and adversity that she has to face: "Most of the time I'm not ok, to be honest. I'm not ok. So, sometimes I just ... want to be alone.... I just need to be alone. I don't want to talk to people and I don't want someone to talk to me. And when I feel fine, I just come out and talk to the people. No problem."

The trauma of the pregnancy as a result of rape also affects her relationship with her daughter. "She knows I love her so much. I like her. I have been there for her all her life and she understands me. It cannot be fine with her, but I do my best. Yaah. And I cannot blame myself because that's how I feel. Sometime I feel like I hate myself. I hate me. I hate everything."

Beatha's descriptions suggest that in personal or public interactions, she is addressed as a refugee, or as a survivor of genocide, war and rape, or as an HIV positive person, but she is never addressed as a migrant single mother. A key dimension of her identity—being the mother of a daughter and a single mother—becomes invisible. Although single parents in German society have gained visibility, including in research and public policy, migrants, and especially forced migrants, still do not feature in this context. Aware of this, Beatha said that she takes the issue further as mother of a daughter who will never know who her biological father was. She deliberately agreed to give the interview as an opportunity to contribute to the visibility of refugee women's multiple traumata "When you called me and when you asked me about my life, and I thought about this yesterday night and I said maybe people need to know about this. People need to know about, how people who get a baby ... from nowhere or without a father or you are not married, how they feel, how they stand, how they work it out." Beatha makes use of the interview to articulate the unheard and overheard by elaborating and explaining her biography and to pass on her story. She also asked the interviewer to send her the interview transcript to give it to her daughter when she is older. Afraid that in dialogue with her daughter, she may not be able to find the right words, she believes that the document will help—when the time comes—to pass on her knowledge to her daughter.

Beatha's biography is characterized by a lack of protection and access to health care afforded to her in various countries: three African and two European. As an asylum seeker, she has not received constant protection from the European refugee regime. The permission for her and her daughter to stay is at risk; she is not allowed to take part in the educational system and, legally, she is not entitled to work and to earn money. Beatha articulated her wishes in the following manner: "To have my own work. To work, to be busy the whole day, come back at home in the afternoon or in the evening ... In the future I would like to be busy. This is what can help me." But for the time being, Beatha is not allowed to develop perspectives in Germany for herself or her daughter.

ESCAPING CONTROL AND TRANSGENERATIONAL SEXUAL VIOLENCE: THE INTERVENING WELFARE STATE

Fatma is thirty-nine years old and is of Turkish origin, but she was born in Germany and speaks German fluently. She has three children, two teenagers with her first husband and a toddler with her second husband; both men are Turkish nationals. Fatma lives in a flat in a German city and is working as a cleaner. Her older daughter Sara, at times, actively participated in the interview, sitting with us in the living room, along with Fatma's mother.

Fatma got divorced from her first husband after more than ten years. She married again, and in her narrative, she primarily refers to this second husband, who came as a marriage migrant from Turkey to Germany and turned out to be despotic and controlling towards Fatma and her children. He once said to her: "You are no mother; you never think of your children; I am the one who is always thinking of them." He used to control the food in the kitchen, the amount of food that was eaten, and the clothes that were bought. He controlled other dimensions of Fatma's life, including her relationships with friends and family. The children were afraid of him and had many sleepless nights.

While Fatma was pregnant with her third child, her husband and father of the unborn, sexually abused her teenage daughter

Sara, his stepdaughter. Initially, Sara was afraid to tell her mother what had happened to her more. The abuse happened more than one time, mostly during her mother's long-term hospital stays because of her critical pregnancy. After the husband attacked Sara and threatened to kill her by holding a piece of broken glass to her throat, she ran away from home, and the *Jugendamt*—the governmental office for children, youth and family affairs—got involved. Fatma was ordered to expel her husband from the house and separate from him, otherwise the children would be taken into state care. A week later, Fatma did as was requested. Only after the attacker had left the house did Sara share with her mother what she had gone through. Sara's fear to inform her mother about the abuses and insults were connected with her stepfather's prohibition of intimate dialogue between mother and daughter. Sara explained:

> It was like that, when I had problems with him, I was not allowed to talk with my mother. We always talk with each other in German, and he didn't understand. And then he thinks, even if we talk about something totally different, that we talk about him. Although that's not right, he immediately had to know what was going on. Even when we were whispering in the kitchen, he heard everything, and he immediately said: "What are you talking about?" ... When I had problems with him, I was not allowed to talk with her.

Fatma explained her own point of view:

> As mother and daughter we have secrets, and of course, as mother I will listen to her, and so I went to her room, so that not everybody listens, especially not him. I entered the room, and he was knocking. "What are you doing there?" "Talking with my daughter." "No, you will come right now." "No, my daughter has problems, and I want to talk with her." "No, you will not. If she has something to say, she will do it in the living room." Only after a while I understood why he didn't want me to talk to my daughter

> in another room because he had something to hide. He was afraid that it would be uncovered.

During the interview, Fatma repeatedly referred to the sexual abuse that her daughter had to experience: "I didn't know that. That evening, when she told me everything, the end of my world had come." Sara interrupted her to explain: "I burst. I couldn't go on any longer.... I know, that it was not my fault, this is why I told her everything. I can't describe how she felt this evening; her whole body trembled. She didn't know what to do."

Though brief, such sequences are much more than mere pieces of information on acts of violence. During the interview, Fatma and her daughter spoke with each other, negotiating between them their perceptions of what had happened to them both. At the same time, however, they shared their views and opinions with the interviewer, going beyond the private and intimate, as both were aware that parts of the anonymized interview would be published.

Fatma now lives together with her three children, and there are plans to move her mother in. She is proud of herself and her children and their personal developments: "I am proud of how I educated my children and that I chose the right way with the divorce. I have done something right, and I do not regret, I am proud that I have these children." Nonetheless, she still has not come to terms with her responsibility concerning what had happened to her children, and she suffers from her earlier inability to give them a safe and relaxed life. The children, however, seem to absolve her and give her words of comfort. During the interview and in the presence of her mother, Fatma admitted that her father sexually abused her when she was young and that her mother did not protect her. Fatma feels the obligation to protect her children, and this is the reason that she will never marry again, as she has promised them. Her desire to protect them is also reflected in her fear to leave her daughter alone with her friends in their families. Fatma does not allow overnight stays, although she knows that she should give her daughter more freedom. The tensions and understandings between mother and daughter are apparent in the following exchange:

> Sara: There are limits for children at every place. Everything is fine, as long as you know how to deal with your children. But if you say: "I leave my child alone, I don't want to discuss this with her, do what you want," then this is not a real family life.
> Fatma: It is good that you are able to think this way.
> Sara: I always think this way.
> Fatma: A couple of months ago it was very hard with her. She could never understand me. As I said before, now she understands me, thank God, and what I mean with this staying overnight with friends and why I am afraid. And that there need to be limits, otherwise it doesn't work. There is no family life without limits.
> Sara: Yes, if there are no limits you feel that people don't care about each other.
> Fatma: But you are very important to me, I need to protect you.

This dialogue demonstrates that mother and daughter are able to speak with each other and to express and respect their views and feelings, namely those related to their experiences of violence and vulnerability. Their interaction can be interpreted with reference to Martha Nussbaum's approach to identify the crucial elements of a "good" human life. Nussbaum's "list of capabilities" means real opportunities based on personal and social circumstances. This includes the capability to form a conception of the good and to engage in critical reflection about the planning of one's life ("practical reason") and the capability to live with and towards others, to recognize and show concern for other humans, to engage in various forms of social interaction and to be able to imagine the situation of another ("affiliation").

The exchange between mother and daughter is also important regarding its connection to Fatma's migration context. Fatma is of Turkish origin, and the public perception of Turkish families in Germany is (still) influenced by Orientalist stereotypes. In media and public opinion, the generalized perception of the majority if not all migrant families is that they are characterized by a *backward and patriarchal system of family honour*—as recently was once again key topic of Sarrazin's bestselling book. As was explained, Sara is not allowed to stay overnight with her friends, but this is not to protect her "chastity." In the interview, Fatma did not even mention "Turkish" culture or religion; clearly, she is indifferent to community rules or dominant social perceptions of her as a "Turkish" mother. Instead, her order to refrain from overnight stays is based on her and her daughter's experiences of sexual violence.

In the case of Fatma and her children, the initial intervention of the *Jugendamt* as an institution of the welfare state and the legal provisions in place eventually became an empowering experience and an important resource for both mother and daughter. Since the 1970s, the women's movement has initiated a public conversation on domestic violence in Germany, which has led to many improvements, such as the establishment of women's shelters. Although in the early period, women's shelters were almost exclusively approached by German women, this has changed: in 2012, migrant women encompassed around 50 percent of those receiving shelter and support (Bericht der Bundesregierung 16). This cannot be interpreted as a higher prevalence of violence in migrant families—as migrant women may lack other forms of support accessible to German women—but it is a strong indicator that migrant women are increasingly able to access the resources of the welfare state that protect their rights. Sexual violence against children became a focus of public discourse and policy development in Germany in the 1990s.

What actually worked for Fatma and her daughter has been in place since 2002: For both women and children, the new *Protection against Violence Act* (*Gewaltschutzgesetz*) made it possible to achieve a court order that forbids the perpetrator from entering the dwelling of the aggrieved person, in this case Sara. This new development in the German context means that the aggressor must leave the home and not the victim (although the option to move to a women's shelter remains). Against this backdrop, the intervening welfare state in Fatma's case did not try to uphold the conventional family model but encouraged and supported the emergence of mother-headed family, which paved the way for healing between Fatma and her children.

LIVING INSIDE-OUTSIDE AN EXTENDED FAMILY—OVERCOMING THE TRAUMA OF FORCED MARRIAGE AND MARITAL RAPE

During our interview, Maryam spoke extensively about her personal experiences with forced marriage and her current situation. She is thirty-eight years old, of Arab origin, and lives in a German city with her extended family. She has two children, a boy with her former husband and a daughter with her current companion, whom she meets from time to time but does not want to live with.

When she was a teenager, her family forced her to marry a friend of the family, who was twice her age. Although—or because—her voice was not listened to in the family, she decidedly resisted: "I had to do something, you know. If nobody is interested in you, you know, if you say, you don't want him, you can't live with him." One month after the wedding, she escaped by committing herself to a health institution. She spent more than a month there and, subsequently, left her husband and broke off all contacts with her family of origin. For Maryam, her decision was more of a logical consequence of her situation than a conscious act of rebellion. Presently, she is back on speaking terms with her family of origin, but it remains a strained relationship. The family does not approve of her relationship with the father of her daughter—the "Iraqi," as she calls him during the interview. I did not have a lot to do with my family. And then my family didn't want to have a lot to do with me, because they said: 'Either the Iraqi or us.' Then I said: 'Okay, this time I decide in favour of the Iraqi' because before [when she was forced to marry] they did not decide in favour of me." Maryam opposes the family rules and restrictions by making her own decisions, but regarding her family, she still speaks in terms of "allowing" and "permitting": "My parents allowed me to marry him the Islamic way." In German law, this is not a legally recognized marriage, so Maryam chose a rather unconventional path: she does not live together with her partner.

She desires to have a sexually active lifestyle and to be independent: "I am just a woman.... Before going to someone strange [to have an intimate relationship], I don't like that.... In our way it is halal, it's not a sin, and then I also have some peace.... I mean, I like it with him like that, and so, why not?" Maryam can practise sexuality within a clear framework, and, at the same time, she avoids marital shortcomings, burdens, and duties.

Her decisions, attitudes, opinions and lifestyle deeply affect her relationship with her family of origin: "I only speak with them superficially, only what I allow them to know." She visits her family from time to time to show her presence in the neighbourhood: "Sometimes I only go to check the situation and see ... they are all sitting here, so I can invite friends.... I'm not afraid, but I don't want that they make so many problems in front of my children. That's it. I'm not afraid of anyone."

Not only with regard to her current marriage, she combines two contradictory strategies: resistance and symbolic conformity. Her distancing herself from her family of origin may well be called a conscious act of undermining dominant images of "proper behaviour" in her community. Furthermore, she consciously uses secrecy to lead the life that she wants. With her children, she celebrates Christmas without the knowledge of the Muslim community. She plays sports—just tolerated by her partner—but in another city so to avoid neighbours or family members seeing her. On the other hand, she explicitly rejects and distances herself from other family members' secrecy and hypocrisy: "When I sit at home and I see my cousins, how they talk with each other—I only observe that from far away—and they say: "I am decent," and they do everything secretly, then I always say: "I am not like that." I am this and this and this, and I admit to what I'm doing." Her ambivalence and contradictory stance regarding her resistant attitudes are an integral part of her narration and, perhaps, even her identity construction. "My hobby has always been swimming. But since 2008, I have been wearing the headscarf. Out of love for him, you see. Stupidity, really." Also, her general self-perception is that she is not silent, that she decides for herself while avoiding conflicts.

> I am not like that, that I shut up and keep silent. I don't let them say anything to me. I always want to avoid conflicts because I know that we will have arguments.... They like

> the woman always to ask the man, but I can't do that anymore, because I learnt the other way. Life made me like that, automatically, that I decide for myself. I ask and answer myself, and I think, it's right this way, so I'll do it this way.

Maryam, as she describes it, gives to her children everything that she did not get when she was young: she always talks to them, and she never beats them. She points out that her education practices are not like "theirs" (i.e., the Arab community's). Other family members notice and recognize how she deals with her children, which leads to the question: does national or ethnic belonging matter when migrant mothers express their perceptions and views of motherhood and caring? Maryam clearly divides between "German" and "Arab" behaviour: "I deal with them like the Germans do: they have to stay in, I forbid play station. This goes down well, because they understand: 'Oh, mama forbids the best thing, oh, that cannot be.'" The son has to tidy his room, carry the garbage downstairs, clean the living room—all according to a weekly cleaning plan. For Maryam, this is important because "With us, with us Arabs it is not like that, that a boy has to tidy his room. 'This is mummy's and sister's job.' But not with me." Thus, Maryam dissociates herself from the Arab community on various levels—primarily to come to terms with her former experience of violence—but on other levels, she identifies with it.

Maryam elaborated on some experiences with her own extended family: "When I see how they talk to their mothers ... I swear, they don't do anything. 'You are a woman. Boys don't do things like that.' They sit there, 'bring me this, bring me that!'" Her son once tried to copy this attitude: "'Mom, bring me water!' [Her son said to her] So I went to him: 'Where are your feet? Where are your hands? So get up and get your water yourself. If you are ill and you can't get up, I will be happy to serve you. But not like that.' And then he noticed: 'Oh, I can't deal with her like that.'"

To interpret her experiences, Maryam refers again to the before mentioned binary of "German" and "Arab", but, this time, adds another aspect, which is linked to her lone-parenting status:

> When he goes to his father, he can "do the foreigner." There he can do what he wants. But not with me. I am not a bad mother; the child has everything. I offer him everything, but with limits. This is better for his schooling, for their future. Because as a foreigner's child, it is always hard in Germany, everywhere. Because many foreigners indeed behave badly, and all are lumped together.

Maryam has created a space for herself that allows her to dissociate from her community of origin on various levels, including the way that she cares for and educates her children. But she also identifies herself as part of this community, as a foreigner. Her message—drawing on K. Crenshaw's approach—might be interpreted as a request for a perspective of diversity and intersectionality. Maryam presents herself not primarily as a victim; rather, she discloses a complex biographical narration, including self-reflection, resistance, and agency while addressing numerous contradictions and discontinuities.

LIFE IN MOTHER-LED FAMILIES: THE END OF VIOLENCE?

How do the interviewed women evaluate their situation? Do they speak of an end of violence? As for Beatha, her traumatic experiences remain with her, aggravated by the insecurity about where she will live and if she will have access to HIV prevention and treatment. Her situation may be interpreted as characterized by structural violence: although her decade-long persecution and the continuous failure of several states to protect her basic human rights is beyond question, this is still not sufficient to grant her asylum. For Beatha. as for the other interviewed women, physical violence or co-habitation with an abusive husband is over but fear is not. Fatma explained in the interview that

> I always feel threatened. I told the judge: I tell you, as soon as his residency is set, he will take revenge.... Because I complained against him to the police. Because we had this confrontation. He will take revenge, I know that, because I know him very well.

But there are also women who feel that they and their children are now safe. Maryam is committed to raise her children without violence or forced marriage.

> Now, I have everything what I want. I went through a lot, though, to get that. But I have two healthy children; I have my own life. I live the way I want. Don't obey anyone. It is too late, though, but you learn by your experiences. I would never get anyone married by force or do anything with a child, what she doesn't want. Because this destroys a person psychologically, really. Because you get in conflicts if something like this happens.

As we learned earlier, she found a way to escape the control of her extended family. Moreover, she extensively explained her efforts to educate her son as a person who does not reproduce patriarchal and violent attitudes but acts with care and respect.

Although each interviewed person perceives life to be hard, challenging, and precarious, it is striking that the majority of the interviewed mothers state that their quality of life has decidedly improved.

Many prefer a life as single mother and reject the idea of marrying again or even having a new partner—although they do talk about the deep wish for partner by their side. Fatma put this wish into words:

> That you always have to be strong, even if you can't. That you have to laugh, even if you don't want. That's hard. And everything alone, without someone who is accompanying you through your life. I tried twice, and it came even worse. This is the main problem I'm suffering of. Although I always try to hide, but during the evenings, when I'm always alone, everything appears again. Especially during the evenings, when you really need this warmth and when you really don't want to stay alone. That you have someone who says, "Darling, I love you" or "You are not alone, we will manage everything." I don't have it, it doesn't work, and I don't dare.

Against the backdrop of the long struggle to escape violence, the dimension of poverty might recede in biographical narratives but remains a daily challenge because there is an actual material price to be paid by mothers and children living without a husband, a father or an extended family. The statistical data referred to earlier—with poverty rates of more than 60 percent for certain groups of migrant one-parent families—illustrate this. There is ample evidence that poverty is connected to multiple exclusions. Welfare state regulations guarantee survival, but they do not alleviate poverty, which means that most single migrant mothers and their children will remain caught in this form of structural violence, even if their residence permit is not at risk or if they have acquired citizenship.

CONCLUSION

Beatha, Maryam, and Fatma have built lives as single mothers as a result of different experiences of gender-based violence: rape in political conflict and war, forced marriage, and domestic violence. To be able to choose single parenthood is an important resource, which allows them to build a good life in a way most of the capabilities that Nussbaum addresses feature in the narrative: life; bodily health (including adequate shelter); bodily integrity (including being able to move freely from place to place, to be secure against all dimensions of violence); senses, imagination, and thought (including adequate education and freedom of expression); emotions (love those who care for us, experience anger); and practical reason and affiliation (Nussbaum 77).

Beatha, Maryam, Fatma and many more ALMIN interviewees seized the opportunity of the interview to break the silence about gender-based violence, which is a global problem occurring across all social strata. To speak out is a courageous and powerful act to overcome victimization. Kavemann elaborates prerequisites to communicate about violence: only what can be heard can become a research topic and there has to be a memory of what has happened, then it is necessary that there is no stigmatization and furthermore communication can only happen if to narrate is not too shameful and not too loaded with guilt. These lines had to be crossed by the interviewees. Kavemann also develops categories of access to persons concerned: communication can only happen if access was successful, and it happens primarily with those who are in safety and with those who have a motivation to co-operate with researchers. The motivation to break the silence can be attributed to all three narratives—and to be able to live as a single-parent family in Germany provides safety. For Beatha and Fatma, there is an additional motive: both see the interview as a mode to communicate with their daughters. Beathas intent is to keep the interview transcript to share it with her daughter when she is coming of age, and Fatma and Sara use the interview situation for a personal dialogue.

The fact that so many interviewees spoke up is also a strong message to researchers. What was stated with regard to migrant single parents—that they are omitted in "general" research on one-parent families—partly recurs in research on gender-based violence. There are various specialized studies, on family violence or forced marriage in migrant communities (Baobaid and Hamed; BMFSFJ "Gewalt"; BMFSFJ "Zwangsverheiratung"; Schröttle and Khelaifat; Uslucan), but "general" studies on the prevalence of gender-based violence do not include migrants—and the specific forms of gender-based violence that they experience, including rape in wars and political conflict or forced marriage. In 2014, the first representative study on violence against women in the EUwas published—with the claim to be representative for the EU and each of the twenty-eight member states (European Union Agency for Fundamental Rights/FRA). The survey of forty-two thousand women comes with a brief section on "Prevalence of Violence by Migrant Background," but the "proxy indicators" used are rather unspecific and so are the results.[5] The forms of violence addressed do not include violence experienced in war and political conflict, forced marriage, or forms that might be linked to (forced) migration. Schröttle (116) summarizes that there have been first efforts to integrate intersectional perspectives in studies on the prevalence of gender-based violence, but that to date, there is no systematic, focused research and theorization. Qualitative data as presented here might contribute to develop this.

Living in a one-parent family becomes a preferable—though

not desirable—family form and an alternative to a life beset with a continuous threat of physical violence. In order to escape gender-based violence, migrant women in Germany increasingly use separation, divorce, and setting up a single-parent family as a coping strategies. For many, this is a migration-related resource as a legal system committed to gender equality and provisions of the welfare state would not be available in their home country. They deliberately claim agency and, concurrently, undermine—and sometimes employ—stereotypes when negotiating the relations between self, migrant community and host society. The interviews show that many of the mothers are well aware of the services and supplements offered by the state, but they also experience its limitations and ambivalences.

NOTES

[1]ALMIN refers to the terms "migration background" and "migrant" according to the definition of the Federal Statistical Office (*Statistisches Bundesamt*):

> The population group with a migration background consists of all persons who have immigrated into the territory of today's Federal Republic of Germany after 1949, and of all foreigners born in Germany and all persons born in Germany who have at least one parent who immigrated into the country or was born as a foreigner in Germany. The migration status of a person is determined based on his/her own characteristics regarding immigration, naturalization and citizenship and the relevant characteristics of his/her parents. This means that German nationals born in Germany may have a migration background, too, be it as children of Ethnic German repatriates, as children born to foreign parents (in accordance with the so-called ius soli principle) or as German nationals with one foreign parent. This migration background is exclusively derived from the characteristics of the parents. And those concerned cannot pass the migration background on to their offspring. As regards immigrants and foreigners born in Germany, however, they can pass their background on. In accordance

with the relevant legal provisions concerning foreigners, this definition typically covers first to third generation immigrants. ("Persons with a Migration Background")

[2]ALMIN (*Alleinerziehende Migrantinnen und Migranten in Niedersachsen Lebenslagen und Fähigkeiten im Spannungsfeld von Armut und Selbstbestimmung* [*Migrant One-Parent Families in Lower Saxony—Living Conditions between Poverty and Self-Determination*]), 2012-2016, www.almin-project.de, funded by Niedersächsisches Ministerium für Wissenschaft und Kultur (MWK), Lower Saxony Ministry for Science and Culture, Germany.

[3]Underlying data bases are from the German micro census 2012 (Statistisches Bundesamt, "Bevölkerung").

[4]All names are pseudonyms; in order to protect anonymity other biographical data were also changed. The interview with Beatha was conducted in English, interviews with Fatma and Maryam were conducted in German and translated to English by the authors.

[5]Even more so, although according to Eurostat the share of foreign nationals in the total population of the EU is about 6.8 percent, their share in the survey is only 4 percent.

WORKS CITED

Baobaid, M. and G. Hamed. *Addressing Domestic Violence in Canadian Muslim Communities: A Training Manual for Muslim Communities and Ontario Service Providers.* London, ON: Muslim Resource Centre for Social Support and Integration, 2010. Print.

Bundesministerium für Familie, Senioren, Frauen und Jugend BMFSFJ (Hrsg.). *Gewalt gegen Frauen in Paarbeziehungen. Eine sekundäranalytische Auswertung zur Differenzierung von Schweregraden, Mustern, Risikofaktoren und Unterstützung nach erlebter Gewalt.* BMFSFJ: Bielefeld, 2009. Print.

Bundesministerium für Familie, Senioren, Frauen und Jugend BMFSFJ (Hrsg.).*Zwangsverheiratung in Deutschland, Band 1 der Forschungsreihe des BMFSFJ.* BMFSFJ: Berlin, 2011. Print.

Crenshaw, Kimberlé. "Mapping the Margins. Intersectionality, Identity Politics, and Violence Against Women of Color." *The Feminist Philosophy.* Eds. Alison Bailey and Chris Cuomo. New

York: McGraw-Hill, 2008. 279-309. Print.

European Union Agency for Fundamental Rights/FRA. *Violence Against Women: An EU-Wide Survey. Main Results*. Luxembourg: Publications Office of the European Union, 2014. Print.

Kavemann, Barbara "Erinnerbarkeit, Angst, Scham und Schuld als Grenzen der Forschung zu Gewalt." *Forschungsmanual Gewalt*. Eds. Cornelia Helfferich, Barbara Kavemann, and Heinz Kindler. Wiesbaden: Springer Fachmedien VS, 2016. 51-67. Print.

Nussbaum, Martha. *Women and Human Development. The Capabilities Approach*. Cambridge: Cambridge University Press, 2000. Print.

Sarrazin, Thilo. *Deutschland Schafft Sich Ab. Wie Wir unser Land aufs Spiel Setzen*. München: DVA, 2012. Print.

Statistisches Bundesamt. "Bevölkerung und Erwerbstätigkeit. Bevölkerung mit Migrationshintergrund. Ergebnisse des Mikrozensus." Statistisches Bundesamt: Wiesbaden, 2013. Print.

Statistiches Bunesamt. "Persons with a Migration Background." *Destatis*. Statistisches Bundesamt Wiesbaden, n.d. Web. 6 June 2016.

Schröttle, Monika. "Methodische Anforderungen an Gewaltprävalenzstudien im Bereich Gewalt gegen Frauen (und Männer)." *Forschungsmanual Gewalt*. Eds. Cornelia Helfferich, Barbara Kavemann, and Heinz Kindler. Wiesbaden: Springer Fachmedien VS, 2016. 101-120. Print.

Schröttle, Monika, and Nadia Khelaifat. "Gesundheit—Gewalt—Migration: Eine Vergleichende Sekundäranalyse zur Gesundheitlichen und sozialen Situation und Gewaltbetroffenheit von Frauen mit und Ohne Migrationshintergrund in Deutschland."

Universität Bielefeld im Auftrag des Bundesministeriums für Familie, Senioren, Frauen und Jugend. BMFSFJ: Berlin, 2008. Print.

Uslucan, Haci-Halil. "Cultural Contexts of Domestic and Juvenile Violence: A Cross-Cultural Perspective from Germany, Turkey and Norway." *International Journal of Criminology and Sociology* 2 (2013): 257-270. Print.

14. I Play, Therefore, I Am

Resisting the "Work" of Single Motherhood in a Culture of Labour-Intensive Parenting

ELIZABETH BRUNO

IN THE EARLY MORNING hours, when the light is barely breaking in, my six-year-old finds my body. She tucks her arms around me and whispers, "My momma, my warmth." Most days, this serene scene lasts for just moments before the wiggling—and imaginary play—begins. My daughter is suddenly sinking her teeth into my sleeve; she has transformed into an incorrigible puppy who wants to be called Chocolate. Or she's imploring that I reprise my role as her twin piglet, Sleepy. She's asking me to become the slow-moving Slothy, or transporting us to France, where I've become Pierre, the easy-going, chocolate-croissant devouring waiter who drives a red Vespa, has a pet squirrel, and defends Parisian children from kidnappers. In these frolicsome moments, as the day cracks open, I love my empty bed—the way it becomes a floating raft or a secret woodland cave or a snotty French café. My bed and my body become whatever my child and I want them to be. My most intimate and private spaces unfold into forests and castles and mountaintops. In many ways, these are the most real moments of my life: the moments when I am most myself. These are precious, empowering minutes, where I escape the stigmas and restraints of being a single mother, when my inner realities unfold and interact with someone else's inner realities.

"Life must be lived as play" (19) wrote Dutch historian and theorist Johan Huizinga. In *Homo Ludens* (1938), he argues that what makes us human is not intelligence or labour but how we play. We are not *homo sapiens* ("wise men") or *homo fabers* ("man the creator") but *homo ludens* ("man the player"). Play creates order—in fact, *is* a kind of order—and systems of law, art, war, religion, and language have all arisen as particular forms of play. Play stands outside the "boundaries of time and space" and "promote[s] the formation of social groupings" (13). As philosopher Daniel Dombrowski rightly notes, Huzinga's ideas are deeply Platonic: "When Huizinga talks of play being *outside* of ordinary reality, he sometimes means *above* ordinary reality in a higher realm, a 'mystical' or ecstatic (literally *ek stasis* 'outside of one's normal place') realm, in his usage" (Dombrowski 106). According to Huizinga, play is a response to "an imperfect world [of] confusion" that can bring "limited perfection" (Huizinga 10).

In 1975, sociologist Dennis Orthner examined how *Homo Ludens* was affecting family studies, particularly attending to "an offshoot of this concept [that has] led a number of recreation groups to adopt the slogan: 'the family that plays together, stays together'" (Orthner 175-183). This idea—what he calls *familia ludens*—is rooted in the belief that play in families facilitates integration or solidarity. In line with Huizinga's insistence that play must exist outside "material interest and no profit can be gained by it" (Huizinga 13), Orthner objects to Huizinga's concepts being applied to the overly structured (and often segregated) play activities of the middle class; to him this "play" was infiltrated by a work-ethic mentality that made free time anything but "free."[1] Not only was "working at play the norm," but activities like golf and Little League separated children from adults and males from females, which, ultimately, removed play's potential to build family communities.

In contrast to the ideals of middle- and upper-class play, Orthner advocates leisure, calling it "a new source of family integration." Quoting social psychologist John Neulinger, he argues that leisure is "not non-work ... not the time left over from work, [but] a state of mind ... a way of being at peace with oneself and what one is doing" (Orthner 177). In other words, he asserts that family play or leisure is not dependent on external realities but internal ones. Orthner goes on to explain that leisure can prompt change from the inside out: through play, humans can see each other in expanded, new, or different ways. Games, camping, and many forms of play, he conjectures, allow people to "explore their environment with greater freedom," which prompts new encounters and connections. This kind of play could induce "the realization of the other beyond the constraints of a particular role" in a way that "improves the level of understanding and offers further possibilities for exchange" (Orthner 177). Put another way, play functions to build community, not just because it brings people together but because it exposes them to one another. Without this uncovering, play's potentials remain untapped.

Although Orthner's text suggests strong family play can exist regardless of class and financial considerations, he, nonetheless, pictures it only in terms of nuclear family life. In fact, he draws on many thinkers who suggest that the foundation of good family leisure must start with "the marital dyad," including Norman Miller and Duane Robinson's assertion in *The Leisure Age* (1963) that sexuality is the "greatest, most beautiful form of play we know" (Orthner 179). Orthner follows suit with Miller and Robinson, asserting that "husbands and wives can increase their understanding of one another through sharing some of their leisure together" and that then "parent-child communication can likewise be enhanced" (Orthner 180). In arguing for the primacy of marital play, Orthner suggests good leisure starts in the adult realm and leaks down into the larger family unit.

The cultural shifts over the last forty years make Orthner's elevation of marriage seem odd, perhaps even offputting; most middle-class American women no longer see themselves primarily as wives, instead considering their primary family role as a mother. Even considering this shift, however, Orthner's definition of leisure in family life does not even begin to consider how play might function in a family where marriage and/or sexuality is not a component of family life. In the case of lone parents, for example, there may not even be a separate adult realm. The absence of an adult partner, generally discussed foremost in terms of financial strain and time restriction, also has meaningful impacts on the duration, quality, and nature of play. In my case, I do not have less time to play, but rather more; because I do not have to juggle adult relationships as a part of my parenting, I am able to more constantly and consistently play. Family leisure does not sneak out of my romantic partnership. To to the contrary, I remain immersed in play because I do not have a romantic partnership.

Regardless of its nature and type, maternal play is often frowned on. It is the cake of parenting; the sweet, sugary and non-nutritious option that should be side-stepped for more healthy options, such as musical lessons, STEM education, and physical exercise. In many ways, this distate for play is intimately related to the ways in which maternal pleasure has become strangely taboo in both mainstream and academic contexts. Over the last decade in particular, most discussions of parenting higlight difficulties. In her recent non-fiction text *All Joy and No Fun*, journalist Jennifer Senior addresses sociological findings that parents are no happier than non-parents (and, in certain cases, are considerably less happy). Rufus Griscom and Alisa Volkman started their online parenting magazine *Babble* to address the "false advertising" around parenting, particularly addressing dissatisfaction and disconnection, isolation, and loneliness for parents in society.[2] These are only a few of the myriad examples of attempts to unmask motherhood and address the less than ideal aspects of parenting. As Sara Ruddick so eloquently suggested to Andrea O'Reilly, after twenty years of new discussions of motherhood, it may be "easier to write about ambivalent feelings about children and about the happiness of lives with children, [but] it may be more difficult to write about the delight, the pleasures" (qtd. in O'Reilly 22).

There is more to the unspoken prohibition against discussing maternal joy than the need to honestly address and expose maternal realities that have been previously hidden or repressed. The joy of maternal play is dangerous because aligning oneself with anything childlike is risky if women want to be taken seriously. As children's literature scholar Beverly Lyon Clark so eloquently notes, "Adulthood is exactly what many feminists want to claim" (5). Many women distance themselves from anything juvenile and work diligently to present themselves as valid human adults. It is no exception with single mothers, who are all but mandated to prove they are not lazy, social dependents by exhibiting superhuman feats of serious, adult responsibility.

Play appears at odds with notions of self-sufficient super-workers. In *Single Mother: The Emergence of the Domestic Intellectual*, Jane Juffer asserts that although there is no typical single mother, the cultural ideal of single motherhood is wrapped up in labour;

"Single mothers in the United States at the turn of the century all live with the imperative to demonstrate self-sufficiency" (3). What Juffer does not note is that this notion of self-sufficiency is dependent on concepts of "good" or "true" adults as labourers. In fact, political condemnations of single motherhood often shame or belittle women for being childlike or dependent; single mothers are "takers" not "makers" (Sargent). Takers avoid serious, productive (and masculine) adult labour. Mitt Romney linked single mothers to gun violence (Marcotte); Rick Santorom called single mothers the primary threat to the "fabric of our country," who were "breeding criminals" (Murphy and Kroll); and Dan Quayle famously said single mothers by choice "mock[ed] the importance of fathers." In each of this cases, single motherhood is chastised for threatening proper "adult" society.

As single mothers are so rarely taken seriously, discussions of play and joy in lone parent family life hardly seem prudent. In addition to political leaders disregarding single mothers as dependent or childlike, society itself remains hesitant to react favourably. A 2011 survey of 2,700 Americans suggests single motherhood is the least favourable lifestyle—far less acceptable than unmarried parents, gay and lesbian parents, couples who cohabitate, working mothers, interracial marriage, and childless women (Morin; "Split Verdict"). Although the notions of who constitutes a "nuclear family" have shifted since the 1950s—interracial families, gay and lesbian parents, unwed parents are now all included—the two-parent nuclear family still overwhelmingly dominates our conceptions of acceptable family life. In this chapter, I will suggest the lack of favorability is linked to a particular understanding of parenting rooted in a kind of economic logic: single mothers are assumed inferior because they can "invest" less time and money.

By addressing single parent play, I aim to offer an alternate means of discussing lone parent life. This discussion is rooted in my own observation of the stark contrast between my joyful daily experiences and the cold and broken visions of single motherhood that society has offered me. If I apply Orthner's ideas of play creating strong family life, I see many single mothers whose worlds are full of deep connection, honest communication, and profound solidarity with their children. In my case, the robust play life that I experience exists not despite a missing spouse but, perhaps, because of it. Of course, this is not some sort of Peter Pan existence; as with every other single mother I know, there is not a day that passes that I'm not engaged in stressfully making financial ends meet and creatively juggling time demands. These are very real (and often pressing) realities, however they are certainly not the only realities of single parent family life.

As I have argued elsewhere, there are real risks in evaluating single mothers based primarily on their labour identities; understanding hard-working non-dependent single moms as "good" super heroes and, conversely, casting them as lazy or dependent social villains if they receive support is a false dichotomy. Moreover, it is one that serves society—not single moms who are offered the looming carrot of social acceptability by performing these identities (Bruno). Although it may seem an improvement over nineteenth and twentieth century condemnations of single mothers based on sexual morality mores, confining any human's value to their labour roles is problematic. For single mothers, the ideal of self-sufficiency is unrealistic to say the least. In America, single mothers experience triple the poverty rate of the rest of the population, the highest rate of low-wage employment, the worst wage gap, the lowest net worth, and the highest risk of bankruptcy (Faludi). Just as feminists often battle stereotypical representations of themselves as angry, man-bashing women, so too do single mothers battle sensationalized (and even romanticized) images of the selfless and all-American super-labourer and/or the anti-American non-labourer.

It is sensible for single mothers in this environment to avoid exposing anything vulnerable or tender—anything that could be seen as potentially childish or idle. However, this chapter argues that single mothers (and other marginalized groups) should have the freedom to not just play, but discuss and think about play as an important part of their life and parenting practices. According to the influential twentieth-century pediatrician and psychoanalyst D.W. Winnicott, play is the only place "the child or adult is able to be creative and to use the whole personality, and it is only in being creative that the individual discovers the self" (73). I join

Winnicott (and Orthner) in understanding play to go beyond recreational or development activity appropriate for children. Play is not nonsense or immaturity but often a deeply mature way to respond to reality. Selma Freiberg's groundbreaking text *The Magic Years* (1959) establishes that play is the process of working out and coping with the world, not escaping it. She argues,

> We must not confuse the neurotic uses of imagination with the healthy ... contract with the real world is *strengthened* by his periodic excursions into fantasy. It becomes easier to tolerate the frustrations of the real world and to accede to the demands of reality if one can restore himself at intervals in a world where the deepest wishes can achieve imaginary gratification. (23)

Play is an important way human beings navigate life and its challenges. For single mothers, play can offer the chance to respond to numerous kinds of scarcity and challenges in the home. However, as aspects of single motherhood that seem childish are quickly brushed under the rug or condemned—and as the joys of maternal reality are more broadly taboo—play is under-considered.

Sadly, there sometimes seems little room to academically discuss the potentials of this kind of play, regardless of how kind and positive maternal scholarship is towards lone mothers. For the most part, this appears to follow efforts to validate single motherhood. Editors of the collection *Dilemmas of Lone Motherhood*, Randy Albeda, Susan Himmelweit and Jane Humphries, open their collection by linking single motherhood with the growing literature on "family structure, the division of responsibility for caring work, welfare policies, pay discrimination, and gender-segregation in labour markets, all of which act together to perpetuate women's economic dependence." They go on to assert that an exploration of lone motherhood touches on each of these things and "highlights one of the key questions of our era, how to raise children while earning a living" (1). Here single motherhood is validated as serious business; it touches on all of the most important adult questions. However, simultaneously single motherhood is conflated with other issues, albeit important ones, and shaped or defined by those questions that people outside of single motherhood find interesting or important.

Even creative, probing pieces that address the unexamined daily realities of single mothers often focus on work and effort in a way that leaves daily reality far behind. In "How Men Matter: Housework and Self-Provisioning Among Rural Single-Mother and Married-Couple Families in Vermont, U.S.," Margaret K. Nelson argues that single mothers are disadvantaged in ways that income levels alone do not fully capture; single mothers must cope with household responsibilities, such as home, car, and lawn maintenance. In response, she catalogues the four major techniques single mothers employ to face these home-labour expectations: lowered standards and avoidance, purchasing necessary goods and services, skill acquisition, and reliance on others (Nelson). Despite Nelson's careful consideration of daily life, there is not a single mention of play or leisure. There is only a vision of struggle against society.

Although there are good reasons to discuss the difficulties single mothers face and understand single motherhood is tied to larger philosophical and social questions, we cannot do so at the expense of ignoring the unique, interesting, and important differences single parents may experience in daily parenting. Although middle-class structured leisure may be difficult or even impossible for single mothers to access, free play in the home can and often does remain a central part of family life, even if it remains hidden and obscured by the tendency to collapse single mothers into labour identities. This chapter suggests that play can be a tool for single mothers to create localized values, purpose, and a family culture. This is no small matter. As Huizinga notes, "A play-community generally tends to become permanent even after the game is over" (23). There are real consequences from play—and the potential consequences of lone parenting play are worth considering.

Play can offer resistance to cultural expectations and, sometimes, misleading standards of American parenting. In this chapter, I examine contemporary expectations concerning single parenting, and further consider its place within the broader expectations of what Sharon Hayes first called "intensive parenting," elements of which I situate under the rubric of "investment parenting." Exploring how parenting has recently become compared to economically productive labour, I suggest that this ideology of investment parenting undergirds contemporary understandings of single mothers and their worth. When culture imagines that single mothers are super-labourers, it does so within the framework of investment parenting in which parents understand their role to be "depositing" time and money into children.

I suggest that lone mothers need not be valued only based on a super-labourer status; they can be respected and regarded (and their relationship with their children can be valued) outside of investment logic. This work can benefit single mothers, their children, and their communities. As psychologist Ruth Linn has suggested, single motherhood is a unique because it invites women to become "moral subjects" and to enact "moral resistance"from the margins of their society (140). In struggling against the normative expectations of culture, single mothers can rub up against the specific dimensions of social expectations and create new routes. Single motherhood offers a noteworthy (and I argue important) vantage point from which the values and structure of parenting in American society can be reconsidered. Play is not just taboo for (serious) single mothers, but, more broadly, for all parents. This intersection suggests that single mothers' play can speak more largely to our concerns and confusions about the role play should have in childrearing practices.

Rather than simply addressing single motherhood as a liability, it is important that the positive potentials of single parenthood are discussed. This chapter does not wish to ignore the often overwhelmingly difficult realities of lone parenting and the practical injustices that single parents experience daily all around the world. Rather, it attempts to address some of the conceptual frameworks that contribute to and perpetuate the way that these injustices are maintained. Many single mothers cannot honestly express their realities but must perform socially acceptable labour identities; this is an additional burden single mothers carry that society is deeply oblivious to. The discursive fantasy of the super-single mother does not serve single mothers in the end, although it may provide temporary relief from judgement. Asking single mothers to be self-sufficient, therefore, is not simply asking them to assume responsibility for themselves. It asks them to assume responsibility for maintaining the illusion that self-sufficiency is possible—and is the best way of organizing a society. Although validating single mothers for being hard workers may offer them social acceptability, this narrow stereotype creates and maintains a safe distance from their real experiences; class inequality becomes preserved without considering potential injustices and flaws in the system.

Although in this chapter I am putting forward imaginative role play as ripe with civic and ethical potential for children and adults, I do not wish to portray this kind of parental engagement as somehow innately superior. Adults who do not connect with children in exactly the way I am describing are in no way precluded from rich communication, mutual problem solving, and civic engagement. I am only touching on one of the two primary modes of play Huizinga outlined; I only address representational play without discussing the "contest" aspect of play (Huizinga 13). Because young children often extend representational play toward their parents before more organized forms of competitive play take place, I will focus on this form. Representational play offers a mode of mutual engagement and connection that speaks back into daily life from the earliest ages. That being said, both competitive and representational play correspond to group dynamics and have lasting effects on groups, not just individuals. This understanding of play is far more than the narrow framework of play as developmental activity; play does far more than just build (or deposit) physical, emotional, and cognitive skills into individual children. This model makes children passive rather than acknowledging how children actively extend into their communities through play. Taking play seriously means taking children seriously and taking seriously what they have to offer our communities.

For me, engagement in representational play has not come out of intentional plans, childrearing books, or expert opinions. In fact, it is quite the contrary: when all my (admittedly over-cognitive) approaches failed, I discovered my daughter reaching out to me through play. Responding to problem-solving techniques children offer can provide surprisingly effective results and can resist investment parenting standards that see adults as the active family member who must fix or control "bad" activity children engage in. Responding to play is a narrative, not theoretical, approach to parenting. It asks parents to listen to the stories their children are telling them and to be active co-creators in the stories a family is going to tell about themselves and the world around them.

WHEN (SINGLE) PARENTING BECAME WORK

The term "single mother" did not come fully into popular usage until the 1980s, appearing at a conspicuous moment when our parenting ideals were being overhauled. Just prior, the term "female head of household" was popular, as it appeared on official documents, such as tax and consensus forms. Before either term was used, lone motherhood was described using a wide variety of phrases. Lone mothers were not a unified group but were seen as different kinds of mothers; they were described as "bastard bearers" (particularly popular in seventeenth-century England) or as "unwed mothers," "deserted women," "separated wives," "widowed mothers," or, on occasion, "divorced women" (Bruno 386-388). In light of this, the almost exclusive usage of the term "single mom" in mainstream representations is of note. It reflects not only the increased dominance of nuclear family life but the emergence of a unifying concept that previously had not linked these mothers.

Single mothers came to be understood as a consolidated group as the moral distinctions that formerly separated them became less essential in understanding women and mothers. In addition to shifting sexual mores, changes in how motherhood was understood and civically valued contributed to these changes. In *Mom: The Transformation of Motherhood in Modern America*, Rebecca Jo Plant artfully demonstrates that motherhood in interwar America started to shift away from being understood as a civic and moral duty and became something more private. In the 1920s and 1930s, conceptions of motherhood clashed; modernists challenged traditionalists who imagined motherhood was a sacred estate that women entered, an institution that was "the fundamental pillar of the nation's social and political order" (5). Eventually modernists won, and the idea that mothers were private producers grew increasingly common. Plant suggests this shift is particularly evident in the vocabulary shift; the casual and personal term "mom" replaced the civically charged notion of "mother" and the force of maternal morality.

In the 1980s, the term single motherhood came to represent not just a woman's "single" marital status but the idea of solo labour; she was a singular labourer engaged in the private work of raising a child. This concept rests on the earlier shift away from moral motherhood and towards privatized mothering and, further, emerging ideals of shared parenting labour among the sexes. During the late 1980s and early 1990s, maternal labour became understood as not just private but shared between male and female counterparts; the term "single" mother emerged in line with increased expectations that two parents would engage in double labour to raise children, who should share domestic and economic labour.

In many cases, shared parental responsibility was advocated through a reliance on the language of "work." Marilyn Waring's groundbreaking text *If Women Counted: A New Feminist Economics*, published in 1988, calls attention to the invisible and unpaid work that has traditionally been done by women. Dismissing the notion that women know little about economics, Waring argues that it is false to understand women as "reproducers not producers, welfare cases not workers" (10). Waring validates mothers and women as intelligent labourers who attend to grossly undervalued areas. She argues that this labour must become visible: "The system cannot respond to values it refuses to recognize" (3). Rather than redrawing lines of labour exclusively in the workplace, Waring implores her audience to consider all the places where labour lines are drawn. Similarly, in *The Second Shift*, from 1989, sociologist Arlie Hochschild describes parenting and domestic tasks as second jobs. She asserts that, "Just as there is a wage gap between men and women in the workplace, there is a 'leisure gap' between them at home. Most women work one shift at the office or factory and a 'second shift' at home" (4). At the time, Hoschschild's reframing of domestic tasks as a second job was part of the effort to level the playing field for women in the private sector, not just the public realm. She wanted men to step up and enact equality in the home and to share in the domestic labour for which women were traditionally responsible.

The language of "work" even came from feminist philosophers at this time, such as Sara Ruddick, who raised the importance of the intellectual labour of motherhood. Unsurprisingly, Ruddick employs the language of mothering "work" in her indispensable *Maternal Thinking*. She argues that parenting is not about who is doing the work but the work itself; "The universal need of human children creates and defines a category of human work" (14). For Ruddick, parental care arises out of the needs of children, not the identity (biological or otherwise) of the parent. Despite having used the word "work" in her text, Ruddick later reflects an awareness of its limitations. In the preface to the second edition of *Maternal Thinking*, published six years later, she suggests that there are "deficiencies" with the idea of mothering as work. She writes, "Generally the idea of 'work' does not give weight to the myriad cultural, domestic, and personal *relationships* that structure anyone's experience" (xii). Ruddick's awareness of the limits of the term work is worth noting, particularly because she contrasts the concept of work with relationships. She wisely worries that using the term "work" totalizes children and "obscures differences in children and therefore in mothers, [and in the] relationships to the social worlds they inhabit" (xiii). As a concept, "work" can assume simplistic and/or universalizing notions that get away from individual situations and circumstances.

In this chapter, I will address Ruddick's concern and argue that although using the word "work" allows for a critical re-examination of gender expectations (which remain unresolved), this word choice is not without its risks and difficulties. Levelling the parental-gender balance (and challenging the notion that caregivers should be exclusively female) has been an important recent development. However, it is worth considering if how this balance was argued for has had unintended and, perhaps, detrimental consequences, particularly for less privileged demographics. Has elevating "women's work" to the status of paid labour made it harder rather than easier for women (and perhaps men) to parent? Has it made it easier for poor mothers or immigrants? Has it obscured or conflated goals and aims or minimized the relational aspects of parenting? Have the attempts to address gender inequality in the social (adult) realm resulted in limiting possibilities in the private (child-adult) realm? Are parents more or less able to understand their children?

I argue that the notion of motherhood as labour is so foundational that it dominates how lone mothers are discussed, labelled, and understood; they have become "single" workers who are judged less for sexual morality and more for their self-reliance in a system in which two parents are expected to juggle the two realms of domestic and economic labour. This shift to describing (and valuing) single mothers as solo labourers originated in the late 1980s and early 1990s as "work" became the normative nomenclature to describe childrearing. Not coincidentally, this was also the moment that many sociological and maternal experts point to as the origin of "intensive-parenting" ideals. Professor of human development Sarah Harkness first starting hearing middle-class parents discussing the importance of investing in "special" or "quality" time, which was meant to stimulate children, in the 1980s (Day). Considering the broader issues at play, it might be helpful to describe these budding practices as parts of the larger logic of *parenting as investment*. That is, the expectations for parents to "invest time" (and "spend" it wisely) are nested within the larger shifts of understanding parents as private workers. The expectation for time and money to be invested into children is not isolated from this shift but a part of it; children are understood as products who are made as a result of proper environments. Parents must not just invest time; they must invest the right or superior things that will "make" their children superior specimens.

Early literature on intensive parenting suggests that poor or immigrant mothers were not initially wrapped up in the standards and practices that middle-class mothers began experiencing in the 1980s. However, in the last decade scholars have increasingly suggested that these standards quickly spread. As Andrea O'Reilly notes, by the twenty-first century the "New Momism style of mothering" was becoming normative across "transcending geographical and class boundaries" (35). Although individual single mothers (who exist across class, race, and national lines) may not have initially experienced intensive parenting ideals, general attitudes and social posturing towards single motherhood in North America have long entangled single mothers in these ideals. By categorizing single mothers as a unified group distinctive for domestic and economic labour, single mothers are automatically ensnared in larger questions and confusions about motherhood as intensive labour. Single mothers are socially devalued based on their supposed inability to meet these standards. A 2010 report from The Economic Mobility Project at Pew Charitable Trusts, for example, discusses the risks of single parenting using investment logic: "Married couples ... provide more supervision as well as more support. In other words, on average, a married couple has more money and time to invest in their child, which should, among other things, increase the skills of the child that are valued in the labour market, the child's human capital" (DeLeire and Lopoo). By suggesting that the role of all parents is to increase a child's "human capital" by the investment of time and money, single mothers are understood as automatically inferior where childrearing is concerned. The nuclear family is understood to be superior because it provides the greatest chances for the right "investment" to be made into child repositories.

Much of the moral judgment around single mothers as human beings seems to have lessened—so much so that John Ifcher and Homa Zarghamee have suggested that "changes in the stigma associated with being a single mother" explains marked statistical increases in happiness for single mothers over the last thirty-five years (Ifcher and Zarghamee 1219). Nonetheless, the economic standards of investment parenting remain overwhelmingly condemnatory. Single mothers can earn their social keep by proving they are hard-working citizens, but this labour has not redeemed them as parents. In fact, quite the contrary. Under investment parenting standards, mothers who clothe, feed, and co-exist with their children are no longer good enough. North American society may have pardoned (some) single mothers as citizens, but it has certainly not absolved them as parents.

THE LIMITS OF THE INVESTMENT PARENTING METAPHOR

The logic of investment parenting, which evaluates and condemns single mothers and partnered mothers alike, has been perpetuated and bolstered by a prominent comparison between mothering and economic labour. In many ways, the comparison makes sense:

mothering involves the responsibility, long hours, and physical exertion experienced in paid labour. However, as the original purpose of this metaphoric comparison was to validate what mothers do, the rise of unbearable parenting standards now experienced is paradoxical to say the least. To address investment parenting standards, and their negative repercussions, how this metaphor operates in North American society must be better understood.

The comparison between motherhood and economic employment has become prevalent in social commendations of mothers. A prime example is the 2014 award-winning American Greetings ad project "World's Toughest Job," created by Boston-based advertising agency Mullen Lowe. After advertising a bogus job under the title "Director of Operations," interested parties were interviewed via webcam. In the advertisement, interviewees are shown being shocked by the job description: 135+ hours a week, constant standing and bending, no holidays, no breaks, and no pay. Before discovering the position is motherhood, interviewees describe the expectations as "crazy," "intense," "cruel," "insane," and "inhumane." When they discover that motherhood is being described, the participants' outrage quickly turns to tears and whoops of joy. Many participants even start expressing thankfulness for their own mothers (Nudd). Jennifer Rooney, who reviewed this campaign for Forbes, suggests the success and popularity of the ad campaign was due to the its ability to "cause people to reconsider Mom as the amazing professional she is" (Rooney). By reframing the labour of mothers in language used to describe economically generative labour, the tasks of motherhood are ostensibly illuminated and, thus, able to be valued more fully.

However, does this comparison actually illuminate motherhood? Beyond creating a way to cognitively grasp the physical exertion motherhood may potentially pose, does this metaphor truly create social support for all that motherhood entails (and does not entail)? Does it create a further need to perform motherhood as intense labour in order for mothers to be valued? Although this metaphor—mothering as unpaid work—validates the physical labour motherhood may require, it relies and reinforces, at the same time, a very specific logic and understanding that parents are valuable primarily as intensive labourers. It feeds into looming standards of investment logic that devalue and underestimate children as passive products who consume their parents' time and money.

The metaphors used in culture have immense, and often unaware, effects—and the parenting as unpaid labour metaphor is no exception. Over the last twenty-five years, cognitive linguist George Lakoff and philosopher Mark Johnson have been working with metaphor, and they argue that people automatically and unconsciously acquire a vast number of metaphors that structure their reasoning, experiences, and everyday language. In *Philosophy in the Flesh* (1999), they draw on neuroscientists' work to show that metaphoric thinking starts with young children conflating ideas and physical experiences, such as conflating warmth with affection, or size with importance. Even though children eventually differentiate between these, cognitive links remain in the neural pathways of their minds. Size remains linked to importance and, consequently, it is used to metaphorically communicate about importance: "Tomorrow is a *big* day. No *biggie*." Likewise, temperature is used to convey affection: "She greeted him *warmly*. He gave her the *cold* shoulder." According to Lakoff and Johnson, language reflects how both language and bodily experience align in the brain; the neural pathways in the mind join subjective and sensorimotor experiences.

Thinking of parenting as unpaid labour is a complex, conceptual metaphor, one adult society employs to validate parents, particularly women. In 2001, the website *Salary* started putting out an annual "Mom Salary Survey," a monetary assessment of the "jobs" of motherhood, based on data from how more than fifteen thousand mothers spend their time. In 2014, the job titles that they used to describe and elevate maternal labour included: housekeeper, cook, daycare teacher, janitor, psychologist, CEO, computer operator, facilities manager, laundry operator, and van driver. In this report, describing mothering as unpaid labour offers a way of comprehending the tasks mothers do, and it validates mothers by comparing what they do to the economic sector. In other words, it is not meant to help understand parenting itself but the worthiness of mothers because they are hardworking. This metaphor praises mothers but based on the commonly held belief that a person's value is derived from his or her economic labour. Such economic language suggests that there is an increasing overlap in the cognitive framework between parenting and paid labour. Lakoff and Johnson suggest our culturally based metaphors do just this; they combine physical experience with "cultural models, folk theories, or simply knowledge or beliefs that are widely accepted in a culture" (60). We accept and rely on this metaphor because it connects the physical experience of maternal labour with larger cultural ideals of human worth being tied to superior (economic) labour.

Complex metaphors are powerful and unconscious driving forces in the world. They offer not just a single connection but a whole web of ideas that shape perceptions. That is why it is particularly important to attend to their implications. After all, this particular metaphor may offer social validation and may help parents feel validated for their effort, but does it help parents understand their children or engage more deeply in their parenting practices? Does validating mothers as "professionals" help women address challenges in motherhood not found in the workplace—the agony of teaching a child thankfulness or self-control, struggling with an illness or disability, creating a language of morality, explaining death or suffering? Where, in this metaphor, is the intellectual work of motherhood? Where is play and the oh-so-unprofessional realities of pretending to be a rideable donkey in order to move an unmovable child?

Understanding motherhood as unpaid work can limit how women conceptualize and engage critically with their day-to-day activities and can misconstrue the relationship between parents and children as a one-way exchange. This is particularly evident when the metaphor is taken to its full extent. When the website *Upworthy* posted the "Mom Salary Survey," they chose the title "It's Pretty Shocking How Much Money this Person Would Make If They Didn't Love Their Client So Much" (Lamour). Children are described as "clients," not unlike the American Greeting company campaign that labelled them "associates." The professionalization of mothers is also a professionalization of children. Rather than being understood as active human beings, they increasingly become understood as demanding consumers who must be appeased and struggled with. Under this logic mothers are providing free services rather than engaging in a two-way relationship.

The professionalization of children is, of course, not entirely new. In her influential *Pricing the Priceless Child* (1994), sociologist Viviana Zelizer famously outlines how between the 1800s and 1930, children became "sacralised" in Western society; they became "economically useless but emotionally priceless" consumers who gobbled up education and other resources (57). In 2014, fellow sociologist Dalton Conley invoked Zelizer in an interview about his new book, *Parentology*, to contend that her distinction still holds: children are still "a big sinkhole of our time, attention and money" that "require a huge parental investment" of time and energy "from birth and before." He further suggests that the Affordable Care Act's extension of children's dependence on their parents to the age twenty-six has all but codified child's dependence into law (Shin). As Conley inadvertently suggests, it seems children are no longer just "sacralised" but professionalized to the point that the law has been rearranged to support to this logic.

In her book Zelizer suggests that our system is not sustainable, asserting that "the sacred, economically useless child may have become a luxury or an indulgence that the contemporary family no longer values, nor in fact, can afford" (208). Zelizer's concern seems have fallen on deaf ears, as children have only become increasingly dependent on parents over the last twenty years. Going beyond just economic dependence, children are now seen to be emotional reliant in unhealthy ways on their parents. Hara Estroff Marano, editor-at-large and former editor-in-chief of *Psychology Today,* describes the results of "invasive parenting" in her 2008 text, *A Nation of Wimps,* and suggests that parents are raising indecisive, anxious, emotionally fragile, and weak children. In April of 2014, Hanna Rosin's cover story in *The Atlantic* likewise implored parents to leave their children alone and spelled out some risks in parental overprotection, including a lack of independence, bravery, and risk-taking. These critiques rightly challenge intensive parenting standards, but they do not recognize the complexity of how intensive- and invasive-investment parenting standards are embedded into larger social values. In fact, they (somewhat ironically) feed into the logic that parents should do a better job.

Rather than focusing on how children could or should be active, these interventions feed on parental anxiety and focus only on improving parenting techniques and ideals of superior labour.

It is a challenge, as Andrea O'Reilly so nicely puts it, "to validate the important work of mothering while at the same time show that maternal work, as it is currently defined under intensive mothering, is not necessary or required" (35). In part, the difficulty of validating the "work" of parenting is because this language—and the underlying metaphor it reflects—creates an endless cycle of responsibility for adults. In this way, the concerns that Zelizer so appropriately raised about children as consumers may offer a point of intervention. If we go beyond thinking of children as inactive products, we have a chance to re-imagine what parents are doing.

ACTIVE CHILDREN AND THE IMPORTANCE OF TWO-WAY EXCHANGE

A fundamental flaw in imagining parenting to be (unpaid) labour is that parenting can be thought of as only a one-way task. This misunderstands basic realities, even on a biological level. Cell migration from baby to mother across the placenta is well documented (Dawe, Tan, and Xiao); a fetus's cells persist as a live part of the mother's body in her blood, bone marrow, skin, kidney, and liver for decades (including Y chromosomes if she is pregnant with a male child) (Bianchi, et al.). These cells are powerful and affect a mother's autoimmune system, healing heart weakness (Kira et al.) and providing protection against certain kinds of cancer (Fred Hutchinson Cancer Research Center) .The ability of children's cells to so powerfully affect a woman's body suggests that parents are not simply producers who "make" a child. Mothers mix themselves with children, socially, emotionally, spiritually, and even physically.

In 1982, the great Canadian author Margaret Atwood addressed this reality in her short story "Giving Birth," which challenges the idea that a mother "gives" birth to a child. The narrator follows Jeanie, a first-time mother who is mentally battling the stereotypes of delivering a baby while she is in labour. Afterward Jeanie looks at her baby and realizes this event was far more complex than the phrase "giving birth" could ever account for the exchange she has experienced; "Birth isn't something that has been given to her, nor has she taken it. It was just something that has happened so they could greet each other like this" (321). Atwood frames birth as a meeting place: an encounter between two beings and not the manufacturing of one being by the other. In doing so, she challenges the logic of production she has inherited from her society, noting it simply cannot address the complexity of her experiences.

Narratives that challenge the idea that motherhood is simply one-way production are rare, even in children's literature, where children are meant to be considered. Instead of thinking about children's active role, twentieth-century children's books are rife with narratives that re-enforce the idea that children are passive consumers. For example, Dr. Suess's *Horton Hatches the Egg* (1940) revolves around a child so inactive that she absorbs her non-biological mother's physical image. An elephant, who invests his time by sitting on a bird's egg, diligently and tirelessly depositing himself into this child, is rewarded when the bird hatches and is a flying elephant. Here labour is shaping a child and the intensive investment Horton offers marks superior motherhood. Similar logic dominates Betty MacDonald's highly successful Mrs. Piggle-Wiggle books, published from 1947 to 2007, which feature a widow who feeds disobedient or naughty children magical candy, which, once consumed, fixes bad behaviour and transforms them into superior children. Armed with a chest full of magical cures left by her deceased (pirate) husband, Mrs. Piggle Wiggle offers cures for children who are, for example, bullies, crybabies, whisperers, show-offs, or slowpokes; she offers peppermint leadership pills that help bullies whose "bodies [have] grown faster than their patience and kindness," or whisper sticks that robs gossiping girls of their voices, or "crybabytitus" tonic that "tastes delicious, sort of like vanilla ice cream with caramel sauce" but causes someone who starts crying to be unable to stop (MacDonald 35). In these books, children are consumers who literally eat their way to better behaviour. How different these good or bad children are that can be (magically) changed by what is deposited into them from the child Atwood finds infused with all the mysteries of life.

One of the risks of imagining children to be consumers in these narratives is that a child is seen as a product that adults must control and fix. In a Mrs. Piggle-Wiggle story, a child's bad behaviour is automatically understood as a product flaw that must be improved on. The idea that this behaviour might also reflect the problems in the environments and communities that these children occupy is utterly lost in this model. Children are not potential problem solvers; they are potential problems. Although this may not seem particularly troubling in a light-hearted children's book, the fact that unborn children are monitored in strikingly similar ways is worth noting. The tests and scans that are standard in medically monitored pregnancies aim to ensure that nothing is wrong with a child; even before someone is born, the goal is to fix and improve them. In *Conceiving Parenting,* ethicist Amy Laura Hall argues that the sustained eugenic underbelly of these practices suggests contemporary parenting is entangled in bigger, older ethical questions: "Who is my neighbor? Am I my brother's keeper?" (4). Questions related to parenting are also ethical questions about responsibility and power over others and about how much control people do (and should) have over others. How much control and responsibility should parents have over their offspring? How much responsibility do we have to "fix" or "create" other people?

Seeing children as inactive products also presents risks for parents. Mothers who see themselves as one-way producers may become inactive as well. Psychologist Daniel Miller suggests that one of the marks of contemporary consumer motherhood is how mothers attempt to understand and communicate about themselves through their children. In "How Infants Grow Mothers in North London," he close-reads the behaviour of well-educated and professional middle-class mothers in London, including their shopping and spending habits. Noting that mothers suppress their own desires, choosing to splurge and buy children's clothing when they want something, Miller links these women to religious practitioners who engage in "ritual purifying through pain" (34). He asserts that the "cult of the infant" has replaced religion as the fundamental experience of "transcendence of one's individuality" and that women use it to "replace consumption as a superior form of self-construction through a new social relationship" (48). In depositing themselves into children, mothers actually blend into their children.

Miller, of course, is not the only person to suggest that parenting is a cult that women can lose themselves in, but he is astute to note that it can offer a potential escape from consumerism and the demands of society. Although this is only one among many reasons a parent might give their time and attention to children, it is worth considering the larger implications of parenting as "depositing." Social advocate and educator Paulo Freire famously addressed social problems that emerged out of an investment (or banking) model of education. In *Pedagogy of the Oppressed,* Freire suggests that the idea of a teacher as someone who deposits information into students actually perpetuates inequality by creating a system in which the "younger generation" is brought "into the logic of the present system," bringing about "conformity" (64). Central to Freire's work is the idea that students need to be understood as active participants and teachers need to be understood as more than bankers; he suggests the terms student-teachers and teacher-students. In the case of parents, the same insight applies. It is not simply important to understand children as active, but to also grasp that parents are more than just investors. Understanding childrearing as a process of depositing (or "investment") maintains a deeply unhelpful hierarchy. Children are not taught to solve problems, to trust themselves, or to be innovative. Rather, they are taught to accept the situation that they find themselves in and the values of the world around them. The same can be said of parents who remain trapped, though in a different location. Not only does the investment model understand children as problems to be fixed, but it also suggests that parents need to be utterly self-sufficient in this work.

Before Freire described the banking model of education, progressive American educator John Dewey argued the concept of all-supreme and independent individuals actually conflicted with creating a healthy democracy. In *Democracy and Education*, published in 1916, he argues that dependence and cooperation—and not self-sufficiency—were essential not only for education but also for social progress:

> From a social standpoint, dependence denotes a power rather than a weakness; it involves interdependence. There

> is always a danger that increased personal independence will decrease the social capacity of the individual … it may lead to aloofness and indifference … to develop[ing] an illusion of being really able to stand and act alone—an unnamed form of insanity which is responsible for a large part of the remediable suffering of the world. (50)

Dewey asserts that dependence creates cooperation, whereas the illusion of independence creates isolation and suffering. Like Freire's model, this description is strikingly apt where investment parenting is concerned. Notions of self-sufficient motherhood are creating a sense of suffering for a variety of mothers who live under the onus that to prove themselves valuable citizens they must operate like economic labourers who are paid based on their individual performances. In reality, parenting is never a one-way street and we need a logic that more fully addresses these complex realities.

PLAY AS INTERDEPENDENT PROBLEM SOLVING

We imagine children as inactive products because we see them as separate and distinct from adults. Adults are labourers, whereas children are pre-labourers who still require skill development to reach their fulfillment. Although this idea has led to important advancements, such as labour laws and compulsory education, it still allows us to devalue children. Beverly Lyon Clark notes that although we idealize childhood in many ways, our disdain of play and immaturity remains so prevalent that adults continue to shame each other through accusations of immaturity and play: "Members of the middle class are apt to think of members of the working class, whether they act out aggressions or seem shy, as adolescents. Members of the middle class may also apply to male members of the upper class, the idle rich, a term that doubly inscribes juvenility: *playboy*" (12). For Clark, this method of disparaging others by associations with immaturity suggests we maintain a disdain for children that allows us to ignore children and their perspectives: "We are so adult centered that the only child we adults can see is ourselves; we do not recognize what it means to attend to children's perspectives" (7). Maintaining that children "play" and adults "work" allows humans to keep distance from children and not fully consider, respect, or value children.

In line with Freire's acknowledgement that teachers are always learning and students teach them too, we must acknowledge that adults also play and children also work. The false dichotomy that adults are good "workers" and children are good "players" needs to give way to a more honest acknowledgement that adults and children alike are working players and playing workers. Moreover, we must acknowledge that we still devalue play itself as inferior, despite long-standing attempts by educators and activists to value play and childhood. Long before feminists were comparing mothering to economic labour, educational innovators and advocates like Maria Montessori were describing play as the "work" of children in order to validate and elevate children and their rights.

In the early twentieth century, play became an important concept for educational thinkers, such as Caroline Pratt, Lucy Sprague Mitchell, and Maria Montessori. Following in the footsteps of nineteenth-century Swiss educational reformer Johann Pestalozzi and the German pioneer of kindergarten Fredrich Froebel, progressive thinkers began to emphasize how each aspect of a child's life—including play—contributed to their formation. Play was no longer contrasted with learning but thought of as the means through which learning was accomplished and the means through which children could arrive successfully at proper social adulthood. Play became valued in a similar way that work was – for the individual benefit it offered the worker.

In the early twentieth-century Maria Montessori's reframing of children's physical play as their "work" was welcomed in America as part of our larger eugenic aims to create superior children. When investigator Josephine Tozier first introduced Montessori to America in 1911, she described her as "an educational wonder-worker," whose scientific teaching would "insure the [child's] development, under freedom, to his highest capacity." Repeatedly emphasizing her scientific approach, Tozier credited Montessori with "the rediscovery of the ten fingers" and declared "the modern baby [is] no longer the plaything of its parents" (123). The idea that understanding children from a developmental and scientific perspective would make parenting serious (and superior) is a notion that continues to undergird our understandings of childrearing. Montessori's method was heralded as being able to craft superior future workers by manipulating children's play to their advantage.

Developmental psychologists, such as Jean Piaget and Erik Erikson, further developed and expanded these notions, articulating them in terms of cognitive and developmental growth. For Piaget, play was an adaptive behaviour that allows children to practise and consolidate skills, such as hand-eye co-ordination and sensory-motor skills. In Erikson's eight stages of development, play corresponds to developmental progress. In the second stage, where autonomy is being developed (ages one and a half to three), Erikson argues that play corresponds to the development of the will. In the third stage, known as the "play stage" (age three to six), he suggests that children develop agency and purpose by using imaginary play to test ideas and imagine the future. In the fourth stage, (age six to twelve), children build competency and industry, start to play with greater interest in precision and skill, and develop a sense of pride and self-worth. In this way, play becomes understood as a separate (and inferior) reality.

Investment parenting imagines play is immature activity children engage in on their way to maturity; it is valuable as a stepping stone toward better things. Although validating children's play as "work" allowed Montessori and others to elevate and prioritize children in the classroom, and to draw attention to children in ways that had not been previously considered, seeing play as a stepping stone still devalues it as lesser. Valuing play as children's "work" suggests it is only meaningful as preparation for adult work. However, as Huizinga and other scholars establish, play is anything but just childishness. It is a fundamentally human way to create meaningful, complex social structures: a way in which not just children, but adults experiment, process, communicate, and respond to the world around them. Perhaps even more importantly, play is an essential part of creating new meaning and new systems. As Georges Bataille suggests in *The Accursed Share*, published in 1949, this process of stepping outside systems is a common and important adult activity. He argues that through art, fashion, eating, sexuality, luxury, and even death we engage in *dépense* (expenditure) and break out of our normal restrictive economies

(10). In this way, play is not merely about the individual gaining skills, but about continually working out how to respond to the systems we find ourselves a part of.

Although individual skills are gained within acts of play, the tendency to imagine play as valuable only in terms of individual skill acquisition is troubling. Play is not, as Freud might suggest, a kind of masturbation or an isolated act of self-pleasing. Playing can be communal and has purposes and results far beyond self-pleasing and individual skill building. As D.W. Winnicott puts it in *Playing and Reality,* playing happens in a "potential space" between people. "Playing has a place and a time," he writes, "It is not *inside* ... nor is it *outside,* that is to say, it is not a part of the repudiated world" (55). Play creates a new space to encounter others and decentre the "repudiated" world. It creates new rules and casts off the regulations that are normally followed. Play creates new contexts, and, with these new contexts, new possibilities.

Play is not simply the ability to imagine—it is the capacity to encounter others and come into relationships of greater equality through mutual engagement and responsibility. In *Rabelais and His World* (1940), Russian semiotician and literary scholar Mikhail Bahktin discusses the role of carnivals in Renaissance society and suggests that through collective play members of a group became equal: "Here, in the town square, a special form of free and familiar contact reigned among people who were usually divided by the barriers of caste, property, profession, and age" (10). In families, where adults are understood to be all-important depositors of time, money, and goodness, play operates in the same way—drawing lines of communication across divides. As Orthner's work on *familia ludens* rightly suggests, this is possible, in part, because play exposes people in a way that offers new points of connection.

Investment parenting standards cannot offer truly active family membership to children, but engaging in play prompts communication and engagement out of which mindful adults can learn to take their children and their concerns seriously. Moreover, when understood as social and political resistance, play can offer both parents and children the ability to engage with inherited social systems of meaning – and even create new systems of meaning. For minority or marginalized families, this offers something that subservient acceptance of unfair labour standards cannot. In the case of single mothers, who are teasingly promised social acceptability as citizens if they prove themselves extreme super-labourers, using play can offer new ways of imagining self-worth. Play as creative engagement is the act of intellectual bricolage: working from the ground up with what is present. Rather than beginning with abstract ideals such as those imposed by society, play creates new meaning out of the people present. Engaging in play can allow parents to go beyond the model of investment, seeing children as something more than inactive, undeveloped pre-adults.

CONCLUSIONS: WHEN SINGLE MOTHERS PLAY

Shortly after my daughter learned to ride her bike, we started commuting to and from her school by bike. The first morning, she felt insecure and afraid, particularly about potholes and dips in the road. After cautiously crossing one or two, she loudly announced to me that potholes were actually lava. We laughingly avoided them all the way to school. In this case, and a thousand other like it, my daughter actively used play to solve a problem she was experiencing. Play is something she utilized to address difficulties in the present moment. In this way, play must be understood as something more than developmental activity children accidentally perform out of some biological need. Importantly, my daughter did not use play to address her fears by internally imagining the potholes as lava but by creating an external system that collectively acknowledged and addressed her fear through a structure of play.

Play is a form of problem solving that deserves to be taken seriously not simply for building skills that lead to successful future employment. Play rests on the ability to both think critically, innovate, and communicate: skills which are, perhaps unsurprisingly, currently lacking in adult American culture. In 2009, New York Times correspondent Kate Zernike reported that these capacities of thinking, communicating, and being creative are what on the Association of American Colleges and Universities found employers wanted to see more of in college graduates: "89 percent said they wanted more emphasis on 'the ability to effectively communicate,' 81 percent asked for better 'critical thinking and analytical reasoning skills' and 70 percent were looking for 'the ability to innovate and be creative'" (Zernike).

Because play is the practice of entering into a situation without a known outcome, it requires attentiveness to people and to problems. In contrast to content knowledge, which we imagine people carry with them, the skill based activities of communication, critical thought, and innovate are not necessarily internally contained. Regardless of someone's position in society, these skills are essential. A doctor who has a profound knowledge of the human body in abstraction must also be able to problem solve through interaction and attentiveness to the particular body in front of him or her. A mother with a profound knowledge of ideal human development must also be able to interact with and attend to their particular children. Play is a paramount means of engaging with what is present, and for that reason exists outside our often simplistic models of education and childrearing as investment.

When we play, we communicate, think, and innovate from the bottom-up, not from the top down. As a mother, on a daily basis I must choose to either respond to my daughter's active problem solving or to ignore it. I do not "teach" her to be a problem solver; I either prevent it or allow it. However, even if I manage to respond on a regular basis and honour my child's work to creatively engage with the world around her, I am aware that under the standards of investment parenting, I remain socially understood as an inferior parent. Under this logic, I cannot make my child superior because I do not invest superior materials. It is for this reason that justice for single mothers requires more than granting a small slice of acceptability for them through notions of extreme labour. Because the ideals of super-labour stem out of our larger systems of value, this requires a recognition that the profoundly unfair and limiting ideals of investment parenting falsely see rearing children in line with economic production.

Although single mothers may successfully practise parenting outside of nuclear family investment standards, they are still not free to express or further develop these practices because anything that does not fall within an understanding of super-labour is deemed suspect: a sign of laziness or deficiency. The idea of single mothers with active kids may prompt grim images of the child labour, rather than the more honest reality that active children have unique chances to develop skills such as communication and critical thought. Active children are not necessarily neglected children. In contrast to the deep disdain of childhood implicit in investment parenting logic, where children are inferior vessels who need to be improved to reach adulthood, allowing children to be active and valid problem solvers offers respect. Play respectfully responds to children and supports active skills that are already present. To play with one's child is to encounter and listen to them, but it is also to be willing to support their natural ability to create systems of meaning that correspond to their perspective.

Play is scary to us, however, not just because we associate it with immaturity, but with vulnerability. Whereas scholars, such as Dewey, see vulnerability as a social strength, society generally treats it as a liability, weakness, or sign of undesirability. This knee-jerk reaction to vulnerability, indeed to death and loss itself, runs consistently throughout North American culture on almost every level. Alongside dismissing vulnerable single mothers and their children, we also tuck our elderly out of sight and refuse to see their aging bodies and minds. We create communities for people with disabilities and avoid any potential discomfort of encountering them in the worlds that we build, where they are not welcome. We even hide death and vulnerability on own our bodies, removing any blemish we find (or imagine) with plastic surgery and endless other means of manipulation to remove any "fault" or vulnerability. The ideals of post-industrial capitalism are ideals of hiding or overcoming vulnerability with power and self-improvement. They are deeply unlike systems of play, which acknowledge and respond to individual vulnerabilities rather than hiding or removing them.

Single mothers will remain offensive if they remain vulnerable. This is not even particularly personal; society is simply keen on avoiding people who remind us of our own humanity. In his 2008 text *Violence,* Slovanian philosopher and cultural critic Slavoj Zizek argues that the primary impulse in Western society has become this right to avoid other people; "What increasingly emerges as the central human right in late-capitalist society is *the right not to be harassed,* which is a right to remain at a safe distance from others" (41). By asking single mothers to live up to investment logic, we also ask them to keep vulnerability – and thus themselves – safely out of sight. A culture of self-improvement is a culture of separation and our parenting paradigm is reliant on these ideals of self-perfectibility. We separate valuable adults from not-yet-valuable children who can (and should) be perfected. We raise children to rise above their inferior childhood state to reach superior adulthood. Instead of coming close to understand the vulnerable perspective of children – and allowing the natural human tendency to be problem solvers – we ask children to overcome and hide their vulnerabilities. In doing so, we actually squelch intelligent solutions and systems that our communities could profoundly benefit from.

The democratic problem solving that Dewey, Freire, and others discuss require communication, interaction, and even interdependence. Single mothers are often in unique positions to practice these skills because their vulnerabilities allow them to focus on realities rather than ideals. The value of these practices goes beyond narrow ideas of super-labour, in which responding to difficulties is merely beneficial because it is hard work. As Dewey writes in *Democracy and Education* (1916), attending to what is actually happening, just as bees or ants do, is what successful civic engagement requires. Dewey argues that animals working without blueprints or plans can collectively create superior systems and structures because of their attention to the collective work they are engaged in:

> When the bees gather pollen and make wax and build cells, each step prepares the way for the next ... the essential characteristic of the event is, namely, the significance of the temporal place and order of each element; the way each prior event leads into its successor while the successor takes up what is furnished and utilizes it for some other stage. (101)

In other words, Dewey suggests that democratic action is co-operative attention (and response) to what is present. Bees do not draw up idealist plans; they pay attention. Dewey argues that this "careful observation of the given conditions to see what the means available for reaching the end" and a willingness to accept new possibilities as they unfold rather than holding onto "a single outcome [that] has been thought of" are paramount (102). Play replicates this pattern. It is active engagement with what is present. The value of this engagement goes far beyond the limited praise we offer single mothers when we suggest they are simply good super-labourers who work hard.

Although we happily praise orphans in literature for being plucky and showing ingenuity in problem solving—orphans such as Harry Potter, Huck Finn, Pollyanna, Little Orphan Annie, Oliver Twist, Pip, Jane Eyre, Heidi, Anne of Green Gables, Dorothy (of Wizard of Oz fame), Peter Pan, and Mowgli—we are not nearly so kind to vulnerable people living in society. We want single mothers and their children to be quiet and hidden rather than be active problem solvers who are interdependent in their communities. We need to consider if these measures are truly just.

In the end, I suspect single mothers—like all mothers—will still come under fire for one reason or another. However, when these mothers play with their children and allow them to be active two-way participants in their mutual life, they are doing something strong and lovely. They are creating systems democratically. They are resisting false, unjust, and unfair expectations based on systems of power that limit and flatten human beings. They are engaged in profoundly important intellectual activity by creating systems that respond to realities rather than to ideals.

I began this chapter with my own experiences as a single mother and, in the end, those experiences are the best that I have to offer. I realize that they are in no way inclusive of other women's experiences of single motherhood, yet I offer them because they are *my* resistance. Years ago, when I started reading about single motherhood, I was surprised by how accurate and, simultaneously, disconnected these accounts seemed from my life. All the single mothers that I know, even the less privileged ones I meet while volunteering at a domestic violence resource centre, are not the bleak, grim characters of poverty they are supposed to be. They are women who toss their babies in the air and laugh with glee. They are intelligent problem solvers who deftly respond to real life problems—and support their children in doing the same.

The literature seems intent on presenting them as struggling workers, but, like me, their own daily realities are just as much (if not more) dominated by their children than by their economic disadvantage. These are dual realities. And although one reality does not preclude the other, it is, for me, unfair that we single mothers are collectively understood to be such inferior parents. The single women that I know are very brave: brave enough to be vulnerable when they play with their children.

NOTES

[1]Orthner does not unpack Huizinga's ideas, but, nonetheless, his concepts resonate with many of Huizinga's insights, including concerns about when "play becomes business" or become "false" (Huizinga 206).

[2]In their popular December 2010 TED Talk, Griscom and Volkman discuss launching *Babble* after the birth of their first son. They say it "It was really more about our desire to speak very honestly about subjects that people have difficulty speaking honestly about. It seems to us that when people start dissembling, people start lying about things, that's when it gets really interesting, that's a subject we want to dive into. And we've been surprised to find as young parents, that there are almost more taboos around parenting than there are around sex."

WORKS CITED

Atwood, Margaret. "Giving Birth." *Mother Reader: Essential Writings on Motherhood.* Ed. Moyra Davey. New York: Seven Stories Press, 2001. 311-324. Print.

Bakhtin, Mikhail. *Rabelais and His World.* Bloomington: Indiana University Press, 2009. Print.

Bataille, Georges, *The Accursed Share.* New York: Zone Books, 1988. Print.

Bianchi, Diana, et al. "Male Fetal Progenitor Cells Persist in Maternal Blood for as Long as 27 Years Postpartum." *Proc. Natl. Acad. Sci.* 93 (2015): 705-708. Web. 14 Apr. 2015.

Bruno, Elizabeth. "Her Cape is at the Cleaners: Searching for Single

Motherhood in a Culture of Self-Sufficiency." *Mothers, Mothering, and Motherhood Across Cultural Differences*. Ed. Andrea O'Reilly. Bradford, ON: Demeter Press, 2014. 385- 412. Print.

Carroll, Linda. "Gay Families More Accepted Than Single Moms." *NBC News*, 15 Mar. 2011. Web. 8 Jan. 2013.

Clark, Beverly Lyon. *Kiddie Lit: The Cultural Construction of Children's Literature in America*. Baltimore: John Hopkins University Press, 2003. Print.

Dawe, G. S., X. W. Tan, and Z.C. Xiao. "Cell Migration from Baby to Mother." *Cell Adhesion & Migration* 1.1 (2007): 19–27. Web. 14 Apr. 2015.

Day, Nicholas. "Parenting Ethnotheories and How Parents in America Differ from Parents Everywhere Else." The Slate Group. 10 Apr. 2013.Web. 13 Nov. 2013.

DeLeire, Thomas, and Leonard M. Lopoo. "Family Structure and the Economic Mobility of Children." *Economic Mobility Project. Pew Charitable Trusts*. The Pew Charitable Trusts. Apr. 2010. Web. 22 Nov. 2013.

Dombrowski, Daniel. *Contemporary Athletics & Ancient Greek Ideals*. Chicago: University of Chicago Press, 2009. Print.

Faludi, Susan. "Sandburg Left Single Mothers Behind," *CNN*. Turner Broadcasting System, Inc. 13 Mar. 2013. Web. 30 Mar. 2016.

Fred Hutchinson Cancer Research Center. "Residual Fetal Cells in Women May Provide Protection Against Breast Cancer." *Science Daily*. Science Daily, 3 Oct 2007. Web. 14 Apr. 2015.

Freire, Paulo. *Pedagogy of the Oppressed*. New York: Continuum, 2000. Print.

Griscom, Rufus, and Alisa Volkman. "Let's Talk Parenting Taboos." *Ted Women 2010*. Ted Conferences, LLC. Dec. 2010. Web. 14 Apr. 2015.

Hall, Amy Laura. *Conceiving Motherhood: American Protestantism and the Spirit of Reproduction*. Grand Rapids: Wm. B. Eerdmans Publishing Co., 2008. Print.

Hochschild, Arlie. *The Second Shift*. New York: Avon Books, 1989. Print.

Huzinga, Johan. *Homo Ludens: A Study of the Play-Element in Culture*. Boston: Beacon Press, 1955. Print.

Ifcher, John, and Homa Zarghamee, "The Happiness of Single

Mothers: Evidence from the General Social Survey" *Journal of Happiness Studies* 15.5 (2014): 1219-1238. Print.

Juffer, Jane. *Single Mother: The Emergence of the Domestic Intellectual.* New York: New York University Press, 2006. Print.

Kira, Rina, et al. "Fetal Cells Traffic to Injured Maternal Myocardium and Undergo Cardiac Differentiation." *Circulation Research.* 110 (2012): 82-93. Web. 14 Apr. 2015.

Lakoff, George, and Mark Johnson. *Philosophy in the Flesh: The Embodied Mind and Its*

Challenge to Western Thought. New York: Basic Books, 1999. Print.

Lamour, Joseph. "It's Pretty Shocking How Much Money This Person Would Make If They Didn't Love Their Client So Much," *Upworthy.* Cloud Tiger Media, n.d. Web. 14 Apr. 2015.

Linn, Ruth. *Mature Unwed Mothers: Narratives of Moral Resistance.* New York: Klower Academic and Plenum Publishers, 2002. Print.

Marcotte, Amanda. "Romney Blames Single Parents for Gun Violence." The Slate Group. 17 Oct. 2012. Web. 22 Nov. 2013.

MacDonald, Betty. *Hello, Mrs. Piggle Wiggle.* New York: Harper Collins Publisher, 1957. Print.

Miller, Daniel, "How Infants Grow Mothers in North London." *Consuming Motherhood.* Eds. Janelle S. Taylor, Linda L. Layne, and Danielle Wozniak. New Brunswick, NJ: Rutgers University Press, 2004, 31-52. Print.

Morin, Rich. "The Public Renders a Split Verdict On Changes in Family Structure." *Pew Research.* Pew Research Center, 16 Feb. 2011. Web. 9 Jan. 2013.

Murphy, Tim, and Andry Kroll. "Santorum: Single Moms are 'Breeding More Criminals.'" *Mother Jones.* Mother Jones and the Foundation for National Progress, 6 Mar. 2012. Web. 7 Aug. 2013.

Nelson, Margaret. "How Men Matter: Housework and Self-Provisioning Among Rural Single-Mother and Married-Couple Families in Vermont, U.S." *Feminist Economics* 10.2 (2004): 20-23. Print.

Nudd, Tim. "24 People Who Applied for the World's Toughest Job Were in for Quite a Surprise." *Adweek.* Adweek Inc., n.d. Web. 14 Apr. 2014.

Orthner, Dennis, "*Familia Ludens:* Reinforcing the Leisure Component in Family Life." *The Family Coordinator* 24.2 (1975): 175-183. Print.

O'Reilly, Andrea, ed. *Maternal Thinking: Philosophy, Politics, Practice*. Bradford, ON: Demeter, 2009. Print.

Plant, Rebecca Jo. *Mom: The Transformation of Motherhood in Modern America*. Chicago: University of Chicago Press, 2010. Print.

Quayle, Dan. "On Family Values." Address to the Commonwealth Club of California. *Vice President Dan Quayle*. N.p., 19 May 1992. Web. 9 Jan. 2013.

Rooney, Jennifer. "Here's How American Greetings Is Working to Maintain Momentum of Award-Winning 'World's Toughest Job." *Forbes*. Forbes Media LLC, 16 July 2015. Web. 5 Apr. 2016.

Rosin, Hanna. "The Overprotected Kid." *The Atlantic Monthly*, Apr. 2014. Web. 14 Apr. 2015.

Rothman, Barbara Katz. "Motherhood Under Capitalism." *Consuming Motherhood*. Eds. Janelle S. Taylor, Linda L. Layne, and Danielle Wozniak. New Jersey: Rutgers University Press, 2004, 19-30. Print.

Ruddick, Sara. *Maternal Thinking: Philosophy, Politics, Practice*. Ed. Andrea O'Reilly. Bradford, Ontario: Demeter Press, 2009. Print.

"Salary.com's 14th Annual Mom Salary Survey." *Salary*. International Business Machines Corporation, n.d. Web. 14 Apr. 2015.

Sargent, Greg. "Paul Ryan Regrets That 'Makers and Takers' Stuff. Sort of, Anyway." *The Washington Post*, 23 Mar. 2016. Web. 3 Apr. 2016.

Senior, Jennifer. *All Joy and No Fun: The Paradox of Modern Parenthood*. New York: Ecco, an imprint of HarperCollins, 2014. Print.

Shin, Laura, "How to Manage Your Biggest Investment: Your Kids," *Forbes*. Forbes Media LLC, 18 Mar. 2014. Web. 5 Apr. 2016

Tozier, Josephine. "The Montessori Schools in Rome: The Revolutionary Educational Work of Maria Montessori as Carried Out in Her Own Schools," *McClure's Magazine*. Dec. 1911, 123-137. Web. 14 Apr. 2015.

Waring, Marilyn. *If Women Counter: A New Feminist Economics.*

San Francisco: Harper and Row, 1988. Print.

Winnicott, W. D. *Playing and Reality.* New York: Routledge, 2005. Print.

"Worst Off – Single Parent Families in the U.S." *Legal Momentum.* Legal Momentum, 12 Dec. 2012. Web. 22 Nov. 2013.

Zernike, Kate. "Making College 'Relevant.'" *The New York Times,* 29 Dec. 2009. Web. 1 Apr. 2016. Print.

Zilizer, Viviana. *Pricing the Priceless Child: The Changing Social Value of Children.* New Jersey: Princeton University Press, 1994. Print.

Zizek, Slavoj. *Violence: Six Sideways Reflections.* New York: Picador, 2008. Print.

15. Scripting Stories of Resistance

Young Single Parents and Theatre of the Oppressed

DEBORAH L. BYRD AND RICHARD J. PIATT

SINCE 2005, Professor Debbie Byrd and the undergraduate students enrolled in her upper-level women's and gender studies (WGS) course titled "Single Motherhood in the Contemporary U.S.: Myths and Realities" have been supporting a mentoring and empowerment program for pregnant and parenting students who attend or who recently have graduated from her city's large public high school. The course is a community-based learning and research seminar in which non-parenting undergraduate students interact regularly with the young parents and parents-to-be, about 80 percent of whom are female and almost all of whom live below or slightly above the poverty line. The college students are asked to synthesize the knowledge gleaned from the young mothers and fathers with information that they encounter in course readings. These readings consist of personal narratives by poor or once poor single mothers, documentary films, and feminist scholarship that examines the U.S. institutions and ideologies that so profoundly affect the lives of young and/or poor single mothers. Each year, the college students ask the young parents to pinpoint some of their most pressing concerns; the college students then identify ways in which they might help the parents meet some of the challenges that they face. The results have varied widely. The college students have produced health resource manuals and childcare directories, brochures outlining procedures for applying for food stamps or Title XX childcare subsidies, pamphlets on early childhood learning and age-appropriate play, and binders that list scholarship opportunities and academic programs at a number of local colleges and community colleges.[1]

The program the WGS class supports is funded by a non-profit agency, Easton Area Neighborhood Centers, Inc. (EANC), whose staff members collaborate with Byrd, school district nurses, social workers, and guidance counselors. Established in 2000 and formerly called the Family Development Research Program, the program recently has been renamed ASPIRE—an acronym for "Achieving Success Professionally, Intelligently, Respectfully, and Empathetically." Through a combination of in-school "Lunch and Learn" group sessions, individualized case management services, and evening and weekend programming at Lafayette College, the ASPIRE staff strive to promote psychological and physical wellness; foster good parenting skills; enhance self-confidence, motivation, and life skills; and teach young parents how to identify and access social services and other resources. Another important goal of this highly successful program is to ensure that all participants earn a high school diploma or a general education diploma (GED) and consider pursuing college or some other form of post-secondary education.[2] Since the years immediately following high school graduation can be a stressful and challenging time for low-income single parents, participants (who generally enroll in ASPIRE as high school students) can remain in the program through age twenty-two or until their youngest child turns five. Quite a few do so; in fact, most of the young parents who have participated in the Theatre of the Oppressed project, described below, are recent high school graduates.

THEATRE OF THE OPPRESSED AND FORUM THEATER PEDAGOGY

Augusto Boal (1931-2009) was a Brazilian theatre practitioner and activist, who developed the system known as Theatre of the Oppressed (TO) from the early 1960s until his death in 2009. Unlike theatrical practices in which the actor on stage is to provide a cathartic experience for spectators who are passively watching a performance, Theatre of the Oppressed seeks to energize audience members to the point that many choose to participate in the production, thus becoming both spectators and actors—or in TO terminology, "Spect-Actors." For Boal, catharsis is something of a dirty word, as it robs the spectators of their right and responsibility to think and act for themselves. Boal takes a cue from Berthold Brecht's Epic Theatre, particularly the practice of *Verfremdungseffekt* (or alienation effect), which uses a variety of theatrical devices to distance audience members from their tendency to empathize with the protagonist—so they, instead, will engage thoughtfully and critically with the socio-political realities pointed to by the story itself.[3] Brecht's theory of theatre provides a lens through which the community can view, discuss, and potentially engage in the political realities around them. Boal takes this idea further than his predecessor to create a theatrical style that allows the audience and the actors to share the same space in what he, throughout his career, termed a "rehearsal for the revolution." For Boal, it is not enough to invite spectators into dialogue; rather, it is necessary to actively engage the audience in the process of determining what constitutes liberatory action. What was a group of observers becomes a living body of Spect-Actors—a group of people who begin to "invade" the theatrical space in order to rehearse potential ways that they might free themselves from socially generated oppression. In the words of Boal, "The *Theatre of the Oppressed,* in all its forms, is always seeking the transformation of society in the direction of the liberation of the oppressed. It is both action itself, and a preparation for future actions. As we all know, it is not enough to interpret reality: it is necessary to transform it!" (Boal, "*The Aesthetics*" 6).[4]

This transformation of reality is the entire point of Theatre of the Oppressed. TO takes a number of forms, each appropriate in its own right to specific situations. For example, in *Image Theater* Spect-Actors create a series of living, human "photographs" or tableaux to convey meaning, which can then be dissected and discussed by the group. Forum theatre generates and enacts short plays, based on real social ills, in which a protagonist wrestles with multiple conflicts and obstacles; in forum theatre, audience members replace the protagonist to try out courses of action different from those in the original scene. In differing ways, each of these forms seeks to empower the Spect-Actor to "occupy his [or her] own Space and offer solutions" to the problems presented (Boal, "*Theatre of the Oppressed*" xxi). The solutions offered are never top-down, predetermined fixes; indeed, all possibilities offered by the gathered Spect-Actors are allowed and encouraged on the stage, then explored and critically examined through discussion. Out of all of this role playing of discriminatory behaviours and practices, this enacting of individualized and systemic barriers to self-realization, self-sufficiency, dignity, and safety, it is hoped that participants will begin to identify and adopt strategies for change that will create better situations for themselves and for their communities. Boal explains:

> the Spectator [is] to take on the role of Actor and invade the Character and the stage ... The stage is a representation of the reality, a fiction. But the Spect-Actor is not fictional. He exists in the scene and outside of it, a dual reality. By taking possession of the stage in the fiction of the theatre he acts: not just in the fiction, but also in his social reality. By transforming fiction, he is transformed into himself. This invasion is a symbolic trespass. It symbolizes all the acts of trespass we have to commit in order to free ourselves from what oppresses us.... To trespass is to exist. To free ourselves is to exist. (Boal, "*The Aesthetics*" 6)

The workshops in which the young parents and the college students participated most closely resemble Boal's image theatre and forum theatre. The workshops were conducted by Richard J. Piatt—an alumnus of the college where Byrd teaches and an assistant professor of visual and performing arts at Merrimack College. Piatt, who is also a Roman Catholic priest in the Order of St. Augustine and whose scholarly field of expertise is Theatre of the Oppressed, led participants through some warm-up exercises, designed to stimulate the imagination, free the body, and warm up the voice. Out of these, the participants then began to engage in image theatre. For example, using the childhood game "red light, green light," participants were instructed to partner up and remain in physical contact with their partner at all times. When red light was called and all participants froze, a few of the "statues" were singled out and explored. What did participants see, objectively and subjectively? Who might these "characters" be in real life? What might they be doing? What is their relationship to each other, and which character seems to have more power or be in control? The newly created characters were then brought to life with lines of dialogue given to them by the Spect-Actors, and a mini-play was born! This exercise allowed participants to understand the base from which they could create images and scenes from their own lives, including symbolic and real roadblocks to their potential growth as parents and as human beings.

Next, Piatt introduced the workshop group to forum theatre—with some departures from conventional Boalian practices that will be explained in more detail below. In forum theatre, members of an oppressed group (in this case, young, low-income parents) are invited to share with one another and their allies their personal experiences of injustice: the young parents are encouraged to recount specific instances in which they were negatively stereotyped, discriminated against, or treated unfairly. As they tell their individual stories, it becomes clear that there are many shared experiences; at some point, the group decides to focus its critical and creative attention on one story—a story that might centre on one kind of oppression but usually puts into play multiple obstacles and challenges that are drawn from several participants' stories.

Once the setting, central conflict and issues, and antagonist(s) are selected, volunteers from the group (Spect-Actors) begin to enact a reality-based but fictional young parent's encounter with one or more oppressors. Participants do not play themselves; indeed, our role-playing scenes often began with a non-parenting college student assuming the role of protagonist and the recent high school graduates playing the character (or characters) who block a young parent's access to important resources. In these Forum Theater mini-plays, the antagonist might be a stranger who makes condescending and negative comments about "babies who are having babies," a teacher who wants to demote a good student to a lower-level math class because the pregnant girl has missed some classes and assignments due to morning sickness and doctor's appointments, or even a grandmother who is assuming that her daughter or son (the young parent) is not capable of making wise childrearing decisions. After the scene is enacted, others in the group are invited to comment and reflect on the action: was the scene realistic? Is this an experience that others can relate to? Did the young parent get what she wanted out of the encounter? Did she remove the obstacles in her path, effectively meet the challenges she faced, and deal with this situation in the way you might deal with it? As the group begins to address the latter series of questions, a Spect-Actor who imagines a different way of responding to the oppressor is asked to assume the role of protagonist; she or he is asked to demonstrate—not just talk about—an alternative course of action.

As the above account suggests, a group of young, low-income parents can benefit in several ways from *Forum Theater* enactments. Young parents can learn that they are not alone in experiencing a specific form of injustice, can collectively analyze an encounter and identify precisely what is problematic about the antagonist's words and deeds, and can experiment with a variety of strategies for coping with a specific kind of discrimination—with each member of the group determining which strategies she or he may personally employ in such a situation.[5] In short, Theatre of the Oppressed is what Paulo Friere would call a form of critical education that can inform and inspire revolutionary action; it promotes group solidarity; engenders a careful analysis of what constitutes an oppressive person, institution, and/or ideology; and empowers the oppressed by allowing them not only to reflect on but to practise a variety of resistance strategies. And if allies participate in the forum theatre performances, the young parents become aware that there are people in the community who support their determination to be treated with dignity, respect, and fairness.

MODIFYING TO PRINCIPLES ... BUT FOR GOOD REASONS

Students in the single motherhood course mentioned at the beginning of this chapter often do a research project near the end of the semester to educate themselves about a topic of interest to the young parents—how to apply for college financial aid or how choose a childcare facility, for example. The college students then share the results of their research with the young parents by "packaging" the information in a concise and teen-friendly format. In fall 2012, Byrd suggested that one group do a different kind of project. They were to conduct research on the principles and goals of the Theatre of the Oppressed (a pedagogy that at that point Byrd had only read about, not participated in) and then use that knowledge to create short scripts based on stories the young parents had shared with them over the course of the semester—stories about being negatively stereotyped or facing difficult challenges and obstacles.

Most of the scenes that the college students created ended up having two versions: a version depicting a teen parent unsure of how she should deal with an oppressor, and a version in which an empowered young parent successfully overcomes the obstacle or self-confidently "talks back" to her oppressor. In other words, the first pseudo-TO scripts tended to present the young parent first as an insecure and helpless victim, then as a person who only had to assert herself to get a desired result—convincing a landlord not to evict her, even though she was not paying her rent on time, for instance. The lack of realism and the victim-superhero dichotomy were, no doubt, due to the fact that the scripts were not generated by a group of young parents sharing and collectively analyzing and performing their own stories but were based on scattered conversations the college students had had with several young parents over a period of three months. This top-down approach to scripting young parents' dilemmas and their coping and resistance strategies was not working.

To begin to rectify this situation, the following semester, one of the college students who had helped to develop the initial TO scenarios did a for-credit internship under the supervision of Beatriz Rios, the newly hired ASPIRE program co-ordinator. Significantly, Rios is a twenty-two-year-old mother of two who, until her hire, had been an active participant in the ASPIRE program. Together, the two revised the TO scenarios to make them more realistic, then combined the skits to create a mini-play that could be called *A Typical Day in the Life of a Teen Parent*. That same semester, Byrd learned that Piatt was a specialist in the Theatre of the Oppressed pedagogy and asked her former student if he would be willing to collaborate with her on a TO project. Thus began a delightful and incredibly fruitful collaboration between a women's and gender studies professor and a trained and experienced Theatre of the Oppressed "joker" (the TO term for a workshop facilitator).

NEW SPECT-ACTORS, NEW SCRIPTS, AND NEW PERSPECTIVES

Byrd sent Piatt the script of the mini-play, and they decided to make use of that text in two TO workshops that Piatt would facilitate in September and October 2013. Byrd invited four teen moms and four of her current WGS students to the first workshop; the goal was to introduce the group to some key TO techniques so that in a few weeks, they could help Piatt facilitate an interactive workshop and discussion with a larger group of young parents. After Piatt conducted warm-up exercises and explained that the group would begin by reading aloud and enacting scenes based on stories that other young moms had shared, we turned to the revised *Day in the Life* script. After a read through, the group determined that many of the "fictional" protagonist's struggles did, in fact, represent life as they and other young parents experienced it. These were their stories with a protagonist very much like themselves. The teen moms decided that the scene that they wanted to focus on was an encounter with a lazy, ill-tempered welfare office employee, who clearly had no interest in helping the young parent access the services to which she was entitled. Interestingly, the mom most eager to show an alternative strategy for responding to such an antagonist was a young woman who had quietly announced at the beginning of the workshop that she would discuss others' performances but was highly unlikely to do any acting herself. But because the script's antagonist so closely resembled a welfare office worker that Maria had encountered two weeks earlier, and because the young mother had succeeded in getting what she wanted despite the woman's unpleasantness, Maria was eager to model for others the resistance strategies that she had employed so successfully. In fact, it was shy Maria who turned out to be the most active Spect-Actor at this particular workshop.

A few weeks later, ten young parents and and a dozen of Byrd's non-parenting college students attended Piatt's second workshop. The procedure was similar to that used in the "training" workshop, except this time, we used a script that had been further revised to reflect the experiences of the four moms who had undergone training, and we asked the larger group of young parents to pick four scenes rather than one scenario for further development. We formed four groups, each consisting of some college students and some young parents, and each group began discussing the issues raised in their skit. Piatt urged group members to share how each of them might have handled the situation, then use that discussion to alter the script. The results were fascinating. One script presented two forty-year-old women who, while grocery shopping, speak disparagingly about and to a teen mom they had never met before. This workshop group chose not to alter a single word of the original script; instead, they completely eliminated most of the words and reduced a three-page scene to the opening half page. As one young mom explained, "I run into people like this almost every day. If I tried to defend myself every time I met some jerk who thinks I must be lazy, slutty, and a bad mom just because I'm a teenager, I'd never get anything else done. Talking to ignorant people like that is a total waste of my time." Most of the young parents in the workshop nodded their heads in agreement—they might have tried to correct misperceptions the first couple of times, but now they would rather put their energy elsewhere.

Group two worked with a scene in which the baby's grandmother is critiquing some of the childcare decisions that are being made by her daughter, the young mom. Although few, if any, of the students had ever heard the term "subtext," creating a subtext to go with the original dialogue is exactly what they did. Two members of the group read the scene's original lines, in which the grandmother criticizes her daughter's parenting and the young mom expresses her resentment of her mother's interference. The other two members stood behind the mother-daughter pair and immediately after each character had spoken a piece of dialogue, interjected new lines that conveyed what the characters were actually thinking and feeling but not saying. The grandmother was questioning her own abilities as a parent, as she was feeling that she must have done something wrong since her daughter had gotten pregnant as a teen. The daughter's rejection of her mom's hard-won knowledge of parenting was only exacerbating the mother's feelings of inadequacy. The daughter, on the other hand, believed that she had let her mom down by getting pregnant at such a young age. She also was feeling overwhelmed by the responsibility of caring for an infant, but she was convinced that she would just further disappoint her mother if she were open about her fears and self-doubts. This led to a discussion about their own personal experiences with individuals vacillating between the roles of antagonist and supporter (friends, family members, teachers, coaches, etc.). The group concluded that in some circumstances, words that often go unspoken need to be said out loud if the protagonist-antagonist relationship is to evolve into one of protagonist and ally.

WORKSHOPS WITH ASPIRE PROGRAM HIGH SCHOOL GRADUATES

In fall 2014, Byrd and Piatt resumed their collaboration, holding one workshop in September and a second in October. Participants included ASPIRE case manager Rios, four of the college students enrolled in the fall 2014 offering of Byrd's single motherhood seminar, and seven ASPIRE participants who are high school graduates (five moms and two dads, ranging in age from nineteen to twenty-two). Two of the young moms had participated in the fall 2013 workshops, and one of these, along with a college student from Byrd's 2013 seminar, alternately participated in and filmed the two workshops. At the end of the semester, this pair produced a twelve-minute documentary film that explained and illustrated how the Theatre of the Oppressed pedagogy can benefit both young, low-income parents and their non-parenting college student allies.

Byrd and Piatt had not decided in advance to work exclusively with high school graduates, but those were the young parents who ended up attending the September workshop. New participants were not invited to the October session for two reasons: we wanted to build on the knowledge generated and the interpersonal relationships established in September, and we discovered that it was an advantage to work with young parents who have a richer set of experiences and more maturity and self-confidence than most of the high school parents were likely to have.

The first 2014 workshop began like the previous year's workshops: with warm-up exercises and the "red light, green light" image theatre exercise. We then did a quick oral read through of the six scenes in the latest version of the *Day in the Life* mini-play. This group of young parents immediately identified two scenarios as ones they would like to enact and discuss in more detail: a grocery store scene in which a young parent encounters two very judgmental middle-aged, middle-class mothers, and a scene in which a high school math teacher responds to the academic challenges being experienced by a pregnant teen in a punitive rather than a supportive manner. Because there were only ten workshop participants (plus the two filmmakers), we collectively explored the issues of power, privilege, and oppression embedded in the two scenes rather than divided into smaller groups. The opening discussion was amazing; the parents were eager to share their experiences and the conversation was punctuated with comments like "wait 'til you hear what happened to me," "my English teacher was just as horrible as that math teacher," and "if you think the woman who went off on you was obnoxious, wait 'til you hear what happened to me last week when I was out at a restaurant with my son and my mom." One of the most moving moments was when a young mom talked about how shocked—and pleased—she was when an older woman came up to her in the mall and actually praised her for the constructive way in which she had just disciplined her unruly three-year-old; all agreed that positive encounters of this sort are extremely rare.

As in earlier workshops, the group revised the original script by incorporating details from the stories that they had just shared with one another; then, they enacted the new scenes, with the college students initially taking on the role of the young parents and the parents playing the parts of the oppressive and obstructionist antagonists. If a workshop participant suggested a resistance or coping strategy different from the one the current protagonist had employed—speaking in a more assertive tone of voice or bringing an older adult ally to a student-teacher conference, for example—that participant was asked to demonstrate and model another strategy to deal with the unpleasant person or difficult situation.

In the second 2014 workshop, Piatt introduced participants to some new TO techniques. After the group came to a consensus about the topic for exploration—financial issues—the Spect-Actors divided into two groups. Each participant was invited to create a moving image by posing other members of the group and then giving each a few lines to repeat, thereby creating a speaking tableau that dramatized the financial stresses and difficulties that were experienced. At one end of the tableau were Spect-Actors portraying the desired "goal" (a better job, a college degree, and so forth) and at the other was, "me," the protagonist. Between her and the goal, each protagonist placed individuals whose views or demands were threatening to block her path to success. The actors representing obstacles tried to physically prevent the protagonist from reaching her goal while uttering refrains commonly heard by young parents: "I have to cut back your hours from fifteen to ten a week"; "you can't do that now that you have a child"; "your tuition bill must be paid in full by July 1"; "you should have thought about that before you got pregnant"; or "there's a third form you were supposed to fill out so you're going to have to come back in next week."

Perhaps the most moving and powerful moving image scenario was one created by a young mom, Kaitlin, whose goal was to achieve economic self-sufficiency by pursuing a college degree. In this instance, lack of safe, affordable childcare was preventing Kaitlin from getting a twenty-hour a week job, which she needed both to qualify for Title XX subsidized childcare and to cover some of her education-related expenses. Kaitlin, her partner, and their two young sons were living with Kaitlin's parents, but Kaitlin's mother was unable to help out with childcare due to a serious medical condition. Kaitlin's father not only was unwilling to provide any childcare assistance but also was constantly telling his daughter that both college and a job in the paid labour force were totally out of her reach until both children entered kindergarten.

When enacting the moving image that she had created, Kaitlin tried to refute her father's claim, but it was clear that she was feeling frustrated and somewhat defeated. At this point, another young mom, Aaliyah, asked if she could assume the role of protagonist. She then proceeded to calmly but firmly explain to "her" dad how she and her boyfriend were managing to cover the cost of subsidized childcare while juggling college coursework and jobs in the paid labour force. If one needs proof that the Theatre of the Oppressed can empower individuals to overcome obstacles in their lives, this incident provides an excellent case in point. The week after this workshop, Kaitlin found and took a part-time night job; her partner is home with the children in the evenings, and she is able to care for them during the day. Although Kaitlin is rather sleep deprived, she has started working towards her goal of having the financial means to enroll in college and to provide her children with quality childcare. Aaliyah's "acting" infused Kaitlin with hope and determination. When the TO group reconvened a few months later, Kaitlin told her friends that she was so grateful that she had participated in the TO project: "We can learn a lot from each. We are really dealing with a lot of the same issues and need a lot of the same things."

A CONCLUSION ... AND A BEGINNING

In spring 2015, Byrd took the group to New York City to see a troupe of young LGBTQ youth, who do public performances of forum theatre. By experiencing a fully realized forum piece and by being able to participate in that piece as Spect-Actors, the young parents and their non-parenting college student allies were able to see what they themselves might be able to accomplish by forming their own TO troupe geared toward teenagers in their own city. It is our hope that such a troupe will have a positive influence not only on emerging adults but also on teachers, administrators, school boards, elected officials, and all those whose lives and decisions have a direct or indirect impact on the success of the next generation.

Clearly, this is just a beginning: the start of what has been a useful dialogue and what might become something more. No one in the group is under the illusion that participating in the Theatre of the Oppressed will magically solve every problem. What it can do, and what it has done in this context, is open up a space for sharing, for critical analysis, and for actually seeing the possibilities for a different, more fruitful future. The immediate future of this particular group is to explore the possibility of using TO, not only to help themselves but also to empower and educate others.

NOTES

[1]See publications by Byrd in the works cited for more information about ways she and her WGS students support and collaborate with ASPIRE program staff and participants.

[2]Nationally, about 30 percent of U.S. teen moms drop out of high school, and many are still without a high school diploma or GED at age twenty-two. By contrast, almost every year 100 percent of ASPIRE seniors graduate with their class. And over 40 percent go on to take college courses or pursue some other form of post-secondary education.

[3]For more information on Brecht's concept of *Verfremdungseffekt*, there are a wide variety of sources available. We would suggest John Willett's *The Theatre of Bertolt Brecht*, *Brecht on Theatre*, edited by Willett, and *Brecht Sourcebook*, edited by Carol Martin and Henry Bial.

[4]For additional information on the theory and practice of Theatre of the Oppressed, see works cited.

[5]A variety of factors can influence an individual's choice of strategy, since each person has a unique personality and value system and since a given course of action may put into serious play issues of risk and safety for one individual but not for another with differing life circumstances.

WORKS CITED

Boal, Augusto. *The Aesthetics of the Oppressed.* Trans. Adrian Jackson. London: Routledge, 2006. Print.

Boal, Augusto. *Games for Actors and Non-Actors.* 2nd ed. Trans. Adrian Jackson. London: Routledge, 2002. Print.

Boal, Augusto. *Theatre of the Oppressed.* New Edition, Trans. Charles A. and Maria-Odilia, Leal McBride, and Emily Fryer. London: Pluto, 2000. Print.

Byrd, Deborah. "If You Build It, They May Not Be Able to Get There: The Challenges of Mentoring Teenaged and Low-Income Single Mothers through an Undergraduate Service-Learning Course." *Journal of the Association for Research on Mothering* 9.1 (Winter/Spring 2007): 111-24. Print.

Byrd, Deborah, and Rachel Gallagher. "Avoiding the 'Doomed to Poverty' Narrative: Words of Wisdom from Teenage Single Mothers." *Journal of the Association for Research on Mothering* 11.2 (Fall/Winter 2009): 66-84. Print.

Emert, Toby, and Ellie Friedland. *"Come Closer": Critical Perspectives on Theatre of the Oppressed.* New York: Peter Lang, 2011. Print.

Martin, Carol, and Henry Bial. *Brecht Sourcebook.* London: Routledge/TDR, 2000. Print.

Willet, John, ed. *Brecht on Theatre.* London: Methuen, 1964. Print.

Willet, John. *The Theatre of Bertolt Brecht.* London: Methuen, 1977. Print.

16.
Single Mothers' Activism against Poverty Governance in the U.S. Child Welfare System

SHIHOKO NAKAGAWA

THIS CHAPTER EXPLORES how the U.S. child welfare system has become a site for poverty governance. Poverty governance refers to the ways that governments employ a variety of policy tools and administrative arrangements in order not to end poverty but to secure, in politically viable ways, the co-operation and contributions of poor people for the smooth operation of societal institutions through civic incorporation, social control, and the production of self-regulating subjects. The burdens of people who live and work in poverty are indispensable for the quality of life that most people expect (Soss, Fording, and Schram). This chapter explores how poverty governance is executed at the frontlines of child welfare services—how racialized single mothers are regulated—and how mothers themselves respond with activism.[1] How is this governance achieved discursively and materially in child welfare policy and its common practice? How has it affected families headed by single mothers? And how have they responded?

Social welfare policy is an area in which the state has long intervened in gender relations. The neoliberal restructuring of welfare states is a more recent intervention, particularly through the creation of workfare—enforcing work while residualizing welfare (Peck 10)—for persons in need of income support. In the U.S., Temporary Assistance for Needy Families (TANF), which was introduced in 1996, is a notable example; TANF replaced Aid to Families with Dependent Children (AFDC). Many single mothers lost their entitlements as full-time care providers, which AFDC had assured since 1935. Single mothers must now work full-time (thirty hours or more) as work requirements to receive TANF in most states (Hill 39).

Simultaneously, foster care caseloads expanded very rapidly throughout the late 1980s and 1990s (Berrick 28) and more than doubled from 1985 to 2000 (Swann and Sylvester 309).[2] The growth in foster care caseloads has mainly affected families headed by single mothers (Slack et al. 518; Paxson and Waldfogel) and among these, has disproportionately affected racialized mothers (Roberts). Moreover, there is an apparent overlap between families receiving public assistance and families involved with child welfare services (Courtney et al.). This overlap reflects how the child welfare system tends to equate poverty with neglect (Roberts 26-27) and follows the neoliberal trend of criminalizing and punishing the poor (Wacquant).

The poverty experienced by families headed by single mothers, however, has been taken for granted. Even more, the dominant discourse of dependency attributes poverty to single motherhood itself. In the U.S., in 2011, 70 percent of children with single parents (22 percent of children overall) lived in poverty (Addy, Engelhardt, and Skinner). Surely, poverty has negative effects on child well-being in the form of "family and environmental stresses, lack of resources and investments, and the interplay of social class/cultural patterns and poverty" (Danziger and Danziger 263). However, historically, it is also a fact that single motherhood and neglect were mutually and simultaneously constructed as social problems; many of the defining indices of neglect were essential to the survival of families headed by single mothers (Gordon 84). Given this, what are the exact connections between child poverty, child well-being, neglect, and single motherhood? Is poverty neglect? Is single motherhood neglect? What is child well-being? Who decides how we define child well-being? And does the current child welfare system actually work for children?

The remainder of this chapter is structured as follows. Firstly, I give an overview of the U.S. child welfare system. Secondly, I discuss single mothers' activism against the child welfare system. And finally, I analyze cultural frames and meanings that the child welfare system both depends on and produces.

AN OVERVIEW OF THE U.S. CHILD WELFARE SYSTEM

The U.S. child welfare system is comprised of thirty to forty separate child welfare programs (Greenberg et al.),[3] which are influenced by a number of public policies, in addition to the *Personal Responsibility and Work Opportunity Reconciliation Act* (PRWORA) of 1996 (P.L. 104-193) which introduced TANF. These child welfare programs include adoption, child protection, income support, education, early intervention, family support, foster care, medical care (Pecora and Harrison-Jackson 80),[4] along with anti-poverty policies and programs (Shanks and Danziger).[5] Child welfare practices, procedures, and legislation rest on family-state relations—intersected with social, political, and power relations between dominant and subordinate groups (Swift, *Manufacturing "Bad Mothers"*)—as well as state-market relations, as neoliberalism has extended market rationality to new domains, including social services (Soss, Fording, and Schram 177).

In 2011 in the U.S., there were approximately 742,000 instances of confirmed child maltreatment, whereas, approximately, 407,000 children were in foster care (USHHS, "Child Welfare Outcomes 2008-2011" 2). Most child maltreatment cases (more than three-quarters), however, involve neglect (USHHS, "Child Maltreatment 2012" 20),[6] and "a rather smaller number of children live in family situations that are so harmful or pose such extreme risk that they are separated from their parents, either temporarily or permanently, by the states.... Children placed in foster care are more likely to come from families with single parents with very low incomes" (Berrick 23). Existing research identifies inadequate financial resources as an important factor in children's out-of-home placement, in addition to the "race"of parents, the age of children, and caregivers' substance use (Bhatti-Sinclair and Sutcliffe 1749). Indeed, poverty, "race," and single motherhood are the three key factors disproportionately affecting family involvement with child welfare services.

Historically, the child welfare system has focused on the question of parental fitness, on safety, and permanency. Safety is ensured by "the protections of children from abuse or neglect in their own homes or in foster care," and permanency means "children having stable and consistent living situations ... continuity of family relationships, and community connections" (USHHS, "Child Welfare Outcomes 1998" 2-1; Shireman 52-53). Well-being became paired with safety and permanency as an expected outcome when child welfare services are delivered, especially when the *Adoption and Safe Families Act* (ASFA) of 1997 (P.L. 105-89) was passed (Wulczyn et al.). Well-being means "families having the capacity to provide for their children's needs, children having educational opportunities and achievements appropriate to their abilities, and children receiving physical and mental health services adequate to meet their needs" (USHHS, "Child Welfare Outcomes 1998" 2-1; Shireman 53). Well-being is a much broader concept than safety and permanency and is influenced by factors that are often beyond the direct control of parents and cannot be accommodated logically within a system of rules based on whether parents have fulfilled their role as caregiver (Wulczyn et al.).

On the other hand, adoptions (for children in foster care) have been promoted by several policies. The provisions of the 1993 federal legislation (the Family Preservation and Family Support provisions, P.L. 103-66) offered a mechanism for funding support services to birth families. In contrast, federal policies in 1994, 1996, and 1997 were less concerned with children's birth families and more with children's opportunities to live in new families created through adoption (Berrick 24-25). The *Multi-Ethnic Placement Act* of 1994 (P.L. 103-382) and the Interethnic Adoption provisions of 1996 (P.L. 104-188) promoted transracial adoptive placements for racialized children. ASFA established shorter timelines for termination of parental rights (Zell 85) and provided additional funding for states, such as through adoption incentive bonuses; states that do not comply with its provisions risk losing a portion of their Title IV-E and Title IV-B funds (McGowan 42). The Adoption Incentive Program,[7] introduced by ASFA, has been reauthorized to provide payments to states that increase the number of children adopted from the public out-of-home care system (four thousand dollars for each child adopted). Meanwhile, no fiscal incentives exist for parents for who successfully reunify (Berrick 27).

These two points contributed to expanding the definition of neglect[8] at its implementation. Even before these changes, neglect was the most difficult form of maltreatment to define,[9] as it is not necessarily a mechanical result of poverty and should be assessed in light of the family's economic circumstances (Paxson and Waldfogel 441). However, child welfare case workers, service providers, and legal professionals,[10] in their day-to-day practices with families and children, were able to make decisions in the name of "the best interests of the child" by taking child well-being into consideration, especially because of the impact of fiscal incentives and/or risks and privatization of child welfare services. In fact, "[a] substantial proportion of reports are related to issues that bear on well-being, such as exposure to domestic violence, school nonattendance, and conduct disorders" (Wulczyn et al. 10).[11]

Through these policies, the discourse embedded in policy and the common practices of child welfare professionals shape the very definition of what child well-being and neglect are and of who is a "good" mother and who is a "bad" mother. "[T]he decline of maternal instinct was the commonly identified source of the policy problem" (Campbell 170). Child intervention is used not only negatively, to patrol against transgressorsbut also positively, to promote specific family structures and relationships (Gordon 83). Child welfare practices can be thought of as reactions shaped by feelings of fear—fear of the decline of maternal instinct and perceived "traditional" nuclear family structures, in addition to the fear that racialized people will no longer occupy subordinate social positions (Campbell 176). Swift points out, "[i]f the underlying schema of neglect rests on the ideal of a two-parent, middle-class, dominant-culture family, it is quite logical that parents not matching this ideal are the most likely to become clients of the child welfare system—the poor, single mothers, and those who are culturally different" ("Contradictions in Child Welfare" 260).

Racism

Racism is a key component in contemporary definitions of child neglect. Racism, together with classism, regulates the ontology of motherhood in the U.S. and produces an unjust disproportionality in child welfare. Black or African American children account for 29 percent of the foster care population but account for only 16 percent of the total national population. Meanwhile, White children account for 41 percent of the foster care population (USHHS, "AFCARS Report #18" 2) but 74 percent of the total national population in 2010 (U.S. Census Bureau). Although the higher poverty rate among Black or African American children contributes to their disproportionate representation in foster care caseloads, in reality, the disproportionality also shows who can "deserve" to be a mother, a fact underscored by the controlling of Black or African American women's bodies. To regulate motherhood and deny single motherhood through child welfare policies, Black or African American women's bodies are signified as a sign of a "bad" mother, and, at the same time, their bodies are materially separated from their own children. Black or African American children are twice as likely to be removed from their homes and less likely to be given family-based safety services (Rivaux et al. 153) to avoid the emotional damage and physical risks of foster care placement. This is because "[g]overnment authorities appear to believe that maltreatment of Black children results from pathologies intrinsic to their homes and that helping them requires dislocating them from their family" (Roberts 17). Racialized children taken from their homes are usually put in White foster or adoptive families (Child Welfare League of America). Andrea Smith claims that the current child welfare system is a legacy of the boarding/residential school systems in the U.S. and Canada because it functions as a racist and colonialist genocidal policy to give "civilizing" instruction to racialized children through cultural genocide. The rate of indigenous children in the U.S. in foster care also shows a disproportion (USHHS, "AFCARS Report #18").

The National Incidence Study of Child Abuse and Neglect reports consistently finding a powerful relationship between family structure or socio-economic characteristics and maltreatment rates. Black or African American and White children are also found to differ significantly on some risk factors (USHHS, "Supplementary Analyses" 7-10).[12] Nevertheless, other studies report finding no "race" differences in the actual incidence of maltreatment, which suggests that racism shapes racial disparities in the child welfare system (Miller and Ward 216-217; Rodenborg 111; Shireman 121). What is different is the response of the child welfare system. Parenting classes and therapy are usually provided for impoverished mothers involved with child welfare services in order to "correct" their "problematic" behaviours as child welfare services. However, these services never address the actual factors that have brought these mothers to the child welfare system: a lack of resources for income, employment, transportation, housing, or childcare. The definition of neglect, which is intertwined with poverty and "Black maternal unfitness" through mother-blame, decides what kind of services is provided for which mothers (e.g., family preservation or adoption). As Jeanne Flavin argues "the failure to ensure reproductive justice lands hardest on the most vulnerable members of society" (182). Therefore, to find the causes that have brought disproportionality to family involvement with child welfare services, the focus needs to be on the differences in the ways that the system treats racialized families (Roberts 26) and also on poor families and families headed by single mothers.

SINGLE MOTHERS' ACTIVISM AGAINST THE U.S. CHILD WELFARE SYSTEM

Welfare rights and single mothers' organizations—such as "Welfare Warriors (WW)" in Milwaukee, WI[13] and "Every Mother is a Working Mother Network (EMWMN)" in Philadelphia, PA, and Los Angeles, CA[14]—have actively organized against the child welfare system. WW distributes copies of their quarterly newspaper, *Mother Warriors Voice*, across the U.S. so that many mothers can share their child welfare "horror" stories and survival guides. This has encouraged some mothers to create their own groups, for instance, "Mothers of the Disappeared" in POWER (Portland Organizing to Win Economic Rights, located Portland, ME) and "Stand for the Children" (HI) (Gowens, "DHS").

Collectively, mothers have demanded their own local child welfare services to develop proper legal procedure, such as providing evidence of neglect or abuse and fair hearings to mothers, which are usually not followed. The lobbying done by these organizations (and the American Bar Association) prompted Representative Gwen Moore in 2012 to introduce a bill "to provide funds to

State courts for the provision of legal representation to parents and legal guardians with respect to child welfare cases," (*Enhancing the Quality of Parental Legal Representation Act* of 2011) (WW, "Congresswoman Gwen Moore" 33). However, this bill was not passed (H.R. 3873, 112th Cong. 2012). Meanwhile, in Wisconsin, mothers are usually given a public defender (PD) from a county list of private lawyers, who routinely conform to the decisions of the district attorney (DA) and case workers (WW, *Photo Bus Tour* 6). Thus, mothers cannot exercise their legal rights when their counsel will not fairly defend them.

Many mothers (across the U.S.) have contacted WW to get help regarding government removal of their children because they never abused or neglected their children. Although there should be conflict between mothers and child welfare agencies over allegations of mothers' abuse or neglect, the disproportionality of the population involved with child welfare services, regarding their classes, "races," and marital statuses, indicates the upper hand of child welfare professionals and the ease with which decisions of child removal are made without substantial proof.

Let us now explore how the child welfare system actually works in Milwaukee (WI). According to WW (*Photo Bus Tour* 6), a case usually begins when an angry ex-partner, relative, or neighbour makes a call to the Bureau of Milwaukee Child Welfare (BMCW).[15] Alternatively, medical doctors, teachers, or other mandated reporters[16] call BMCW, usually when mothers challenge the authority of the mandated reporters. BMCW decides, generally based on personal bias and not state statutes, if the child is safe or not. If the child is deemed unsafe, the child is placed in foster care. However, in special cases, the child is allowed to return home only if services are provided to families. Within forty-eight hours of removal, BMCW and the DA must file a CHIPS (Children in Need of Protection or Services) petition[17] in children's court (48 Wis. Code. Sec. 299 [4] [b]), which is allowed to include hearsay evidence and unsubstantiated allegations of abuse or neglect.[18] In CHIPS cases, BMCW and the DA need only prove with a preponderance of the evidence that abuse or neglect occurred (48 Wis. Code. Sec. 981[3] [c)] 4),[19] although they rarely need to prove this, since no evidentiary hearing is ever held.[20] Most often, the mother is not informed that she has a right to a jury trial within thirty days of the children's removal in order to make the state prove the allegations (48 Wis. Code. Sec. 305). Instead, mothers are urged to agree to the court's jurisdiction (48 Wis. Code. Sec. 13 [4]).[21] Then they must agree to meet a list of conditions that BMCW and the judge impose to get her children back.

At this point, according to WW (*Photo Bus Tour* 6), child welfare workers, mostly employed at contracted private agencies (multiple supervisors for each visit, case workers and supervisors, child advocates, parent aids, foster care supervisors, etc.), begin to enter into the mothers' and children's lives. These interactions are shaped most by whether they like the mother or not (if CPS finds that the mother is good or bad). Mothers find themselves having to repeatedly attend classes and therapy until the workers are willing to "give up the income that the mothers bring in" (6)—that is, to decide that the mothers no longer need classes and therapy provided by these professionals. The children are usually required to go to psychiatrists and often must take medications. Moreover, mothers repeatedly return to court.

> However, 8 judges, 15 DAs, 69 GAL [Guardian Ad Litems]'s, and 38 PDs never hold a legal hearing or trial to prove the allegations of abuse or neglect against the mother. Instead they gossip about her at each "hearing." The "legal" proceedings are done in secret, forcing the mothers to be subjected to a gang-bang. And this secrecy breeds the corruption which has taken over these proceedings. (WW, *Photo Bus Tour* 6)

If BMCW decides to terminate the parental rights, the mother is finally allowed a trial. Often, however, she is bullied into giving up the children. The entire process functions to make mothers feel powerless, disturbed, and/or depressed. The children are finally allowed to go home, but only after all parties approve of the mother.

Mothers' groups have organized many protests, demonstrations, events, vigils, speak outs, and support groups in response to the child welfare system. For example, in 1992, WW created a weekly support and advocacy group for "Mothers and Grandmothers of

Disappeared Children (MaGoD)."[22] They created survival plans for themselves. They made up a telephone tree so that they could call one another after a visit with their children, since they suffered the loss of their children the most after the visits. In addition, they shared the names of the rare, helpful professionals and attended one another's court cases whenever possible (although they are not allowed to go inside the courts of other members) (Gowens, "DHS"). WW also tries to inform mothers (across the U.S.) to "demand a jury trial, if they take your child" because by the time mothers find WW, they have usually already lost their right to a trial by either judge or jury (Gowens, "DHS"). EMWMN created the eighteen-minutes film "DHS: Give Us Back Our Children," in which mothers and a grandmother talk about their battles to reunite their families after the Philadelphia Department of Human Services took their children illegally (Gowens, "DHS"). This film has become an important vehicle in the activists' tactics to bring about change (Gowens, "DHS") and is used to educate people about the grim reality of the child welfare system. These groups also organized the first annual international week of Stop the War on the Poor in July 2014 and demanded the end of the wrongful removal of children in Washington, D.C., Milwaukee, Los Angeles, Philadelphia, San Francisco, Ireland, and London, England.[23]

Although these groups have played a pivotal role in fighting for the rights of mothers and children in poverty, they have received few support from other advocacy groups and activists as well as from the general public. Feminist and welfare rights activists have shaped the U.S. welfare system but, more recently, U.S. welfare politics have also shaped activism (Ladd-Taylor 139). Ellen Reese points out that "policymaking does not end when legislation is passed—policy implementation is policy making" (168). In such a way, grassroots activists mobilize to shape the state and local implementation. However, resources are usually allocated for particular kinds of feminist or welfare issues and not others (Reese 32). In negotiating with and responding to the state and the public, some forms of activism have historically marginalized and excluded racialized single mothers in order to achieve their own goals (Nakagawa, "Mothers'/Women's"). The area of child welfare is no exception.

GREED AND PREJUDICE WORK TOGETHER AS POVERTY GOVERNANCE IN THE U.S. CHILD WELFARE SYSTEM

According to Joe Soss, Richard Fording, and Sanford Schram, racial disparities in poverty governance "do not flow directly from social structures.... They depend, ultimately, on what specific human agents decide and do in the process of governing. As a result, one must specify how race operates, not just as a social structure coordinating human relations, but also as a cultural frame structuring perception and choice," which strongly relates to policy design and implementation (14). Through frames of poverty governance, frontline child welfare services are provided with meanings of "race," class, and gender; at the same time, these meanings are culturally shaped and produced in these very practices.

Pat Gowens, the director of WW, points out that greed (functioning as selfish desire for one's own upward mobility) and prejudice work together in the child welfare system (Gowens, Personal interview); child welfare professionals' greed for a particular professional standing and prejudice against poor people work together to hurt families. Importantly, the greed and prejudice are not necessarily rooted in every individual professional but are symptomatic of the system and policies in place. Greed and prejudice are systematically structured and institutionalized to shape the policy choices of actors and of frontline interactions in order to make poverty governance operate in the child welfare system. In this section, I explore how poverty governance is executed at the frontlines of child welfare services with a focus on the cultural frames of child welfare implementation and the cultural meanings of "race," class, and gender that are produced through implementation. In doing this, I rely on Gowens's analysis of greed and prejudice in the child welfare system.

Greed

Neoliberalism has produced new relationships between the nation-state and its citizens, between employers, between service providers and their clients, and among citizens (Dominelli 15). Specifically, neoliberal market doctrines control administration and professionalization in social services. As long as the professionals are managerially competent and financially successful, and know little about the area they are investigating, the better suited to the tasks that governments deem them to be (Dominelli 19). This has resulted in the growing popularity of directive or supervisory approaches to dealing with poor people (Bashevkin 137), as a treatment and "a set of regulatory practices that attempts to bring individuals into conformity with the state's ideal of the productive citizen" (Campbell 177). As a result, the frontlines of child welfare services become a site to discipline poor racialized single mothers based on white middle-class values carried through by policies.

On the other hand, the total U.S. child welfare spending in 2012 was twenty-eight billion dollars (four hundred and sixty million dollars in Wisconsin). This spending is for child welfare activities and services, such as protective, prevention, in-home, foster care, and adoption services, and administrative costs. However, the vast majority of federal funding (Title IV-E) can only be accessed once children have already been removed from their birth families (DeVooght, Fletcher, and Cooper). More significantly, federal adoption incentive bonuses introduced by ASFA (four thousand dollars for each child adopted) spurred states to put pressures on agencies to move more children into adoptive homes, such that federal adoption assistance expenditures rose to 1.3 billion dollars in the fiscal year of 2002 (Hansen 1412). However, most children in foster care were removed from their homes because of poverty-related "neglect," and most of the children intended for adoptions by congressional sponsors of ASFA were Black or African American (Roberts 109). At the frontlines, professionals investigate, interpret, and judge cases and mothers, then arrive at appropriate decisions about children. It is important to remember that in this context, adoptive placements are financially rewarded. In addition, there are many constraints in the child welfare system that can shape child welfare professionals' decisions, and studies show the association between such constraints and out-of-home placements (Roberts; Smith and Donovan; Zell; Kemp et al.).[24]

The privatization of child welfare services—mostly contracting out (Freundlich and Gerstenzang 15)—under these conditions, specifically the government removal of children from poor racialized families, has resulted in "a job-creation program for job-hungry professionals and a child trafficking system to procure free infants and young children for baby-hungry white suburbanites, straight and gay" (WW, "HELP Stop the War" 28). After Kansas fully privatized its child welfare services in 1997, other states began following suit (Crum 48), and child welfare privatization initiatives were identified in twenty-two states in 2000 (Collins-Camargo, Ensign, and Flaherty 73).[25] However, private agencies respond to the incentives or risks in the contract with the state (Zullo 26), and critics warn that privatization may create incentives for the agencies to increase profits by providing less costly and potentially less effective services (Hubel et al. 2050). Wisconsin's child welfare system has been highly privatized since 1997. For example, BMCW provides only access (to take referrals on cases of alleged child abuse/neglect from the public) and initial assessment services. All other services are provided by private agencies.[26] Its three big contractors have been St. Aemilian-Lakeside, Inc., Integrated Family Services, and Children's Service Society of Wisconsin.[27] For example, St. Aemilian-Lakeside's annual expenses of 2013 were about sixteen million dollars (Saint A, "Financials"). Davis Tobis claims that one of the complicating factors for the child welfare system is that it serves as a resource for agencies that receive money from government to provide services. Agencies receive a specific amount for each day a child is in their care, and once a child is discharged, the money stops coming in. This creates a disincentive to discharge children (xxvi). The negative impact of this schema is reinforced through the combination of privatization and adoption incentive bonuses. Moreover, current models of contracting out often involve performance-based targets and incentives, which "connect payment to the achievement of pre-established goals, whether in the form of process indicators, outputs, or outcomes" (Freundlich and Gerstenzang 17-18). A private agency in Boston was given a quota by the state to double the numbers of children it usually placed for adoption (Roberts 111).

Specifically, the imposition of mandatory conditions on mothers to win the return of their children creates jobs for workers or, specifically, a middle-class salary for professionals, even in non-profit agencies. Money is to be made from supervised visits, psychological evaluations, parenting classes, nurturing classes, domestic violence classes, anger management classes, alcohol and other drug abuse classes, individual therapy, family therapy, drug therapy, parental aid, and group meetings with case workers, visit supervisors, and parental aides (WW, *Why the Federal Government* 2). These mandatory conditions "have been increased dramatically as non-profits/professionals have become dependent on funds generated by providing mandatory services. These 'services' are routinely and repeatedly mandated regardless of the parents' situations" (2). The conflict of interest between service providers and mothers is so obvious that, to name one example, "visit supervisors had to delay [the] return of children simply to continue their own paycheck" (Veronica, former visit supervisor, qtd. in Gowens, "DHS"). Former Georgia Seneator Nancy Schaefer, who introduced a bill [S. 415, Georgia, 2008] to reform the child welfare system, reveals in "the Corrupt Business of Child Protective Services" that

> There is a huge bureaucracy made up of judges, court appointed attorneys, Guardian Ad Litems, social workers, state employees, court investigators, therapists, psychologists, psychiatrists, foster parents, adoptive parents, and on and on, who are looking to the children in state care for their job security ... the federal and state financial incentives ... have turned CPS into a business that takes children and separates families for money.

WW has an annual photo bus tour of the BMCW Empire on international women's day ("Exposing the Child").[28] In fact, Title IV-E waiver demonstrations—flexible funding waivers that support placement prevention, reunification or post-permanency supports—have provided significant positive changes in child welfare practices, including the overall decline in out-of-home placement populations in Florida and Ohio. Due to the positive outcomes of the waiver demonstrations, the *Child and Family Services Improvement and Innovation Act* of 2011 (P.L. 112-34) allowed ten waivers in each of the fiscal years from 2012 to 2014 (Crayton; Casey Family Programs).

On the other hand, the child welfare system becomes a "child trafficking" system as well. One visitation supervisor felt too guilty about her "child trafficking" job, quit her job, and became an activist for the MaGoD Project. She shared one typical trafficking case, for which she felt guilty to be paid twenty dollars an hour to manage. She was asked to take a six-month-old racialized baby to visit her birth mother, who is poor, young, uneducated, on SSI (Supplemental Secutiry Income), and a mother of seven. The visitation supervisor drove the baby from a beautiful, ranch style home in a suburb, where two very clean, White, tidy, nurturing lesbian women were caring for the child. She was reminded by the case workers and others that the well-to-do couple will "give her a better life," yet she spoke of how they did not love the little girl more than the birth mother. The privatized child welfare agency forced the couple to adopt two other siblings in order to keep the baby that they had received two days after birth, and the couple adopted the other siblings, although they kept complaining about it. The former visitation supervisor claims that

> Money is exchanged for these children and everyone is getting paid except the parents who created the children. These children are being trafficked by the state like slaves were torn from their mothers—separated forever without a trace. Why do I feel guilty? I was being paid to help richer, privileged people tear a poor, young black woman from her infant and other children. (WW, "First Annual" 8)

Prejudice

The law does not provide clear guidelines as to when a decision to remove children from their birth parents should or should not be taken. Studies have found that the factors most closely related to the decision are the features of the parents, especially those of the mother. The parental variables include the parents' poverty, physical or mental health problems, poor household management, lack of parental cooperation with the child protection worker, and single parenthood (Arad 47-48). Again, this is not to argue that specific child welfare professionals are problematic but rather that the child welfare system has become one site for poverty governance, in which the material and symbolic interests of dominant agents and major social institutions are implicated (Wacquant xx). The child welfare system has been developed and shaped by federal and state policies, and "[p]olicy is embedded in the culture that produces it, and is best seen as a cultural practice of governance" (Campbell 7) with "a dual process of subject formation that simultaneously constitutes those who govern and those who are governed" (Campbell 44).

There are both historical-cultural traditions of blaming the poor for their poverty (Gowens, "Interview") and blaming mothers for not being "perfect" (Caplan). Embedded prejudice against the poor and mothers, coupled with racism, supports child welfare agents' views and treatment of mothers, all in order to satisfy quotas to keep their agencies funded. These cultural frames were set as governing mentalities that "derive their power to compel from both symbolic and material registers. They are cultural process[es] of formation and figuration that shape public policy debates and outcomes" (Campbell 50). CHIPS petitions are usually full of hateful comments, including lies about the mother by case workers, which are based in their classism, racism, and sexism.[29] The case workers mostly only go to poor racialized neighbourhoods for investigation. They frequently believe that children can have a better life with middle-class (which means "good") adoptive families rather than in poor (which means "bad") birth families. These cultural frames need to be constantly reconfirmed and reinforced to be "cultural norms," so they need to be mobilized through day-to-day frontline child welfare practice.

In social welfare discourses, single motherhood has been discursively constructed as "Other" in order to buttress white middle-class work and family values as "normal" and "normative." At the same time, the bodies of single mothers have been materially regulated. Single motherhood— which subverts patriarchal, heterosexist family norms inside the home and in labour markets—is the policy problem. Single mothers' difficulties to provide caregiving, which are caused by poverty, social structures, and actually policies themselves, are instead interpreted as evidence of their "bad" motherhood and/or Black "pathology." Interpreted in this way, single motherhood becomes child maltreatment itself rather than the cause of child maltreatment.

In reality, to deny single motherhood is important for poverty governance and is needed for the current economic system under neoliberalism. Firstly, to deny single motherhood constructs "good" motherhood as resources (e.g. Edin and Kefalas 166).[30] Moreover, it constructs "good" motherhood as parenting based on two-parent nuclear families with men as the primary breadwinners reinforcing women's dependency on men (Gordon 113) and ensuring that women absorb the tasks and costs of social reproduction privately. Secondly, to deny single motherhood reinforces white supremacy in order to secure racialized populations for a low-wage work force, but, at the same time, denies the parental and reproductive rights (an issue tied to the rights of citizenship) of racialized people to determine the society and citizenship as racist, colonialist, sexist, and class oppressing. In other words, poor racialized single mothers are discursively and materially regulated in the child welfare system as poverty governance, but they are also used to produce and reinforce other discourses to regulate the poor for other specific material goals of poverty governance. In fact, Representative Glenn Grothman, who was on the Wisconsin State Child Abuse and Neglect Prevention Board, proposed a bill [S. 507, Wisconsin, 2011] to list single parenting (non-marital parenthood) as a contributing factor to child abuse and neglect (Gowens, "Child Welfare and Senator" 53). Long after the welfare reform of 1996, the state continues to attack single motherhood because of its subversive characteristics in relation to dominant socio-cultural and governance norms and racialized and gendered class hierarchies (Nakagawa, "More 'Us'").

CONCLUSION

When statistics or studies show that children who are poor, racialized, or living with single mothers are more likely to be involved with child welfare services, we are made to believe that poverty, "race," and single motherhood are the roots of neglect or abuse. In other words, neglect and abuse are believed to happen more in these families than in other families. On the one hand, poverty can have negative effects on the ability of families to provide basic material needs to children, if material needs are taken as the definition of child welfare.[31] Studies also show that "impoverished families face a higher degree of stress, disorganization, and other problems compared to more affluent families" (Seccombe 51).

However, many cases of child intervention are the opposite: many child interventions do not happen because of poverty-related problems. They happen, foremost, because the mothers are poor—they cannot afford to hire private lawyers to defend their cases, even if they never abused or neglected their children in the first place. The point is that mothers' poverty, "race," and single status do not always predict neglect or abuse, yet these factors become understood as doing so in the child welfare system. Poverty, "race," and single motherhood become identified as neglect in the system because welfare agents and institutions receive strong financial incentives to make these connections. In contrast, homeless children tend to be ignored by child welfare services because their cases do not produce the kind of financial incentives as do cases wherein children are removed from their mothers. Thus, classism, and the ideological fabrications represented by "good" motherhood, and Black "pathology" are culturally reinforced through implementation. Meanwhile, many mothers, and also their children, suffer mentally and physically, especially when children are placed in foster care. However, the state and case workers usually have minimal supervision over foster care (Koehler). Moreover, the children who need protection the most cannot get help if agencies allow greed and prejudice to fuel their interventions (Wexler 22). The problem of single mothers in child neglect cases defies any clear distinction between agency bias and objective reality (Gordon 95). The answer is clear: mothers must be able to exercise their rights for a trial so to make the state prove allegations of abuse or neglect against the mothers in a court of law, and family and/or children's court must be open for fair hearings. Otherwise, the system clearly infringes not only on mothers' rights but on children's rights as well.

NOTES

[1]This chapter is a part of my dissertation project, "Single Moth-

ers and Child Welfare in the U.S.: Post-1990 Welfare Reforms" (tentative title). My research relied on mixed methods, including face-to-face interviews, discourse analysis, and analysis of secondary data. My face-to-face interviews with the parents involved with child welfare services and their advocates were completed during a fieldwork trip to the Welfare Warriors in Milwaukee, Wisconsin from June to July 2013. In this chapter, I incorporate a case study of one state in particular, Wisconsin, although each state across the U.S. has a different child welfare system.

[2]However, foster care caseloads did decrease by 23.3 percent between 2002 and 2011 (USHHS, "Child Welfare Outcomes 2008-2011" 2).

[3]The major programs are the Child Welfare Service Program, the Promoting Safe and Stable Families program, the Foster Care Maintenance program, the Adoption Assistance program, the Independent Living program, the *Child Abuse Prevention and Treatment Act,* and other federal programs including the Social Services Block Grant, Medicaid, and TANF block grants (Greenberg et al. 43).

[4]For example, the key policies enacted after PRWORA are the *Adoption and Safe Families Act* of 1997 (Allen and Bissell), the Foster Care Independence Act of 1999, the *Keeping Children and Families Safe Act* of 2003, the *Adoption Promotion Act* of 2003, and the *Fostering Connections to Success and Increasing Adoptions Act* of 2008 (Pecora and Harrison-Jackson 82-84).

[5]The current federal anti-poverty programs are Subsidized Housing (1937), Supplemental Nutrition Assistance Program (1964) (changed from the food stamp program in 2008), Women, Infants, and Children (1972), Supplemental Security Income (SSI) (1974), Section 8 (1974), Earned Income Tax Credit (1975), Hope VI (1993), Child Care and Development Block Grant (1996), TANF (1996), and Workforce Investment (1998) (Shanks and Danziger 34-45).

[6]According to the U.S. Department of Health and Human Services, "More than three-quarters (78.3%) of victims were neglected, 18.3 percent were physically abused, and 9.3 percent were sexually abused.... In addition, 10.6 percent of victims experienced such 'other' types of maltreatment as 'threatened abuse,' 'parent's drug/alcohol abuse,' or 'safe relinquishment of a newborn'" ("Child Maltreatment 2012" 20).

[7]The program is now renamed as the Adoption and Legal Guardianship Incentive Payments Program.
[8]The usual presentation of neglect is ideological in form (Swift, "Contradictions in Child Welfare" 246).
[9]"[I]t is often split into subcomponents that relate to physical, medical, and educational neglect" (Paxson and Waldfogel 441).
[10]I refer to all of them as child welfare professionals in this chapter.
[11]WW claims,

> States routinely fail to comply with statutory definitions of abuse and neglect. Instead they remove children based on bias. Examples of common unlawful reasons for family separation: home is messy...; moms left children alone briefly while doing grocery shopping etc....; moms have been battered by a male partner...; moms have an illness...; moms have spanked the children...; moms challenged school authorities, police, or medical authorities ...; moms are homeless...; children have missed doctor or dental appointments...; children have missed days in school...; relatives make unproven allegations (gossip) against parents (*Why the Federal Government* 1).

Wisconsin statutes (Children's Code) define abuse and neglect as the following:

> "Abuse" means (a) physical injury inflicted on a child by other than accidental means, (b) sexual intercourse or sexual contact, (c) sexual exploitation of a child, (d) permitting, allowing or encouraging a child for prostitution, (e) causing a child to view or listen to sexual activity, (f) exposing genitals, pubic area, or intimate parts, (g) manufacturing methamphetamine at a child's home, and (gm) emotional damage for which the child's parent, guardian or legal custodian has neglected, refused or been unable for reasons other than poverty to obtain the necessary treatment or to take steps to ameliorate the symptoms. "Physical injury" includes but is not limited to lacerations, fractured bones, burns, internal injuries, severe or frequent bruising or great bodily harm (14g). "Neglect" means failure, refusal or inability on the part of a caregiver, for reasons other than poverty, to provide necessary care, food, clothing, medical

> or dental care or shelter so as to seriously endanger the physical health of the child (12g). "Emotional damage" means harm to a child's psychological or intellectual functioning. "Emotional damage" shall be evidenced by one or more of the following characteristics exhibited to a severe degree: anxiety; depression; withdrawal; outward aggressive behavior; or a substantial and observable change in behavior, emotional response or cognition that is not within the normal range for the child's age and stage of development (5j) (48. Wis. Code. Sec. 02).

[12]In 2006, 56.1 percent of Black or African American children with specific family risk conditions lived in single-parent households, compared to 20.8 percent of their White counterparts; 45.9 percent of Black or African American children with the conditions lived in a family of low socio-economic status, compared to 15 percent of their White counterparts (USHHS, "Supplementary Analyses" 7-10). "The child is classified as in a family of low socioeconomic status if the household income was less than $15,000, the parent(s) were not high school graduates, or the household participated in a poverty program" (USHHS, "Supplementary Analyses" 8).

[13]The Welfare Warriors (WW) is a nonprofit organization of mothers and children in poverty, established in Milwaukee, Wisconsin in 1986. In their mission, they claim,

> We work to create a voice for mothers in poverty through our own organizations and media. Through street activism, advocacy, and our newspaper, *Mother Warriors Voice (MWV)*, we fight for the creation of a federal program to guarantee that all children have support to the age of 18. We educate and agitate until all communities recognize that "Motherwork IS Work" and must be paid and prioritized by the community and in the workplace. We actively protest the devastation being caused by "welfare reform." ("Our Mission")

They have a mothers' hot line, a monthly meeting, and have organized many demonstrations and events for mothers and children, funded by donations, some grants, subscription fees of *MWV* and their own fund raising events.

[14]Every Mother is a Working Mother Network's "roots are in

the welfare rights movement of the 1960s and 1970s and in the International Wages for Housework Campaign (WFH) which has campaigned for recognition and payment[s] for caring work since 1972." They claim, "We fought for and won a resolution in the Platform for Action of the 1977 U.S. Conference on Women in Houston Texas (a conference mandated by Congress)" (EMWMN "About Us: History"). They submitted a testimony to be included in the record of the Senate Finance Committee's hearing on *Welfare Reform: A New Conversation on Women and Poverty* (111th Cong., 2nd sess., September 21, 2010) (EMWMN, "Testimony to Senate").

[15]BMCW was changed to the Division of Milwaukee Child Protective Services.

[16]States differ in their definitions of mandated reporters (Paxson and Waldfogel 442).

[17]For example, in Minnesota,

> after the CHIPS petition is filed by the CPS and county attorney, a preliminary case plan aimed at issues that led to the maltreatment is drawn up by CPS. Once the case is adjudicated (i.e. allegations of child maltreatment are found to be true), a mandatory case plan comes into effect. The goals of the court include ensuring that the caregiver compiles with the case plan and that the case is resolved in a timely manner. Federal and state guidelines prioritize family preservation as the preferred outcome; however, alternative plans are considered at the same time in case family preservation does not work. The case usually ends with a permanency disposition for the child (e.g. family preservation, transfer of custody to a relative, adoption) (Karatekin, Gehrman, and Lawler 64).

[18]Federal laws require social workers to present evidence to a judicial officer in dependency court demonstrating the child's harm or risk of harm (Berrick 24).

[19]"States differ in the level of evidence required to substantiate a report of maltreatment: some require 'some credible evidence,' while others require 'a preponderance of evidence'" (Paxson and Waldfogel 442).

[20]A chief judge of children's court in Milwaukee, WI (Joseph Don-

ald), admitted at a meeting with WW that he had never had a jury trial in his two years as chief judge, although two mothers in the group had demanded a jury trial of the judge. Moreover, a district attorney told WW that "he has never had a jury trial in a child welfare case in his 18 years working in children's court" (qtd. in Gowens, "Child Welfare Officials" 33).

[21]Parents are encouraged to sign the petition requesting jurisdiction of the court, before a plea hearing and fact-finding hearing, for the involuntary removal of a child.

[22]The MaGoD Project of WW "was founded in 1992 to provide support and legal advocacy to moms whose children have been wrongfully removed by Social Services. This Project also works to change the practices and laws that allow the government to needlessly remove children from loving homes, their siblings, and their mother" ("MaGoD Project").

[23]It demands 1) passage and implementation of the *RISE Out of Poverty Act* (H.R. 814, 113th Cong. 2013-2014) and 2) the *Social Security Caregiver Credit Act* (H.R. 5024, 113th Cong. 2013-2014), 3) child welfare agencies' stop removing children from families because of poverty, racism, sexism or other bias, 4) living wage for mothers and other caregivers, and 5) resources for the care of people, not war and occupation (EMWMN, "First Annual"; WW, "First Annual" 6-9).

[24]For example, child welfare case workers face accountability pressures on reporting requirements, court expectations, and the risk of being held personally responsible for a tragedy (B. Smith 256). Lee et al. demonstrate the common difficulties of CPS investigation processes: limitations of the intake process, difficulty coordinating with various systems, limited time and resources, policy and practice misalignment, and difficulty in the use of risk assessment tools. Family preservation services require high levels of collaboration with families, which is associated with adequate supervision, job clarity, and worker autonomy (Kemp et al. 109). In response to organizational resource limitations and time pressures, case workers may do what they can, which often involves deprioritizing work with parents (Smith and Donovan 558). In addition, in response to expectations from their supervisors, judges, attorneys, public officials, and even local media, case workers seem to do what they

are expected to do, conforming practices to those that bring legitimacy so that this also contributes to promoting adoption (558).

[25]The increased interest in statewide privatization led the federal government to put forth a framework of recommendations and in conjunction with the U.S. Department of Health and Human Services, the Office of the Assistant Secretary for Planning and Evaluation, created the Child Welfare Privatization Initiatives Project (Hubel et al. 2050).

[26]All other services are case assignment and placement, intensive in-home services, ongoing case management, staff development and foster parent training, family intervention, support and services, kinship care, and independent living (BMCW).

[27]In 2014, St. Aemilian-Lakeside merged with its child welfare subsidiary, Integrated Family Services, to create Saint A (Saint A, "About Us.").

[28]The bus tour is to problematize "125 million dollars to fund 850 Bureau and private staff, 169 private agencies and therapists, and 98 lawyers who take and keep 2774 children away from their moms each year on unproven allegations of abuse and neglect" (WW, *Photo Bus Tour* 1).

[29]In this chapter, I do not analyze them in detail. Many existing studies explore the relationships between a variety of factors (e.g. mandatory work requirements, low-wage employment, parental economic circumstances, domestic violence, housing and school instability, child welfare reforms, and privatization) and child well-being, parental child maltreatment, and child protective intervention, specifically. However, I wanted to provide a feminist structural analysis to comprehend the current child welfare system, based on the perspectives and experiences of impoverished mothers involved with child welfare services, and social movements and activism, regarding child welfare services.

[30]Especially, in a capitalist society, poor mothers "are under constant pressure to view what neoliberals sometimes construes as 'desires' as normal needs of children growing up in a capitalist economy" (Swift and Birmingham 107).

[31]However, financial inability to provide for child is excluded from the definition of neglect in thirteen states, including Wisconsin (State Child Welfare Policy Database).

WORKS CITED

Addy, Sophia, Will Engelhardt, and Curtis Skinner. "Basic Facts about Low-Income Children: Children under 18 years, 2011." *National Center for Children in Poverty.* NCCP, Jan. 2013. Web. 27 Mar. 2015.

Allen, Mary Lee, and Mary Bissell. "Safety and Stability for Foster Children: The Policy Context." *The Future of Children* 14.1 (2004): 48-73. Print.

Arad, Bilha Davidson. "Parental Features and Quality of Life in the Decision to Remove Children at Risk from Home." *Child Abuse and Neglect* 25.1 (2001): 47-64. Print.

Bashevkin, Sylvia. *Welfare Hot Buttons: Women, Work, and Social Policy Reform.* Toronto: University of Toronto Press, 2002. Print.

Berrick, Jill Duerr. "Trends and Issues in the U.S. Child Welfare System." *Child Protection Systems: International Trends and Orientations.* Eds. Neil Gilbert, Nigel Parton, and Marit Skivenes. New York: Oxford University Press, 2011. 17-35. Print.

Bhatti-Sinclair, Kish and Charles Sutcliffe. "What Determines the Out-of-Home Placement of Children in the USA?" *Children and Youth Services Review* 34.9 (2012): 1749-1755. Print.

Bureau of Milwaukee Child Welfare (BMCW), State of Wisconsin. *Bureau of Milwaukee Child Welfare: Serving Families in Milwaukee County.* Milwaukee: Bureau of Milwaukee Child Welfare, n.d. Print.

Campbell, Nancy D. *Using Women: Gender, Drug Policy, and Social Justice.* New York & London: Routledge, 2000. Print.

Caplan, Paula J. "Mother-Blaming." *"Bad Mothers": The Politics of Blame in Twentieth Century America.* Eds. Molly Ladd-Taylor and Lauri Umansky. New York: New York University Press, 1998. 127-144. Print.

Casey Family Programs. "Levels of Research Evidence and Benefit-Cost Data for Title IV-E Waiver Interventions." *Casey Family Programs.* Casey Family Programs, 5 May 2014. Web. 27 Mar. 2015.

Child Welfare League of America (CWLA). "Transracial Adoption and the Multiethnic Placement Act." *The Hill.* Capitol Hill Publishing Corporation, June 2007. Web. 27 Mar. 2015.

Collins-Camargo, Crystal, Karl Ensign, and Chris Flaherty. "The National Quality Improvement Center on the Privatization of Child Welfare Services: A Program Description." *Research on Social Work Practice* 18.1 (2008): 72-81. Print.

Courtney, Mark E. et al. "Involvement of TANF Applicant Families with Child Welfare Services." *Social Service Review* 79.1 (2005):119-157. Print.

Crayton, Christina. "New Title IV-E Waivers: Improving Outcomes and Stepping Closer to Comprehensive Finance Reform." *Policy & Practice* 70.2 (2012): 17-20. Print.

Crum, Tina. "The Shift Toward Private Sector Service Delivery: Restructuring Child Welfare Systems in the Name of Children." *Journal of Children and Poverty* 4.2 (1998): 39-59. Print.

Danziger, Sandra K., and Sheldon Danziger. "Child Poverty and Antipoverty Policies in the United States: Lessons from Research and Cross-National Politics." *From Child Welfare to Child Well-being: An International Perspective on Knowledge in the Service of Policy Making*. Eds. Sheila B. Kamerman, Shelley Phipps, and Asher Ben-Arieh. New York: Springer, 2010. 255-274. Print.

DeVooght, Kerry, Megan Fletcher, and Hope Cooper. "Federal, State, and Local Spending to Address Child Abuse and Neglect in SFY 2012." *Child Trends*. Child Trends, 2014. Web. 27 Mar. 2015.

Dominelli, Lena. "Neo-liberalism, Social Exclusion and Welfare Clients in a Global Economy." *International Journal of Social Welfare* 8.1 (1999):14-22. Print.

Edin, Kathryn, and Maria Kefalas. *Promises I Can Keep: Why Poor Women Put Motherhood Before Marriage*. Berkeley: University of California Press, 2005. Print.

Every Mother is a Working Mother Network (EMWMN). "About Us: History." *Every Mother is a Working Mother Network*. EMWMN, n.d. Web. 16 Jan. 2014.

Every Mother is a Working Mother Network (EMWMN). "First Annual International Week Stop the War on the Poor, July 14-20." *Every Mother is a Working Mother Network*. EMWMN, 10 July 2014. Web. 10 Jan. 2014.

Every Mother is a Working Mother Network (EMWMN). "Testimony to Senate Finance Committee Hearing on TANF" *Every Mother is a Working Mother Network*. EMWMN, 15 Oct. 2010. Web. 16 Jan. 2014.

Flavin, Jeanne. *Our Bodies, Our Crimes: The Policing of Women's Reproduction in America*. New York: New York University Press, 2009. Print.

Freundlich, Madelyn, and Sarah Gerstenzang. *An Assessment of the Privatization of Child Welfare Services: Challenges and Successes*. Washington, D.C.: CWLA Press, 2003. Print.

Gordon, Linda. *Heroes of Their Own Lives: The Politics and History of Family Violence*. New York: Viking Penguin Inc., 1988. Print.

Gowens, Pat. "Child Welfare and Senator Grothman's Women Hating." *Mother Warriors Voice* Spring (2013): 53-54. Print.

Gowens, Pat. "Child Welfare Officials Speak and Admit Their Lawless Practices." *Mother Warriors Voice* Winter (2013): 33. Print.

Gowens, Pat. "DHS, Give Us Back Our Children: Feminists Organizing to Protect Children from Child Protective Services." *Rain and Thunder: A Radical Feminist Journal of Discussion and Activism* 57 (2013). Print.

Gowens, Pat. Personal interview. Tape recording. Milwaukee, WI. 24 July 2013. Audio.

Greenberg, Mark H., et al. "The 1996 Welfare Law: Key Elements and Reauthorization Issues Affecting Children." *The Future of Children* 12.1 (2002): 26-57. Print.

Hansen, Mary Eschelback. "State-designated Special Needs, Post-adoption Support, and State Fiscal Stress." *Children and Youth Services Review* 29 (2007): 1411-1425. Print.

Hill, Heather D. "Welfare as Maternity Leave? Exemptions from Welfare Work Requirements and Maternal Employment." *Social Service Review*. 86.1 (2012): 37-67. Print.

Hubel, Grace S. et al. "A Case Study of the Effects of Privatization of Child Welfare on Services for Children and Families: Nebraska Experience." *Children and Youth Services Review* 35 (2013): 2049-2058. Print.

Karatekin, Canan, Richard Gehrman, and Jamie Lawler. "A Study of Maltreated Children and Their Families in Juvenile Court: I. Court Performance Measures." *Children and Youth Services*

Review 41 (2014): 62-74. Print.

Kemp, Susan P. et al. "Engaging Parents in Child Welfare Services: Bridging Family Needs and Child Welfare Mandates." *Child Welfare* 88.1 (2009): 101-126. Print.

Koehler, Andrea. "The Forgotten Children of the Foster Care System: Making a Case for the Professional Judgment Standard." *Golden Gate University Law Review* 44.2 (2014): 221-256. Print.

Ladd-Taylor, Molly. *Mother-Work: Women, Child Welfare, and the State, 1890-1930*. Urbana: University of Illinois Press, 1994. Print.

Lee Shawna J. et al. "When Practice and Policy Collide: Child Welfare Workers' Perceptions of Investigation Processes." *Children and Youth Services Review* 35 (2013): 634-641. Print.

McGowan, Brenda G. "An Historical Perspective on Child Welfare." *From Child Welfare to Child Well-being: An International Perspective on Knowledge in the Service of Policy Making*. Eds. Sheila B. Kamerman, Shelley Phipps, and Asher Ben-Arieh. New York: Springer, 2010. 25-47. Print.

Miller, Oronde A., and Kristin J. Ward. "Emerging Strategies for Reducing Racial Disproportionality and Disparate Outcomes in Child Welfare: The Results of a National Breakthrough Series Collaborative." *Child Welfare* 87.2 (2008): 211-240. Print.

Nakagawa, Shihoko. "More 'Us' Than 'Them': Welfare Reform According to Congressional Hearings and the Welfare Mothers Voice." *MP: Feminist Online Journal* 2.3 (2009): 3-26. Web. 27 Mar. 2015.

Nakagawa, Shihoko. "Mothers'/Women's Rights in Welfare Rights Activism: Feminist Organizations' Engaging with Child Welfare 'Empire.'" Presentation at National Women's Studies Association 33rd Annual Conference. National Women's Studies Association, Oakland. 11 Nov. 2012. Conference presentation.

Paxson, Cristina, and Jane Waldfogel. "Work, Welfare, and Child Maltreatment." *Journal of Labor Economics* 20.3 (2002): 435-474. Print.

Peck, Jamie. *Workfare States*. New York: Guilford Press, 2001. Print.

Pecora, Peter J., and Markell Harrison-Jackson. "Child Welfare Policies and Programs." *Social Policy for Children and Families: A Risk and Resilience Perspective*. Eds. Jeffrey M. Jenson and Mark W. Fraser. London: Sage Publications, Inc., 2011. 57-112. Print.

Reese, Ellen. *They Say Cut Back, We Say Fight Back! Welfare Rights Activism in an Era of Retrenchment.* New York: Russell Sage Foundation, 2011. Print.

Rivaux, Stephanie L. et al. "The Intersection of Race, Poverty, and Risk: Understanding the Decision to Provide Services to Clients and to Remove Children." *Child Welfare* 87.2 (2008): 151-168. Print.

Roberts, Dorothy. *Shattered Bonds: The Color of Child Welfare.* New York: Basic Civitas Books, 2002. Print.

Rodenborg, Nancy A. "Services to African American Children in Poverty." *Journal of Poverty* 8.3 (2004): 109-130. Print.

Saint A. "About Us." *Saint A.* SaintA, n.d. Web. 23 Mar. 2015.

Saint A. "Financials, St. Aemilian-Lakeside 2013 Annual Report." *Saint A.* SaintA, 2015. Web. 23 Mar. 2015.

Schaefer, Nancy. "The Corrupt Business of Child Protective Services." Presentation at World Congress of Families. Amsterdam, the Netherlands. 15 Aug. 2009. Conference presentation.

Shanks, Trina R. Williams and Sandra K. Danziger. "Anti-Poverty Policies and Programs for Children and Families." *Social Policy for Children and Families: A Risk and Resilience Perspective.* Eds. Jeffrey M. Jenson and Mark W. Fraser. London: Sage Publications, Inc., 2011. 25-56. Print.

Shireman, Joan. *Critical Issues in Child Welfare.* New York: Columbia University Press, 2003. Print.

Slack, Kristen Shook et al. "Child Protective Intervention in the Context of Welfare Reform: The Effects of Work and Welfare on Maltreatment Reports." *Journal of Policy Analysis and Management* 22.4 (2003): 517-536. Print.

Smith, Andrea. *Conquest: Sexual Violence and American Indian Genocide.* Cambridge: South End Press, 2005. Print.

Smith, Brenda D., and Stella E. F. Donovan. "Child Welfare Practice in Organization and Institutional Context." *Social Service Review* 77.4 (2003): 541-563. Print.

Smith, Brenda. "Service Technologies and the Conditions of Work in Child Welfare." In *Human Services as Complex Organizations.* Ed. Yeheskel Hasenfield. Thousand Oaks: Sage Publications, Inc., 2010. 253-267. Print.

Soss, Joe, Richard C. Fording, and Sanford F. Schram. *Disciplining the Poor: Neoliberal Paternalism and the Persistent Power of Race.* Chicago: The University of Chicago Press, 2011. Print.

State Child Welfare Policy Database. "State Child Welfare Policy Database." *Child Welfare Policy.* Child Trends, 2011. Web. 16 Jan. 2015.

Swann, Christopher A., and Michelle Sheran Sylvester. "The Foster Care Crisis: What Caused Caseloads to Grow." *Demography* 43.2 (2006): 309-335. Print.

Swift, Karen. "Contradictions in Child Welfare: Neglect and Responsibility." *Women's Caring: Feminist Perspectives on Social Welfare.* Eds. Carol Baines, Patricia Evans, and Sheila Neysmith. Toronto: McClelland & Stewart Inc., 1991. 234-271. Print.

Swift, Karen. *Manufacturing 'Bad Mothers': A Critical Perspective on Child Neglect.* Toronto: University of Toronto Press, 1995. Print.

Swift, Karen, and Michael Birmingham. "Location, Location, Location: Restructuring and the Everyday Lives of 'Welfare Moms.'" *Restructuring Caring Labour: Discourse, State Practices and Everyday Life.* Ed. Sheila M. Neysmith. New York: Oxford University Press, 2000. 93-115. Print.

Tobis, Davis. *From Pariahs to Partners: How Parents and Their Allies Changed New York City's Child Welfare System.* New York: Oxford University Press, 2013. Print.

U.S. Census Bureau. "Annual Estimates of the Resident Population by Sex, Age, Race, and Hispanic Origin for the United States and States: April 1, 2010 to July 1, 2013, 2013 Population Estimates." *U.S. Department Commerce.* U.S. Department of Cimmerce, n.d. Web. 21 Oct. 2014.

U.S. Department of Health and Human Services (USHHS). "AFCARS Report #18." *Children's Bureau, An Office of the Administration for Children and Families.* USHHS, 30 June 2011. Web. 29 Mar. 2015.

U.S. Department of Health and Human Services (USHHS). "Child Maltreatment 2012." *Children's Bureau, An Office of the Administration for Children and Families.* USHHS, 17 Dec. 2013. Web. 29 Mar. 2015.

U.S. Department of Health and Human Services (USHHS). "Child Welfare Outcomes 1998: Annual Report." *Children's Bureau, An*

Office of the Administration for Children and Families. USHHS, 2000. Web. 12 Mar. 2015.

U.S. Department of Health and Human Services (USHHS). "Child Welfare Outcomes 2008-2011: Report to Congress Executive Summary." *Children's Bureau, An Office of the Administration for Children and Families.* USHHS, 16 Aug. 2013. Web. 29 Mar. 2015.

U.S. Department of Health and Human Services (USHHS). "Supplementary Analyses of Race Differences in Child Maltreatment Rates in the NIS–4 (Fourth National Incidence Study of Child Abuse and Neglect, NIS–4)." Eds. Andrea J. Sedlak, Karla McPherson, and Barnali Das. *Office of Planning, Research, and Evaluation, An Office of the Administration for Children and Families.* USHHS, Mar. 2010. Web. 29 Mar. 2015.

Wacquant, Loic. *Punishing the Poor: The Neoliberal Government of Social Insecurity.* Durham: Duke University Press, 2009. Print.

Welfare Warriors (WW). "Congresswoman Gwen Moore Introduces Legislation to Provide Trained Lawyers for Parents in Child Welfare Cases." *Mother Warriors Voice* Spring (2012): 33. Print.

Welfare Warriors (WW). "Exposing the Child Welfare Empire to Celebrate International Women's Day: 'Stop the War on the Poor. Reunite Our Families.'" *Mother Warriors Voice.* Spring (2009): 28-32. Print.

Welfare Warriors (WW). "First Annual International Week to Stop the War on the Poor." *Mother Warriors Voice* Summer (2014): 6-9. Print.

Welfare Warriors (WW). "HELP Stop the War on the Poor." *Mother Warriors Voice.* Fall-Winter (2013-2014): 28-30. Print.

Welfare Warriors (WW). "MaGoD Project." *Welfare Warriors.* N.p., n.d. Web. 12 Mar. 2013.

Welfare Warriors (WW). "Our Mission..." *Welfare Warriors.* N.p., n.d. Web. 12 Mar. 2013.

Welfare Warriors (WW). *Photo Bus Tour of the Bureau of Milwaukee Child Welfare EMPIRE.* Milwaukee: Welfare Warriors, 2009. Print.

Welfare Warriors (WW). *Why the Federal Government Needs to Overhaul Child Welfare.* Milwaukee: Welfare Warriors, n.d. Print.

Wexler, Richard. *Wounded Innocents: The Real Victims of the War*

Against Child Abuse. Buffalo: Prometheus Books, 1990. Print.

Wulczyn, Fred et al. *Beyond Common Sense: Child Welfare, Child Well-being, and the Evidence for Policy Reform*. New Brunswick: Aldine Transaction, 2005. Print.

Zell, Maristela C. "Child Welfare Workers: Who They Are and How They View the Child Welfare System." *Child Welfare*. LXXXV.1 (2006): 83-103. Print.

Zullo, Roland. "Is Social Service Contracting Coercive, Competitive, or Collaborative? Evidence from the Case Allocation Patterns of Child Protective Services." *Administration in Social Work* 30.3 (2006): 25-42. Print.

About the Contributors

Dwayne Avery is a postdoctoral fellow in the Department of Film at York University. His research explores the "place of motherhood"—the ways in which motherhood ideologies are tied to specific geographical locations, from the domestic home to the urban apartment. Avery received his Ph.D. from McGill University's Department of Art History and Communication Studies in 2011. He currently resides in Montreal, QC.

Nancy Bressler, Ph.D., is an assistant professor of communications at Wheeling Jesuit University. Her research focuses on pedagogical advancements, specifically the development of students' media literacy skills and how instructors can incorporate media activities into the classroom. In addition, her media studies and critical-cultural research examines how media representations influence and contribute to American identities, cultural norms, and social perceptions. Nancy Bressler's research is featured as a refereed journal article in *Discourse: The Journal of the SCASD* and as book chapters in *Communication Theory and Millennial Popular Culture, Home Sweat Home,* and *Teaching From the Heart: Critical Communication Pedagogy in the Communication Classroom.*

Elizabeth Bruno is a third year doctoral student at the University of Oregon, where she studies early twentieth-century American children's literature, motherhood, pedagogy, and rhetoric. She holds a Master's degree from Yale in Religion and Literature. Her chapter

"Her Cape is at the Cleaners: Searching for Single Motherhood in a Culture of Self-Sufficiency" appears in *Mothers and Mothering across Cultural Differences* from Demeter Press.

Linda M. Burns is professor emerita of sociology at Carlow University in Pittsburgh, Pennsylvania. She is a single adoptive mother.

Deborah Byrd is professor of English and women's and gender studies at Lafayette College, where she also serves as director of the Center for Community Engagement. She publishes on nineteenth-century British poetry, feminist, community-based learning pedagogy, and support programs for teenage and low-income single mothers.

Lara Descartes received her doctorate in anthropology from the University of Michigan in 2002. She was faculty in the University of Connecticut's Department of Human Development and Family Studies from 2002 to 2008 and is currently a Professor in Family Studies at Brescia University College in London, Ontario. Her areas of research have included parenting, sexual minorities, health, popular culture and media, work and family, and social support.

Dino Di Nella is a lecturer in the Sede Atlántica at the National University of Río Negro in Argentina. Di Nella, who is pursuing a Ph.D. in sociology at the University of Barcelona, holds a master's in gender equality policies and a postgraduate diploma in gender and equality from the Autonomous University of Barcelona. Di Nella also holds a degree in law from the Universidad Nacional de La Plata and is a member of the Group Copolis.

Ellen Hauser currently teaches at Carthage College in Kenosha, WI. She holds a Master's Degree in Political Science and a Ph.D. in Development Studies from the University of Wisconsin Madison, and has worked on international development issues in China, Uganda, Rwanda, and with the U.S. government in Washington, DC. In addition to her academic work, she writes creative essays on her experiences as a single mother. She is the mother of an amazing daughter, and her hobbies include improv theater and poetry."

Rachel Lamdin Hunter is a registered nurse specializing in child, family, and women's health. She now teaches in the Bachelor of Nursing and Postgraduate Health and Social Practice programs at Waikato Institute of Technology in Hamilton, New Zealand, and is undertaking a Ph.D. at the University of Waikato, studying the well-being of women and children in mother-led households. She is mother to three daughters.

Lara Martin Lengel, Ph.D., began her research on transnational gender, women's, and cultural studies as a Fulbright Research Scholar in Tunisia. She is Professor in the School of Media and Communication and the Women's, Gender and Sexuality Studies program at Bowling Green State University. Her refereed research appears as lead articles in *Text and Performance Quarterly*, *Journal of Communication Inquiry*, and *Convergence: Journal of Research into New Media Technologies*, and in *Gender & History, Feminist Media Studies, Studies in Symbolic Interaction, International Journal of Women's Studies, International Journal of Communication, Journal of International and Intercultural Communication,* and *Communication Studies*. Her books include *Casting Gender: Women and Performance in Global Contexts* and *Intercultural Communication and Creative Practice: Music, Dance, and Women's Cultural Identity*. She is mother and step-mother to four children.

Ulrike Lingen-Ali is a lecturer and researcher at Carl von Ossietzky University of Oldenburg. From 2012 to 2015, she was a researcher in a project on migrant one-parent families in Lower Saxony, Germany (ALMIN), and she has teaching experience in migration, education, and gender Studies. She completed her Ph.D. in Education at Oldenburg University. Her thesis adopts a transcultural perspective and analyzes agency and biography in Palestinian and German feminist contexts. Ulrike Lingen-Ali is a member of the working group Migration—Gender—Politics, the Centre of Interdisciplinary Research on Women and Gender, and the Center for Migration, Education and Cultural Studies at Oldenburg University. Her research interests focus on migration and family structures; concepts of identity and belonging; intersectional research on violence; orientalism, othering, and Islamophobia; and gender dynamics.

Katherine Mack is an associate professor of English at the University of Colorado, Colorado Springs. She is the author of *From Apartheid to Democracy: The Truth and Reconciliation Commission of South Africa* (Penn State University Press, 2014). She has also published essays in *Reception: Texts, Readers, Audiences, and History* and the *Journal of the Council of Writing Program Administrators* as well as in various edited collections.

Rosa Ortiz Monera is pursuing a Ph.D. in sociology at the University of Barcelona. She holds a master's in gender and women studies from the University of Barcelona and a postgraduate diploma in international development co-operation from the Autonomous University of Barcelona. Monera also holds a degree in economics from the Pompeu Fabra University (Barcelona). She is a researcher in the Group Copolis.

Maki Motapanyane is an associate professor of women's and gender studies in the Department of Humanities at Mount Royal University. She is the editor of *Mothering in Hip-Hop Culture: Representation and Experience* (Demeter Press, 2012), and co-editor (with Roksana Badruddoja) of *"New Maternalisms": Tales of Motherwork (Dislodging the Unthinkable)* (Demeter Press, 2016). Her research spans the fields of feminist theory, motherhood and cultural studies, with academic publications featuring a range that includes feminist theory, transnational feminist research methods, mothering and motherhood, racialized comedy in Canada, and gender in Hip-Hop culture.

Lee Murray is currently an associate professor at the College of Nursing, University of Saskatchewan. She is also a clinical nurse specialist (CNS) in adolescent mental health, in particular suicidal adolescents and adolescents with developmental disabilities. Dr.

Murray's clinical practice, research and teaching are in the areas of adolescent mental health, individual and group counseling, inter-professional practice and leadership, and school health in context of the role of a mental health nurse in schools. She also has a great interest and curiosity regarding "mothering." To satisfy this curiosity, she uses auto-ethnography as methodology to explore the normative discourse of mothering in the context of her own experiences as a mom.

Shihoko Nakagawa is a Ph.D. candidate in gender, feminist, and women's studies at York University, Canada. Her research areas are gender, poverty, public policy, and social movements, and her research focuses on single mothers' movements and social welfare policy in the U.S., Canada, and Japan.

Fr. Richard J. Piatt, O.S.A, is a professor of practice at Merrimack College where he teaches acting, directing, script analysis, the politics of performance, and American musical theatre. He is on the board of directors for Pedagogy and Theater of the Oppressed, Inc. and co-edits that organization's peer reviewed *Journal of Pedagogy and Theatre of the Oppressed*. Fr. Piatt is also a member of the international Sciology of Theatre and Performance Research Group, a reviewer for the online journal *Praxis*, and the director of the Rogers Center for the Arts at Merrimack College.

Lydia Potts is a social scientist with specialization in migration studies as well as in gender studies. She teaches political science, intercultural education and women's and gender studies at Carl von Ossietzky University Oldenburg, Germany and has also vast experience in transnational research, teaching and curriculum development with European, Arab and African partners. Dr. Potts directs the working group Migration—Gender—Politics, based in the Department of Cultural Studies and the EDULINK project African Migration and Gender in Global Context—Implementing Migration Studies. Since 2010, she has co-ordinated the Erasmus Mundus Master Course European Master in Migration and Intercultural Relations (EMMIR), and since 2012 she has been the co-ordinator of the research project ALMIN (Migrant One-Parent

Families in Lower Saxony/Germany). Her main fields of research are global migration and gender, migrant families, migration and ageing, single migrant mothers, and travel literature by women. She was visiting professor in the U.S. and held an HCM-fellowship at the London School of Economics and Political Science in 1995. She is co-founder of the Centre of Interdisciplinary Research on Women and Gender at the University of Oldenburg. She is author of "The World Labour Market: A History of Migration," co-author of "Frauen—Flucht—Asyl" and co-editor of "Women's Studies im internationalen Vergleich," "Societies in Transition: Challenges to Women's and Gender Studies," "Mann wird man: Geschlechtliche Identitäten im Spannungsfeld von Migration und Islam," and "Kabbo ka Muwala: Migration and Mobility in Contemporary Art."

Danielle Russell is an associate professor in Glendon College's English Department. Her publications include chapters on *The Color Purple*, *The Song of the Lark*, the legacy of *The Madwoman in the Attic*, the work of Neil Gaiman, and children's literature; she is the author of *Between the Angle and the Curve: Mapping Gender, Race, Space, and Identity in Willa Cather and Toni Morrison.*

Elisabet Almeda-Samaranch is a professor at the Department of Sociology at the University of Barcelona in Spain. She is the director of the Group Copolis and holds a Ph.D. in sociology from the Autonomous University of Barcelona and a master's in social welfare and social planning from the University of Kent in Canterbury. She also holds a degree in economics and business from the University of Barcelona. Her research and teaching have centred on three main areas: systems of criminal justice (social control, women's delinquency and women's prisons), changes and family policies (one-parent families and comparative family policy), and memory and identity.

Natasha Steer is the fortunate mother of an adventurous twelve-year-old boy. She is currently pursuing a masters degree in Social Justice Education at the University of Toronto. In the four years that they have lived overseas, Natasha and her son have travelled to thirty-eight countries in five continents. Her time raising her son overseas has taught her that it is good to take risks and that single parenthood need not follow convention.

Christin Quirk is a Ph.D. candidate at Macquarie University in the Department of Modern History, Politics and International Relations. Her thesis examines dominant discourses and culturally contested conceptions of motherhood in the period 1969-2008 by focusing on the experiences of single and lesbian mothers. Her previous research, commissioned by the Royal Women's Hospital, investigated past adoption practices in the post-war period and informed an apology to women who lost a child to adoption. Christin has lectured in Australian immigration history, historical perspectives on the family, and social issues and social policy. She was a member of the editorial collective for *Lilith: A Feminist History Journal* from 2011 to 2014 and is currently the joint events and social media co-ordinator for Oral History Victoria.